iCon

Books by Jeffrey S. Young

Steve Jobs: The Journey Is the Reward

Forbes Greatest Technology Stories:
Inspiring Tales of the Entrepreneurs and Inventors
Who Revolutionized Modern Business

Cisco UnAuthorized

Inside MacPaint: Sailing through the Sea of Fatbits

Books by William L. Simon

Beyond the Numbers

As Coauthor

The Art of Intrusion

A Cat by the Tail

In Search of Business Value

The Art of Deception

The Afterlife Experiments

Winning in Fasttime

Driving Digital

Lasting Change

High Velocity Leadership

On the Firing Line

Profit from Experience

iCon

Steve Jobs

THE GREATEST SECOND ACT
IN THE HISTORY OF BUSINESS

Jeffrey S. Young
William L. Simon

WILEY

John Wiley & Sons, Inc.

Copyright © 2005 by Jeffrey S. Young and William L. Simon. All rights reserved

Published by John Wiley & Sons, Inc., Hoboken, New Jersey
Published simultaneously in Canada

Design and composition by Navta Associates, Inc.

For general information about our other products and services, please contact our Customer Care Department within the United States at (800) 762-2974, outside the United States at (317) 572-3993 or fax (317) 572-4002.

Wiley also publishes its books in a variety of electronic formats. Some content that appears in print may not be available in electronic books. For more information about Wiley products, visit our web site at www.wiley.com.

Library of Congress Cataloging-in-Publication Data:

Young, Jeffrey S., date.
    iCon : Steve Jobs, the greatest second act in the history of business /
Jeffrey S. Young, William L. Simon.
        p. cm.
    Includes bibliographical references and index.
    ISBN-13 978-0-471-72083-6 (cloth : alk. paper)
    ISBN-10 0-471-72083-6 (cloth : alk. paper)
    1.   Jobs, Steven, 1955—Adult biography. 2. Computer engineers—United States—Biography—Adult biography. 3. Apple Computer, Inc.—History—Adult biography. I. Simon, William L. II. Title.
    QA76.2.J63Y677 2005
    338.7'6100416'092—dc22

                                                                                                    2005006841
    ISBN: 978-0-471-72083-6

10 9 8 7 6 5 4 3 2 1

For Janey, Alyssa, Fiona, and Alistair
For Arynne, Sheldon, Victoria, and David

Contents

Prologue

Charisma, a gift given to few people, is a complex skein of many threads. Nature bestowed that gift on Steve Jobs, along with a spellbinding ability to captivate a crowd that is the hallmark of evangelists and demagogues. To witness one of his hours-long performances is to watch a master showman deliver an unscripted, free-ranging monologue about nothing but technology—and the world according to Steve Jobs.

Once, when Jobs was younger and more callow, skeptics said this bravura performance art was all he had. There was an arrogance about the young prince of technology on his first ascendancy at Apple that made him seem cold and empty, even as he pushed the envelope of what was possible with a personal computer. He attracted followers, but it was a cult.

Fifteen years in the wilderness after being rejected by his own company changed all that: it made him human.

Nowhere was that more clear than in January 2000 at the MacWorld Expo in San Francisco's Moscone Convention Center. At that event, on that frosty morning, Steve Jobs reached an emotional watershed, one that few people had thought would ever happen for him. And as with everything else about this man's larger-than-life world, he did it in front of thousands of observers.

For those who were attentive enough to hear what he said, Steve Jobs let the world see how much he had changed. Nearly drowned out by applause and shouting, his confession took place in one unscripted and unhyped moment at the very end of the presentation.

Making a presentation at the annual Macintosh trade show and "love-in" in San Francisco is an essential part of the life of an Apple chief executive. Steve had started doing it years earlier; after he was kicked out of the company his successors carried the tradition forward. But no one did it like Steve, and by the time he was back at Apple he had honed these presentations to a fine performance art.

Now balding and bespectacled, Steve had built to the finale. A black mock turtleneck and a well-worn pair of jeans demonstrated his continuing disdain for corporate uniforms. With a diffident and self-deprecating smile, Steve brought up one last slide on the giant fifty-foot Big Brother screen behind him. On it was his title, Interim CEO.

Pacing back and forth, alone onstage and in the warmth of the lime-light, he acknowledged how hard everyone at Apple had been working since his return and spoke of his dual jobs running both Apple and Pixar. "After two and a half years," he said, "I hope that we've been able to prove to our shareholders at Pixar and our shareholders at Apple that maybe we could pull this dual CEO thing off. So I'm not going to change any of my duties at Pixar or at Apple.

"But I am pleased to announce today that I'm going to drop the 'interim' title."

The crowd erupted with shouts of "Steve! Steve! Steve!" At first, a core handful of Apple-lovers started the chant. It built, rising out of the center of the auditorium. The pace of clapping hands quickened, then feet stomped, and, finally, the crowd gave him a standing ovation.

"Steve! Steve! Steve!" The noise level reached a crescendo and drowned out everything else. Onstage, the prince himself at first didn't quite catch what was happening. Then, after cupping his hand to his ear to hear better, he suddenly realized: thousands of Apple fanatics, owners, developers, and faithful were telling him something he wanted to hear. The entire audience was pouring out its love for him.

For the first time in his public life, there, onstage, at the end of a remarkably well orchestrated two-and-a-half-hour show, Steve appeared genuinely touched. With a sheepish smile, he felt and basked in love that flowed freely all around him.

Perhaps he wasn't brash and cocky anymore. Maybe four kids, and the complete failure of one company and the near failure of another, had taught him something. There on the stage at the Moscone Center, Steve was genuinely moved. With a lump in his throat, he fought back tears and mumbled something to make it clear that, yes, we all can change. Yes, even Steve Jobs had made the transition into a world where feelings and passion could partner with business and technology.

"You guys are making me feel real funny now," he started. "I get to come to work every day and work with the most talented people on the planet, at Apple and Pixar. The best job in the world. But these jobs are team sports."

His eyes misted up. A team sport. Fifteen years ago it would have been a lie, but now everything was different. Time, that great leveler, had eroded his invincibility and his elitism, and made him realize just how human and how lucky he was, and now he could stand in front of thousands and honestly, genuinely thank the many people who had worked long hours to make him look good.

With grace and a deft touch, he whispered one last thing to the audience: "I accept your thanks on behalf of all the people at Apple."

There it was. This was a new Steve Jobs. Humbled by failure, elevated by the birth of his children, mellowed with age, yet still as headstrong and perhaps even more certain of his own decision making than ever before, he now understood that it really was the many others who did the work: "Apple is a team sport."

He was the person who, more than any other, had made technology seem freighted with promise for every person. It had been a masterful romp through a collection of marginal and incremental technologies that made everything seem new and shining and important when infused with his infectious enthusiasm, his passion for the Macintosh, and his genuine thrill with the journey of redemption itself—for himself, for Apple, and for the personal computer industry. His charm, his relish at the triumph of the moment, and his easy manner coalesced in a tour de force that recalled all the old slogans—"Insanely Great!" "Let's Make a Dent in the Universe!" "The Journey Is the Reward!" "Let's Be Pirates!"—and replaced them with new ones: "This Is Going to Be Huge!" "Beyond the Box," and, finally, "Reinventing Apple," "Think Different," and a noisy parade of characters from Buzz Lightyear to the clown fish Nemo to the family of Incredibles.

Steve wasn't the only one who was emotionally touched that day. Off to one side of the auditorium, sitting by himself and barely recognized, was the other Steve, Steve Wozniak, the one known as Woz, the once and former partner, the genius behind the Apple II who had created the original cult of Apple with inspired and quirky feats of engineering.

As Woz watched his former partner gently, even humbly, accept the applause and the praise being showered on him, tears ran down Woz's cheeks. Walking out of the hall, he told a reporter that "it felt just like the old days, with Steve making announcements that shook my world." If Woz could forgive Steve, so could anyone. It had been a long time since Steve had first made him cry.

But lots had changed since that time. As Steve Jobs basked in the moment, the giant loudspeakers came to life. He slipped off the stage, and the Macintosh faithful streamed out of the auditorium, enveloped in Steve's reality-distortion field, while the sounds of one of his heroes whispered all around them. The song was "Imagine" by John Lennon, who was killed so close to the day of Apple's IPO in December 1980:

> You may say I'm a dreamer,
> But I'm not the only one.

Yet no one could have imagined Steve's own story.

PART ONE

Flowering and Withering

1

I think it's clear that Steve always had a kind of chip on his shoulder. At some deep level, there was an insecurity that Steve had to go out and prove himself. I think being an orphan drove Steve in ways that most of us can never understand.
—Dan Kottke, one of Steve Jobs's closest friends

Roots

We all tend to lose track of just how much change—as a country, a society, a civilization—Americans weathered in the twentieth century: the shock and chaos of two world wars, the hopeful uncertainty of the 1950s, the upheavals of the 1960s, the reconfigurations of the 1970s and 1980s, the technology-inspired turmoil of the 1990s. The parade of powerful events in these decades altered the way Americans work, think, play, and even love. In hindsight, we recognize the inevitable shifts in what we consider socially acceptable behavior, and they surprise us by having defied our own conventional wisdom.

One practice that has remained constant and yet changed in the years since the birth of Steve Jobs is adoption. It was far more common in the mid-1950s and earlier than it is today. The differences can be simply explained: back then, single parenthood was a disgrace, and abortion was not only illegal but, if available at all, too often deadly. The advent of widespread birth control in the 1960s changed the equation forever: arguably the Pill ranks with penicillin as the greatest medical developments of the twentieth century. In conjunction with the women's movement, birth control changed our moral compass. Back in the 1950s only one respectable avenue was open for a single woman who was pregnant: giving her newborn up for adoption. Agencies dedicated to bringing together childless couples with women who were "in the family way" became something of a cottage industry.

Steve Jobs was born on February 24, 1955, in San Francisco, California. Beyond that one fact, he knew virtually nothing of his birth parentage until he was already grown and famous. Within weeks of his birth, the mother of "Baby John Doe" signed over legal custody of her infant son to a San Francisco couple, Paul and Clara Jobs, who had been thwarted for nearly ten years in their hope of having children.

Paul Jobs had been through several lives before landing out West. He was a man of imposing demeanor, a farmer's son raised with a no-nonsense midwestern Calvinism. It was enough to steel him for the decade-long Depression that would mark his young adulthood and define his choices. He dropped out of high school and wandered the Midwest for several years, searching for work during the height of the Depression and living something close to the life of a hobo. Eventually, Paul opted for the relative certainty of service in the military over the unsettling inconstancies of the open road, enlisting in the U.S. Coast Guard—the "Hooligan Navy," in the popular phrase that he often used—and mastered the skills of an engine-room machinist. Like his midwestern upbringing, his Coast Guard experiences stayed with him in tangible ways: the tattoos on his arms, the short crew-cut hairstyle. Though he was always conscious of his lack of formal education, he exuded the hearty, robust personality of a proud, productive, blue-collar American.

Paul Jobs landed in San Francisco when his Coast Guard ship steamed into port to be decommissioned. By then, with the war and the Depression behind him, Paul was looking for the same thing that other men all over the nation were: a new beginning. He made a bet with a shipmate that "in the shadow of the Golden Gate" he would be able to find himself a bride. He was soon dating a local girl and promptly asked her to share his life. Paul and Clara married in 1946 and headed back to Paul's roots in Indiana, where the mechanical skills he had learned in the service helped him land a job with International Harvester.

Paul's tinkering abilities extended into his hobbies as well. He found nothing more relaxing or rewarding than buying an old, beat-up jalopy and spending his weekends underneath the hood repairing it and getting it roadworthy again. When the work was done, he'd sell it and buy another, pocketing a profit each time. His austere background made him a tough negotiator, especially when it came to his auto deals.

Yet the attraction to California was too strong. In 1952 Paul and Clara packed up and moved back to San Francisco, into an apartment overlooking the Pacific Ocean. Paul was soon hired as a kind of strong-arm man by a finance company that sought help collecting on auto loans—an early repo man. Both his bulk and his aggressive personality were well suited to this somewhat dangerous pursuit, and his mechanical bent enabled him to pick the locks of the cars he had to repossess and hot-wire them if necessary.

Three years later, following the adoption of the baby boy they named Steven Paul Jobs, the family moved to a house in South San Francisco, an industrial town with a number of new housing tracts for returning veterans. Even at three years old, Steven was shaping up to be quite a handful, what polite folks today tactfully call a "hyperkinetic" child. He often started his day at four in the morning and had a gift for getting into trouble. Once he and a playmate had to be rushed to the hospital after they decided to see what ant poison tasted like. In another incident, Steve jammed a bobby pin into an electrical socket and got a nasty burn for his curiosity. Nonetheless, his antics didn't dissuade his parents from adopting another child, a daughter, Patty, two years younger than Steven.

Perhaps Steve needed a bit more supervision than most children, but he was obviously bright and in many ways seemed much like any other American kid in the mid-1950s. He mugged for the camera in neighbors' Super 8mm home movies, roared around the neighborhood on his tricycle, and watched unhealthful amounts of television—perhaps an early sign that he would turn into a youngster who didn't make friends easily.

Not long after Steve was born, the Nobel Prize for Physics was awarded to John Bardeen, Walter Brattain, and William Shockley for their invention of the transistor. Paul and Clara Jobs could not have imagined how this invention would change their son's life and would lead him to change the lives of so many others.

. . .

By the time he was ten, Steve's interest in electronics was patently obvious. He was attracted by the practicality of electronic gadgets, using his youngster's imagination to see their nearly unlimited potential. By now, his dad had moved the family down the peninsula to Mountain View, a bedroom community for the electronics companies sprouting up around Palo Alto, where Paul Jobs continued working as a repo man. The neighborhood Steve's parents had chosen was particularly suitable, being filled with engineers employed by Hewlett-Packard and other electronics firms. On weekends, they could be found at their garage workbenches, where they usually welcomed the lonely boy looking to learn and keep busy. It was one of these neighbors who let Steve play around with a simple carbon microphone that he'd brought home from the lab. Steve was fascinated with the device and asked many perceptive questions. Soon, he had spent so much time at the engineer's home and had so impressed the man with his precocity that he was given the microphone for his own.

From his peers, though, Steve reaped nothing but trouble. He was already a renegade. Much later, a schoolmate would describe him as a "loner, pretty much of a crybaby." The two were on a swim team together, one of Steve's only ventures into team sports. "He'd lose a race and go off by himself and cry. He didn't quite fit in with everyone else. He wasn't one of the guys."

Steve's youthful penchant for mischief and willfulness rapidly developed into something else. He was suspended from school several times for misbehavior and defying his teachers, refusing to do any schoolwork or assignment that he felt was a "waste of time." According to Steve himself, "I was pretty bored in school, and I turned into a little terror." He was the ringleader in a group that exploded bombs and let snakes loose in the classroom. "You should have seen us in third grade," he said. "We basically destroyed the teacher." That those words convey a sense of pride and satisfaction in giving pain offers another clue to what Steve would become. It is no surprise that he was eventually expelled.

Steve soon came under the influence of a fourth grade teacher who changed his life: Imogene "Teddy" Hill. "She was one of the saints of my life," he said. "She taught an advanced fourth grade class, and it took her about a month to get hip to my situation. She bribed me into learning. She would say, 'I really want you to finish this workbook. I'll pay you five bucks if you finish it.' That really kindled a passion in me for learning things."

Steve learned more that year than in any other year in school. His teachers wanted him to skip fifth grade and go straight to middle school. Eventually his parents reluctantly agreed. He entered Crittenden Middle School a year early, but the school district made no provisions for the social adjustment of gifted kids, plunking them down with the older children.

At the same time, things weren't going well for Paul Jobs. He had quit the repo business and become a real estate salesman in the booming world of the peninsula. His brusque personality wasn't suited to the mix of obsequiousness and aggression required to be a successful realtor. One day during Steve's fourth grade year, Teddy Hill asked her class, "What is it in the world that you don't understand?" She recalls that Steve's hand shot up and he replied, "I don't understand why all of a sudden we're so broke!"

In time, Paul Jobs, after fifteen years away from the trade, returned to work as a machinist. Though he had to reenter at the bottom and work his way up, he quickly climbed the ladder and the family breathed a little easier financially. Paul went to work for Spectraphysics, where he eventually worked on developing the system of mirrors that read bar codes on products in just about every supermarket in the world.

Steve, however, was absolutely miserable at his new school. Mountain View's Crittenden Junior High was much tougher than the grade school, and it was on the wrong side of the tracks to boot. The local police were often called to break up fights, and the troublemaking of Mountain View hooligans made Steve's pranks seem tame by comparison.

His free spirit and immense intelligence went unnoticed against the backdrop of all the commotion, and he grew increasingly unhappy and frustrated. The situation became so dire, to Steve's mind, that he simply decided not to return to Crittenden the following year. He informed his father of the decision that summer. After much discussion, Paul and Clara accepted the reality that their son, already a discipline problem, was on the verge of becoming a full-blown juvenile delinquent. They understood that they had to make a choice.

"He said he just wouldn't go [back to that school]," recalled Paul Jobs. "So we moved."

At eleven years old, Steve was already able to demonstrate enough strength of will to convince his parents to resettle. His trademark intensity, the single-mindedness that he could apply to remove any obstacle to his progress, was already evident.

In 1967, the Jobs family moved to the flatlands of Los Altos and found themselves smack in the middle of what may have been the largest assemblage of science wonks ever gathered in one place since the Manhattan Project. Los Altos and the surrounding towns of Cupertino and Sunnyvale were sown through with electrical engineers and their families. At the time, Lockheed was booming as the prime contractor for NASA in the space race, and all through the area a profusion of electronics companies was springing up to service the moon shot. It was also ground zero for a wave of innovation and entrepreneurial activity that exploited the world of electronic miniaturization ushered in by the invention first of the transistor, and then of the integrated circuit, or IC, which crammed hundreds of those transistors onto a single "chip." In every garage there was a welcoming brain for Steve to pick and a box or two filled with spare parts or obsolete equipment that could be taken apart after school. In contrast to rough-and-tumble Mountain View, this was heaven.

At Cupertino Junior High School, Steve met Bill Fernandez, the slight, intense son of a local attorney, who was as much of a misfit as the young Jobs. Neither one was even vaguely athletic—they were both skinny, scrawny, and relatively uncoordinated—but they each had a discernible intensity, viewed as oddness by their classmates. Electronics was the perfect outlet for these outsiders. They could pursue their interests in the calm solitude of the neighborhood garages and workshops, while relegating the usual adolescent dilemmas of peer acceptance, sports prowess, and boy-girl turmoil to another world for hours on end. They may have been oddballs to their fellow students, but Fernandez and Jobs had tapped into the sensibilities of the surrounding community of engineers and scientists.

"I have this vivid memory of Steve Jobs," recalled Bruce Courture, who attended both Cupertino Junior High and Homestead High—six years of school—with him. Courture was voted "Most Likely to Succeed" in the senior class and is now living up to this expectation as a partner at one of the most successful high-tech law firms in Silicon

Valley. "It's one moment that has always stuck in my mind. It was a very foggy day. All us boys in our freshman class were running a couple of laps around the track. And all of a sudden Steve, who was ahead of me, glanced back across the field at the PE coach, who was hidden by the fog, and saw that he couldn't possibly see the far side of the field. So [Steve] sat down. Well, I thought that was a pretty good idea. I joined him. The two of us just sat and watched everyone else run by us. When they came back around for the second lap, we stood up and joined them.

"We had to take some ribbing, but he had figured out how he could get away with half the work and still get credit for the whole thing. I was really impressed, especially that he had the guts to try it, even though he was just a freshman. I would never have thought to do that on my own."

Living directly across the street from the Fernandez family were the Wozniaks. The father, Jerry Wozniak, was an engineer with Lockheed, and since Fernandez's parents had nothing to do with electronics, Jerry had been Bill's mentor and tutor in the subject. Jerry's son Stephen also shared in the passion for electronics and on occasion pitched in with Fernandez on science fair projects, despite being five years older.

Steve Jobs entered Homestead High School in 1968, an important year for the United States. The country was wracked by conflicting sentiments about the war in Vietnam and civil rights, and college campuses were convulsed by protests, demonstrations, and riots, with newsworthy hotbeds at the northern California schools of UC Berkeley and San Francisco State.

Meanwhile, Steve Wozniak, a freshman at the University of Colorado, was leaving his own mark on the campus. In a series of confrontations, the daring and able computer prankster had challenged the school's administration. After one memorable episode on Election Day, the campus computer kept generating an irreverent message, over and over. That was the last straw, as far as the dean of students was concerned, and once the culprit's identity was revealed, Wozniak was able to stay only long enough to finish one academically lackluster year. He left campus knowing that he would not return.

Though the affair with the campus computer might indicate otherwise, he was, in his own mother's words, "a square." He didn't seem to notice girls and was athletically challenged.

"Woz," as he'd been called since grade school, was a generally obedient youngster despite his tendency to be willful in certain circumstances. He also had the ability to focus, completely and utterly, on whatever interested him and often became so absorbed that his mother's only recourse was to rap his head with a pencil if she wanted his attention. Few things held Woz's attention besides electronics and the science and math that constituted its basic elements. He could spend endless days designing circuit boards for various gadgets, but when it came to more mundane subjects like literature or social studies, his lack of interest held him back from doing even the simplest homework assignments. It was the classic personality profile of genius: brilliant in one area, bored in all others. By his senior year in high school, he was nearly failing English and history.

Still, Woz was secure in his knowledge of electronics and cocky enough to let everyone know it. In class, he talked back to his electronics teacher, catching him in errors and challenging him before the other students. His smug superiority made him equally unpopular with staff and classmates, leaving him isolated and with few friends, but his hearty sense of humor was appreciated.

The friends he did have were invariably younger. There was something about him—precision, single-mindedness, and a generosity of spirit—that appealed to youngsters looking for a role model. His best friend through high school was a boy two years younger, Alan Baum, another bright electronics whiz, who eventually went on to MIT. Woz was also a dyed-in-the-wool prankster. He honed his practical-joking skills while developing his talent for electronic design.

Despite his academic shortcomings and pranks, Woz soon became the best technician in the Cupertino neighborhood and was a figure of worship to kids like Bill Fernandez.

In the summer of 1969, Woz and Alan Baum spent a few months filling a folder with schematics and specification sheets for a computer. Then, when Baum left to attend MIT, Woz decided to build the device himself, scavenging parts from surplus stores or directly from sympathetic companies. He convinced Bill Fernandez to help, an attractive idea since the methodical Fernandez had a neat, carefully designed, and eminently accessible workbench in his garage across the street.

"I wanted to design a machine that did something," Wozniak said years later. "On a TV, you turn a knob and it does something. On my computer, you pushed a few buttons and switches, and lights would come on." That was his goal and he succeeded: things could happen. At least, until the power supply exploded as the two boys were demonstrating their machine to a reporter from the *San Jose Mercury News*. It may not have been a sophisticated device, but Wozniak had built it five years before the first hobbyist computer kits appeared on the market.

They called it the "Flair Pen or Cream Soda computer," said Fernandez. "Woz was always drawing schematic designs with them. He said you could tell a real engineer by the Flair pens in his shirt pocket. Purple was the color of choice that year. And all we drank was cream soda in bottles. We were so broke that we would save up the bottles and walk over to Safeway to get the deposits back so we could buy another."

One day Fernandez invited Steve Jobs to see the computer that he and Woz had built. It was the first meeting between Woz and Jobs, and it was by no means auspicious. At eighteen, Wozniak was a bona fide electronics whiz, while Jobs and Fernandez, five years younger, were just a couple of kids who didn't know much of anything practical about the subject. Sure, they liked to play with gadgets, but they were much more interested in doing tricks with lasers and mirrors than they were in doing something worthwhile. Wozniak, on the other hand, had already designed circuit boards on paper for more elaborate computers and regularly visited the Stanford Linear Accelerator library to pore over the most advanced materials he could find.

Jobs was awestruck by the ability represented by the project. Though he had long felt unrivaled in his knowledge of electronics, he was sobered by his realization that Woz was "the first person I met who knew more electronics than I did."

Steve Jobs had already heard about Wozniak from Fernandez and knew his reputation as a highly accomplished prankster. His most famous high school stunt had resulted in Homestead High's principal running out on the athletic field holding at arm's length a heavy and ominously ticking gym bag that had been snatched from a student locker; the bag contained bricks and an alarm clock. This little episode earned Woz a night in Juvenile Hall—and a standing ovation from the student body upon his return the following day.

Steve Jobs and Steve Wozniak seemed to be cut from the same cloth. They both were solitary, self-absorbed, and isolated, neither joiners nor jocks. Their five-year age difference was trumped by the passions they shared. Wozniak had an ardor for electronics that made his sentences run together like a speeding train when he tried to explain a concept or a principle that held his interest.

Jobs also had an intensity, driven by whatever his latest passion might be. He would stand very close to whomever he was talking to, invading the person's space as he poured forth about his newest discovery, and he was nearly impossible to avoid once he made up his mind to buttonhole you. Much later, an acquaintance said of him, "Trying to have a conversation with Steve Jobs is like trying to sip water from a fire hose." Steve had a sharp wit but rarely laughed—not as a boy or even later when he was on top of the world. At times, he was seen to smile, but real, uninhibited laughs were few and far between.

This was always a major difference between the two. Steve Wozniak had a quick wit and loved sharing a joke—it was one of the few things for which he'd take a break from technology. (A few years later, he ran a free Joke-a-Day service in San Jose, and even now he sends out jokes and cartoons almost daily to a select list of friends.) Woz was immersed in computers and electronics, while Jobs was immersed in himself.

Jobs almost certainly knew by then that he was adopted, and this knowledge seemed to have fueled a quest for something that would give his life meaning. The machine that Wozniak and Fernandez were completing was one early element to fill that void.

Woz may have had the know-how, but Steve Jobs certainly had the gumption. When Jobs had an objective, nothing stood in the way of his reaching it. One thing that didn't change over the years was his chutz-pah, his aggressive personal willingness to wade right in, to go for the top person, the decision maker. After the family's move to Los Altos, he began a project to build a frequency counter—a device to track the occurrences of a given electrical frequency in a circuit. When he found that he needed more parts, he picked up the phone and placed a call to Bill Hewlett, one of the founders and principals of Hewlett-Packard. "He was listed in the Palo Alto phone book," explained Jobs. "He answered the phone, and he was real nice. He chatted with me for, like, twenty minutes. He didn't know me at all, but he ended up giving me some parts, and he got me a job that summer working at Hewlett-Packard, on the line assembling frequency counters. . . . Well, 'assembling' may be too strong. I was putting in screws. It didn't matter; I was in heaven."

But as puberty worked its hormonal alterations on Jobs, he began to realize there might be more to life than electronics. "I remember my first day on the assembly line at H-P," he recalled wistfully. "I was expressing my complete enthusiasm and bliss at being there for the summer to my supervisor, a guy named Chris, telling him that my favorite thing in the whole world was electronics. I asked him what his favorite thing to do was, and he looked at me and said, 'To f——k!' "I learned a lot that summer."

Between his sophomore and junior years, Steve Jobs also discovered marijuana. "I got stoned for the first time; I discovered Shakespeare, Dylan Thomas, and all that classic stuff. I read *Moby-Dick* and went back as a junior taking creative writing classes."

Steve marched to his own tune, and as the United States changed from the conformity of the sixties to the individuality of the seventies, he quickly assimilated the countercultural values that interested him— individuality, a refusal to follow the rules or be intimidated by them, and an enthusiasm for mind-expanding drugs. Steve managed to embrace all of this without embracing the hippie ethic of putting out the least possible effort.

Homestead High School was a low, squat school thrown up in the post-war boom that hit the valley. It sits hard by two freeways and is the kind of campuslike school that California specializes in. Land was never much of a problem, so new classrooms were just tacked on to the rest of the school. When classes began in September 1968, Steve Jobs and Bill Fernandez arrived as freshmen.

The two friends from Cupertino Junior High School shared their enthusiasm for technology, but both felt at a distinct disadvantage because they didn't come from heavily scientific households. The school offered an electronics class—John McCollum's Electronics 1—and the pair determined to enroll in it together.

They became "wireheads." The slang name that Silicon Valley high school kids gave to electronics club members had a hip connotation. The name combined the drug orientation of the time with electronics and avoided the bumbling connotation of "nerds." In Silicon Valley, it was "cool" to be into electronics.

Four years earlier, Steve Wozniak had thrived under the authoritarian and practical regimen of the school's science department. He had become the prize student in the electronics classroom—the president of the math and the electronics clubs, a winner of science fair awards, and the designer of endless electronic schematics. For Jobs, the subject never quite caught fire, and as he went through high school, he grew less interested in science and more interested in other things.

"I only vaguely remember Jobs," recalls McCollum. "He kind of faded into the background. He was usually off in a corner doing something on his own and really didn't want to have much of anything to do with either me or the rest of the class.

"But I do remember that one day he was building something and needed some parts that I didn't have, which were only supplied by Burroughs. I suggested that he call the local number for the company, talk to the public affairs people, and see if they wouldn't let him have one or two of the components for his school project.

"The next day he came in as pleased as could be and told me that Burroughs was sending him the parts, and they should arrive very shortly. When I asked how he had managed that, he said he had called the main office, collect, and told them he was working on a new electronic design. He was trying various components and was considering using theirs.

"I was furious. That was not the way I wanted my students to behave. And sure enough, in a day or so the parts arrived by air freight. I didn't like the way he had done it, but I had to respect his results."

As his sophomore year came to a close, the fourteen-year-old Jobs started to drift in new directions. Electronics had begun to lose its appeal, and swimming team practice at the Mountain View Dolphins took up too much time, so he switched to water polo. But that was a short-lived interest. He found that he just didn't have the aggressive killer instinct that it took to "be a jock. I was always a loner." He was looking for something to get involved with. Something interesting.

A shop in Mountain View called Haltek was full of abandoned, rejected, obsolete, and unsorted electronic components. In Silicon Valley, components could be rejected for any number of reasons: a flaw in the paint, too high an incidence of failure in a particular batch, or a newer design that renders obsolete an entire warehouse filled with perfectly good product. More often than not, these orphaned parts showed up at Haltek—and so did all the garage designers and high school kids working on their own projects or experiments. Steve managed to talk his way into a weekend job there during high school.

When Fernandez shared details about the computer that he and Wozniak were building, Steve was already employed at Haltek on weekends and had started to develop a nose for electronics components and their prices that would stay with him for years. The Fernandez-Wozniak project caught his interest, and Jobs started to spend more time at the Fernandez garage. A friendship began to flourish between him and Woz.

They bonded in part over their love for pranks. Woz would design a scheme, and Jobs, with his almost compulsive willingness to be an outlaw, was more than willing to carry it out. His friendship with renowned prankster Wozniak gave him a certain cachet among his peers.

By age sixteen, Steve Jobs wore his hair shoulder-length, and his appearances in school became more and more rare. He was on the periphery of a band of technologically savvy hippies who had discovered how to fool AT&T's long-distance switching equipment. Dubbed "phreaks," the youngsters had learned techniques for completing calls by playing certain frequencies of tones into telephone receivers.

One of the most infamous of these phreaks was a character nicknamed Cap'n Crunch, who discovered that a whistle included in boxes of the cereal could fool the phone company's computers. Steve wanted to meet him, so he tracked him down. Eventually Crunch showed up and took the two amateur outlaws, Steve and Woz, through the world of phone phreaking, spending an evening calling all over the world for free. The two decided they would build their own electronic machine to do the same thing that Crunch did with a whistle.

One approach for doing this involved a homemade device called a blue box. After some research in the Stanford Linear Accelerator library and a number of false starts, Woz came up with a design for a better blue box than any that the other phreaks were using. For one thing, it needed no on/off switch but automatically came to life whenever one of the keys was pressed. This kind of innovation would characterize a Wozniak design for years to come.

"We were ecstatic," said Jobs. "We thought it was absolutely incredible that you could build this little box and make phone calls around the world." None of the phreaks considered the free phone calls a form of stealing—the only loser was the phone company, a synonym for "the establishment." What, they reasoned, could be more honorable than that?

They showed the prototypes to friends, and the interest was obvious and immediate. Everybody wanted one, and the two Steves, now full-fledged phreaks themselves, garnered all sorts of attention.

Jobs, with the gift of persuasion he'd learned from his father, convinced Woz that they should start selling the units. With Jobs using his nose for bargains in buying the parts, their out-of-pocket cost for the first boxes was $40 apiece. Woz, now attending the University of California at Berkeley, did the assembly work in his dorm room; Steve sold the units throughout the buildings on campus. They charged $150 per unit but sweetened the deal with a guarantee of free repairs should any problems arise. As the machines became more and more popular, Jobs demanded as much as $300 from people who looked like they could afford it. Students, however, still qualified for the original price.

His princely income was a major factor in Jobs's declining interest in finishing high school. It was around this time that he met Chris-Ann Brennan, a fellow student working on her own animated movie who avoided any school supervision of the project by doing much of her work at night. In this rejection of authority, Jobs saw a like mind. Soon they were lovers, and he and Chris spent many afternoons taking long walks, drinking wine, and smoking pot. One day, choosing a wheat field as an appealing spot to take some LSD, Jobs recalled that "all of a sudden the wheat field was playing Bach. It was the most wonderful experience of my life up to that point. I felt like the conductor of this symphony with Bach coming through the wheat field."

Wozniak didn't understand any of this. His idea of a good time was to talk about esoteric points of electronics.

Their blue box venture had been fun at the outset, but the scene quickly began to change. The phone company took aggressive steps to combat the scam, and things turned dangerous. One evening Steve was making a sale in a pizza parlor parking lot when he felt a gun being pressed against his body as a crook decided to rip off the rip-off artists. "There were eighteen hundred things I could do, but every one had some probability that he would shoot me in the stomach. I handed over the box."

Jobs's enthusiasm soon cooled. He was interested in expanding his vistas and making money, while searching for answers to something that smoldered inside him. They weren't answers he could discover with a blue box.

Jobs made the journey from Silicon Valley to Berkeley two or three times a week. The ambience in the heart of hippiedom was to his liking, as he traveled through the Bay Area, delving into ideas, practices, and people he rarely encountered in Silicon Valley. Jobs would soon be heading off to college himself, and what he saw in Berkeley profoundly influenced the type of place he chose.

The school that Steve Jobs decided on was Reed College in Portland, Oregon, the Pacific Northwest's premier liberal arts college. Private and expensive, it has always had a reputation for attracting and fostering brilliance and individuality. His parents were aghast—not only at the price, but at the distance from home. Still, "Steve said that Reed was the only college he wanted to go to," recalled his mother, "and if he couldn't go there, he didn't want to go anywhere." Once again, the headstrong boy prevailed over his parents. They bit the bullet, dipped into their savings, and sent him off to Reed.

Steve managed to leave his mark at Reed, not academically but through the sheer force of his personality. His studies came in a distant second to other pursuits. By autumn of 1972, Steve decided to abandon his experimentation with hallucinogens and opted instead for the philosophies of the East as a path to higher awareness. "I was interested in Eastern mysticism, which hit the shores about then. At Reed, there was a constant flow of people stopping by—from Timothy Leary and Richard Alpert to Gary Snyder."

His first-semester grades were poor, so, with his characteristic directness, he dropped out of school and got a refund of the tuition. Yet he remained on campus, living in dorm rooms vacated by other students who'd left to pursue other interests. Reed, being a good liberal school, didn't mind, especially since Jobs had become friends with Jack Dudman, the school's dean of students. "Steve had a very inquiring mind that was enormously attractive," Dudman remembers. "You wouldn't get away with bland statements. He refused to accept automatically received truths. He wanted to examine everything himself."

Steve's decision to drop out but live off the school's bounty made him a celebrity. When the next school year started, he continued to live at Reed. "He very shrewdly perceived that he could get just as good an education without the credit," explained his long-time friend Dan Kottke, who met him as a fellow student at Reed, "and who needs the credit?" Jobs was tired of being poor and idle and still felt like an outsider, even in his group of close friends. Something else was driving him.

"I think it's clear that Steve always had a kind of chip on his shoulder," said Kottke. "At some deep level, there was an insecurity that Steve had to go out and prove himself. I think being an orphan drove Steve in ways that most of us can never understand."

In the spring of 1974, as both Watergate and the end of the Vietnam War played out, Steve was back at his parents' house. While idly leafing through the *San Jose Mercury News*, he saw an employment ad from Atari, a company that, even in forward-looking Silicon Valley, was considered a bit outrageous. Because of the stunning success of the company's landmark video game Pong—the game's installation at one tavern in Sunnyvale caused block-long lines—Atari was in need of electronic technicians. In an ad that became famous in the world of high tech, the company offered the opportunity to "have fun and make money." Steve Jobs applied and, to his shock, was hired.

At the time, Atari was experiencing an exponential growth spurt. Al Alcorn, the chief engineer, remembers, "We were used to folks showing up and saying, 'Hi, I'm going to work for you.' It was part of the brashness of the Valley. Atari was growing fast, I'd hear what their skills are and more often than not I'd say, 'That's it, you're great, you've got a job.'"

One day the personnel director came by and told Alcorn, "We've got this weird guy here. He says he won't leave until we hire him. We either call the cops or hire him." Alcorn replied, "Bring him in."

Jobs was brought in, "dressed in rags basically, hippie stuff. An eighteen-year-old drop-out of Reed College. I don't know why I hired him, except that he was determined to have the job and there was some spark. I really saw the spark in that man, some inner energy, an attitude that he was going to get it done. And he had a vision, too. You know, the definition of a visionary is 'someone with an inner vision not supported by external facts.' He had those great ideas without much to back them up. Except that he believed in them.

"I gave him to Don Lang, who said, 'Oh, no, what are you giving me this guy for? He has b.o., he's different, a goddamn hippie.' But we wound up cutting a deal with him. Jobs could come in at night and wouldn't bother anybody."

Steve was given a number of minor tasks. Then one day he came to Alcorn requesting to be allowed to go to India "to see his guru." At the time, the company was having a problem with its games in Germany. Alcorn decided that Steve could correct whatever problems the Germans had on his way East. So Alcorn gave Steve a quick primer on the situation at the German facility and sent him to the last place you'd expect to find a juvenile hippie who was en route to search for a mystic. Alcorn recalled, "Here are the Germans, you know, 'Snap to! Attention!' And here comes Jobs off the airplane, just scuzzy. [But] I had given him a two-hour course [and] he solved their problem in two hours."

Before leaving, Steve approached his friend Dan Kottke about joining him in India. Kottke was as unusual in his own way as Steve was. Soft-spoken, diffident, and gentle, with a cascade of frizzy, tangled hair that surrounded his head like a mane, he was a superb pianist (his cousin is the pop guitarist Leo Kottke) and was smart enough to have won a National Merit Scholarship. What's more, he wasn't a Californian but hailed from the New York area.

Steve's devotion to the philosophies of the East seemed to be tied to his quests for other truths—the absolutes and the loopholes of science and electronics—and tied as well to his own identity. He was "totally determined to go," said Kottke of the planned trip to India. "He felt some kind of unresolved pain over being adopted. That was the same period that he hired a private investigator to try and track down his mother. He was obsessed with it for a while."

Steve's suggestion that Kottke be his traveling companion raised a problem. "I didn't have any money," Kottke said. "He had this great job at Atari, and he had thousands of dollars. So he offered to pay my airfare, which was very generous. And indeed, had he not offered it, the trip probably wouldn't have happened. I was very dubious about it, and he said 'Come on, I'll pay your way,' because he wanted someone to travel with. So I called up my parents and told them, 'I'm going to India with my friend, and he's going to pay my ticket.' So, of course, my parents, who were worried that I would never come back, gave me a round-trip ticket and plenty of money."

After the stop in Germany, Jobs arrived in India barefoot and threadbare. This was how he chose to dress, as an expression of a specific ideal or aesthetic. In India he was confronted for the first time with people who were poor—not the way California hippies were poor, by choice, but poor by fate. It was an eye-opener for him, as it had been for numerous others before him. The complete contrast with the material comforts of American life was intense and shocking, and it challenged everything he thought he knew up to that moment.

His clothes may have been ragged, but they were Western clothes, and he had something more than "going native" in mind. His idea was to make the journey as a mendicant—a spiritual beggar dependent on the kindness of strangers. He immediately traded his T-shirt and jeans for a lunghi, a loincloth that is the traditional Indian garb for mendicants, and gave away everything else he had. Joined by Kottke, he headed north from Delhi toward the Himalayas, the legendary center of spirituality in India.

They slept in abandoned buildings and bought what food they could in the villages they passed through. True to form, Jobs bargained hard. "He looked at prices everywhere, found out the real price, and haggled. He didn't want to be ripped off," recalled Kottke. His aggressiveness with a woman who sold them watered buffalo milk nearly caused them to be run out of one town.

Completely by chance, the two lucked upon a guru and his followers in the mountains. As Jobs told the story:

"I was walking around in the Himalayas and I stumbled onto this thing that turned out to be a religious festival. There was this baba, a holy man, who was the holy man of this particular festival with his large group of followers. I could smell good food. I hadn't been fortunate enough to smell good food for a long time, so I wandered up to pay my respects and eat some lunch.

"For some reason this baba, upon seeing me sitting there eating, immediately walked over to me and sat down and burst out laughing. He didn't speak much English and I spoke only a little Hindi, but he tried to carry on a conversation and he was rolling on the ground with laughter. Then he grabbed my arm and took me up this mountain trail. It was a little funny, because here were hundreds of Indians who had traveled for thousands of miles to hang out with this guy for ten seconds and I stumble in for something to eat and he's dragging me up this mountain path. We get to the top of this mountain half an hour later and there's this little well and pond at the top of this mountain, and he dunks my head in the water and pulls out a razor from his pocket and starts to shave my head. I'm completely stunned. I'm nineteen years old, in a foreign country, up in the Himalayas, and here is this bizarre Indian baba who has just dragged me away from the rest of the crowd, shaving my head atop this mountain peak."

Jobs was discovering his own truths. "We weren't going to find a place where we could go for a month to be enlightened. It was one of the first times that I started to realize that maybe Thomas Edison did a lot more to improve the world than Karl Marx and Neem Kairolie Baba put together."

The pair of traveling mendicants took off again after only a month in Kainchi. It was the summer high season when India is hottest. The dust was in their teeth and their hair, and they had grown weary of the poverty they saw everywhere. It would always be remembered by both travelers as a country of constant hassles. Kottke took up the narrative: "There's a very famous story in India about a guru called Baba Ji. He's kind of like Davy Crockett over there. He's a well-known mystical yogi who keeps reincarnating and [he's] hundreds of years old.

"Well, presently he was incarnated as this guy Harikan Baba, and we decided that we would go visit him. And that was a real quest. It was a ten-mile hike up a dry desert riverbed, over boulders and along a trail that was almost impossible to follow, and our feet were rubbed raw from the sandals, and all we had on were the lunghi, so the sun was merciless. And finally we found this cliff, with a stairway up, and it was the ashram.

"We'd been going so long, and put so much effort into it, we weren't about to go away. Even though when we got there we both thought the guy was a bit of a bozo. After a couple of days we had had enough. I'm sure he was a very far-out guy, but he was very much into wearing colorful saris, he was really into his wardrobe, changing his clothes all the time. And he was very flowery with his language too. All 'the essence of existence is so and so.' Which did not impress us one little bit.

"We had no idea what we were doing. So when we left, even though we knew it was a long journey, we did so in the afternoon. Then that night, as we were sleeping in the dry creek bed, along came a thunderstorm. And I mean a real thunderstorm, like nothing I'd ever seen before. There we are in our flip flops and thin cotton shawls and the rain is beating on us, and the thunder is roaring, and the lightning is breaking all over us. And it got so intense, and the two of us were both so kind of out of it, that we decided to cover ourselves in the sand.

"There we were, wearing next to nothing, and I remember us hunkering down in the sand trying to defend ourselves from the rain pelting down, trying to dig a hole that we could crawl into so that the rain wouldn't destroy us. I'm sure that was the high point of the trip, because I remember us praying. Out there in the dry creek bed, in the middle of India, completely disoriented, all our rhythms and beliefs shattered, where we were sure a flash flood would come through any moment, the two of us praying to any god that could hear us: 'Dear God, if I ever get through this, I'll be a good person. I promise.'"

They survived to continue their journey. They ate food in bazaars. Kottke finally cut all his hair, not out of some inappropriate fashion statement but because the lice and the fleas and the filth drove him to it. They wanted to see Tibet, so they headed up the mountains. Each contracted scabies in the town of Menali, the site of a famous spa, to go along with the dysentery they'd had for a while. But Kottke also had his traveler's checks stolen. This was the end of the journey. When he went to the bank in New Delhi, it refused to refund the checks to him. Jobs, who was leaving in a few days, gave Kottke all the money he had left—$300.

The whole experience in India had been intense and disturbing. It had been entirely different from anything Jobs had expected, anything he had known in booming Silicon Valley. But it had not been the answer. The inner fire wasn't satisfied. Jobs came back determined to work toward the root of things in a different way.

When Steve returned, he was rather distant and very spaced out. Wearing saffron robes and sporting a shaved head, he drifted into Atari and asked for his job back. This blissed-out kid in an orange toga might have prompted most companies to call for security as soon as he approached the door, but this was Atari, in California, in the 1970s. Atari said, "Sure."

Steve's return to Atari found him torn between the memories of his search for truth in the East and the new reality of electronic game playing and engineering. He remained true to the hippie aesthetic, which was easy enough because Silicon Valley was so close to the hippie meccas of San Francisco and Berkeley. He renewed his relationship with Woz, though soon he slyly began to redefine the relationship, trumping Woz's technical knowledge with his own business skills.

Woz, now working at HP, took advantage of his friend's being back at Atari. The company had put out a game called Gran Track, "the first driving game with a steering wheel," explained Jobs. "Woz was a Gran Track addict, so I would let him in at night and let him onto the production floor, and he would play Gran Track all night long. Then when I came upon a stumbling block on a project, I would get Woz to take a break from his road rally for ten minutes and come and help me. It was a great way to get terrific engineering for free."

It worked like a charm. Woz had no hunger for glory; all he wanted was to do something neat, like design a computer or play more video games. Jobs was the hustler, the man with the plan, the man who knew how to generate the income.

. . .

There was something about Jobs that Nolan Bushnell, the founder of Atari, responded to. "When he wanted to do something, he would give me a schedule of days and weeks, not months and years. I liked that," said Bushnell.

One day, according to Alcorn, Bushnell "grabbed Jobs and made a deal on the side. On his blackboard, Nolan defined the game of Break-Out, how the game would work, the details. Then Alcorn, the head of engineering, took over with the logistics—Jobs could build it as long as he worked at night when none of the other engineers were around. "He said that for every [computer chip] under fifty—or some number—I'm going to give you, like, a thousand dollars or something as a bonus to salary."

In Break-Out, the player would constantly fight a brick wall, trying to "break out" of it to win. Mastering the game turned out to require total concentration upon the task at hand, determination to succeed, and a driven attitude—all of which Jobs and Woz had in their blood.

The design for Break-Out was completed in one forty-eight-hour stretch. The company thought Jobs was designing it, but it was entirely Woz's work. "Steve's role was to buy the candy and cokes while Woz did all the design," said Randy Wigginton, a very young camp follower who would end up at Apple.

True to his past achievements, Woz managed to do the work using a ridiculously small number of chips. Alcorn was impressed and paid Steve the $1,000 he had offered. But Steve went back to Woz and said that Atari had paid only $600. He gave Woz his "half." So Woz, who had done all the work, ended up with $300, while Steve Jobs pocketed $700.

Afterward, Alcorn found that he had a problem. "We could not understand the design. And since Jobs didn't really understand it and didn't want us to know that he hadn't done it, we ended up having to redesign it before it could be shipped."

Woz didn't learn the truth about that transaction until a year later, and the story became a wedge between him and Jobs. On an airplane, Woz spotted Al Alcorn and went over to talk to him. Enough time had passed that Woz thought he could admit that he was the one who had designed the circuitry for the Break-Out game that had used so few chips. In that conversation, Alcorn made a passing mention of the $1,000 he had paid for the design. Woz realized that his friend and partner had shortchanged him. The knowledge was so painful, one source said, that it made Woz cry.

According to Alex Fielding, a longtime friend of both Steves, when Jobs read that story in *On the Firing Line* by Bill Simon (co-author of the present volume), he was highly annoyed and called Woz to complain. "I don't remember that," Jobs insisted, as if "I don't remember" meant "It never happened."

Steve used the money from Atari—whatever the amount—to afford a break, heading for All-One, an apple farm in Oregon where his New Age buddies from Reed hung out. Steve Jobs was in a fantastic frame of mind as he headed north. He was working in the electronics industry, realizing his lifelong dream. Finally, he was actually doing something, actually helping to build something. With his nose for component prices—the result of his time at Haltek, the blue box period, and his father's example in rebuilding and selling cars—plus Wozniak's uncanny abilities, they had a good thing going. They'd done it once before with the blue boxes, so it seemed as if they could probably build something else and sell it. But what should it be?

With the publication of a *Popular Electronics* article in January 1975 announcing the introduction of an Altair computer kit, the first arguably "personal" computer had appeared. All it did was light up a string of bulbs across its front to demonstrate the answers to binary arithmetic questions that had been laboriously hand-coded into the machine's memory banks with a series of switches. But one local teacher with foresight, Bob Albrecht, decided with some cohorts that it was time to issue a call to form a club. Menlo Park was the hub of the "Free University" movement, which Albrecht had spearheaded, developing it out of the offices of the *Whole Earth Catalogue* (a kind of New Age manifesto and how-to guide to the back-to-the-earth sustainability movement). Together with a few like-minded enthusiasts, they put together a computer hobbyists' group to share tips and information, calling it the Homebrew Computer Club. Because of the hefty price tag the kits carried, the members decided that people who already had machines would share them with others who were not so fortunate.

Membership quickly ballooned from the original thirty members to more than one hundred enthusiasts, and the meetings were moved from an alternative school housed in an old mansion in Menlo Park to the Stanford Linear Accelerator Center's auditorium on the edge of the Stanford University campus.

In early 1975, as more of the kits appeared, Steve Jobs was already thinking about how he and Wozniak could profit from this new field. He had to find an angle. When he discovered it, the magic came about pretty much by chance.

2 I had learned one thing about the
electronics business by then: you can't
judge anybody by how young they are
or how they look. The best engineers don't
fit any mold.

—Dick Olson, talking about Steve Jobs in 1976

A Company Is Born

The split personality of Steve Jobs—wannabe businessman
and Zen devotee—showed itself intensely in 1975. He was
deep into the fruitarian, mucusless diet of Ehret, alternating that with
fasting, like a nonconformist leftover from the flower-child era.

Jobs began to attend meditation retreats while employed at Atari.
The nearby Los Altos Zen Center had attracted his attention as a place
to practice Zen. During his spiritual reading period at Reed, Steve
had been drawn by the emphasis on experience, intuition, and self-
fulfillment through inner consciousness. Zen was not an exterior religious structure, and it suited his quest for something more. He'd been
left emotionally reeling from many unsatisfactory answers about his
parents and was searching for spiritual truths. Zen Buddhism provided
satisfactory substitute answers. "Chris-Ann [Steve's high school girl-
friend] was living in a tent up there," Dan Kottke said. "And there was
this Zen master there by the name of Kobin Chino. Steve and I used to
go visit him a lot, mostly in his house, which was near the zendo. And
we would have tea, and sit, and talk.

"Kobin was a very far-out guy, but he had only just arrived from
Japan, and his English was atrocious. So we would sit there and listen

31

to him, and half the time you'd have no idea at all what he was going on about. Well, I thought it was sort of fun and took the whole thing as a kind of light-hearted interlude. But Steve was really serious about it all. This was the time in his life when he became really serious and self-important and just generally unbearable.

"But I remember one time we were sitting there, and all of a sudden Steve says to Kobin, 'What do you think of speed? You know, doing things fast?' He was really serious about it and was really into this idea that the quicker you could do something, the better a person you were. But Kobin just looked at him and started to laugh, which is what he did whenever he thought that something was irrelevant. I thought it was pretty irrelevant, too."

Yet Steve was hooked. He studied with Chino for several years and considered him one of the most important influences in his life. (Years later, Chino became the official "roshi" of Jobs's second company, NeXT, and eventually officiated at Steve's marriage.) The Zen master's secret—the ability to answer a question with whatever is on his mind, impulsively—became a lifelong habit for Jobs. Some people might say that his management style started with Chino, because his study of Zen began the year before he founded Apple. Zen, with its emphasis on the spontaneous and the intuitive, synchronized smoothly with the chaotic style of Nolan Bushnell at Atari, which was the only place Jobs ever really worked.

To a personality that already was essentially unbridled and uncensored, a personality looking for a method to make sense of the madness of the universe and to answer some deep-seated questions, the attraction of Zen Buddhism was enormous. It offered a self-directed approach to religion, which was crucial to a terribly self-important young man. He had no need to depend on anyone else for guidance. Zen fought rational, analytic thinking by elevating intuition and spontaneity. For a young man who had essentially no formal education in anything, this was important. And Zen was mystical and concerned with the big issues—Zen koans like the "journey is the reward" appealed to Steve's sense of truth. He embraced Zen Buddhism more deeply than ever, and Kobin Chino became his master.

At the same time, however, Steve wanted to be a businessman. He wanted a business of his own.

Too young and definitely too inexperienced to know what he couldn't achieve, and ruled by the passion of ideas, he had no sense of why something was impossible. This made him willing to try things that wiser people would have said couldn't be done. He had a force of personality that could simply overrun objections, and his lack of real-world experience kept him from knowing what pitfalls might lie ahead.

The willingness to attempt the unlikely or the unachievable was one trait—perhaps one of the few—that he and Steve Wozniak shared. Woz delighted in doing something better, with fewer parts and more elegant engineering than anyone believed possible. He would go to one of the biweekly Homebrew meetings, pick up an idea or be spurred by a challenge that someone had posed, and work feverishly on a new schematic so that he could stand up and talk about it at the next meeting.

By the fall of 1975, Woz was proudly showing the pieces of a new printed circuit board, and by the end of the year he had built the second of two boards, both designed to drive a color display. Steve Jobs was impressed. Maybe this was what he had been looking for—maybe here was a product that he could build a business around. Of course, in the hothouse environment of the Homebrew Club, Woz was just another energetic enthusiast, and as other members started to mount businesses built around making personal computers, Woz's rough "breadboards" (engineering slang for rough mock-ups of products) attracted little attention.

Steve knew better, and he had faith in his friend's engineering prowess. He talked to Woz about turning it into a business, and Woz agreed to build printed circuit boards that a hobbyist could buy and then load up with components to create a "computer." Meanwhile, Woz continued working at HP and Jobs continued his night work at Atari.

When they were selling the blue boxes, everyone just called them by that name—"blue boxes"—but other hobbyists were already selling circuit boards. Wozniak and Jobs would need a name, a challenge that proved tougher than they'd imagined. Wozniak had his head in circuit design. Steve Jobs, the marketing guy, couldn't come up with anything that either of them much liked. One idea was a second-string choice that grew out of Jobs's admiration for pop lyrics and all the time he'd spent with back-to-the-earth friends on the apple farm in Oregon. Besides, "Apple" would come before "Atari" in the phone book. In the end, with a self-imposed deadline for delivering partnership papers to the local newspaper for publication, they went with the gentle, non-threatening, hardly serious name of Apple Computer. (Eventually Apple would fight a long-running battle with the Beatles over the name, a battle that grew much worse once the iPod made its appearance and Apple moved to dominate the music industry.)

Wozniak bought in on the name but still had doubts about the partnership. Steve Jobs, the hard charger, had to keep his partner pumped up about the project. Woz didn't want to give up his day job, and his family questioned whether Steve Jobs was someone they wanted their son to hang out with, much less start a business with. Jerry Wozniak couldn't understand why his son should have to go fifty-fifty with a kid "who hadn't done anything." And Wozniak's new wife, Alice—he had gotten married a few months earlier at age twenty-five—was fed up with the way Woz had turned their apartment into a spare parts depot.

On April 1, 1976—April Fools' Day—Wozniak finally gave in, signing the ten-page document that gave him and Steve Jobs equal shares in the company, with 10 percent going to Ron Wayne, a Jobs buddy from Atari who had agreed to lend a hand. But none of the three, not even Steve Jobs, saw this as any grand venture. They weren't taking on the world; their big vision was to build the computer boards for $25 and sell them for $50. They hoped to make enough of a profit to earn back what they'd already spent on having Woz's circuitry turned into a professional design for a circuit board that could be built for sale.

Still, they weren't blind to the future possibilities. They called their first product the Apple I, clearly announcing their sense of more apples to fall not far from the tree.

The first challenge facing the intrepid entrepreneurs was the same one that has faced most entrepreneurs before and since: capital. Together, they could come up with only $1,000 cash. Woz sold his HP 65 electronic calculator for $500. Steve Jobs sold his Volkswagen bus for twice that, but the buyer paid only half because the van blew its engine within weeks of the sale. Together, this added up to a very meager bankroll. The picture didn't look any brighter when they took their printed circuit board to a Homebrew meeting one Thursday in April.

Woz stood up, showed the board, talked about the features, and sat down to a thunderous lack of interest.

Then the situation suddenly brightened, setting the stage for everything that lay ahead. As Steve Jobs later described it, "The guy who started one of the first computer stores told us he could sell [our circuit boards] as fully stocked boards if we could make them up and deliver them. It had not dawned on us until then" that the boards might have a bigger market if the purchaser didn't have to solder parts in place himself. The offer was all the more surprising because the man Steve was talking about—Paul Terrell, who had started what would become the first chain of retail computer stores, the Byte Shops—had met Steve at Homebrew meetings and had always avoided him. "You can always tell the guys who are going to give you a hard time," Terrell said later.

The Byte Shop needed product. Terrell was impressed by one demo at a Homebrew meeting and told Steve to "keep in touch." Steve showed up at the Byte Shop the next day, barefoot, to test the level of interest. Jobs was bowled over by the response. Terrell said he would pay $500 for Apple computers. And he wanted *fifty* of them—an order worth $25,000.

"That was the biggest single episode in all of the company's history," said Wozniak. "Nothing in subsequent years was so great and so unexpected." They were in business!

Or almost. Before they could build the computers, they had to have parts, and before they could buy the parts, they had to have money or at least credit. With the order in his back pocket, Steve traveled tirelessly all over the Valley, looking for funding. After a string of turndowns, he approached a big supply house, Kierulff Electronics. Bob Newton, the Kierulff manager, remembers Steve as "an aggressive little kid who didn't present himself very professionally." But he was impressed by Steve's driving intensity and said he would check with Terrell to confirm the order.

Anyone less determined than Steve Jobs would have said, "Okay, I'll call back in a few days," and left. Steve refused to leave until Newton had made the call. Terrell, it turned out, was at an electronics convention, where Newton finally reached him and got confirmation that the skinny youngster sitting at his desk really did have a purchase order for $25,000. That was good enough. Newton gave Steve a credit line to purchase up to $20,000 worth of Kierulff products, but the credit was for only thirty days. Somehow, Steve would have to either deliver finished computers and collect the money to pay for parts or come up with another source of money within a month. Either too rash to understand the risk or too unconcerned to care that he might not be able to raise the money in time, Steve accepted the terms.

Perhaps the best description of high tech in that era came from Dick Olson, whose company assembled circuit boards by "stuffing" (attaching electronic components to them). The barefoot Steve Jobs, in his usual torn jeans, walked in one day to buy Olson's services on credit. Olson wasn't put off, commenting later, "I had learned one thing about the electronics business by then: you can't judge anybody by how young they are or how they look. The best engineers don't fit any mold."

Not long afterward, Steve showed up at the Byte Shop in Palo Alto with a dozen working computer boards—one quarter of the Terrell order. Terrell was not happy. It was a small matter of miscommunication: he had ordered computers. What Steve tried to deliver were plain boards. No cases. No power supplies. No keyboards. No monitors. As far as Steve and Woz were concerned, a fully loaded circuit board was "a computer."

Yet despite the misunderstanding, the boards gave Terrell one more product to offer customers. He accepted the boards and wrote a check for $6,000. That represented a profit for the partnership of $3,000.

By the end of the year, the fledgling company had delivered about 150 Apple Is, representing nearly $100,000 in revenue. Wozniak made almost as much from Apple as he had from his day job at HP. Yet he had no thoughts of walking away from the security of the regular HP paycheck.

In the fall of 1976, Steve Jobs worked very long days at finding the best hardware deals and drumming up new retail outlets. He was also looking for investors and for reliable people to help build the growing company. He was back together again with his high school girlfriend, Chris-Ann. She and Steve were still pursuing the way of Zen Buddhism, and at the zendo they occasionally ran into California governor Jerry Brown, another Zen devotee.

By this time, the Apple I wasn't selling very well at the Byte Shops, and Paul Terrell was thinking of dropping the line. That didn't deter

Steve. Competitors were making headway, and he was determined to outdo them. Meanwhile, Woz, much to the continuing chagrin of his wife, had covered nearly every surface in their kitchen with pieces for the new computer he was designing, which eventually became the Apple II. He had come up with a clever way to send color signals to a television set and was determined to provide plenty of extra expansion slots that would enable users to add cards to increase the functionality of their machines. That turned out to be a brilliant decision, but not for a reason anyone would have guessed at the time. The expansion slots would give developers an opportunity to coattail on the success of the Apple II by providing cards for the computer, increasing the value of the purchaser's machine while building huge revenues for one company after another.

Woz and Jobs also made a key decision about the operating system. The competitive Altair computer used a version of the BASIC programming language that had been written by a Harvard dropout, Bill Gates, and his sidekick Paul Allen, which they were selling to computer manufacturers at $500 for each machine it was installed on, a cost the buyers had to foot. The two Steves determined to provide a language that would be free to the user and would be stored on a chip on the circuit board. Instead of the customer having to first load the operating system each time he or she turned on the computer, before being able to do anything useful, the Apple II would load its operating system automatically, making startup much easier and more intuitive for the nontechnical user. This made the Apple machine the toast of a new generation of hackers who could write programs for the computer as soon as they unpacked it and set it up. Because Microsoft supplied this version of BASIC too, the Apple II was the Seattle company's most profitable computer platform until the IBM PC came along.

Another key innovation grew out of Steve Jobs's decision that the new computer should be *quiet*: it would have no fan. That was a fairly radical notion. Anyone else might have thought the idea absurd, but Steve just charged ahead.

His conviction grew as a result of all the time he'd spent studying Zen and meditating. He found the noise of a fan distracting and, in his intuitive way, was certain that consumers would be much more willing to buy a computer that didn't sit on the desk and churn loudly.

The main source of heat in a computer was the power supply. Getting rid of the fan wouldn't be possible without a different type of power supply. There was just one problem: no suitable unit was available anywhere. That didn't deter Steve. He simply went on a hunt to find somebody who could design one for him.

The man he found was Rod Holt, a forty-something, chain-smoking socialist from the Atari crowd who wanted to charge $200 a day. "We can afford you. Absolutely no problem," Steve assured him, even though they were essentially out of money. Undeterred by reality, Steve was trying to bring the Apple II to life on nothing more than moxie and energy.

"He just conned me into working," Holt said. And work he did—days, nights, and weekends. Week after week, the time that Holt ordinarily would have been out racing motorcycles he instead spent inventing a new power supply for Steve Jobs. To replace the conventional linear unit, which was heavy, hot, and based on technology more than fifty years old, Holt struck out in a new direction. He created a switching power supply that was much more complex but was also lighter, smaller, and cooler. The design substantially reduced the size required for the computer's case and met Steve Jobs's demand of making a fan unnecessary. It also revolutionized the way that power was delivered to electronics products.

In October, two men from Commodore came to see Jobs at the garage where Apple had moved its operations, and they wanted to talk buy-out. A Canadian calculator company, the firm had bought another hobbyist computer based on the same chip that the Apple II used—the MOS 6502—and was looking to expand. Steve was willing to consider it. He named the price: $100,000, Commodore stock, and salaries of $36,000 for both Woz and himself. The deal fell through, but you have to wonder what Steve Jobs and Steve Wozniak would have done with the rest of their lives if Commodore had paid the price and made Steve and Woz employees.

By summer 1976, Woz had made significant strides in designing the II. With the success of the Apple I the two friends had created, as well as the cash their fledgling business had already generated, they were primed to bring their improved machine to the world. That Labor Day weekend, they flew to Atlantic City for the first Personal Computer

Festival. They took along a working mock-up of the Apple II plus a cassette interface card (the precursor of disks) to store data that never worked very well. For the two Steves, the world's first personal computer festival became a very humbling experience.

It started on a red-eye flight to Philadelphia. On the plane, in addition to Jobs and Wozniak, were a number of other West Coast computer-niks. Most significant was the team from Processor Technology in Berkeley, whose members had with them a working version of the "Sol." Sheathed in a sleek metal stamped case with a built-in keyboard, the Sol was the first of the new generation of personal computers. It was self-contained and complete; it came fully assembled and ready to plug into a power supply and a monitor—and since it used the same microprocessor as the Altair, it was basically compatible with programs written for that predecessor. By comparison, the crude "cigar box" mock-up of the Apple II that the two guys from Cupertino carried with them was positively amateurish.

During the flight, Lee Felsenstein, the emcee of the biweekly Homebrew Club meetings, leaned over the back of his seat and talked to Jobs and Woz. Felsenstein, who had been a design consultant to the folks at Processor Technology, took one look at the crude circuit board, with its drastically minimized number of ICs and chips, and decided that "it was thoroughly unimpressive. All they had was a cigar box. I thought that Wozniak might be riding for a big fall. And I wasn't about to get in his way."

The convention was held in a decaying Atlantic City at a time before casinos appeared to revitalize that seaside resort. The buzz on the floor was all about what would happen to Ed Roberts and MITS, the company that had created the first hobbyist computer. The founder of Altair was casting about for buyers, and rumors swirled. Worried by the competition that suddenly erupted all over the industry, Roberts wanted out—but he was shrewd enough to know that he could probably still sell out for a substantial bundle of cash. Some of the biggest names in the retail electronics business were looking at the personal computer market—notably, Tandy, with its chain of Radio Shack stores, and Commodore, known for its aggressive marketing of calculators with inexpensive Texas Instruments chips during the early 1970s. Roberts was looking for a buyer.

While Roberts looked for cash, dozens of hobbyists and engineers wanted to take over the number-two position in the business. The Altair was still unquestionably the premier personal computer, but the explosion of retail stores and computer kit sales made it obvious by the fall of 1976 that there was a market for computers. The scramble for dominance was underway.

At that show, numerous new computers were on display. It was impossible to know who would succeed. But for Steve Jobs, a few things became evident as he walked around the convention floor. First of all, the new Apple had to be a complete, self-contained device to satisfy the new wave of computer buyers. Terrell, of the Byte Shops, had told him this, but as Steve saw for himself the second generation of machines that reflected this wisdom, he had to accept the message. A keyboard, too, was essential for input and programming, and since several of the new machines included keyboards, it was clear that to be competitive, the new Apple had to have one, too.

Then there was the matter of promotion. Apple had a booth that was fronted by a card table and framed by a row of yellow curtains, with another shoestring operation on either side. Its booth was decorated with a laminated copy of an article about Apple Computer in a hobbyist magazine and a single printed name card. It was far from impressive. Add the open-necked shirts, long hair, scraggly beards, and mustaches sported by Jobs, Wozniak, and Dan Kottke, who was helping out, and it all added up to an operation that didn't inspire much confidence. MITS and the newest companies on the block, IMSAI and Processor Technology, had enormous booths with all the flash, dazzle, and sizzle of trade-show hype—miniskirted girls, hourly demonstrations, three piece–suited marketing sharpies, and button-down engineers. While Apple was off to the side, where only dedicated enthusiasts bothered to go, the leading companies were out in the high-visibility center of the floor. None of the power brokers came to visit the Apple booth. The most unconventional of the computer companies, the one from deep in the heart of Silicon Valley, was all but invisible in the ballooning hype of the hobbyist electronics business.

Jobs and Wozniak's first complete circuit board, which they had thought of as "the Apple I Computer," even without the case, the power supply, the monitor, or the keyboard, cost around $250 per unit for parts and assembly. That was difficult enough for the two fledgling businessmen to raise. With the ambition of adding all the elements that the market seemed to require, Jobs knew that he'd have to find another source of capital. If he truly wished to make the kind of market splash that he envisioned for the Apple II, it would cost a lot of money. Furthermore, it required an expertise in public relations and advertising that neither Jobs nor Wozniak had ever encountered.

By the time Jobs left the Personal Computer Festival, he understood that to succeed with the new computer Wozniak had designed, he would require a new orientation to the business of computing.

Steve Jobs later explained the computer he led Woz to create as a result of attending their first computer show. "The real jump of the Apple II was that it was a finished product. It was the first computer that you could buy that wasn't a kit. It was fully assembled and had its own case and its own keyboard, and you could actually sit down and use it. And that was the breakthrough of the Apple II: that it looked like a real product. You didn't have to be a hardware hobbyist with the Apple II. That's what the Apple II was all about."

As pressure mounted in late 1976 to get the Apple II ready for market and to continue building the company, Steve Jobs showed an awareness of his own limitations, combined with an almost uncanny ability to hunt down exceptional people and cajole them into joining the effort. He had a salesman's enthusiasm for the product, an evangelist's bible-thumping passion, a zealot's singularity of purpose, and a poor kid's determination to make his business a success. In that stew of characteristics lay both the seeds that would make Apple a success and the poison that would turn so many people into Steve Jobs's enemies.

One unanswerable question is, Where does good taste come from? That fall, the semiconductor company Intel ran a clever, attention-getting advertising campaign that ignored the usual technical claims for its products and instead relied on symbols—poker chips, hamburgers, and race cars. Steve Jobs was immediately struck by the imagination that this represented and the way it spoke directly to the reader. This one ad would shape his attitudes toward advertising for all the years ahead. He called the Intel marketing department and managed to find out that the Regis McKenna Agency had created the campaign.

Steve called the agency and asked to speak to McKenna but was instead shunted to the man responsible for handling new accounts, Frank Burge. Frank listened politely to Steve's description of his company and where he wanted to take it, and then he tried to explain why Apple wasn't yet ready to be represented by an agency with the stature of McKenna.

Undissuaded, every day for the next week Steve called Burge and badgered him about coming over to see the new Apple product. Finally, Steve simply wore him down.

"As I was driving over to the garage, I was thinking, 'Holy Christ, this guy is going to be something else. What's the least amount of time I can spend with this clown without being rude and then get back to something more profitable?'

"For about two minutes I was just thinking of escaping. Then in about three minutes, two things hit me. First, he was an incredibly smart young man. Second, I didn't understand a fiftieth of what he was talking about."

"Incredibly smart" wasn't enough, however, and the agency still turned him down. Steve was determined, though. He called McKenna's office three or four times a day. McKenna's secretary probably got fed up answering the calls and, just to stop the persistent young man from bothering her, pressured her boss. McKenna took the call and was persuaded to let Jobs come in and talk to him.

The two Steves went together. During the conversation, Jobs mentioned an article that Woz had been working on for a hobbyist magazine, and McKenna asked to look at the draft, advising that it not be too technical. Wozniak, bristling, blurted out, "I don't want any PR man touching my copy!" To which McKenna retorted that then they had both better get out. Jobs calmed the ruffled feathers and convinced McKenna that they were indeed a viable company, with a superb product, and that he should take them on. When McKenna proved reluctant, Jobs pulled his now-customary tactic of refusing to leave the office until McKenna consented to handle the account.

Steve was so persuasive that Regis McKenna, in a decision that would turn out to be hugely beneficial for all of them, agreed to accept Apple Computer as a client.

· · ·

For Regis McKenna, it was clear from the beginning that Apple would be able to grow its sales only by reaching beyond the hobbyist market. And this path would require advertising in a widely seen, visible publication where no electronics company had dared to go before. McKenna wanted national attention, to make the media sit up and take notice of the little company with the garage-built computer. Where would you advertise to achieve a goal like that? Regis had the answer. All of his studies showed that computers were bought by men, so the advertising should go somewhere with a high male readership. He chose *Playboy* magazine.

Apple Computer now had a capable, brilliant agency and an astute media selection. There was just one problem: the company didn't have enough money to advertise in *Playboy*.

Money means something different in Silicon Valley; it simply does. The annals of the Valley are filled with stories of people who were at the right place at the right time. Still, finding working capital was another matter. Getting those lucky enough to become wealthy in Silicon Valley to open their wallets was a dance of an altogether different kind, which eventually would be called Venture Capital. Back then it was just difficult. McKenna suggested that Steve talk with a board member of his agency, a man who was also on the board of Atari: Don Valentine.

Jobs called Valentine and convinced him to come over and look at their garage operation. A self-made man, the son of a truck driver, and an ex-Marine, Valentine had successfully headed the marketing departments of both Fairchild and, subsequently, National Semiconductor. In the early seventies, he quit working for others and started a venture capital group. His reputation in the closed world of Silicon Valley was as a no-nonsense guy who knew the electronics world and wasn't about to be taken in by any hype. He also knew that some of these strange engineering start-ups were going to redefine the world.

Don drove a Mercedes Benz and was neat, well-heeled, and well-tailored, wearing Brooks Brothers suits in a business filled with engineers dressed in open-necked polyester shirts. When he showed up at Jobs's parents' house, the pair of scruffy thinkers he encountered were not his idea of a good business bet. After looking at their newest product and listening to their plans for selling a few thousand computers a year, he told them that neither one knew anything about marketing, neither had any sense of the size of the potential market, and they weren't thinking big enough, as he recalled later. He would be willing to talk about investing only if they brought in someone who had marketing expertise. Jobs, with characteristic directness, asked him to recommend some of the people he had in mind. Valentine demurred. After a week of three or four phone calls a day from the persistent Jobs, the venture capitalist finally cracked open his Rolodex. Valentine suggested three names to him; one of them was Mike Markkula. (The venture capitalist learned his lesson, however—many years later when Valentine was approached by an equally odd couple, the founders of Cisco Systems, he agreed to put up the money to start the company.)

At the time that Steve Jobs called him, Markkula was enjoying a life of leisure. While a marketer at Intel in the early seventies, he had acquired stock options from other employees, in addition to the ones he himself had earned. When Intel went public, those options made Markkula rich overnight. He was casually looking around for other ventures to involve himself in, but with two small children, houses in Cupertino and Lake Tahoe, and enough money to keep him going indefinitely, he was in no hurry. Nonetheless, he agreed to come to the Cupertino garage.

When Markkula arrived, Jobs and Woz found him to be a short, slender, lithe man—he'd been a gymnast in high school. He was quiet, reserved, and precise, with wire-framed glasses and a diffident manner. He played the guitar, wore an expensive gold watch, and drove a gold Corvette. Like Woz and Jobs, he was a loner.

There was one very big difference: Markkula understood the effect that the microprocessor might have on the world. He understood that it was only a matter of time before someone came up with the right computer—one that made use of the microprocessor and did something more thrilling than display the time or add lines of numbers. And because he had worked for a company that supplied the consumer electronics world, he sensed how explosive the development of a new item could be. When the partners showed him their new machine and ran through a few displays, Markkula forgot about how Jobs looked. He forgot about where the company was headquartered. He forgot about all the reasons he shouldn't get involved. And he offered to help them draw up a business plan and get the venture off the ground. Woz was leery about bringing someone new into the venture, but Jobs knew that he needed help to make Apple into the kind of successful business he had imagined at the Personal Computing Festival. And in Markkula, he recognized the type of quiet, relaxed, unassuming guy that he knew he could overpower.

Steve Jobs showed Markkula the vision and convinced him that they could change the world by selling computers to homes and offices. Markkula decided that he was right. He started to come by the garage. An engineer by training, he soon became intrigued by writing software and quickly developed into a full-fledged amateur hacker. He talked things over with Jobs, Wozniak, and Rod Holt, the power-supply engineer who had decided it was worth hanging around. (Ron Wayne, their original partner, had long since departed. "Steve Jobs was an absolute whirlwind," he said, "and I had lost the energy needed to ride whirlwinds." He's never had any regrets. "I made the best decision with the information available to me at the time." As of 1999, he was living in Tucson and still working in technology.) Pretty soon, Markkula was convinced that they could put Apple onto the Fortune 500 in less than five years. Time would prove him right.

Richard Melman, who had gotten to know Markkula when they were both at Intel, remembers a lunch the two shared late in 1976. "He told me that he had these two kids, and they were going to build microcomputers." Markkula pulled out his business plan, and Melman remembers it distinctly. "He told me that the company was going to be a billion-dollar business, and he showed me all his charts and graphs proving it. I remember walking away, thinking, 'That guy is crazy! How could anybody have the gall to say that he was going to build a billion-dollar company? That was bigger than Intel. He was nuts.'"

Markkula was convinced and very sure of himself. He started by offering Steve Jobs business advice, drew up that business plan mostly on his own, and stayed on to become Apple's principal early investor. His initial backing amounted to $91,000 in cash, with a personal guarantee on a bank line of credit for another $250,000—in return for equal one-third ownership with Woz and Jobs and 10 percent to Holt, who became a company engineer.

The founders gathered poolside at Markkula's home on January 3, 1977, where Mike and the two Steves spent the day arguing before finally signing the papers that turned Apple Computer Company into a corporation. Part of the deal that Markkula insisted on was that Steve Jobs and Woz would become full-time Apple employees; Woz would finally have to bite the bullet and leave the security of his job at HP. But there wasn't any need to discuss the name: "Apple" was already too well known to even think about changing it.

Markkula introduced the team to Mike Scott, an executive at chipmaker National Semiconductor. Quite the opposite of amiable Markkula, Scott had the rough edges and sharp qualities of a streetsmart guy who had succeeded on guts and determination. He and Jobs were cut from different cloth. Jobs didn't like Scott, and what loomed ahead was years of management struggle.

Nonetheless, Scott was hired with the title of president. Because there was already a Mike, he took the nickname Scotty and joined Bill Fernandez, Randy Wigginton, Chris Espinosa, and Rod Holt as the earliest employees in the trenches. The presidential salary would be $20,001. This was $1 more than any of the three major shareholders earned, but the power resided with Woz, Jobs, and Markkula, and Scott knew it.

Jobs and Scott fought over many things, some important, some trivial—who would sign the purchase orders, how the offices would be laid out, the color of the workbenches. They even fought over the awarding of employee numbers. Jobs was upset that he was designated employee number two, to Wozniak's number one. In tears, he demanded that he be given "number zero." (Jobs finally won that round, but not until a good deal later, when Scott was fired.)

At one point, Scotty took Jobs out into the parking lot for a walk, which was where most of the company's important decisions were made. But this wasn't about a company decision. Scotty brought up the delicate matter of body odor. Jobs, deeply dedicated to the fruitarian diet, was sure that because of the fruit, he didn't need to shower. The gist of the message was that no one in the office could stand to work near him.

As Apple sprang to life as a corporation, two Steve Jobs traits came into focus: his drive for perfection and the twin trait of impatience. He couldn't understand why everything he wanted seemed to take so long. This was especially true about the mysterious art of writing software—an even greater problem because Steve had so little understanding of the process and even less awareness of the equally demanding chore of combing the lines of code for bugs. Worse, the company's entire programming staff was made up of two kids who were even younger than Steve.

Randy Wigginton started programming for Apple while still in high school, and he remembers, "I was just this kid to him. I was working for $2.50 an hour. And I'd get up at 3:30 in the morning and work from then until I went to school, then come back after school and work until 7 or 7:30 at night." But Randy had his eyes open when things started to come unglued between the two Steves. "The friendship between Woz and Jobs dissolved in that period. By the time of the Apple II introduction, there was not much pretense left. [Steve Jobs's] strength was that he was always concerned with the end-user—how things would look onscreen, what the case was like. But the way he went about telling us was so superior that we hated him."

If they couldn't agree on much else, at least Jobs, Woz, Markkula, and Scotty were all in accord that the company needed to make a major splash at the upcoming West Coast Computer Faire, the first major trade show on the West Coast. Jobs had had the foresight to sign up early—early enough to capture a booth position directly opposite the entrance doors, the first thing people would see as they walked in.

Markkula spent $5,000 on booth design alone, which was a lot of money for a small company in 1977. It featured a smoky back-lit Plexiglas panel with the company name and logo on it. Black velvet draperies wrapped the booth, which held three brand-new Apple IIs (the only three in existence) and one large-screen monitor displaying the antics of the games and the demo programs that Wigginton, Wozniak, and the other programmer, Chris Espinosa, had written. The contrast would be enormous between the Apple display and the folding tables with handwritten signs that other companies would be using—the same kind of makeshift arrangement that Jobs and Woz themselves had set up at their first show with the Apple I only six months earlier.

At the last minute, the new plastic cases for the Apple IIs were finally delivered. Steve had decided that the Apple II had to look like a KLH stereo—an integrated dorm unit then popular that had an appealing physical design. When he saw the cases, he was furious: they looked dreadful. He set the small crew of the faithful Apple employees to work sanding, scraping, and spray-painting.

The next morning, when the doors to the Faire were thrown open at 10 A.M., the first visitors to stream in found themselves face-to-face with the sleekest, most handsome, most professional-looking personal computer the world had ever seen. And when the guys manning the booth pulled the cases open, the hobbyists, the nerds, media people, and others saw the most advanced motherboard anyone had ever dreamed of. Woz had outdone himself once again, with a design that crammed onto the board sixty-two chips and ICs—an unheard-of achievement. And Jobs's overbearing demands that every solder connection be done with a neat, attractive straight line gave the workmanship a quality look that was as pleasing and surprising as it was unsurpassed.

People crowded around, unwilling to believe that the electronics in those small boxes could possibly be responsible for creating the dynamic images in vivid color on the giant television screen. Steve Jobs, looking almost dapper in his first suit, had to continually whip away the draperies to prove that there was no big computer hidden out of sight.

"After the Faire, we had a sense of exhilaration for having pulled off something so well, not just for Apple, but for the whole computer movement." That was the view of programmer Espinosa, at the time still a junior in high school.

Within months, Apple had received three hundred orders for the Apple II, already triple the number of Apple Is ever sold. But Steve saw to it that owners of the original Apples could upgrade; it was the kind of issue he intuitively understood. For all of his personal complexities, he always held to the ethic of "what was right," even when it was costly to the company. The upgrade policy would remain in place until Steve left Apple.

That summer, Steve Jobs lived in Cupertino with his friend Dan Kottke. Steve's on-again/off-again girlfriend, Chris-Ann, who by this time worked as an assembler at Apple, moved in with him. But an old problem followed them, a problem that has plagued many entrepreneurs and would plague thousands in the high-tech industry in the years ahead: the difficulty of a wife or a girlfriend competing with the mistress called "work." Chris-Ann was low on Steve's list of priorities. The problems between them grew worse when late in the summer she became pregnant.

For reasons that have never been clear, for years Steve Jobs denied that he was the father and refused to have anything to do with the idea of being a father to a child. Chris-Ann smashed the dishes, wrote on the walls, and broke doors and windows. Steve put up with her justified but unruly behavior until at last she adamantly refused to have an abortion. At that, Steve gave up on the relationship, and Chris-Ann quit her Apple job and headed up to the apple farm in Oregon.

Dan watched all this in disbelief. Through the years, he had listened to so many anguished distress messages and sermons from Steve about being abandoned by his parents. Now Jobs was willing to let one more fatherless child come into the world? To Dan, it just didn't make sense. Their friendship cooled.

On top of the battles with Chris-Ann at home, Steve continued his battles with Scotty at work. The standard warranty in the electronics business was ninety days; Steve insisted that they needed to sell the Apple II with a one-year warranty, understanding instinctively that you built a loyal body of customers by treating them well. Scotty was adamant. Steve started to cry. Scotty took him outside for another walk around the parking lot. When they returned, both had cooled down, but Steve prevailed: the warranty would be for one year.

Steve could infuriate his employees but at the same time stand on a pedestal as the creator of the dream and the culture, the crusader leading the charge. He was the guy who kept the Apple polished.

He could be the toughest son of a bitch in town, able to outmaneuver smart, experienced men twice his age. One day programmer Wigginton, working feverishly on a new version of BASIC, found that his six weeks of work had vanished from the Call Computer time-sharing system where Apple maintained an account. On its own, the firm could not yet afford the large computers needed for storage. Wigginton tried frantically to recover his work but couldn't. The time-share center had done a routine back-up, he learned, and somehow thousands of lines of his code had simply disappeared. He phoned the company and asked its employees to mount a tape reel with the previous back-up; though it wasn't very recent, it would at least mean that he wouldn't have to start from scratch. Alex Kamradt, the head of the company, refused. He hadn't liked the way that Jobs and Woz had treated him in the past.

Worse, Apple was going through a cash-flow crunch and hadn't paid its bill for several months.

Steve Jobs stepped in, cooled Kamradt down, and offered to pay him on the spot if he would come over and pick up the check. Kamradt agreed. Just before Kamradt hung up and started out the door, Steve convinced him to load the tape reel so that Wigginton could go back to work.

While Kamradt was driving over, Wigginton downloaded the back-up file, signed off the system, and left the building, followed by the rest of the staff, who guessed what was about to happen. When Kamradt showed up, Steve told him there was no check, he wasn't going to get paid because his computers had wiped out weeks of work, and he could go to hell.

It took guts for Steve Jobs to talk that way to a man like Kamradt, an ex-boxer with cauliflower ears, a mashed nose, and a short temper. Jobs, the skinny vegetarian for whom Zen meditation was the closest thing to exercise, stood his ground; if he ever knew fear at moments like this, he never showed it. Kamradt backed down and stalked out, furious but empty-handed.

When Steve had needed to make a decision about a case for the Apple II, he figured on selling about the same number of units they had with the Apple I, and he chose a less expensive process. Now the decision came back to haunt him: the machine tooling for the Apple II case gave out, and just at a time when customers were demanding machines, suppliers were demanding payment, and cash flow had dwindled to a trickle. Scotty had tried his best to juggle by making purchases on forty-five or sixty days' credit to delay the outgo, while selling to customers on thirty-day terms. But no cases meant no computers, and that meant no income.

Steve showed his usual business acumen by coming up with a scheme to solve the crisis. He offered the case manufacturer a bonus of $1,000 per week for every week ahead of schedule that he delivered. It worked. The new tooling was quickly finished, Apple had cases again and went back to shipping, and the desperate cash situation soon cleared up. The company had been within a hairbreadth of bankruptcy, only a few days from closing its doors.

Disaster had been averted, but Markkula realized that he'd have to find venture capital earlier than he'd intended. Between them, he and Scott loaned the company more than $200,000 as a stopgap while Mike "went to the well," searching for venture capital.

At the same time, Steve Jobs was undergoing a change—at least, in outward appearance. Though twenty-three years old, he was rich, if only on paper. His hair was just as long but now carefully styled, as he grew into the "wonder boy" role that the media labeled him with at Regis McKenna's urging. When Markkula and Scott flew to New York to present Apple's venture capital pitch in front of the Venrock investment group, they took the newly presentable Steve Jobs along with them.

The early computer boards—the kind that Woz and Steve showed at Homebrew meetings—had zero appeal to anyone but a hobbyist. Now, in 1977, with Apple sales humming along, the company still faced the main challenge that had plagued Apple and its competitors from the start: what's a computer good for? A number of people and groups were working on software packages that would begin to provide an answer, but until those useful packages appeared, consumers continued to see the computer as a toy.

Another problem was more fundamental. In operation, a computer must carry out streams of instructions in sequence, handle lots of incoming data, and spew out reams of results. At the very beginning of the computer age, instructions and data had been entered by throwing switches or plugging in patch cords. Advances had brought first the punch card, then reels of magnetic tape. Woz's earliest designs had involved typing in everything by hand, then using a cassette tape to store data. For personal computers, the disk drive, which used a big floppy disk made of magnetic material encased in a paper or plastic sleeve, was beginning to look like the solution of choice for storage.

At a landmark meeting of the Apple staff in December 1977, Mike Markkula turned to Wozniak and told him that Apple had to have a disk drive ready in time for the upcoming Consumer Electronics Show (CES) in Las Vegas. The show was one month away.

No one would have even presented such a challenge to anybody but Wozniak. The timetable was impossible, but *impossible* was a word that

Woz didn't seem to have in his vocabulary. With the kind of gusto he relished, he tapped young Randy Wigginton as a teammate and threw himself into the project.

"Christmas Eve of 1977," Randy said, "Woz and I finally got the disk drive to write and read something. And to celebrate, we went out and got a milkshake.

"The night before CES, we got to Las Vegas and it still wasn't finished. The hardware was working, but the software wasn't. So Woz and I would work on it for an hour, then go out and gamble for an hour. I was seventeen at the time, and we were out there throwing craps. We did that all night long, and I got no sleep. About seven o'clock in the morning I finally got it working, and Woz said, 'You had better back it up,' and I backed it up in the wrong way and destroyed what we had done in the last hour, and we had to do that over again."

Somehow they got it working in time, and the drive became the runaway sensation of the show. As usual it had the Woz touch: it used far fewer components than anything else on the market. The emcee of the Homebrew meetings, Lee Felsenstein, remembers seeing it there. "I nearly dropped my pants," he said. "It was so clever. I thought, 'We better keep out of the way of these guys.'"

On May 17, 1978, at the All-One farmhouse in Oregon where Steve Jobs liked to hang out with his Zen buddies and pick apples, Chris-Ann gave birth to the baby that Steve had tried so hard to deny. Steve appeared a couple of days later, stayed long enough to help select the little girl's name (they decided on Lisa Nicole), and promptly left. Over the next few months, he voluntarily contributed child support, then stopped. Chris-Ann let it be known that she would agree to a settlement of $20,000. Markkula encouraged Steve to up the figure to $80,000 and be done with it. Steve again insisted that he wasn't the father and refused to let Chris-Ann have any settlement at all.

Steve Jobs was a young man who had set the rules in life from a very early age. By refusing to go to high school, he had forced his parents to move to a new neighborhood. He had convinced them to let him attend a more expensive college than they could afford—then he dropped out. In business, he had coerced one established professional after another to work for him, extend terms that he insisted on, or in some other way yield to his demands. Now he was faced with someone who wouldn't let him set the agenda. Chris-Ann had refused to get rid of the child, refused to acknowledge someone else as the father, and refused to disappear. This was bitter medicine. With the birth of the child, Chris-Ann had tied him down and thrown her anchor around him, and no matter how far Steve might run or climb, this child would always be there to remind him of that period of his life. For the first time, Steve was powerless.

He was still living in Cupertino in the house he shared with Dan Kottke, where they had had a long string of roommates, including a pair of strippers and a gun enthusiast who liked to shoot his Colt .45 pistols into the air.

Locating another lady to prove to Chris-Ann that their connection was broken became Steve's priority. Finding a new woman, however, was harder than finding a roommate. Steve had never been a woman-izer. He found dating uncomfortable, small talk difficult, and the whole dating scene unappealing. So, instead of dating, he simply chose a woman he had already been thrown into contact with.

For Steve Jobs, the offices of his public relations guru, Regis McKenna, were proving an attractive place to visit. Any good PR man knows about keeping his clients happy, and Regis wasn't just one of the good, he was one of the great, continually coming up with strategies that broke the mold.

Part of the Regis formula for keeping his clients in a positive frame of mind dictated his staffing policy. Regis wasn't bashful about being obvious: if elegant, unusually attractive young women could help keep a smile on the clients' faces, then that's who he would hire. The McKenna staff was well supplied with head-turners. As part of the required uniform, McKenna demanded a cashmere blazer. One touch would signal the luxurious, sensual elegance of success.

One day Steve Jobs met a member of this McKenna harem, Barbara Jasinski, a striking beauty with a heritage that combined Polynesia with Eastern Europe. The combination was stunning. It wasn't long before Steve began heading to Barbara's tiny bungalow in the hills on most evenings.

By this time, while he still considered drugs an essential element in gaining perspective, he had all but given up using them. That represented quite a change. Chris Espinosa, recalling how it had been at first, when he was still a teenager, said, "Every time I saw him, for years, he asked me if I had a girlfriend yet, or if I had dropped acid. That was all he cared about. It got so that I would be embarrassed before he even opened his mouth because I knew what he was going to ask. And since I had done neither, I dreaded it."

But if Steve's attitude toward drugs had now changed, his relationship with Apple president Scott had not. Things had grown so bad that their knock-down, drag-out confrontations had come to be known around Apple as "the Scotty Wars." One typical example: for Apple's first Christmas party, in 1977, Steve went wild when Scotty refused to tell the caterers that they should plan a vegetarian menu.

Scott got some of his own back when he learned that to relax the tensions of a tough day, Steve liked to immerse his feet in the toilet bowl and flush. The tale spread throughout the company, making Steve the butt of many jokes.

By 1978, the company had grown to a workforce of about sixty people, orders continued to pour in, and cash-flow problems were a thing of the past. Steve Jobs and Mike Markkula were looking ahead. They thought that the Apple II had about reached saturation; it was time to think about a new machine.

Customer feedback had already pointed out some needed improvements. Though it's a little hard to grasp this concept now, the Apple II displayed only capital letters, on rows that were only forty characters wide. Both of these shortcomings would need to be corrected if the machine was going to be considered a serious business computer. Plans were laid for an interim machine, dubbed the Apple II Plus, and for a major upgrade that would be released as the Apple III.

Steve would later say that you could start a new company with A players, and they would hire other A players, but that as soon as you hired a B player, he would hire others, and before long you had a company filled with B players and C players. In the view of Apple marketer Trip Hawkins (who went on to cofound Electronic Arts, the game maker), that was already happening. Apple had become a company that could do no wrong, Trip believed. "It was the Camelot of business. Basically, market demand propelled the growth of the company, and it covered up a lot of mistakes. So you could have incompetent people running around spending a lot of money and it wouldn't be noticed because the demand for the Apple II was so strong." Inside the company, old timers called it the Bozo Explosion.

That problem of incompetent people infected the Apple III but wasn't the main source of difficulty. "Steve Jobs got involved in the Apple III in a way that was really disruptive," Trip explained. Steve had taken it on himself to design the external package, but he'd made it too small for everything the team had designed to go in the box. Steve refused to consider changes in the configuration of the case. When the Apple IIIs were shipped, they never worked properly. The fault was at least partly Steve's, but by then he was off to other things and had washed his hands of anything to do with the new product. The blame fell on the engineers.

In late summer of 1979, Apple sold $7,273,801 worth of stock privately, purchased in large blocks by sixteen buyers, among them some of the largest venture capital and merchant banking companies in the world.

One of the investors was Xerox Development Corporation, the strategic planning, acquisition, and venture capital arm of Xerox, where two men shared the task of finding venture-investing opportunities. One of them, Stevan Birnbaum, remembers that Jobs "projected the feeling that he was going to succeed with or without us and we'd better get on board." Despite the scruffy appearance of Steve and his partner Woz, the Xerox men decided to take part. Birnbaum's recollection is that "we invested $1,050,000." It proved to be a decision they wouldn't regret.

With a market now available for his shares, Steve Jobs sold just over a million dollars' worth of his personal holdings. At twenty-four years old, as a result of his own drive but partly despite himself, Steve Jobs was a millionaire.

He bought a house in the hillside town of Los Gatos, nestled up under the Santa Cruz mountains, and left it practically undecorated except for a painting by Maxfield Parrish, a well-known illustrator whose works now hang in New York's Metropolitan Museum of Art and elsewhere. The house was testimony to Steve's asceticism. It had no furniture other than cushions and a mattress on the floor of his bedroom.

He also bought the first of his Mercedes coupes. He added a BMW motorcycle with orange pom-poms on the handlebars, and he and Kottke went for extended spins through the mountains and back roads behind Stanford, skinny-dipping in a reservoir that was hidden by a slight rise from the stream of nine-to-fivers whipping past along Route 280.

The money Steve spent did not all go toward self-indulgence. He generously financed a charitable organization that provided assistance to blind people in Nepal and India.

The change in lifestyle was accompanied by a change in his outlook. Steve made a conscious decision to become more of a businessman. He was determined to learn what he could about running a company by paying closer attention to the business side of Apple and trying not to buck the system. He didn't give up Zen meditation, but he continued to keep his hair as neat as it had been for the investment bankers' session in New York, and he wore suits when he needed to.

By the late 1970s, most high schools in the country, in a perhaps misdirected effort, were attempting to prepare their students for the computer age by teaching BASIC programming as a standard part of the curriculum. A vast educational market developed for the Apple II, a market completely unanticipated by the company and never even mentioned in the original business plan. After students used the computers at school, the Apple II quickly became the brand of choice for most high schoolers bent on convincing Mom and Dad to buy them a computer for Christmas. In the early years, this surprise market sustained Apple.

It was also the year that a word processing program finally made it onto the shelves of computer stores. Called AppleWriter, it was created by a man named Paul Lukas, a hippie sitting in a cabin high up in the mountains of Oregon. The program worked hand-in-hand with the company's first printer, the Silentype, and heralded the start of a loosely comprehensive set of products. A Dow Jones stock market package had also been finished, as had a checkbook-balancing effort that Mike Markkula had worked on. At last, there were a few reasons for a businessperson to start thinking about owning a personal computer.

By now, the company had grown into a bureaucracy—albeit a benevolent one, with humanistic values, where no one was fired and where topics like the official company culture could be endlessly debated.

That summer, Steve Jobs agreed to a paternity test. In the days before modern DNA analysis, the report came back showing a 94.97 percent chance that he was the father of Lisa Nicole. Steve still refused to accept it and still refused to pay consistent child support. Chris-Ann ended up on welfare. It took a court order the following year, in an action filed by the County of San Mateo, to force his hand. Steve finally agreed to pay support, to reimburse the county $5,000 for welfare payments, and to provide medical and dental insurance.

He could be forced to pay, but the county would not force him to spend time with the child, and he steadfastly refused. Against all reason, he insisted that "twenty-eight percent of the male population of the United States could be the father." He justified his capitulation by saying, "I settled because we were going public, and it was consuming a ton of emotional energy. I had to get it resolved. I didn't want to defend a suit for ten million dollars."

For Halloween in 1978, Apple threw the first of what would become an annual extravaganza: the company Halloween costume party. Steve showed up decked out as Jesus Christ.

He thought it was funny. Most of the rest of the company thought so as well, but not for the same reasons. Those who believed in omens and destiny might have said it was a symbol that Steve Jobs's personality issues lay just ahead.

3
We would have these management retreats
at spectacular resorts. There would be a
couple of days of meetings and at night we
would open the bar and dance until we
dropped. This wasn't like working.
—Phil Roybal

Let's Be Pirates!

In January 1979, the last of several crucial elements fell into place.

A time would come later on when Steve Jobs would be tightfisted about letting anyone in the company give product away to contractors and supporters who contributed something to the company. In the early days, he was more generous. He sold an Apple II at cost to a man named Dan Fylstra, a Boston-based would-be software entrepreneur. Now, at the beginning of 1979, Dan returned with a program that two of his colleagues had produced. It allowed the user to enter numerical data in cells, rows, and columns and then manipulate it—multiplying the numbers, finding the average, and so forth. A whole table of numbers could be constructed—say, the sales figures for each month of the quarter for every sales rep in the region. You recognize the description: it was the first of the now-familiar computer spreadsheets. Perhaps most striking for people who saw the program was one essential feature that would make the electronic spreadsheet an immediate success: when the user changed a single number, every result was almost instantly recalculated.

Along with the Apple II's built-in programming language, expansion capability, and disk drive, Fylstra's program, Visicalc, became the last of the essential elements that turned the personal computer into a must-have machine. When Visicalc shipped in the fall of 1979, it transformed the computer into a useful product for business, and it ran only on the Apple II. By the time versions came out for other platforms, Apple had taken over as the unchallenged dominant player in the personal computer market.

In the next year, sales doubled again. Apple Computer effectively had no competition.

Despite the successes, Steve Jobs wasn't happy. The Apple II was Woz's machine. Steve wanted a machine that everyone would know had been created by Steve Jobs. He wanted to show that he could do it, that Woz wasn't the only computer genius at Apple Computer.

Steve had in mind a new machine that would go well beyond anything anyone had ever seen or even dreamed of. He already had a name for it. In one of the strangest, most difficult-to-understand choices possible, Steve Jobs decided to give the computer the same name as the baby he at the time refused to accept as his own: Lisa. For many years, one of the great Apple insider games was for employees to outdo each other in coming up with plausible-sounding explanations for what the letters LISA meant in computerese. Few people were fooled.

The early Apple software developer Bruce Tognazzini understands the powerful frustration that must have driven Steve toward leaping into a project of his own. "Markkula never let Jobs have any power. No one in the early days thought that Steve was running anything. He would show up every once in a while and go on a tirade. But the reason we stayed at all was that none of us were working for him. We were working for Markkula, or Scotty, but not for Steve. If we had been, most of us would have left."

To write the Lisa business plan, Steve turned for help to Trip Hawkins, the marketer who had been hired by Apple with his MBA fresh in hand. The plan, he said, "called for a $2,000 system that would be based around a 16-bit architecture," and was to be a high-end office computer following the model of well-engineered Hewlett-Packard systems. With that vision in mind, Steve hired two HP engineers to take charge of the design.

Fine intentions. Steve's list of must-haves was long and continued to grow. Because he carried the title of vice president of research and development, his demands had clout whether they were reasonable or not.

Meanwhile, he conceived a scheme to pry open the door to Never Never Land, the Holy Grail of computer research: the highly secretive Xerox Palo Alto Research Center, referred to by everyone—often in awed tones—as "Xerox PARC." One apocryphal story says that he approached the Xerox Development Corporation (XDC), the company's venture capital arm, and told its representatives, "I will let you invest a million dollars in Apple if you will open the kimono at Xerox PARC." XDC's Stevan Birnbaum says that didn't happen. However he did it, Steve managed to get an invite for himself and several others. The $1 million that XDC had agreed to invest, in exchange for 100,000 Apple shares, may have been the key.

At the time, PARC was breaking new ground in personal computer technology, but no one within the company had been able to figure out how to build his or her great ideas into an inexpensive personal computer. They were hoping that Apple's interest might lead to some kind of joint effort. It didn't turn out that way.

After several meetings to lay the ground rules for admission to the inner sanctum, the day came when Steve, Scotty, computer scientist extraordinaire Bill Atkinson, and four other Apple guys were escorted into the demo room. PARC scientist Larry Tessler figured that "these were a bunch of hackers, and they didn't really understand computer science. They wouldn't really understand what we were doing, just see pretty things dancing on the screen."

Instead, Tessler witnessed a very different scene. "Atkinson was peering very closely at the screen, with his nose about two inches away from it, over my left shoulder . . . looking at everything very carefully. And Jobs was pacing around the room, jumping up and down and acting up the whole time. He was just very excited.

"Then when he began seeing things that I could do onscreen, he watched for about a minute and then he was just jumping around the room, shouting in the air, saying, 'Why aren't you doing anything with this?! This is the greatest thing! This is revolutionary.'"

Tessler was just as bowled over by the Apple crowd as they were by the PARC technology. "Nobody else who had ever seen the demo cared as much about the subtleties. Why the patterns were there in the title of the window. Why the pop-up menus looked the way they did."

Atkinson explained the group's awe. "I was aware of the theories behind most of what they were doing from the trade press. But the thing was, it was working. It looked nearly complete. If they could do it, then we could do it. It energized us. It gave us something to strive for."

What Apple saw that day was a display on which the user made selections, not by typing out cryptic commands, but by moving a pointer to designate the desired onscreen object. And individual windows for different documents. And onscreen menus. Today, this is the standard way that most people interact with computers, but then it was extraordinary. Up until that time, computers were controlled by typed commands, and the screens generally displayed nothing but letters and numbers. Here was a graphical user interface (GUI, as it would later become known) unlike anything ever seen on a computer screen before, and better yet, it was working. As if that wasn't enough, the computer (the Alto) also had a word processing program that displayed pages as they would look on a printer, had an art and drawing program, and featured a new kind of networking scheme—called Ethernet—that allowed many machines to share files and information in an office.

Most startling of all, a gadget was moved by hand across the desktop to control the insertion point onscreen: a mouse. While this wasn't brand new—a visionary named Douglas Englebart had created the prototypes in the 1960s at a project for the Stanford Research Institute (SRI) and the Defense Advanced Projects Agency (DARPA)—it was the first time it had been refined into an electronics product as opposed to a demo.

Larry Tessler had put on demonstrations for a lot of folks since arriving at PARC, but this crowd was truly different. "What impressed me," Tessler said, "was that their questions were better than any I had heard in the seven years I had been at Xerox. From *anybody*—Xerox employee, visitor, university professor, student. Their questions showed that they understood all the implications, and they understood the subtleties, too.

"By the end of the demo, I was convinced that I was going to leave Xerox and go to Apple." He did, becoming a vice president with the additional title of chief scientist.

On the drive back to Cupertino, Steve Jobs, still pumped and supercharged from the visit, turned to Bill Atkinson and asked how long it would take to bring what they had just seen over to the Lisa. Atkinson, a brilliant programmer but short on experience with operating systems and user interfaces, guessed. "Oh, about six months." He was off by five years.

The enthusiasm generated by that visit to PARC would prove to be a blessing for everyone who uses a personal computer today, but it was not very good for the fledgling Lisa project at Apple.

The people who came together to build the Lisa manifested an elitism that was quickly obvious to the rest of the company; unless you were wearing an orange badge, you couldn't even enter their quarters—a spanking new building along Bandley Drive in Cupertino. But elitism doesn't guarantee results. "We just went crazy," said Hawkins. "Everybody. Steve included. Lisa became a kind of kitchen sink where we were trying to do everything that could possibly be done with a computer, and suddenly the cost factor, which in the original document was set at $2,000, just went out the window. The computer was eventually $10,000 when released.

"We made two radical underestimations: one was of how much things were going to cost; the other, how long it was going to take to do them."

Here, that stunning contradiction in Steve Jobs's personality was in full play. He could infuriate people he worked with every day, he could change his mind with startling frequency, yet he could keep the fires burning in the heads and hearts of the brightest people in the company. "One of his favorite statements about Lisa," Trip Hawkins said, "was, 'We'll make it so important that it will make a dent in the universe.' Now, on its face, that is a completely ridiculous idea. But people would rally around stuff like that, especially engineers who've spent their lives bottled up in a lab somewhere, missing out on all the fun.

"Steve has a power of vision that is almost frightening. When Steve believes in something, the power of that vision can literally sweep aside any objections, problems, or whatever. They just cease to exist."

The reason that Apple succeeded, Hawkins insisted, "is that we really believed in what we were doing. The key thing was that we weren't in it for the money. We were out to change the world."

That would happen, of course. But not with the Lisa.

.   .   .

By 1980, Apple had burgeoned to 200 employees, then 600, then more than 1,000, with plants in Texas, Ireland, Singapore, and California. For most of the employees, it was no longer a place powered by passion but something that looked good on the resume.

In the late summer, Apple's organization suddenly changed again. The company had grown so large that the structure was unwieldy. Working in secret, Scotty and Markkula, together with only a couple of key managers, plotted a new structure of three divisions. There would be an Accessories Division, handling printers, add-on circuit boards, and especially a new disk drive the company was developing. The Apple II and Apple III product lines would be combined in a group to be called Personal Computer Systems.

Finally, there would be a Professional Office Systems division with one flagship product, Steve Jobs's Lisa. After the trip to Xerox, Steve had come back determined to build all he had seen into the new Lisa. But the team of "professional" computer scientists disagreed, and they fought him tooth and nail. Eventually Steve would win that battle, but he lost the war. Instead of putting Steve in charge of the Professional Office Systems division, the plan handed the responsibility to John Couch, who until then had been the vice president of software. The plan was announced to the management team, including Steve, at an executive retreat in late summer, and it came as a public slap in the face. Steve had been gunning for the title of vice president, New Product Development, which would have made him the unquestioned commander of the Lisa project. Now it had all been taken away from him, removing him from any day-to-day operating role in doing what he loved to do, the only thing he knew, his only real skill: building new machines by inspiring, and infuriating, small teams of hand-selected engineers.

To soften the blow, the new plan made Steve the chairman of the board. Scotty and Markkula tried to tell him he was needed in that position for the public stock offering now in the planning. Having a twenty-five-year-old as the head of what was by now a hundred-million-dollar company, especially a good-looking, media-darling twenty-five-year-old, could generate enormous publicity and pump up the stock price for the IPO.

Trip Hawkins remembers, "Steve's feelings were really hurt. He was unhappy about the way that Scotty had pulled this stunt without informing or consulting him—it was his company, after all! And he was really upset about losing direct involvement with Lisa. He was just really bent out of shape."

Worse, John Couch made it clear that he didn't want Steve meddling in the affairs of the Lisa any longer. Period.

It was Steve's first great humiliation. There would be others to come, but for someone to whom life had been so sweet, someone who was already becoming a media star, that first one must have tasted especially bitter. In another sense, though, his fortunes were about to change. Literally.

The second week of December 1980 was a time that seemed to have no anchor for Steve. On Monday, ex-Beatle John Lennon was murdered by a crazed fan. On Friday, Apple stock became publicly traded.

Apple Computer's 4.6 million public shares were sold within an hour. It was the most successful public stock offering in history up to that time and the most oversubscribed initial public offering since the Ford Motor Company went public in the mid-1950s.

The early private investors did very well. Among them, Xerox sold its Apple shares not long afterward. Xerox venture capitalist Stevan Birnbaum said, "Normally, a company provides us with a five-year plan as part of the investment process. The good companies accomplish the five-year plan in seven years. In the case of Apple, they had more than accomplished the objectives in eighteen months." The Xerox investment of $1 million brought a return of "over $30 million," Birnbaum said. To this day, he's still impressed with "how two very young men without college degrees, money, or experience" went on to build a Fortune 500 company in less than five years.

Overnight, Steve Jobs was worth $217.5 million dollars, making him one of the country's richest self-made men. He had moved into the rarefied territory of storied wealth. In a much-repeated quote, with no source ever cited (in other words, maybe he never said this, but it's so good that if he didn't, he *should* have), Steve supposedly announced, "When I was 23, I had a net worth of a million dollars. At 24, it was over ten million dollars. At 25, it was over a hundred million."

When Steve was later asked about the effect of so much wealth, he named "visibility" as the principal factor. "There are tens of thousands of people who have a net worth of more than $1 million," he said. "There are thousands of people who are worth more than $10 million. But the number who have more than $100 million gets down to 100."

He was not only super-rich, but the youngest of the super-rich. To the public he was an icon—a handsome young bachelor with a winning smile, a technology groundbreaker who was defining the new world we would all live in. He was doing it with an exuberance that was still a little coarse, but this would smooth out before too long. It could even be seen as one of his charms.

In material terms, Steve could now have whatever he wanted. More important, the money carried power. Before, Steve had been only as strong as his ideas; if he couldn't convince Scotty, Markkula, and the executive staff, his product ideas and goals came to nothing. Now it would be different. Now he had a cudgel to wield. He would cement his position and gain loyalty. He understood the power of greed, and he would use it.

Somehow, the people who had already given him loyalty were not part of the equation. Steve denied options to many of his peers who had founded the company with him. It was a bizarre, virtually incomprehensible decision that fired up a stream of anger and disgust among the crew who had with little complaint put in the painfully long hours, week after week and month after month, to make the company successful in the early days. Bill Fernandez, the company's first employee, was also first out the door when he discovered that he wasn't getting stock while newly hired engineers were. "I felt I was doing all the donkey work and that I would be a technician forever," he said. (Eventually he returned.)

Chris Espinosa and Randy Wigginton didn't receive any options from the company, either, but they fared better. Out of generosity, as well as a sense of fairness, Woz in 1980 started a private sale and giveaway of his stock that he called the "Wozplan." Under it, he distributed about eighty thousand shares, roughly one-third of his holdings, to his family and a long list of deserving (and even some undeserving) friends and acquaintances, including a real estate developer who had befriended him.

Tightfisted Steve tried to make it sound as if it was his cofounder who had it backward. "Woz ended up giving stock to all the wrong people. Woz couldn't say no. A lot of people took advantage of him." Strange criticism from a man who was incredibly stingy about giving shares that could have made his family and closest friends fabulously wealthy. He even shut out Chris-Ann and Lisa, after making sure that the legal agreement calling for him to support his daughter was signed and sealed in advance of the public offering. For years, on occasions when Chris-Ann found money tight for herself and her daughter and gathered the strength to ask Steve for a little help, he invariably refused.

Steve's longtime college friend Dan Kottke, who had journeyed with him to India and had shared the Cupertino house with him, was still a technician at Apple in 1980. Kottke asked Steve about stock options a few times. "He told me to go see my supervisor." Kottke was so distraught over the situation that early in the countdown to going public, he appealed to Markkula and Scotty. They agreed that he was deserving and granted him two thousand shares. But that was a pittance compared to the rank-and-file engineers, the guys who had come in after Kottke, who were given one thousand shares of "founders stock," which after splitting several times amounted to thirty-two thousand shares on the day of the public offering.

Steve had intentionally kept one of his oldest friends from receiving any stock. It was as if he needed to demonstrate the power he had, to prove that he really was the boss. But there was another, more powerful reason. Kottke, with his gentle manner, had provided Chris-Ann with a shoulder to cry on after the break with Steve.

Somehow, Steve had decided that a sense of *loyalty* was a virtue of overriding importance. Intelligence and loyalty—these were the two qualities he had come to measure people by. Kottke passed the first test but perhaps, as far as Steve was concerned, had failed the second. If Kottke wasn't going to be loyal to Steve, the door would be closed to him.

Freezing Kottke out of the IPO was an early example of the demands that Steve made then, and still makes today, on his friends, associates, and employees. If you are part of Steve Jobs's world, you will be loyal to Steve in all things. In some cases, that has meant being sentenced to a Jobsian Siberia for life.

. . .

As the holiday season arrived in 1980, Steve felt personally unsettled. He had just signed his child-support papers but had not made any effort to see his daughter since her birth. He couldn't seem to finish remodeling the Los Gatos house, and it remained nearly empty of furniture and interior decorations. At work, he could make snap decisions about aesthetics, but when it came to his personal life, he was indecisive. Worse, he was learning that his new role as company whiz-kid-without-portfolio was unsatisfying and unrewarding as the Lisa project scurried along without him.

Then a computer in the R&D phase—one that he had tried to bury several months earlier—caught his attention. The experimental machine was the brainchild of a Renaissance man and computer scientist by the name of Jef Raskin. Raskin had been hired at Apple to create its technical documentation and manuals. He was a former professor at the University of California at San Diego (he had taught Pascal [a computer language] programming to Bill Atkinson) and was a world-class organist. Eventually, with the stock options he received from Apple, he built a concert hall on his property in the Santa Cruz Mountains and hosted small recitals.

Jef was driven by the possibility of creating a small, inexpensive computer for the masses. He had formed a small group and with amazing speed had produced a working prototype over the Christmas holiday of 1979. In keeping with the spirit of the company name, he dubbed his invention "Macintosh," after his favorite type of apple. Yet he had made a mistake: the name of the fruit is spelled McIntosh. He had misspelled it. In the long run, it didn't matter. The computer became far better known than the apple ever was, and since the introduction of the computer, the name of the apple has been misspelled.

Raskin had a vision of a computer that would be a complete "canned" solution and saw his Macintosh as a "toaster," a self-contained appliance with no add-ons. What you bought was all you needed. He also had very strong ideas about ease of use. You would switch on the machine and begin working immediately, without the bother of loading software or entering arcane commands. The machine would be easily portable and would sell for around $1,000, which meant that Apple had to be able to build it for about $300. He saw no need for graphics, however, and certainly no need for a mouse. Of the system he had seen at Xerox PARC, the only thing he liked were the windows.

The circuit board for the new machine had been created by Burrell Smith, a gnomish, self-taught digital hacker who had been discovered wasting his talents in the company's service department. He was the kind of eccentric, off-the-wall talent that serious computer designers disdained. Secretive and aggressively self-assured, he was cut in the mold of Woz, a designer in the hurry-up mode. He also had the raw mental capacity to keep all the elements of a circuit board design in his head at once and then, again like Woz, to minimize. This was the essence of great digital design, and it was close to being a black art.

Burrell was just one example of the kind of people Raskin surrounded himself with. Raskin had assembled a rat pack of computer engineers with fire in their bellies, the kind of talent most companies would not put up with, the kind of talent that made Apple great. Working on the fringes of the corporate freight train that was Apple by late 1979 and 1980, spiriting parts and scavenging components out of engineering labs in the dead of night, Raskin's group made incredibly fast progress.

What they were doing caught the attention of Apple II hacker Andy Hertzfeld, who was working for the company writing programs. He visited their lab in February 1980, saw the Macintosh prototype for the first time, and was captivated. He sat down at the bench and in a single, manic session that same night managed to bring up the first images on the prototype's screen. He wasn't then free to join the team but had instantly become one of them in spirit.

The Macintosh had been in and out of favor for the better part of a year. Raskin's pipe dream would be canceled and then reinstated. Steve was one of the first to abandon the project in mid-1980, when he was in the midst of designing Lisa as a real product. "Jobs said, 'No, you can't do this,'" recalled Raskin. "'This is wrong. Apple needs Lisa, and this will interfere.'" Steve lost that battle; Scotty kept the R&D project alive by hiding it from Steve.

Raskin's team was clustered in the same suite of offices where Apple had started, the space behind the Good Earth restaurant on Stevens Creek Boulevard. Meanwhile, many of the other employees—a still rapidly expanding number—had moved to a row of low-slung, adobe tilt-up buildings along nearby Bandley Drive, under constant construction after 1979.

By early 1981, Steve was looking for a new product to pour his enormous energy into, and despite his earlier resistance, Raskin's Macintosh now caught his eye. Ousted from the Lisa team, and with his money from the IPO and his new role as chairman, Steve needed to find something to do. He was intrigued by Raskin's concept of an appliance computer that was as easy to use as a toaster, but he started pushing for the machine to be built around a different computer chip, the Motorola 68000. The idea of a change at this stage annoyed Raskin, but Steve saw advantages in using the 68000—primarily that this was what the Lisa team had used and it would enable Apple to move the new Lisa graphical look to the machine—and commanded that the new prototype be built with it. Raskin was the sergeant to a lowly squad of soldiers and was greatly outranked by Steve. He could do nothing but smolder inside as his project was hijacked.

In fact, the personal attention of General Steve inspired Raskin's team, but it was a double-edged sword. One Mac team member complained of the change that had taken place in the work environment. Steve Jobs, he wrote in a memo to Raskin, "seems to introduce tension, politics, and hassles."

By Christmas, the tireless Burrell Smith had already managed to get a new design working with the 68000 chip. Steve came by and was pleased to find Burrell at work over the holidays. He appreciated employees who worked ridiculous hours, as he did himself. Smith explained to Steve how his prototype, supposedly for a machine that would be a more affordable baby brother of the Lisa, had a clock speed nearly twice as fast.

With that, the bells went off in the company cofounder's mind.

As Steve looked at the crude working model that Smith had produced, it suddenly became clear that the Macintosh could be the Apple II of the eighties, a computer that could deliver the technology of the future—the ease of use that a graphical user interface and a mouse heralded—at a remarkably low cost. It was an extraordinary design. Iconoclastic, unique, and uncommon, but it worked.

The Lisa, an official project on Apple's books with a workforce of twenty-four hardware engineers and countless software programmers, was slogging forward. Their combined efforts had managed to produce a single working prototype, hidden away in a closed lab in one of the Apple buildings along Bandley Drive. The machine was built around five circuit boards and a number of custom components. Meanwhile, over in a tiny suite of rooms sequestered away from the rest of the company, a long-haired engineer had made a new computer in a few weeks that was twice as fast and could be sold for one-third the price. It relied on a single circuit board and contained nothing but off-the-shelf parts. *And yet it had a graphical user interface, too!*

Marketer Joanna Hoffmann recalls the time vividly. "It didn't take long, once you saw the gleam in Steve's eye, to see the writing on the wall for Jef. Steve was going to get what he wanted."

It wasn't just the machine that fueled this new fire in Steve Jobs's gut. It was the team, this little band of kindred souls, these five people who were working on the Macintosh with such enthusiasm and renegade spirit—the same kind of passion that had created the Apple I and the Apple II. Steve no longer had to subjugate his outlaw spirit to the corporate process, rewarded with little but his unceremonious booting off the Lisa project; here was the kind of dedication he understood, the kind he loved. These were crusaders like himself who thrived on the impossible.

Steve would inspire this little-noticed team in a corner of a forgotten building. He would show them all—Scotty, Markkula, the whole company, the entire world—that he could lead them to produce a remarkable computer. Not the way that the newly bloated bureaucracy had mismanaged the Apple III and threatened to mishandle the Lisa. He set off with guns blazing to make the Macintosh the world's next groundbreaking computer.

Steve began his campaign with Jef Raskin, pitching him the idea of the Macintosh becoming *the* computer, the next giant leap. He made it clear that he wanted to get more involved in the project. Raskin was flattered but worried: the two had already butted heads.

When Raskin took his complaints to Scotty about Steve's interference, the company president saw it as a way to separate the disruptive

Steve from the rest of the company, even at the expense of sacrificing Raskin. At the corporate level, Markkula and Scotty were only too happy to let Steve get involved in Raskin's project. With the Macintosh group housed in an isolated location—an arrangement Jef had originally requested precisely to keep Steve from sniffing around—now that very isolation could work perfectly to keep Steve caged up and out of everyone else's way. Raskin had asked for support and instead got sandbagged.

One of Steve's first acts as general manager of the Macintosh project was to hire the key people who made the Apple II happen: Woz (though this was primarily for show and to lend legitimacy to the team), Rod Holt, Randy Wigginton, Jerry Mannock (who had designed the Apple II case), and even Dan Kottke and Bill Fernandez. The Apple veterans joined Burrell Smith, programmer Bud Tribble, Stanford electrical engineer Brian Howard, and marketer Joanna Hoffmann on the infant project. Steve also commandeered a new space, relocating the team into another building that Apple was leasing, a place known to everyone as "Texaco Towers" because of its proximity to a gasoline station.

The entire group moved into the new quarters in early 1981 and tackled the work of turning the Macintosh prototype into a bona fide computer product. Steve, the master of unrealistic goals, announced that they were to have the machine ready for market in a year. All they had were the basics of the hardware. No operating system, no applications, nothing but a few demos. It was a ridiculous timetable.

Yet Steve had that magical, uncanny power of persuasion. The team drank his Kool-Aid and accepted his timetable. "He has the ability to make people around him believe in his perception of reality," said Bud Tribble a few years later. "It's a combination of very fast comeback, catch phrases, and the occasional very original insight, which he throws in to keep you off balance."

When Steve set up camp with the Macintosh group, the project gained a halo that Raskin never would have been able to bring to it: their own evangelist, someone with the mantle of celebrity who made everything he did seem a little larger than life. Steve had the religion of personal computing, and he was a true apostle. He could rattle the windows, shake the pulpit, and make the congregation stand up and shout, "Praise the Computer!"

But he was more than just a preacher in the religion of Computer; he was chairman of the board of the whole corporation. He could get funding, he could get scarce equipment, and he could protect his team from other managers. If someone from outside the project hassled team members, they had only to mention it to Steve. "All we had to do was complain about someone," one team member said, "and it was like unleashing a Doberman. He would chew the guy's head off so fast that our heads would spin."

Jef Raskin was treading on thin ice and knew it. All through January, Raskin and Steve skirmished with each other. Raskin was no fool; the Macintosh held the prospect of turning into the project of a lifetime. He had conceived the notion of a small, neatly packaged, affordable computer. He had pulled together this remarkable team that had breathed life into the concept. Now an outlander was trying to replace him as head of the team.

In the middle of the Jobs-Raskin wrangle, everyone at Apple was brought up short. Early in February, Steve Wozniak suffered a serious accident. An enthusiastic pilot, he had begun a flight in his single-engine Beechcraft Bonanza when, he now says, he "tried to take off without adequate airspeed." The aircraft stalled—the wings losing their lift—and he crashed. The company waited breathlessly as he lay in the hospital, moving in and out of consciousness. Steve Jobs hired a limo to ferry Woz's distraught parents to the hospital. He could make grand gestures; it was the small ones he had more trouble attending to.

When Woz eventually gained consciousness, he suffered from amnesia and had no recollection of what had happened. He had to ask his wife why he was in the hospital. Though he doesn't like to talk about it these days, he acknowledges that it was five weeks before he could recall the event.

Back at Apple, Steve Jobs continued in his attempts to wrest control of the Macintosh from Raskin. At one point, he had tried to undermine an in-house presentation that Raskin was scheduled to give by trying to convince his rival that the session had been called off. Raskin responded with a closely reasoned memo to Mike Scott, detailing nearly a dozen ways in which Steve wasn't competent to run the Macintosh project. Typical was the item that read:

9. Optimistic estimates. Jobs was wrong on his Apple III schedule, wrong on the LISA schedule, wrong on the cost and price estimates, and he will be wrong on Macintosh. He is a prime example of a manager who takes the credit for his optimistic schedules and then blames the workers when deadlines are not met. His cost estimates are often based on unrealistic assumptions about the elasticity of prices of parts.

Someone showed the memo to Steve, who became furious. That afternoon Markkula got Jobs and Raskin to sit down in the same room with him to find a resolution. Steve was in tears—he was always quick to cry when he couldn't have his way—and announced that he couldn't possibly work with Raskin any longer. Raskin, who must have sensed that the chips were stacked against him, said that he couldn't work for Steve.

By the time the meeting was over, Steve Jobs was the new head of the Macintosh project. Jef Raskin didn't even get a consolation prize; he would take a vacation, probably to save himself embarrassment in the humiliation of defeat.

If the world were always just, Jef Raskin would be remembered as the genius behind the Macintosh. The world is not always just, and history does not always remember those who should be its heroes. In this case, the computer that Raskin imagined was very different from the Macintosh that was eventually produced. The true father of the Mac as the world knows it was Steve, its adoptive father.

It was a couple of days before Steve Jobs's twenty-sixth birthday. He had won yet another battle.

By the winter of 1981, Apple was a four-year-old swollen bureaucracy where the employees acted as if they, not the stockholders, owned the company. Some senior executives felt that too many new hires were taking it easy, assuming that Apple would never get rid of anyone; so far, no Apple worker had ever been formally fired. In the Valley, working at Apple was now looked on as a guarantee of lifetime employment.

First thing in the morning on a dark and rainy Wednesday that February 1981, employees were notified of an all-hands meeting in the company's underground parking garage. Programmer Donn Denman recalls, "Scotty stood up and started talking about how Apple had grown too fat, and he was going to have to fire some people. He was going to be calling people into his office through the morning, he said. And then he dismissed us. The whole place suddenly went silent. Who was on the list? None of us had any idea if we would make it through the day or not."

Employees soon discovered that those who still had their jobs at the end of the first hour weren't in the clear. The firings happened in spurts. Everyone walked around wondering if that day would be his last. Gradually, it became obvious that if your manager got fired, you might as well start packing. Incompetent department heads weren't just fired; their entire workgroup was wiped out, no matter how valuable the contribution that some of the individual workers had made.

Steve Jobs had been consulted in advance about the firings and had given his stamp of approval, but now he tried to distance himself, leaving the impression that Scotty had acted on his own.

The bright young programmer Andy Hertzfeld was devastated. His cubicle neighbor and software project partner had been fired. How could he go on with his project when the other guy working on it was gone? He went to see Scotty the following morning and told him that he was leaving. Scotty asked Hertzfeld what could make him stay. He mentioned several projects, but the only one that mattered to him was the Macintosh. Steve Jobs went to Hertzfeld and shanghaied him: ignoring Hertzfeld's objections that he had to finish up what he had been working on before he could leave, Steve unplugged Andy's computer, put it in the trunk of his car, and drove the bewildered programmer to the Macintosh building. Andy wanted Macintosh, and Steve wanted Andy. It was a done deal.

By February, Woz had been released from the hospital but hadn't fully recovered, and it wasn't clear whether he'd be coming back to work.

Bill Atkinson was the closest thing that Apple had to a mad scientist. With wild blue eyes, a shock of unruly hair, a gentle voice, and retiring manner that often gave way to a prankster's hearty laughter, Bill fervently believed that the computer creator's mission in life was to design machines that would make computing continually easier for the user. Most of all it had to be *fun*.

Unlike the tasks that most people perform to earn their daily bread, programming can be utterly absorbing. A programmer who's truly worthy of the name, when confronted with a particularly arresting challenge, is likely to work straight through without stopping until he has defeated the devils that have hidden the solution from him. Bill Atkinson was that type of programmer. One morning after an all-night session when he had made major breakthroughs, he dozed off in his sports car, drove into the back of a big rig, and sheared off the top of the car.

When he came to several hours later, he was lying in a hospital bed. Sitting at his bedside was Steve Jobs, asking, "Are you okay?" It's not that Steve was worried about possible delays to his beloved Macintosh project—Atkinson was working on the Lisa where he was creating the graphics primitives (essentially the programming routines to draw things onscreen, eventually called QuickDraw) that would allow Apple's next generation of computers to look like Xerox's. Steve revered Bill because he was a certifiable genius; Bill was the first of the superstars. From that day on, Bill Atkinson's heart was with Steve and the Macintosh.

Steve had not wavered from his deadline, still holding to the demand that the Macintosh be ready for the market in twelve months. Because no one had ever written software that displayed graphical images onscreen, the amount of effort required to manipulate every dot (that is, picture element or "pixel") all the time turned out to be prodigious. What made the job so frustrating for the team members was Steve's apparent total inability to overlook any detail of the project. He was a micromanager to the nth degree. He cared passionately about the smallest of items. Eventually the final result was better for it; however, the path was tortuous.

Donn Denman, the young programmer who was working on a Macintosh version of the programming language BASIC, called it "hands-on management." Steve, he said, "would march right into your cubicle, invade your space, sit right down, and start playing with whatever you were working on. He'd make comments and suggestions about making something easier to use or better looking. He didn't really know what you were doing on the technical level, but he was real interested. Then he'd be gone, and you wouldn't see him for a long time."

The team members found that they had to develop a strategy for dealing with Jobs. "The goal," Denman said, "was to do something neat to show him by the next time he came by.

"We all had a joke about Steve. If you wanted to get him to agree to a new idea, something that was a good idea but that he hadn't thought of, you told him the idea, and then just let him reject it. A couple of weeks later he would come rushing over to you and tell you how he had just had a great idea and would proceed to tell you the same idea you had told him before." As far as Steve was concerned, it was now *his* idea, so he had no problem with it being incorporated into the design.

Though the whole team recognized this trick of Steve's, of playing your own idea back to you, no one knew whether it was calculated or something Steve did without even realizing it. A phrase sprang up in the group to describe this annoying tactic. Jef Raskin said, "We called him the 'reality distortion field.'" Who first used the phrase is shrouded by the mists of time; Andy Hertzfeld thinks it was Bud Tribble. But it's colorful enough that writers ever since have continued to regurgitate it to explain a wide variety of Steve's decisions and mistakes.

Yet even though Steve didn't understand the details of the technology, he was still determined to put his own personal stamp on some significant part of the project. The single area that didn't require technical knowledge was the case. He took that as his own domain.

Steve's style of working on a problem was to think about it constantly. If you started up a conversation with him, or, more likely, he started one with you, he would immediately launch into a question about how you thought the problem should be solved. As soon as you reacted, he decided one of two things: either you knew nothing significant that could help him solve the dilemma, which meant that he would say nothing further on the issue and would march away, or you had some insight into the situation. His answer, even if he thought your reply offered a valuable insight, was usually a variation on the phrase "That's s——t"—his stock reply to either situation. If he considered you a worthy person, he would explain why your ideas were garbage and his were the only right way to look at the situation; if he didn't think you were worthy, you'd be left just with the garbage.

One day Steve went into a design meeting with a telephone book, and threw it on the table. "That's how big the Macintosh can be.

Nothing any bigger will make it. Consumers won't stand for it if it's any larger.

"Hey, and there's something else. I'm tired of all these square, squat boxy-looking computers. Why can't we build one that's taller, rather than wider? Think about it." And he walked out.

People in the room took a look at the book and blanched. That phone book was about half the size of any computer ever built. It was impossible, Burrell Smith decided—the electronics he needed could never be put into a box that small.

Steve wasn't someone who took no for an answer, at least not from people who worked for him. His demand, unreasonable as it sounded, was a wakeup call for everyone on the team. Steve expected a revolutionary machine; they would create one for him. It was the same dichotomy all over again—finding Steve annoying, frustrating, intolerable, and yet answering his clarion call, marching to the beat of his drum, willingly, even gladly.

Over the next weeks that spring, various Macintosh case mock-ups were tried out on the team, vertically oriented designs lined up for their inspection and comment. The basic look of the machine was quickly set, and it changed very little over the years. It met Steve's requirements of small and vertically oriented. The basic model that was to become so popular would offer a black-and-white screen and one built-in disk drive with a provision for adding another. In a decision that became the source of continuing controversy throughout all the years of the machine being on the market, there would be no expansion slots to add to the machine's capabilities with hardware cards.

It was as if he had taken part of the toaster idea from Raskin's original concept—after all, there aren't any upgrades to those—and held onto it religiously, even though it was a bad one in light of the computer that the Mac became. Worse, it rejected one of the crucial reasons the Apple II had been a success: expandability. For Chris Espinosa, "rejecting everything Woz" was a big part of Steve's motivation on the Mac. Steve knew the answers, even if they were totally wrong some of the time, and the combined force of his personality, wealth, media fame, and arrogance set them in stone. Of course, what made his abrasive personality acceptable was that more often than not he was right.

. . .

In the aftermath of Black Wednesday, a whispering campaign built up against Scotty, with the flames being fanned from the human resources group, which was appalled by Scotty's treatment of people in meetings. The water-cooler gossip saddled him with sole blame for the firings, while Jobs and Markkula, who had both acquiesced, had left him to take the heat alone. When people turn against someone, little things that they do get blown up into major grievances and add fuel to the fire. Scotty had made a comment one day that Black Wednesday "was just the beginning," leaving a lot of employees walking on eggshells and wondering if they should be updating their resumes. And Scotty probably thought he was showing enthusiasm and encouraging devotion to the company with his little stunt of looking over a cubicle wall and asking, "Are you working your ass off?" The natives were thirsting for blood. Scotty seemed to be sealing his own fate.

When he returned from a Hawaii vacation in late March, Mike Markkula called Scotty to a Sunday evening meeting and told him that the executive staff had requested his resignation. Markkula would take over as interim president.

The decision played right into Steve's hands. Scotty was a potential roadblock for a Macintosh project that had Steve at the helm. Markkula, on the other hand, while smart and shrewd, would never be successful in standing up to Steve's drive and determination. For a chairman of the board with limited real control, Steve couldn't have asked for a better turn of events.

Still as determined as ever to get the Macintosh finished and on sale by his original target date, Steve Jobs demonstrated his commitment to his already frenzied team by betting the Lisa project manager $5,000 that the Mac would ship before the Lisa did. It only made the atmosphere in the Texaco Towers offices even more insane.

Then, in May, Steve came to a decision that in hindsight probably made all the difference between a late, overblown project (or possibly even a complete failure and cancellation) and the stunning success that the Macintosh eventually turned out to be. Instead of developing software for the new machine in-house, Steve turned to outside sources. Like all such pivotal decisions, this one also sowed the seeds of the Mac's losing battle with the IBM PC family of computers for marketplace dominance.

In part, the decision may have grown out of a selfish, power-hungry motivation. On both the Apple III and the Lisa projects, Steve had been pained to discover that the larger and more bloated the teams became, the less control and influence he had. It was standard at this point to have Apple people develop Apple software, but that might mean he would lose control of the Macintosh project as he had of the earlier ones. He was determined not to let that happen. This meant enlisting other companies in the industry to help him write software.

Steve was surrounded by young people. Some of the best Apple talent was even younger than he. Youth seemed to equate with ability, dedication, and forward thinking. When Steve thought "young" and "software" in the same sentence, the name that first came to mind was Bill Gates. Sure, he was something of an enemy, but it's better to know your enemies.

Microsoft was already a success, but compared to Apple it looked more like a wannabe, and Gates himself looked like a wannabe who might be dreaming of being as rich as Steve Jobs someday. Gates had a streak of the daredevil about him and an arrogant show-off attitude that made him appreciate Steve's willingness to espouse the unconventional. He was a reserved and intensely focused young man, but with the twinkle of the Homebrew hacker about him as well.

Up to that point, Microsoft's most important product was a programming language—BASIC—that ran on many computers. It enabled programmers to create applications, but its most successful platform was the Apple II. Woz had included a version of BASIC, licensed from Microsoft, on the motherboard of the computer, and as the machine became the dominant computer, Microsoft's revenues soared. When IBM looked for a partner to help it write the software for its new personal computer—as yet unannounced in 1981—the company's engineers headed to Microsoft.

Steve invited himself up to look around and to sit down with Bill Gates and Paul Allen at their corporate headquarters—then, as now, in Redmond, outside of Seattle. At an early spring meeting, the three talked about their goals for their companies. Then Steve launched into his pitch. He waxed poetic about accessibility, the mouse, and the desktop metaphor.

The two young whizzes disagreed violently about the market for the personal computer. Steve foresaw a loose intellectual coalition of college students and educated, progressive homes, maybe combined with a still-fuzzy constituency of middle managers and secretaries. Gates, on the other hand, was strongly influenced by IBM's centrist view that computers were utilitarian business tools. There was no room in that scene for the emotional attachment to computers that Steve Jobs described.

Steve insisted that words couldn't adequately convey the essence of the machine. Gates and Allen would have to visit his lab in Cupertino and see this remarkable new computer for themselves.

After Steve left, Gates and his team decided to go for it. They were too sharp not to play both sides of the fence. They could see the Lisa as a possible winner, and Steve Jobs's low-cost version just might be a runaway hit.

The Microsoft crowd arranged to troop down to Cupertino and stayed there till late afternoon, now convinced that Apple was onto something special. Bill Gates committed his company to writing major programs for Steve's machine. Their work for IBM involved creating system housekeeping software—essential, but not sexy. Now, application programs—those were the sexy projects that could get a programmer's heart beating fast. Developing the "killer app" was where the glory lay. And that's what Steve dangled in front of them like a carrot. They snatched at it. Microsoft named their project Sand. It was based on a vision that Steve spun for them about a factory sitting on a beach, where sand would go in one side and finished computers would come out the other. (Silicon, the key component of most transistors, is present in sand.) As they were working for the relentlessly unpoetic IBM personal computer, which was about to be released that summer, the Mac gave them something to dream about.

The next month IBM introduced its version of the personal computer. It was exactly the kind of computer that everyone on the Mac team was expecting. It was large and clunky. It introduced no new technology. It was difficult to learn to use. It was the furthest thing possible from Lisa or Macintosh. The Mac guys went out and bought one as soon as it was available, late in August. Then they tore it apart. All of them were relieved that it was as inelegant and unwieldy as it was. They were sure that their new computers would destroy IBM's challenge as soon as theirs were announced the following year.

For his part, Steve saw it as a battle, a race to save the world. It felt right for him to be the underdog, the unlikely David to IBM's Goliath. "It is coming down to Apple and IBM," he said once. "If, for some reason we make some big mistake and IBM wins, my personal feeling is that we are going to enter sort of a computer Dark Ages for about twenty years. Once IBM gains control of a market sector, they always stop innovation. They prevent innovations from happening.

"If you look at the mainframe marketplace, there's been virtually zero innovation since IBM got dominant control of that marketplace fifteen years ago. The IBM PC fundamentally brought no new technology to the industry at all. It was just a repackaging and slight extension of Apple II technology, and now they want it all.

"Apple is providing the alternative."

While Steve downplayed the technology of their computers, Apple also took out a famous ad in the nation's newspapers that combined an elitist sense of the company's destiny with an overblown prose style that was just a teensy-weensy bit too self-righteous and self-serving:

WELCOME IBM.
SERIOUSLY.
Welcome to the most exciting and important marketplace since the computer revolution began 35 years ago. And congratulations on your first computer. Putting real computer power in the hands of the individual is already improving the way people work, think, learn, communicate, and spend their leisure hours. Computer literacy is fast becoming as fundamental a skill as reading or writing. When we invented the first personal computer system, we estimated that over 140,000,000 people worldwide could justify the purchase of one, if only they understood the benefits. Next year alone we project that well over 1,000,000 will come to that understanding. Over the next decade, the growth of the personal computer will continue in logarithmic leaps. We look forward to responsible competition in the

massive effort to distribute this American technology to the world. And we appreciate the magnitude of your commitment. Because what we are doing is increasing social capital by enhancing individual productivity. Welcome to the task.

It was a very smug ad, especially, coming as it did, from a firm less than one-tenth the size of IBM. As events would work out, IBM's release of a personal computer was very good for Apple. It legitimized the market. It brought enormous amounts of publicity to Apple as the only real competition to IBM. It strengthened the company's role as the underdog, a role that many wished to identify with. The year 1981 was the watershed for Apple in terms of name recognition. As the year started less than 10 percent of Americans knew what Apple was. By the end of the year that figure was up to 80 percent. IBM's introduction of its machine, no matter the technology, was the best thing that could have happened. The fact that the two firms were so very different—one Californian and liberal, the other East Coast and buttoned-up—only served to further highlight Apple. The introduction gave the Macintosh and Lisa teams even more impetus to make sure that they brought out their revolutionary new machines soon, to show the world just how stodgy IBM was—and how brilliant Apple was by comparison.

Of course it didn't quite work out that way in the end.

By July, the Macintosh was beginning to shake down. The basic design and the circuit board layout were close to final. The machine would come with an internal disk drive, the same one that was used in the Apple II. It would have 64 kilobytes of ROM—the read-only memory used by the hardware. It would also have the same amount of RAM (random access memory, used by the software), though Burrell Smith had devised a way of doubling the RAM to 128 kilobytes. That was secret knowledge, however, talked about in whispers because it had been done in defiance of Steve Jobs, who had decreed that there could only be one memory configuration.

That same month Steve completed the first draft of the Macintosh business plan. It called for introducing the computer in mid-1982, at the same time as the Lisa and the new model Apple II. The price of the Mac 1 would be $1,500, including software, falling to $1,000 for the

Mac 2. The Macintosh would achieve first-year sales of 500,000 units; Steve had made up the number out of thin air and had repeated it so often that it became accepted as fact.

People around the company were beginning to wake up to a problem that Steve had tried to hide, a problem that now began to smell like a mackerel rotting in the closet. He was targeting the Macintosh for the office environment, the same segment of the marketplace that the Lisa had been designed to reach. It was a disaster in the making: two computers reaching the market at the same time, targeted to the same customers. That was bad enough, but one of them, the Macintosh, would be more compact, faster, and far less expensive. It wasn't a game that any sane product manager would want to play.

The Macintosh was still being carried on the Apple books as an experimental project. The time had come for Steve to go hat in hand to Mike Markkula, still serving as president, and argue for the Macintosh to be accepted as a serious project. When he came to the question of markets in the plan, Steve slighted the topic with a dismissive "Macintosh is aimed at the markets Lisa does not address." To Markkula, who had apparently not yet gotten wind of the problem and besides was no marketing guru, the explanation apparently passed without notice. The power of Steve's vision and the good business sense of selling an inexpensive machine that offered all the power and the features of Lisa carried the day. Backed by Markkula's approval, the executive staff and the company's board approved the change of status. Macintosh was a real product. Macintosh was official.

Steve accepted the need to push back the first shipment date to October 1, 1982. Even with that delay, the schedule was still as unrealistic as ever, but Steve couldn't see it. He still wouldn't let practical realities get in the way of his determination. He was convinced in his own "feel" for the marketplace. Much later, he explained, "We think the Mac will sell *zillions*, but we didn't build Mac for anybody else. We built it for ourselves. We were the group of people who were going to judge whether it was great or not. We weren't going to go out and do market research. Did Alexander Graham Bell do any market research when he invented the telephone? Of course not."

. . .

In February Steve took the Macintosh team to Pajaro Dunes, a posh seaside resort on the ocean a hundred miles south of Cupertino, for the first of what would become a continuing series of retreats. Steve Jobs opened his appearance in front of his group by writing a slogan on the board, a kind of rallying theme for the meeting. This time it was "The Journey Is the Reward." When he was done, he sat down and for the most part just listened. Each group in turn updated the rest of the team on what it had recently accomplished and what challenges it was currently tackling.

These events were already something of a tradition at Apple. "Apple was very much like a club," according to Phil Roybal. "We would have these management retreats at spectacular resorts. There would be a couple of days of meetings, and at night we would open the bar and dance until we dropped. This wasn't like working." In later years, the Macintosh retreats would be imbued with a kind of magic for all participants.

By early 1982, the team was filled with the kind of computer-niks who could find work anywhere in the Valley. Most of them were male, white, and middle class—there were no blacks, few Hispanics, and, other than Steve's personal assistant, no Asians. They were all college educated, bright, and homogeneous. Every new candidate for the team had to pass muster with everyone already in place. Forget the human resources–style psychological tests; Steve had his own set of questions. Two of them were, "How many times have you taken acid?" and "When did you lose your virginity?" He didn't care about the answers; the idea was to weed out the wimps who were no good at thinking on their feet. The other key test was to play one of the videogames in the common area of the Bandley building with Burrell Smith or Andy Hertzfeld: if you were good enough to keep up with them, you were a viable candidate.

Steve was not only very rich but pulling a quarter of a million dollars a year out of the company in salary, yet he refused to let any of his engineers receive more than $30,000 a year, the lowest salaries of any engineers at Apple. He considered anyone working less than eighty hours a week to be wimping out.

They all shared one attribute: they cared more about building an amazing computer and shocking the world with it than they did about anything so ordinary as money, career paths, or tradition.

At the same time, they could laugh at themselves. "One of the requirements for employment was a love of pineapple pizza," Chris Espinoza recalled. "We actually asked that. I mean, if they didn't like the same kind of pizza as we did, how could they come out to dinner with us?"

The relationship between Steve and the team always had plenty of rough spots. He rarely liked people's wives or girlfriends—he thought they could do much better and said so. It had become a running joke within the group that eating out with Steve was an exercise in embarrassment. First, there was the issue of sending plates back. He rarely accepted the first plate brought to him; he would find some reason to send it back. It would be "s——t," or dirty, or not what he thought the waitress had described. Another plate would be brought, and often that one would go back, too. It was like a power trip gone mad. Some screwy internal need made him play out the same pathetic scenario over and over. The waiter had to grovel. It was as though the gods had showered this young prince with money, power, and adulation but had failed to grant him humility or grace. He was an unmannerly brat with $200 million in the bank.

Then there was the uncomfortable ritual about paying a restaurant check. Andy Hertzfeld remembered one typical occasion: "When the bill came, Steve said something like, 'Well, I don't have any cash. All I've got is a credit card.'

"That was all I had as well, so I said so, and he replied, 'Great, you can pay for it then.' It took him years before he paid for anything. He never had cash with him, and whenever we went out with him, we had to pay. I think it had something to do with not wanting to be taken advantage of. Or maybe he was just a skinflint."

Mike Murray offered a bit of his own psychological analysis. "Steve just doesn't have the limits that the rest of us do. Because of his background and his early success, he doesn't have any boundaries. He doesn't know that anything is impossible because, well, he's always been able to do anything he wanted. So even as he's being a jerk, he's got this incredibly seductive aura around him that keeps you bound to him, keeps you near the flame, keeps you on the team."

If Steve hadn't become much more sophisticated in his approach to business, his personal life was a different story. He was managing the transition from rich kid lacking in polish to a smoothly groomed young prince. In 1982, he was named by Governor Jerry Brown to the California Commission on Industrial Innovation, which provided an opportunity for Steve to hobnob with the likes of the chairman of the Bank of America and his childhood idol, David Packard of Hewlett-Packard. The rich are treated deferentially by maitre d's, car salesmen, and other ordinary folk; the very rich are treated deferentially by everyone, even by presidents. Steve found that prominent people wanted to hear what he had to say. He was considered a great innovator. Steve Wozniak, by returning to college to complete his degree, had left the scene of the action, leaving Steve Jobs to garner the praise, the acclaim, and the attention.

On the romantic front, Steve had split up with his long-term girlfriend the year before and was making the rounds with one after another in a string of girlfriends. Mostly blond, not overly made up or aggressive, and often students at Stanford, they were the typical California beauties that a young millionaire might be expected to pursue. Steve was always the center of attention, and the woman lasted only as long as he was interested.

Then singer Joan Baez entered his life. She was older—old enough to have been involved with the Beat Generation and the early counter-culture, but, more to the point, with Bob Dylan, Steve's only enduring cultural fixation. Furthermore, she was a little wild and a little scandalous, having publicly announced, in the midst of the frenzied but still considerably more conservative seventies, that she had slept with a woman. Steve was always trying to be as different as possible, and the entirely distinctive Baez was a good catch. For Baez, always looking for a new experience, Steve and his wild crew were an interesting diversion.

A part of Steve badly wanted to settle down and have children, but another part of him was constantly at war with the notion. He liked his life as it was and didn't want anything to do with a traditional family life. He had at last begun to see his daughter Lisa, however. According to a fictionalized version written by a novelist who hews closely to real life and was in a position to know the true story, the girl at age ten was discovered one day in the yard, curled up asleep, dirty, and ragged. An envelope was pinned to her sleeve, addressed to her father. Nearby sat an old Ford truck, "rusty as something in a junkyard," which she claimed to have driven there herself. The child accepted "Tom"—the Steve Jobs stand-in—as her father, and he didn't deny it.

With Bill Atkinson, Steve admitted to occasional feelings of wanting a family. Over dinner one night with a group of the Macintosh gang, Steve agonized over Baez, lamenting, "If only she were of child-bearing age, I'd marry her." In fact, she was forty-one, an age when many women still have babies.

Steve came to see his Macintosh crew as a gang of pirates, and he was the pirate king. He had shanghaied the best people from the rest of Apple to join his renegade crew. And from the Lisa project he and his gang had stolen everything worthwhile, taking the best ideas worked out by that team over three years, while profiting from the team's worst mistakes by avoiding unproductive paths. His guys worked in splendid isolation, and they did so at a pace that put the rest of the company and the entire computer industry to shame. They would bring the greatest computer ever to market in less than two years.

By the end of June, they had the entire design on a computer wired up on the lab bench, ready for full testing.

"About then, Steve was getting nervous," said Martin Haeberli, a chip designer Steve had personally hired away from Xerox to develop an integrated chip for the Mac. "And Burrell was getting nervous because we still had nothing to show." Steve, though, instead of being frightened by the ticking clock, asked Burrell to investigate whether he could possibly design a Macintosh using a different kind of chip, called a PAL, that would create a greater number of dots on the screen.

"Burrell disappeared for about a month," Haeberli said, "and when he came back had a working design. Meanwhile, I had been shepherding [the original chip design] and we were about to get our first test chips back. Unfortunately, they ran about 40 percent slower than necessary. Ultimately, the decision was to go with the design Burrell had created by himself in a single month."

The company that would have manufactured the original chips, VLSI, was notified that Apple would not be using its chips after all. VLSI had already incurred huge development costs, overrunning the budget by more than 50 percent, because being a supplier to Apple seemed so valuable, and the company wanted to ensure that it would be a long-term relationship. Steve had originally signed the letter of intent committing to a deal worth $250 million; now he offered to settle for $100,000. The offer was an insult, but Jobs was adamant, and VLSI ended up taking a bath and writing off a huge loss.

The Macintosh team that showed up for the second retreat in late September, again held in Pajaro Dunes, was nearly one hundred strong.

The slogan Steve wrote on the blackboard this time accurately captured the spirit of the group: "Let's Be Pirates." It brought a roar of approval. Then he wrote another line that goaded the group, yet fired up their dedication: "Working 90 hours a Week and Loving it!" He could probably have made the slaves building the pyramids or the rowers in a Roman galley thrilled to be whipped, as a reminder that they were taking part in a noble effort.

With the stagecraft of a magician, Steve then pulled out a sweatshirt that had the "pirates" phrase emblazoned on it and pulled it over his head. Soon everyone at the retreat had one.

Of course, no one pretended this was a democracy. A handful of the sweats also had a tiny line of type over the left breast: "Macintosh Staff." They might have been a merry band of pirates, but there was still a distinction between those who swabbed the decks and those who ate at the captain's table.

The retreat was a sharing of information, to bring everyone up-to-date on how each aspect of the development was proceeding. It was also designed to keep the ardor at a fever pitch. Despite all setbacks, Steve was determined that they would ship the Macintosh the following May, no matter what. The schedule had slipped, but he was certain that it was now on track.

Meanwhile, in the fall of 1982, back in Cupertino, the Lisa was nearing release for the following spring. Journalists were brought in for an early look, and their reactions were encouraging. At the same time, dealer orders poured in for Apple II Christmas sales, leapfrogging ahead of any earlier Apple Christmas, even as the company readied the Apple IIe in the wings. Revenues continued to soar, and Steve was in the midst of his infatuation with Joan Baez. The world looked very rosy.

On the downside was the still-unresolved question of the Apple presidency. Steve Jobs didn't doubt that he was fully competent to run the company, but he was the only one on the board who thought so. A lengthy search had not produced any interested candidates strong enough to please the board. Late in 1982, news came that a feeler had been put out to the president of Pepsi, John Sculley. He was told that working in Silicon Valley was the "equivalent of being in Florence during the Renaissance," but it hadn't been enough to convince him even to consider the position.

Another problem was the name: "McIntosh" turned out to be a name already in use by McIntosh Labs, a manufacturer of high-end audio systems. Despite the different spelling, both companies were in the business of manufacturing electronics gear, which meant that the trademark office would not allow Apple's use of a name that, although spelled differently, was pronounced the same. The head of McIntosh Labs, a white-haired gent in his seventies named Gordon Gow, declined to sell the rights. Steve's troops had coalesced around the product named Macintosh; they were emotionally invested in the name, and it had come to symbolize everything they had dreamed of. Having to find a new label for their computer was bitter medicine.

The first issue of *Time* magazine in 1983 featured Steve Jobs's face on the cover. Late in 1982, Time, Inc., had advised Apple that the magazine, for its traditional New Year's issue, would honor the personal computer as "the machine of the year." The magazine's San Francisco correspondent, Michael Moritz, had been given carte blanche by Apple and spent several months around the company researching the story. On New Year's Eve, a courier showed up to hand Steve Jobs the first copy of the magazine to appear on the West Coast. He flipped through the magazine and found a full-page portrait that carried the title "The Updated Book of Jobs."

As Steve started to read it, he felt something was very wrong. The text was clever but barbed with phrases like "a blind faith that would have been the envy of the early Christian martyrs," which seemed to be making fun of him. Wozniak was quoted as saying that "Steve didn't do one circuit, design or piece of code," and someone identified only as "a friend" was quoted as saying, "Something is happening to Steve that's sad and not pretty, something related to money and power and loneliness." Bad enough that this unnamed "friend" was attacking him, but *Woz*—his old companion in pranks, his cofounder. Here was disloyalty in spades.

As if to underscore its point, the article was illustrated with a photo of Steve sitting alone, cross-legged, meditating in a sparsely furnished room of his house. An anonymous employee turned the knife with an incisive, highly quotable phrase: "He would have made an excellent King of France." Any reader would finish the piece convinced that Steve Jobs was a man without creative or design skills who had contrived to make his fortune on the backs of others. (Moritz turned the article into a book about Apple called *The Little Kingdom*; it was the first of the Apple books, excellent and heavily researched, and it fleshed out the unflattering portrait of an unfeeling wunderkind. The author ended up a venture capitalist with Don Valentine's firm, Sequoia Associates, and was instrumental in the start-up of both Yahoo! and Google.)

Few could take such a blow and keep right on going. Steve couldn't, either. He canceled his New Year's plans, stayed home, and spent the night thinking. He wouldn't let it get to him. He would prove they were wrong. He would bring out the Macintosh, and they would eat their words.

At the same time, any thoughtful, introspective person would have paid attention to the criticisms, decided which seemed to have validity, and given some serious thought to making changes in his life. Or at least trying to. But not Steve Jobs.

At 8 A.M. the next morning, New Year's Day 1983, Steve called Jef Raskin. He wanted a shoulder to cry on, and Raskin's was the one he chose. It gave him no pause that Raskin was the man he had forced out of the Macintosh project after a bitter fight. For Steve, the past was irrelevant. Only the present mattered.

He had learned nothing.

May 16, 1983, was another tough day for Steve. From the previous retreat, months earlier, it had been the date that Steve had pinned all his hopes and dreams on—the date that he had promised himself and sold to his loyal team members as the ship date for the Macintosh. It was a date written in stone—or at least on T-shirts, but it wasn't to be. The

Lisa was released then, and the company insisted the Macintosh not be released before its big-sister machine. The delay turned out to be a good thing.

The third Macintosh retreat lacked some of the sizzle of the previous two. For one thing, it was not being held at the fancy Pajaro Dunes but at a motel in Carmel. It also came on top of news about the delayed ship date and a critical problem with the disk drive: the floppy drive for the Lisa, and destined for the Mac as well, was fatally flawed.

For Bill Atkinson, though, the big issue of the day was something quite different. Atkinson now had the title of chief software architect for Apple's graphics and pixel-based displays, and he deserved much of the credit for what made the Lisa and the Macintosh so different from an IBM PC: their on-screen appearance. Now Atkinson was fuming, absolutely beside himself with rage, frustration, and bitter disappointment that he couldn't keep bottled up inside.

Ordinarily mild-mannered and soft-spoken, Atkinson had gained Jobs's trust years earlier when he stood up in a meeting where Steve was spewing some outrageous technical gobbledygook, and yelled, "Steve Jobs, you're an asshole!" and then walked out.

Steve had reacted exactly the opposite from what everyone expected. He called Atkinson the very next day, invited him to dinner, and the two became close friends—or at least as close as Steve ever allowed anyone to become.

Now Atkinson had had enough. "Bill told Steve that he was quitting," said Hertzfeld, the only witness to the screaming match that erupted. "He was upset because in all the publicity about the Lisa, in the hours of interviews, the pages of articles, there wasn't a single mention of his name. He was the guy behind it. Without him, there would have been nothing. Without his breakthrough routines to allow us to quickly and easily draw the screen, there would have been no Lisa and no Macintosh. But it was as though he didn't exist.

"He was crying and screaming. And Steve was screaming back at him. It really tore me apart. Here were the two people I respected more than anyone else in the world, and they were completely out of control."

Steve walked out of the shouting match, down the hall, and into the room where the team was assembled for the retreat. It was like the argument had never happened. He was Steve the magician; Steve the preacher, leading the prayer meeting of the faithful; Steve the drummer, sounding the beat for everyone to march to.

At the front of the room alongside him was the first working big-screen Macintosh, a prototype of the machine they were going to ship. Steve picked up a half-empty bottle of Perrier, walked over to the Mac, and dramatically announced, "I've just been talking to the folks at McIntosh Labs. We got the name.

"So I christen you Macintosh."

And with that, he poured the bottle of mineral water over the machine. The room erupted in pandemonium. Everyone stood and started cheering.

It was absolutely the right thing to do. He hadn't been talking to people at McIntosh Labs, however, and they hadn't agreed that Steve could use the name. He simply knew that he needed a big gesture to galvanize his team for the final stretch, and he was right. It worked.

For once, though, Steve Jobs must have admitted to himself that what he had done was wrong; either that or he recognized that Bill Atkinson was too valuable to lose. He pulled some strings behind the scenes, and within two weeks, Atkinson was named an Apple Fellow—the highest recognition for scientists within the company. The designation brought more than just an honor; with it came a significant jump in salary, a handsome pile of stock options, and the freedom, like a "university professor" at Harvard, to pursue whatever he was interested in.

After the retreat, the "pirates" theme proved to be a powerful glue for holding the team together. It captured a sense of "us against them" that emphasized how different these people were and how different their computer was, setting them apart from the rest of Apple. Someone even tacked up a Jolly Roger pirate flag, complete with skull and crossbones, on the inside of the Macintosh building.

Late on a Sunday night not long afterward, one of the young software engineers on the team, Steve Capps, along with team member graphic artist Susan Kare (who created the look of all the icons for the Mac), came up with the in-your-face idea that the pirate flag should fly from the roof of the building. They found a spare board lying around, fastened the flag to it, climbed up, and mounted the board so the flag was prominent, unmistakable. The next morning it caused a sensation.

To the Macintosh crew, it was a symbol of their uniqueness. To every other Apple employee, it was a challenge. Some found it an insult—especially to the Lisa team, which was located across the street.

Here was a tiny group of people with, yes, smaller salaries but an inordinate number of enviable perks—fruit juices, leased cars, larger office cubicles, video games, Ping-Pong, their own basketball court, and free massages! Here they were looking down their noses at the people who brought in the money that allowed them to have all of those goodies. It was a prescription for internal chaos.

In early March 1983, Steve was in Manhattan, which he had decided to make a second base by purchasing an apartment overlooking Central Park. On one brisk late-winter day, he rounded up John Sculley and the two of them spent an afternoon meandering through the Metropolitan Museum of Art and sharing ideas over coffee in a café.

If the board wouldn't let Steve run the company, the next best choice from his perspective would be someone he felt comfortable with, whom he might be able to control. John Sculley fit the bill on both counts. He was a top-notch, proven marketer who would be highly valuable to Apple. He knew nothing at all about technology—which to John was a drawback but to Steve looked like a blessing. If John were running Apple, who would he look to for technology guidance? Who more likely than the man who had recruited him?

John had been adamantly opposed to the idea from the time it was first broached to him. Now he was wavering. Referring to Pepsi, Steve asked a question that has become part of the legend of U.S. business: "Are you going to sell sugar water for the rest of your life when you could be doing something really important?"

Before the end of the month, the board had laid a deal on the table. John would receive $1 million a year in salary, a $1 million bonus for accepting, and up to $1 million in stock options, performance incentives, and low-interest loans to enable him to purchase a $2 million house.

John Sculley already had a good deal at Pepsi—a powerful position and a stable job at a stable company in a stable industry. To his credit, he chose the challenge over the sure thing. Apple had a new president—and, more important for Steve, a new president who worshiped him.

A month later, when the appointment was announced by Mike Markkula, John Sculley made a statement in which he said, "If you can pick one reason why I came to Apple, it was to have the chance to work with Steve. I look on him as being one of the really important figures in our country in this century. And I have the chance to help him grow. That in itself is exciting."

Wall Street approved of the appointment. In spite of a declining market share and falling profitability in the face of the challenge of the IBM PC, Apple's stock boomed to a high of $63 per share. But the company's corporate insiders were looking at a different story. The previous year, another development project, the Apple III, had flopped, a victim of Steve Jobs's inflexibility and the design-by-committee syndrome. (Randy Wigginton said, "The Apple III was kind of like a baby conceived during a group orgy, and [afterward] everybody had this bad headache and there's this bastard child, and everyone says, 'It's not mine.'") The product had been introduced in 1980, suffered a 20 percent failure rate, and never sold more than a handful of units.

Now the Lisa, too, was a flop. By early summer, orders had fallen to a thin trickle for the $10,000 business machine. When compared to the $3,000 IBM PC, with its Microsoft software and utilitarian focus, businesses were voting with their checkbooks. Cool didn't cut it. Following on the heels of the disaster that was the Apple III, the company had yet another disaster in the making. It looked like John Sculley had arrived in time to be captain of a sinking ship.

He would soon discover the truth about the Macintosh. The dark picture was described by Joe Shelton, a marketing manager who was to promote the Apple-labeled Macintosh software products at the introduction. "When I joined the group," he said, "I heard these ridiculous projections of 70,000 computers in the first one hundred days, and 500,000 Macs in the first year. And I thought it was crazy." Since then, he had been drinking the Steve Jobs Kool-Aid. "Within a few months, I found myself saying the same thing—and believing it. Steve had the most remarkable effect on all of us. We knew what he said was impossible to achieve rationally. But, emotionally, he had us all wanting it so badly to come true that we came to believe it as well."

The handsome price the stock had achieved with the news of Sculley's appointment didn't last. One of John's early duties was to approve the press release acknowledging that the Lisa was not selling anywhere near projections, and that the company would report a loss for the final quarter of the fiscal year. (Apple's financial year runs from September to August.) With that bombshell, the stock price plummeted from $63 to $21.

Not that it affected Steve's lifestyle any, but with the fall in stock price, his net worth dropped, in a matter of weeks, by a *quarter of a billion dollars.*

In November, Apple's *1984* ad for the Super Bowl was completed under the direction of Ridley Scott, who had already directed the films *Aliens* and *Blade Runner* and would go on to do a series of blockbusters that included *Thelma & Louise* and *Black Hawk Down.* Even after Apple moved the production to England to save money, the ad was budgeted at more than $750,000, according to Andy Hertzfeld. Buying the air time on the Super Bowl cost even more; this was to be a one-shot, million-dollar moment. John Sculley later called it a "bet the company" proposition.

A print of the TV spot was flown in and messengered to Apple to show at the monthly board meeting. Steve wanted to share recognition with Mike Murray for his work in creating the piece and arranged for him to come in and present it. Mike said, "I was really proud of it. This was my crowning achievement, and I was finally going to be recognized for my contribution. Afterward, I looked around the room and Phil Schlein had his head on the conference table and was banging his fist on it. I thought, 'Wow. They really liked it.'

"Then he looked up at me, and I realized that he hated it. Right there, they voted to have us sell the time and pull the ad. The board thought it was the worst ad Apple had ever made."

The board wanted nothing to do with it. "The chilling reception from the board compelled John Sculley to ask Chiat-Day to sell back both time slots that they had purchased," Murray said. "But [agency cofounder] Jay Chiat was true to form, and only sold off the thirty-second slot, telling Apple that he wasn't able to get rid of the longer one at so late a date. Apple considered using the slot for a more conventional commercial but in the end decided to take a chance on the *1984* spot."

Steve was ecstatic. It was all going his way.

·   ·   ·

All that money would be worth it if the commercial started conversations and drove thousands of people into stores to see the Macintosh. Obviously, the money would be largely wasted if for some reason the Macintosh wasn't in the stores when the crowds arrived following Super Bowl Sunday. Nothing could stand in the way of getting the finished product into the stores, and not just the hardware itself but the software as well.

On Sunday, January 8, the West Coast software programmers and testers assembled for a conference call with the East Coast product introduction team. Shortly before that, the programming team had faced the hard truth: it had barely more than a week left to finish the software and deliver it for disk duplication, and the team simply wasn't going to make it. The alternative was ugly: ask consumers to buy a great new computer with buggy, unstable software labeled "demo."

During the phone call, when the team announced that the software wouldn't be ready, the reaction wasn't what they anticipated. They expected a typical Steve Jobs explosion. Instead, they got an ego massaging. He told them how great they were and how all of Apple was counting on them. He said that they could make it happen, that they could get the software finished. It was simply impossible to send out demo disks; it would send the wrong message to the marketplace. He was counting on them, and they could do it. And with that, he hung up before they had a chance to argue.

The people in the conference room in Cupertino were stunned. They had pushed so hard already that they were near the point of total exhaustion. There comes a time in mountain climbing when strong men would rather sit down and cry than try to continue. Working for Steve Jobs had the challenges of climbing a difficult mountain, but, like the proverbial Saint Bernard arriving with brandy for the mountain climber, Steve had given them new energy. He had challenged them to rise to the occasion, and he had chosen his people well. They would not let him down. There was little to say. Silently, they got up and went back to their cubicles and back to work. Few of them slept that week.

At the last moment, in the hours before dawn on the morning of the sixteenth, the team arrived at a combination of System and Finder software (the operating system for the Macintosh) that seemed to work. Randy Wigginton feverishly attacked the last few bugs; each time he compiled a new version, it seemed to have worse bugs than the one before. Desperate, unwilling to give up, he kept going until, at last, with minutes to spare, he succeeded. They had software that could go to duplication.

Stories about the soon-to-be-released Macintosh began to appear all over the United States. The computer hit the cover of more than twenty magazines, made it onto the nightly news of the three major networks, and was covered by all the major papers in the country. It marked the first time that the introduction of a new computer was considered national news.

Both Steve and John spoke about "betting the company" on the new Macintosh. Talk like that was guaranteed to appeal to an America where the go-for-broke syndrome had always been a birthright.

When the Super Bowl commercial aired, viewers were treated to an ad unlike any they had seen before. The spot depicted scenes of men with shaved heads dressed in gray, prisonlike garb, sitting in rows on long benches, hollow-eyed, watching as a Big Brother–like figure lectures to them from a giant screen. An attractive young blonde woman, running from goon oppressors, dashes into the chamber, approaches the screen, spins around to build up momentum with the huge sledgehammer she's carrying, and then lets it go, smashing into the center of the giant screen, which explodes in a blinding flash of light. At that point, the brief voice-over begins, emphasized by the same words appearing on-screen:

On January 24th Apple Computer will introduce
Macintosh. And you'll understand why 1984
won't be like *1984*.

The ad was so spectacular, so distinctively different, so stunningly original that television stations all over the country replayed it on their evening news, giving Apple millions of dollars' worth of instant free advertising.

The Macintosh itself was unveiled to the world as promised, on January 24, 1984, at the company's annual meeting, in front of a packed audience of employees, stockholders, and the press. Steve dressed for the occasion in an elegant double-breasted jacket offset by a polka-dot bow tie. This was to be one of his finest hours.

When the lights dimmed, he appeared in a spotlight at the podium, opening the meeting with a shrug of his shoulders and a soft-spoken, flat recitation of a few lines from his favorite poet, Bob Dylan, and the song "The Times They Are a-Changin'."

He was followed by John Sculley, who was greeted with hearty applause as he described Apple's strong cash position with no long-term debt and the strong sales of the Apple IIe, which had broken all records in December.

Then Steve came back out and said he had done enough talking, and it was time to let the Macintosh speak for itself. He lifted a Mac out of a bag. With a prototype voice synthesis program, it said to the audience:

> Hello, I am Macintosh. It sure is great to get out of that bag. Unaccustomed as I am to public speaking, I'd like to share with you a maxim I thought of the first time I met an IBM mainframe: never trust a computer you can't lift!
>
> Obviously, I can talk, but right now I'd like to sit back and listen. So it is with considerable pride that I introduce the man who's been like a father to me—Steve Jobs.

That was dynamite stuff. The audience erupted with applause, both for the amusing speech by the little computer and for the return to the stage of the man most people would forever think of as the creator of the Macintosh, the icon himself, Steve Jobs.

Steve launched into a performance as flawless and seamless as any he had ever given. His presence was powerful, his charisma enticing, his intensity captivating. The only thing missing was a sense of humor.

In the days that followed, customers flocked to shops to see for themselves what all the hype and hoopla was about. Orders poured in, and the critical first hundred days racked up the seventy thousand sales Steve had touted.

It looked as if Steve's overblown sales figures might be on target, after all.

4

We're going to have to do something about
Sculley. He can't stay. He doesn't know
what he's doing.

—Steve Jobs

Learning to Fail

John Sculley's vision was clouded. Steve Jobs could be captivating, exuding an aura that blinded people to his faults. John
still thought that Steve walked on water, and he bought into the vastly
overblown sales forecasts for the newly released Macintosh. The
accepted number was still 500,000 for the first year, 1984, and the early
sales reports gave no reason to doubt it. Two company executives
tried to bring some sanity to the subject: Floyd Kvamme, the executive
vice president of sales and marketing, and Ken Zerbe, the executive vice
president of finance and administration. They were removed.

While the world looked at Apple and thought that it was seeing the
model of how corporations of the future should be run, a power play
was shaping up inside the executive suite that promised to split the
company apart.

After the Macintosh introduction, John had decided to consolidate
the Mac and the Lisa groups under Steve Jobs's leadership. From there,
it all started to go bad. The first day under the new setup, as both groups
gathered in the atrium of the Lisa building, Steve's first words to the Lisa
people were, "You guys really f——d up." It went downhill from there.
"I was embarrassed to be part of the Mac Team," Donn Denman said,

remembering that day. "I looked over at the Lisa people as he was going on with his tirade, and there was pure hatred in their eyes. And I couldn't blame them."

Not all of the Macintosh people felt that way. The tirade generated emotions that were unhealthy for everyone involved. Some of the Mac people thought that Steve's comments were absolutely correct. "I thought it was his finest hour," Andy Hertzfeld said. "It was just what he needed to say. They *had* screwed up."

Steve's willfulness and self-centeredness were rapidly proving to be his undoing. His performance that day was like the prediction of a seer, foretelling of things to come. It bespoke an essential lack of humanity in his vision for Apple and flew in the face of the humanistic values that the company was supposedly founded upon. It announced that he believed he was meant to run all of Apple and that his time was fast approaching.

Jay Elliott, Apple's vice president of human resources and the only other member of the Mac team to sit on the company's executive staff, was a keen observer of people, and he watched the relationship between Sculley and Steve with increasing alarm. "John was the president," Elliott said, "but all the power was with Steve. At exec staff meetings, all you had to do was watch the body language. Steve and John would talk to each other, but everyone else who was supposedly reporting to John spent all their time talking to Steve. He was in charge."

"We hired John to be Steve's mentor," explained Elliott, "and it ended up being the other way around. . . . [I]t was Steve who taught John."

John Sculley was quiet and cerebral, reserved, and clearly unable to stand up to Steve. That inability was compounded by Steve's seeming Midas touch, as the Macintosh looked poised to be the best-selling computer of all time, dominating the marketplace. Meanwhile, Steve himself was reaping the benefits of Regis McKenna's ongoing publicity campaign, which was designed to make the world believe that Steve Jobs was "the inventor of the personal computer." The campaign had succeeded.

Steve, meanwhile, was about to walk straight into the eye of the storm.

The ancient Greeks had a word for Steve's behavior. They called it *hubris*, the insolent pride that humans exhibited when they thought they could challenge the gods. The gods' response was always the same: to strike down the arrogant human with a bolt from the heavens.

In 1984, the catchphase of the year was the line from a Wendy's hamburger commercial: "Where's the beef?" Buyers were beginning to ask the same thing about the Mac. The first hundred days it had stood up on sizzle and flash, but on closer inspection, there didn't seem to be much steak. The machine had no software to speak of. The joke on release was that the machine had six software programs: Macintosh Write, Macintosh Paint, and Microsoft Word—and Write, Paint, and Word. The boys in Redmond had done their work, but no one else—including Lotus, which had the best-selling spreadsheet for the IBM family, Lotus 1-2-3—had been able to master the arcane art of writing software for a visual display–based computer. The Mac was competing with the IBM PC, a computer that had thousands of programs on the shelves. The Mac was seen as a toy, a flaky machine that you could love, but you wouldn't buy.

A massive round of market research provided chilling insight. Retail sales people were showing the IBM PC first; even shoppers who asked about the Mac were steered away from it, back to the PC. Customers disliked the idea that it was not expandable, that it had a small screen, and that there was no color.

One freelance speechwriter remembers sitting in front of a Macintosh with Apple manager Betsy Pace, trying to use the machine to write the speech she was to give the following morning at the general session of Apple's all-important annual sales meeting. He would write a sentence or two and try to save. The machine could save only onto a floppy, but at this point it would spit out the floppy and display a message requesting that the disk containing the Microsoft Word program be put into the drive. That would be done, the floppy would spin for some moments and then be ejected, accompanied by a request that the floppy with the speech file be reinserted. And back and forth, sometimes for minutes on end, to the frustration of the writer and the increasing anxiety of the speech-less manager. The problem was that the computer didn't have enough memory, and the internal hard drive didn't have enough storage space. Apple executives were getting a taste of what their customers experienced. It was called the "Disk Drive Olympics" among the Mac team.

The blame for these problems is not hard to assign. Field and market testing wasn't a part of Steve's makeup. He believed in his intuition and his marketing savvy. Especially in early 1982, when he was flying high and truly felt that he had the golden touch, no matter what anyone else might say, Steve simply decided what the box should contain, and that was it. As Mike Murray said, "Steve did his market research by looking into the mirror every morning."

It would prove to be the Mac's one Achilles' heel. By closing the computer to the outside, by predefining its features, by deciding that he—this kid who had never had a job, who had never worked in a menial office occupation, who had no touch for the common clown struggling to make the mortgage payment and buy food for his kids—knew exactly what the world of buyers needed, he revealed his megalomania. He truly believed that he was in touch with the consumer, that he understood both computers and the public with such clarity that he could single-handedly decide on the configuration of the machine. It came from an arrogance of youth and power—an insolence and a presumptuousness that went far beyond anything he had shown before. It was the first indication of hubris in the project's leader, hubris that eventually led to disaster.

The sales figures for July 1984 were frightening. Macintosh sales appeared to be slowing. At first Steve refused to believe it; he thought it was simply a case of summer doldrums. But when the figures for the second month in a row showed the trend accelerating, panic started to set in. Their nearly thousand-strong organization—a group built to reflect the outrageous optimism of the sales forecasts, not the reality of actual sales—was in no way supported by income. Suddenly Apple had a serious problem, and Steve was a big part of it.

In having kept himself totally isolated from the typical user, he had failed to grasp the most basic fundamentals of the buying equation. He didn't understand that when faced with spending a couple of thousand dollars on a computer, most people didn't care what it looked like, whether it had a mouse or not, or what color it was. All they cared about was whether it did the job.

Resentment began to germinate in Apple's corridors. The Apple II organization—responsible for the popular and brisk-selling Apple IIe and IIc lines—was constantly getting hold of the wrong end of the policy stick, with its members becoming near untouchables in the corporate caste system. Meanwhile, Steve and the rest of the company royalty—the undisputed Brahmins—were in a nosedive with their product, and John Sculley still wasn't reining them in. The company's reputation for industry leadership was rapidly being undone by the erratic behavior of its chairman.

An even bigger blow came when the Mac members began to get wise to what their Lisa counterparts were being paid. Engineers in the Lisa division routinely made more than $50,000 a year, while in the Mac group only Andy and Burrell were in that range. Steve had managed to drum up near blind allegiance to the concept of the Mac, while paying salaries $10,000 to $20,000 less and still expecting his days, nights, and weekends, his "90 hours a week." The situation created not only "extreme depression among the engineers," as one manager wrote in a memo, but also a minor uprising among the Macintosh folks that grew even more heated when some of the more senior Macintosh people began to discover that the people reporting to them, hired later, were being paid more than their bosses.

Steve tried to restore some balance by paying extremely generous bonuses to his Mac people, but that only rankled the Apple II division, since it was the Apple II products that brought in almost all the revenue to pay everyone's salary. Human resources director Jay Elliott tried to convince the Macintosh insurgents that the lower salaries were a reasonable counterbalance for the value of the perks they received, which in some cases even included the cost of a nanny. It didn't wash; the Mac people felt betrayed and used. They had given their hearts to Steve and the Mac, and he had treated them badly. Steve was never able to regain their trust. (In coming years, few of the Mac team worked for Steve Jobs again.)

The battle for the hearts and minds of Steve's own people was only part of the problem. Though Apple was universally considered a leader and an innovator in the world of personal computers, it was widely distrusted as a result of its inconsistent performance, not to mention the behavior of its chairman. In the battle for survival against rival

IBM, Apple was becoming less of a big gun and more of a loose cannon. For consumers, IBM was a name that could be trusted. Apple was not.

Apple had established a tradition of holding an elaborate annual bash for its international sales force—four or five days of entertainment, pump-up-the-troops, technical lectures, and drunken carousing into the wee hours, held at some elegant resort. This sort of affair is well known in the corporate world, and it's important for reinvigorating the sales force with product knowledge and enthusiasm. In some years, the Apple meetings were dazzling in their splendor, but the 1984 meeting, to be held in Hawaii at a resort on tourist-crowded Waikiki beach, presented special challenges.

With Macintosh sales faltering, Steve saw that it was vital to put on an extravagant week to get the sales reps—many of them brand new to Apple—fired up and committed to guaranteeing the product's success. Over on the other side of the house, Del Yokam faced a different challenge. Now running the Apple II product group, Del realized that all the focus would be on the sexy new Macintosh that was making all the headlines but bringing in no money, while his Apple II products produced all the revenue that kept the company afloat. Worse, the Apple II group had no forthcoming products to beat the drums about. The money-making part of the company was in danger of being lost in the shadows of the Mac.

For the highlight production of the Macintosh session at the conference, Steve Jobs greenlighted the concept for a mock-documentary entitled *1944*, both a reminder of the hugely successful *1984* commercial and a parody of every B-movie about the war ever made. The Macintosh army lands and takes the beachhead, presumably against the implacable foe, IBM. Meanwhile, on a set built to look like the Oval Office, President Roosevelt (seen only from behind) gives orders to "the General," played by Mike Murray. The eight-minute, $50,000 production wowed the audience, who greeted the unfolding story with roars of appreciation and howls of laughter.

The capper came at the very end, when the president swiveled his high-backed chair around to the camera, to reveal a man whose makeup gave him a remarkable resemblance to Franklin Roosevelt. The actor held up a cigarette burning in Roosevelt's familiar long-stemmed holder. He was instantly recognizable, despite the impressive makeup: Steve Jobs himself. The sales troops loved it, stomping and whistling in appreciation.

That show was a triumph, yet the Apple II show outdid it. As the two thousand sales people walked into a large auditorium, they immediately recognized the setting: the room was designed in the style of a major political convention, whose members had assembled to choose between two candidates for their party's nomination: the Apple IIe and its smaller cousin, the Apple IIc. In a broadcast booth above the floor sat two commentators who would narrate the meeting: "David Brittle" (a take-off on NBC anchorman David Brinkley) and "Connie Chunk" (NBC reporter and host Connie Chung). The laugh-packed script had the audience roaring almost from beginning to end.

Steve Wozniak agreed to take a short role in the production and showed his own inspired sense of humor. He threw away the professionally written comedy piece that had been specially crafted for him and instead ad-libbed several minutes of on-target gags that fit in perfectly with the theme of the session and kept the audience laughing.

One moment in the twenty-five-minute spectacle became part of Apple legend. A short "nomination speech" was presented for each of the two "candidates." The company's vice president of sales, ex-Columbia University football coach Bill Campbell, delivered the nomination for the IIc. Partway through, he spoke a line that no one reviewing the script had picked up on—but the audience did. Describing the smaller of the Apple IIs, he said, "It's not size that counts, it's performance." The immediate outburst of raucous laughter was deafening.

For the sales force, the Hawaii meeting had been a week of fun, revelry, and carousing. For the executives, returning to Cupertino headquarters was enough to bring on the heartburn. "Steve was incredibly depressed," Jay Elliot recalled. "He thought John [Sculley] was screwing up. He was going to have to take charge of the company because John didn't 'get it,' which was Steve's phrase. He didn't understand the business." It's as if an airplane runs out of fuel and the pilot, who didn't check before takeoff, blames everyone else for the accident.

The sales figures continued to slide, and Steve's mood darkened with each successive report. He became convinced that the only solution for Apple was to form a strategic alliance with another major company. He looked at AT&T, General Electric, and even Coca-Cola for a co-merchandising program. At one point, Steve approached General Motors. He invited Roger Smith, the company's CEO, to tour the Macintosh Division. Steve suggested a buy-in, a strategic alliance, and Smith replied that he knew very little about computers but would send a member of his board out to talk with the board.

The board member who showed up was a guy named Ross Perot, and although they were an odd couple—the young, wild Steve and the straitlaced Texas patriot couldn't have been more different—they got along like a pair of ranchhands at a cookout. Still, in the end, Perot was impressed but couldn't see a fit between the two companies.

Steve then flew a team to Japan to visit Epson, a business machine manufacturer that might provide a better match. The ride out from Tokyo was extremely frustrating; the road was blocked due to an earthquake, so they switched from their limousine to a train, only to learn that the train tracks were blocked as well. When they arrived, the Epson people were gracious even though they had been standing by at the ready for hours. Steve was in a foul mood.

The Epson president stood up to make the product presentation himself. The gentleman had hardly started, having spoken for little more than a minute, before Steve interrupted. According to Jay Elliott, who was part of the team and witnessed the incident, "Steve turned to the president of the company and said, 'This is s——t. Don't you have anything good?' And with that, he marched out."

Later, on the train heading back to Tokyo, Steve began to vent. Rather than using the opportunity to explore the difficulties within Apple, he talked about the problems he was having with his latest flame, the designer of the Vietnam Veterans' Memorial, Yale architecture student Maya Lin. "He couldn't understand why things were always so difficult for him," Elliott said. "He didn't care about the little scene at Epson—that had meant nothing to him. He had forgotten it as soon as it was over. What really counted was love, and he couldn't understand why he couldn't make it work."

The multimillionaire founder of Apple Computer poured out his heart as Japan sped by outside his train window. He was nearing his thirtieth birthday and still longed to start a family but was afraid of what the future held. Finally, he turned to Elliott and blurted out a complaint that might have made sense if spoken by a Rembrandt or a Beethoven: "I'm just an ordinary guy. Why can't they understand that?"

The maelstrom continued to swirl. Sales dipped below ten thousand a month, Steve was having enormous mood swings, and Sculley hadn't taken charge. People weren't buying Macintoshes, in part because there was still no serious software available. By now, the initial Apple IIc rush had died out. Worse, Del Yokam had put in a production order based on the earlier strong sales, and the company found itself stuck with a huge inventory of unsold units. Apple had to announce a write-off of the unsold inventory, which gave Wall Street the jitters. Two hundred thousand of the machines had to be liquidated through a bartering company. Apple was stalled and sinking.

Even so, the Macintosh Division was on a takeover binge, grabbing control of the internal groups responsible for companywide functions like advertising, public relations, distribution, and peripherals. Steve's rationale was that it was the only way that he, as chairman of the board, could be sure that the "right" thing would be done. But it was the inordinate amount of power centered in the Macintosh division that was at the root of the company's problems. The situation was all the worse because it was Steve who wielded that power.

A week after the 1985 annual meeting in Phoenix, Arizona, most of Apple's executive staff headed for another retreat. One morning the company's marketing boss, Mike Murray, found Sculley and PR maven Regis McKenna attending a session. He told them that it was essential he have a private meeting with them, and the urgency of his tone convinced the two to hear him out.

On their way to the elevator, Steve saw the three of them together and asked what they were up to. Murray, trapped, said they were going to have a meeting. Steve indicated that he wanted to join them. For the first time in his three years at Apple, Mike Murray said no to Steve Jobs. Steve was insistent, but Murray stood his ground. Eventually, they left the chairman standing there as the elevator door closed, and headed upstairs. It was Steve's first inkling that something might be up, and he decided he would find out what it was.

Meanwhile, the three conspirators were holed up in Sculley's hotel room, with Murray telling the company president that he thought Steve had to be removed from his position as head of the Macintosh Division. Sculley and McKenna listened carefully while Murray, a trusted lieutenant, an insider, and a loyal subject to Prince Steve, ticked off the reasons behind his conclusion. Finally, the lightbulb started to flicker in Sculley's head: if Murray, who was closer to Steve than almost anyone else, was telling him that Steve had to be removed from the head of the Macintosh Division, then surely something was seriously wrong.

Under Steve's recent power grab, the Macintosh group that had started as a tight-knit clan of pirates committed to the cause had now swollen to a mondo-division of seven hundred people, with barely a trickle of revenue to pay their salaries and driven by a leader who made decisions on the spur of the moment and changed them just as quickly.

It would have been easy to lay blame for these problems at least in part on Murray himself, and perhaps in some ways it was right to do so, because as director of marketing he certainly had a large hand in the decisions that had led to the current mess. After all, the fundamental trouble was that they had missed the market. They thought they could sell machines into the office environment, and they didn't know (or didn't bother to find out) that those computers were normally purchased in groups. Apple had always sold to individuals, tailoring all of its marketing to making a person feel good about choosing to go with Apple.

Steve had convinced them all that their plan was on the money, and he had Sculley completely bamboozled as well. They had all been sure that the strategy was correct, and that the dropping sales were simply a reflection of the computer shakeout, the seasonal softness, or the non-existent software. "He could see the horizon out there, a thousand miles out," explained Jay Elliott, "but he could never see the details of each little mile that had to be covered to get there. That was his genius, and his downfall."

After Phoenix, Steve and his original cofounder, Woz, traveled to Washington for a ceremony at which President Ronald Reagan presented them with the first National Technology medals for their contribution to American technological advances. It was an uncomfortable moment for both Steves, however; they couldn't stand each other anymore and could scarcely contain their dislike.

When Jobs returned to California, he found that Wozniak had publicly quit Apple. In a blast of uncensored comments, Woz berated the company for its lack of support for the Apple II product line and its chaotic management. Clearly relishing the dig at his former friend, Woz ripped the way that the company had ignored the Apple II at the recent annual meeting, even though it was the firm's only money-making product. "We had a shareholders' meeting last week," he said, "and the words 'Apple II' were not mentioned once. I made a very strong complaint about it."

By February 1985, Elliott and Murray had decided that the only person within the organization with the marketing muscle and the vision to replace Steve at the helm of the Macintosh Division was a forty-one-year-old Frenchman by the name of Jean-Louis Gassée.

At the time the head of Apple France, Gassée was a mathematician and a charismatic leader, with several books of murky pop philosophy under his belt. With a reputation as a philosopher and a future-thinker, he was also the head of the only international operation for Apple that was solidly in the black. In the software doldrums of autumn 1984, when nothing other than MacWrite and MacPaint were available for the Macintosh in Europe, Gassée had shown his ingenuity and business sense by sending an employee to New York with tens of thousands of dollars in cash to purchase as much software as possible, which he then distributed to dealers throughout France.

While others were plotting to replace him, Steve was busy drafting a memo offering solutions to the problems of the Macintosh Division. His proposals amounted to offering a Band-Aid to a man having a heart attack. The remedies he suggested included eliminating free beverages and catered food, and flying business class instead of first class.

At the end of that month, Steve celebrated his thirtieth birthday, honoring himself with the kind of bash that only multimillionaires and heads of large companies even aspire to. In the ballroom of the St. Francis Hotel in San Francisco, he treated a thousand of his closest friends and employees to a black-tie dinner-dance; entertainment was provided by Ella Fitzgerald.

By the week of March 11, revenues for the Macintosh were just over 10 percent of the projection. Steve obviously had no grasp of how desperate the situation was, and someone needed to step in fast.

Sculley finally had no choice but to act. He stepped up to the plate and announced the closing of several production facilities. Fortuitously, IBM announced soon afterward that it was ceasing production of its ill-conceived lowball version of the IBM PC, the PCjr computer, which had been a flop all along. The business press had another victim to flog for a change, leaving Apple with a temporary bit of breathing space.

At the same time, Mike Murray was circulating a memo to key members of the executive staff, summarizing the fears he had first expressed to Sculley and McKenna in Phoenix. Under the heading "DO NOT CIRCULATE, COPY, OR SHARE," he described what he saw as the company's "major philosophical problems," laying blame squarely on Steve for "espousing vision . . . at the clear expense of corporate survival."

In fact, Steve was one of the first people he showed it to. Now, with his most loyal people questioning his role as the head of Macintosh, Steve finally began to come to his senses about the reality of the situation. Steve and Murray met constantly throughout that month, with Steve trying desperately to convince his director of marketing that only Steve Jobs understood how to save Apple, and that Sculley should be removed and Steve himself installed as president and CEO. Murray, of course, wasn't buying. He believed in his heart that the only answer was to put someone else at the head of Macintosh and to give Steve a new role in research and development, with an eye toward developing a project that would be as breathtaking as the Macintosh had been three years earlier.

The world of Apple was crashing down around them. People were defecting en masse, and Sculley was worried. With research in hand showing that the Macintosh was *still* being perceived as a yuppie computer and not a serious business machine, Sculley allowed himself to be convinced of the idea that Gassée should take over for Steve. Steve's response was to tell Sculley that he "didn't know a damned thing about computers"—failing to understand, even at this juncture, that the need was for someone who understood business, not technology.

Steve continued to live in his own reality distortion field, unaware of the hurricane that was about to blow him over. Late in March, he appeared at the offices of the German design firm frogdesign—the outfit that had successfully crafted the look of the Sony Walkman. When Steve had first seen the Walkman, he was so taken with the creativity that he gave frogdesign a large contract to create the look of all of Apple's future products. When he arrived in March, he discovered that the company was doing work for Steve Wozniak's new company, Cloud 9, building a universal remote control device that could run any television or stereo equipped with infrared signaling gear.

When Jobs saw the designs lying around on their drafting boards, he hit the roof. In a rage, he demanded that they either send the designs to Apple or destroy all the work. In fact, he was partially within his rights: a clause in Apple's contract allowed the company to approve other frogdesign clients. And Steve Jobs's former partner wasn't acceptable.

The press pounced on the story, making Apple and Steve Jobs look petty and mean-spirited. "Steve Jobs has a hatred for me," explained Woz. The manager of the frogdesign office, Herbert Pfeiffer, offered an apt description: "It's a power play."

The board finally took action on April 11, led by a taciturn investor who had been there from the start. Board member Arthur Rock was a quiet, tall man with a taste for the finer things and an absolute abhorrence for prevarication or hype. Faced with a string of resignations, enormous unsold inventories of both Apple IIs and Macintoshes, and sales of the Mac that continued below one-tenth of forecast levels, he felt compelled to make John Sculley take charge. Sculley's first decision was to cancel development of the Macintosh XL in favor of the less ambitious Mac II. The next was to cancel the struggling, never successful Lisa. Finally and officially, the Lisa was dead for good.

Turning to more pressing matters, the board in effect told Sculley to stop acting like a Steve Jobs sycophant and to assume his proper role of man-in-charge. Sensing the changing winds and realizing that he was close to being cut loose to swing in the breeze, Sculley decided to lay his cards on the table. Mindful that he was speaking in front of Steve Jobs, who as chairman was, of course, at the meeting, Sculley responded that he could turn things around only if he were given the authority to handle the company the way he saw fit. He said he found it hard "to act like a CEO when you're meant to boss the chairman of the board."

Within minutes, the ax had fallen. Steve was no longer running the Macintosh group, the position would be offered to Gassée, and power was consolidated in Sculley's hands.

Steve, shocked and bitter toward Sculley, brushed past him and left the meeting without saying a word.

Looking for a way to recover control, Steve once again displayed his ability to overlook anything in the past. He recruited his close friend, marketing director Mike Murray—the same man who not long before had infuriated Steve by adding fuel to the fire with his memo arguing for Steve's removal. Steve could overlook the past, and he could cast a spell that made others overlook it as well. Together, the two concocted and wrote up a bold billion-dollar plan that would have had Apple becoming a parent to four separate companies. One would be a retail organization, formed by buying up several major computer retail chains, including ComputerLand, with Sculley as its president—shunting him aside and out of Jobs's way. Steve would remain chairman of Apple Computer, Inc., the parent organization.

Saturday morning Murray showed up at his office for a meeting and discovered Gassée sitting outside the door. The Frenchman had, after all, not been offered the position as head of Macintosh but a different post altogether. Standing there face-to-face with Murray, Gassée was embarrassed that no one had yet told Murray and explained that as of Monday morning, he, Gassée, was the new marketing director. He'd been given Murray's position. Murray felt faint; his head was spinning. He'd been working long hours with his good friend Steve on their new grand plan, while at the same time, behind his back, Steve took his job away and didn't even mention it. When Murray had a chance to confront his friend, the only explanation Steve offered was that it "must have slipped my mind."

Sculley, unwilling to lose the talented Murray, arranged a get-together for the three of them—Murray, Steve, and himself—and settled on creating a new position for Mike as vice president of business development. When Sculley excused himself to attend briefly to other business, Steve changed gears and tried to make Murray a confederate again, telling him, "We're going to have to do something about Sculley. He can't stay. He doesn't know what he's doing."

News of Gassée's new position swept through Apple like wildfire that Monday. Not a word was said about Murray's promised new job as vice president of business development.

When Sculley left a couple of days later for a trip to China, Steve continued to plot his overthrow. "I thought they were both being incredibly childish," contended Elliott. "Steve was trying to pull off a palace coup, and John was acting like a spoiled child. The two of them were going to take Apple under." When Steve saw Sculley's reorganization plan at a high-level strategy meeting on Monday, May 20, he became even more frantic. The proposed reorganization consolidated the company under two executive vice presidents—Apple II's Del Yokam heading up operations and Bill Campbell taking over marketing and sales. Steve was listed as vice president of new product development, but that was it.

Steve and Murray took a stroll along Bandley Drive that afternoon, and Murray was amazed to find that Steve was still trying to figure a way to unseat Sculley. Incredibly, Murray offered whatever help he could give. Steve had also clued in Gassée to his designs, albeit vaguely, out of a liking for Gassée and a mistaken trust in him. The Frenchman understandably had greater loyalty to Apple than to Steve. He told Steve he'd think it over, but Gassée had a well-established friendship with the company's chief lawyer, Al Eisenstadt. Over a barbecue dinner that same evening at Eisenstadt's home, Gassée shared the news that Steve was still brewing plans for a coup. Eisenstadt wasted no time in sharing the news with Sculley.

The CEO called an emergency meeting the next morning. He was livid. "I'm running this company, Steve, and I want you out for good. Now!" Caught red-handed, Steve was uncharacteristically silent for once in his life. He stayed under tight control and didn't blow up once during the three-hour ordeal.

As Steve sat there, Sculley polled the executive staff one by one, forcing each man to publicly pledge allegiance to either him or Steve. Jay Elliott remembers being disgusted by the whole thing: "I told John that I thought he was being an ass, and I refused to do it. Right then, I thought they both should get out."

Steve and John both spoke of resigning that day, John to his wife and Steve to his most loyal lieutenants, with tears in his eyes. As he headed for the door, Mike Murray said, "You had better make sure you know what you're doing. The minute you walk out that door, the world will change." Steve finally listened to his friend, and they then spent several hours reviewing his options. They decided that instead of acting hastily, it would be better to give things a few days to calm down. It was the Memorial Day weekend anyway; why not think it over, maybe even talk to Sculley?

Steve drove over to Sculley's house the next morning. Following Mike Murray's advice, he sought to convince John that he had only tried to do the right thing for Apple, and that it wasn't meant to reflect on Sculley himself. Steve was at his most charming, remarkably composed, and not at all strident or aggressive. The two men walked along the winding lanes surrounding Sculley's house as Steve tried to explain himself. He really did want only what was best for Apple, he insisted, and if that meant he had to leave the company, then so be it. He would abide by whatever decision Sculley ultimately made, but he wanted one more chance to stay with the company that he had founded.

The nonconfrontational Sculley was persuaded, saying that he was willing to give it one more go if Steve would vow allegiance to him and agree to work for the good of the company as a public spokesman. No problem, Steve said, that was what he wanted anyway. Several hours later, the two shook hands and parted, Sculley with the impression that he had agreed to consider the role that Steve would play at Apple.

Steve couldn't believe that Sculley had let him pull the wool over his eyes so easily. Before his Mercedes had pulled out of the driveway of Sculley's neo-Tudor estate, he was already plotting a final attempt at a coup. Sculley was a wimp and couldn't be allowed to run the company that Steve Jobs had founded, but Steve knew he had to act fast.

On that beautiful Memorial Day afternoon, Steve's lieutenants gathered and conspiratorially discussed how they would convince Mike Markkula that Steve should be kept as head of Macintosh. Markkula, a quiet, reticent, calculating man, showed up toward the end of the festivities. He was visibly uncomfortable and agreed to listen only as long as Steve didn't say anything. He wanted to hear what the people working for him thought. He listened, thanked them for their input, and left.

Sculley met Jobs in his office early the next morning and told him that he had heard from Markkula. He knew that Steve was again plotting behind his back, even after the assurances offered just a few days earlier. Steve, Sculley announced, would have to leave.

Afterward, Sculley called each board member individually and asked whether he had their support for removing Steve. One by one, they told him he did. At seven o'clock that evening, Sculley called Steve at home and told him that it was all over. He was going ahead with the reorganization and had the votes on the board to strip Steve of any operating role in Apple. Steve was welcome to stay on as a "product visionary," a compromise that was acceptable to die-hard loyalists like Apple vice president Debi Coleman, but he would not be in charge of a division any longer.

Steve, in tears, called Bill Campbell and Mike Murray to tell them the news. It was Tuesday evening, May 28, 1985. Murray's wife was on a long-distance call when an emergency interrupt came through. She told the operator that it "had better be important" and then heard Steve's voice saying, with almost no emotion, "It is." She called her husband to the phone, and Steve told him, "It's all over. John and the board have voted me out of Apple." Before the former marketing director could say anything, Steve hung up.

Murray called back but got no answer. Even though it was ten thirty at night, he was frightened enough to drive up to the house and make sure that Steve didn't do something foolish. With his life's work taken away from him, Mike feared that Steve would commit suicide.

He arrived to find a completely dark house. After climbing an outside staircase that led up to Steve's bedroom, he pushed open the door to discover the chairman lying on his mattress on the floor, completely alone. Silently, he sat down next to him and hugged his friend and former boss. The two of them cried and sat in darkness for an hour, saying little—"What was there to say?"—with Murray doing what he could to offer comfort. Finally, in the wee hours of the morning, convinced that Steve wasn't going to end it all that night, Murray slipped out of the house and drove home.

When Murray returned to check on the situation the next evening, Steve was talking comeback. The following afternoon, Steve finally showed up at work and immediately came to see Murray to discuss how he should handle himself. Should he go away? Should he fight? Should he roll over and die? Should he make bitter public statements? Murray told him that he had two options: He could take the low road, get out now and be bitter, giving the press all the comments they would be looking for. Or he could take the high road, be a statesman, rise above it all, and refrain from backbiting or bitterness. Murray urged him to come to the meeting that Sculley had scheduled for the next day, May 31, Murray's thirtieth birthday, and lend his support to the reorganization. Show that he was behind it. Show that he was bigger than the petty squabbles that had been going on. Steve said that he would sleep on it.

At the companywide communications meeting the next morning, Murray was pleased to see Steve slip into the back row of the auditorium. He had obviously decided, against his most fundamental instincts, to be a team player. As the meeting proceeded, however, Sculley refused to acknowledge Jobs. He introduced all the key members of his new team, including both Gassée and Coleman, but no other members of the Macintosh Division. When he displayed the organization chart, one name was conspicuously missing. There was no mention of the company's former Macintosh Division leader, cofounder, product visionary, front man, and evangelist. The meeting ended without mention of him. For John Sculley and the new Apple Computer, Steve Jobs didn't exist.

One last time, Steve went to his office in a corner of Bandley 3—the building he had built to house his superstars, the Macintosh team. A few minutes later, he walked out to his Mercedes and drove away.

On Saturday morning, June 1, the *San Jose Mercury News* led its front page with the banner headline: "APPLE CO-FOUNDER JOBS DEMOTED." The story also made the front pages of the *San Francisco Chronicle* and *Examiner*. Throughout the rest of the United States, the tale of his fall from grace merited coverage but only on the inside pages or the business section.

Steve switched his answering machine on and spent the day listening to callers' voices as the phone rang continuously. He avoided reporters and editors and talked only to a few friends and family members. With the shades down and the house dark, he listened to Bob Dylan.

By 1985, he had given everything to Apple and the computers they produced, and he wasn't about to fade quietly into the background. Steve was a fighter, a competitor who believed that he knew better than anyone what was right. For a week, he brooded and considered his options. Then he packed his suitcases and caught a flight to Paris to begin a long-scheduled business and pleasure trip. He was stumping throughout Europe for the Macintosh Office and planned to go on to Russia to promote Apple IIs, which had recently been approved for sale behind the Iron Curtain. Perhaps in action he might find some solace.

From Paris, after doing his corporate bit, he headed for the Tuscan hills outside Florence in central Italy, bought a sleeping bag and a bicycle, and camped out under the stars in an orchard in San Gimignano, a medieval village. No one recognized him as he bicycled through the little hill towns of Italy. As he pondered his fate, instead of coming to grips with it, he grew more depressed.

By late June he was in Sweden, still trying to do the right thing for the company. His attitude had mellowed a little. "Things don't always happen the way I want them," he told a Swedish journalist. "Just like Mick Jagger said, 'You can't always get what you want; sometimes you get what you need.'

"Five years ago this would have bothered me. Now I'm sitting back and thinking that maybe there is some wisdom in this. Henry Ford had a couple of difficult quarters, too, in the 1920s.

"I'm not a power-oriented person. I care about Apple a great deal. I put pretty much my entire adult life into building great products and building a great company. So I'm going to give what I can to further Apple. If that means sweeping the floors, I'll sweep the floors. If that means cleaning the toilet, I'll clean the toilet."

He was hardly chastened. "Woz hasn't done much in many years," he answered, in response to a question about the recent departures of several key Apple people. "Andy Hertzfeld is always complaining. He'll come back anyway. What I did with the Macintosh team was to give them recognition for their work: I'm not so sure it was good. I may have made a mistake. It was a good concept, but it went a little too far."

Steve Jobs was down but not out. He continued talking about his team, but it could have been a description of himself: "A lot of it went to their heads. For a few people, it is very difficult when things happen. You have to think very strongly about your inner values—what really is important for you. When things happen very fast, you don't have the time. It can scramble your brain."

By July 4, Steve was in Russia but he felt ready to return to Cupertino. He wanted to patch up his differences with Sculley and get on with his new job, whatever that was. When he arrived back at Apple in the middle of July, however, he found that the corporation didn't want him.

"I was asked to move out of my office," he explained. "They leased a little building across the street from most of the other Apple buildings. I nicknamed it Siberia.

"So I moved across the street, and I made sure that all of the executive staff had my home phone number. I knew that John had it, and I called the rest of them personally and made sure they had it and told them I wanted to be useful in any way I could, and to please call me if I could help on anything.

"They all had a cordial phrase, but none of them ever called. So I used to go to work. I'd get there, and I would have one or two phone calls to perform, a little bit of mail to look at. But most of the corporate management reports stopped flowing by my desk. A few people might see my car in the parking lot and come over and commiserate. And I would get depressed and go home in two or three or four hours, really depressed.

"I did that a few times, and I decided that it was mentally unhealthy. So I just stopped going in. You know, there was nobody really there to miss me."

One person did—the still-loyal, pixieish former Macintosh marketing director, Mike Murray. He had moved into the office next to Steve's. One day Murray gathered his things and joined Steve in the empty offices. No one missed him for a week. In the reorganization, the job that the loyal lieutenant had been promised only weeks earlier suddenly evaporated. Sculley's new minions felt that Murray couldn't be trusted—he was too close to Steve. Nonetheless, ever the sloganeer, Murray had coined the phrase "One Apple" as his last effort to influence the new management. The phrase became Sculley's rallying cry that summer and fall as the company president tried to win back the Apple II corps and win over the remaining Macintosh partisans. Every time he heard it, Mike had to laugh at the irony of it all. (Murray eventually left and joined the archrival Microsoft.)

Still chairman of the board, Steve avoided corporate duties and focused on supervising repairs being made to his house. Then he decided that he wanted to conquer a new dimension—space—and asked NASA if he could ride the space shuttle. He found that being a "global visionary" didn't cut the mustard with the government. He was turned down. Christa McAuliffe, an elementary schoolteacher, was selected instead.

Apple's stock continued to drop, eventually falling as low as $15 a share. Then, for the quarter ending June 28, the company announced its first loss ever: $17.2 million, with a drop in sales of 11 percent from the corresponding quarter a year earlier. It hurt, and he began to blame himself for the troubles the company was experiencing. A few days later, however, Steve was even more stunned by a comment that Sculley made to securities analysts at the company's quarterly meeting to describe Apple's most recent results and future plans. "There is no role for Steve Jobs in the operations of this company," Sculley told the closed meeting, "either now or in the future." The comment instantly leaked to the press, and a couple of days later the president reconfirmed it to a collection of reporters trying to interview him as he slipped into his limousine. Steve was staggered.

"You've probably had somebody punch you in the stomach," Steve explained, trying to describe how he felt. "It knocks the wind out of you, and you can't breathe. If you relax, you can start breathing again. That's how I felt. The thing I had to do was try to relax. It was hard. But I went for a lot of long walks in the woods and didn't really talk to a lot of people."

A few days later, he decided to sell a little more than 10 percent of his Apple shares—850,000—which was the maximum quarterly sale allowed under SEC regulations. The sale netted him around $11 million and squelched rumors of a leveraged buy-out that had been circulating since he had made a call to Morgan Stanley in late May. He just wanted to get out, and the rules of selling founder's shares were such that he had to sell off his stake piecemeal—he still had six million shares, which were worth about $90 million, even at the depressed price. Nonetheless, the sale started a flurry of rumors about his plans. Few people expected the thirty-year-old to quietly accept being sent out to pasture. Speculation centered on Steve either starting an investment fund, launching a new career as a venture capitalist, or starting some sort of new company. He was known to have been pursuing the computer graphics division of George Lucas's empire in the months before the final reorganization. He now had the beginnings of a war chest, but what would he use it for?

The answer wasn't long in coming. With time on his hands, he hired a political consulting firm to help him find a way into politics. It was the same group that had worked with his sometimes role model and fellow Zen Buddhist disciple, former California governor Jerry Brown. But Steve had never voted or belonged to a political party. The group apparently told him that gaining a constituency would be difficult. He started to look in other directions.

"I think what I'm best at is creating new, innovative products. That's what I enjoy doing," he said later that summer, finally starting to understand what those around him had been saying for years. "I enjoy, and I'm best working with, a small team of talented people. That's what I did with the Apple II, and that's what I did with the Macintosh.

"I had a piece of paper one day, and I was writing down the things that I cared the most about, that I was most proud of personally in my ten years at Apple. There's obviously the creation of the Apple II and the Macintosh. But other than that, the thing that I really cared about was helping to set up the Apple Education Foundation. I came up with this crazy idea that turned into a program called 'The Kids Can't Wait,' in which we tried to give a computer to every school in America and ended up giving one to every school in California, about ten thousand computers.

"I put those two together, working with small teams of talented people to create breakthrough products and education."

That summer Steve spent a lot of time wandering around the semi-deserted Stanford University campus and the rolling hills that framed it, searching for an answer to the question that continued to haunt him. He had always felt at home there, starting as a high school junior hanging out in the cafeteria, then auditing physics classes, going to Homebrew meetings, and later preaching to small groups of interested MBA students. Apple photographed many of its Macintosh advertising shots along the covered walkways and bicycle paths of the eucalyptus tree–lined campus. Steve and Sculley had even posed there during happier times. Stanford meant something special to the college dropout and high-tech preacher.

He went into the libraries and began to delve into the world of biochemistry and recombinant DNA research, trying to understand the Bay Area's other rapidly growing industry. He had met Paul Berg, one of Stanford's Nobel Prize–winning biochemists, at a dinner for France's president, François Mitterrand, a year earlier. He called him up and invited him to lunch to ask a few questions. Over a meal in a coffee shop near the Stanford campus, he and Berg talked.

"He was showing me how they were doing gene repairing," Steve said. "Actually, it's straightforward. It's kind of neat. It smells a lot like some of the concepts you find in computer science.

"He was explaining how he does experiments in a wet laboratory, and they take a week or two to run. I asked him, 'Why don't you simulate them on a computer? Not only will it allow you to run your experiments faster, but someday every freshman microbiology student in the country can play with Paul Berg recombinant software.' His eyes lit up."

Berg, for his part, remembers the conversation a little differently. It was Steve whose eyes lit up. The scientist explained to the young entrepreneur that the computers used to run such simulations were presently too expensive and the software primitive. "Suddenly, he was excited by the possibilities," recalled Berg. "He had it in mind to start a new company. He was young and rich and had to find something to do with the rest of his life. This sounded like it."

It had been a long time since Steve felt the surge of energy that he had experienced with the blue boxes, the Apple I and II, the early Lisa, and the Macintosh. With possibilities of something on the horizon, the inspiration started to come through again. It was a new product, a new machine. A fresh love affair. A new trail to blaze.

Just as Steve was getting turned on by this idea of creating a new computer for the university market, in late August something happened at Apple that crystallized what would be the formation of his next project. Gassée canceled the fledgling Big Mac computer in favor of a much less ambitious Little Big Mac. When he took over the Macintosh Division that summer, Gassée expanded the development program for an advanced interim version of the Mac, based loosely on a computer that had been abandoned and was centered in that engineering group. Code-named Little Big Mac, it kept the basic design of the Macintosh and simply substituted a more powerful chip, the 68020.

This contrasted sharply with the Big Mac, which was an extremely powerful machine built around a custom chip set, code-named the Jonathon and created by Rich Page, one of the key designers of the Lisa. When Gassée canceled the Big Mac, Page was miffed. He talked about leaving Apple with his close friend Bud Tribble, the original Macintosh software project leader who had returned after medical school and was again in charge of software development for the Macintosh.

Tribble was one of the first people Steve thought of as he formulated his new venture. Over the Labor Day weekend at the beginning of September, Steve broached the subject of a new company to the soft-spoken manager and was encouraged that Tribble found his ideas intriguing. They discussed the "3M" machines that universities were settling on as the computers of the future: advanced workstations with one million pixels of resolution on screen, one million bytes of main memory, and the ability to process up to one million instructions per second—hence three "M"s. These would be the basis for the workstations of the future, and although machines of this caliber were available from workstation companies and IBM, they presently cost well over $10,000 apiece, much more than the target $3,000 that universities were willing to pay.

Tribble knew just who could build such a machine. He suggested a couple of people at Apple who might be willing to help get it off the ground, including Page and George Crow, an analog engineer who had been a member of the original Macintosh team. Steve also suggested Susan Barnes, the Macintosh controller, for the financial side of things, and Dan'l Lewin, architect of the successful Apple University Consortium, who had been promoted to marketing manager for all higher-education applications during the recent reorganization. When Steve asked each of them, sub rosa, they all agreed to join him. He was at his most inspired and persuasive as he wove the dream of his new enterprise. He was talking to a group of people who had never been at the heart of the Macintosh project—essential yes, but not the key superstars. They were all individualists who, like Steve, were searching for another chance to create something great, this time with their names indelibly linked to its creation, and Apple no longer seemed like the place to do it.

As Tribble said, "Everyone wants to be involved in a start-up." This would be a start-up with a bang that would return them to the roots of

Apple. The way Steve described it, how could it fail? Overnight, he had the kernel of a company.

"We have no business plan. We haven't done anything," Steve said a few days later, when their plans went public. "Now, you might say we're all crazy. But we've all known each other for four years. And we have an immense amount of confidence in each other's abilities and genuinely like each other. We all have a desire to have a small company where we can influence its destiny and have a really fun place to work."

With that, Steve realized that he had better tell Apple about the new venture. A board meeting was scheduled for September 12, and though he hadn't attended them for the last several months, as chairman he was still entitled. As the meeting was called to order, he briefly explained that he had done a lot of thinking about things over the summer and had come to a few conclusions. Although no one recorded the speech, when Steve described his motivations to *Newsweek* a few days later, it sounded like a speech he might have given before:

I personally, man, want to build things. I'm 30. I'm not ready to be an industry pundit. I got three offers to be a professor during the summer, and I told all the universities that I thought I would be an awful professor.

What I'm best at doing is finding a group of talented people and making things with them. I respect the direction that Apple is going in. But for me personally, you know, I want to make things. And if there's no place for me to make things there, then I'll do what I did twice before. I'll make my own place. You know I did it in the garage when Apple started, and I did it in the metaphorical garage when the Mac started.

I helped shepherd Apple from a garage to a billion-and-a-half-dollar company. It took a bunch of rambunctious upstarts, working with very little resources but a certain vision and commitment, to do it. I'm probably not the best person in the world to shepherd it to a five or ten billion dollar company, which I think is probably its destiny. And so I haven't got any sort of odd chip on my shoulder about proving anything to myself or anybody else. I had ten of the best years of my life, you know, and I don't regret much of anything. I want to get on with my life.

Phil Schlein recalled that it was one of Steve's finest moments, and he had seen the charismatic young man sway some mighty skeptical board members before. If the board were inclined to tears, there wouldn't have been a dry eye in the place. Steve was giving a farewell speech, and it was a great performance. He then went on to describe his still-inchoate plans for a new firm and assured them that he had no intention of taking any technology or proprietary ideas out of Apple. He mentioned that he would be taking a few people from the company, but by no means enough to disrupt operations or the products they were working on—and anyway, they would be people who were already leaving. He offered his resignation as chairman if the board thought that the new company would compete with Apple.

The board members asked Steve to step outside while they discussed it. They were sold on his candor and were favorably disposed to letting him take on the building of a quasi-Apple workstation computer. It could be a high-end Macintosh workstation for the educational market, a project that seemed perfectly suited to him and definitely in Apple's best interests. A few minutes later he was invited back in, and Sculley, very friendly, told him that Apple thought it sounded like a marvelous project. They were interested in buying 10 percent of his new venture while keeping him on the board, although not as chairman. Mike Markkula joined in and suggested that Steve and Sculley should discuss it further during the coming week. They made a date for Sculley and Apple's counsel, Al Eisenstadt, to meet with Steve. With good cheer all around, the meeting adjourned.

That night, at Steve's house, the new group met for the first time as a team, sitting beneath a tree in his backyard. Steve told them what had transpired in the boardroom. The group members decided that they didn't feel comfortable drawing things out. They wanted to tell Sculley their names right away and make a clean break. "We decided to cut the umbilical cord and go as a group so there wouldn't be one hit after another," said Susan Barnes. Furthermore, they wanted to sever ties completely with Apple. They didn't want any investment from the company.

At dawn Steve was up. He couldn't sleep that night, so he got into his car and headed for Cupertino. Sculley appeared at 7:25 that morning, Friday, September 13, and immediately encountered the chairman of the board, who was sitting on a sofa outside his office. Steve told him that the group had decided it was best to leave en masse and handed him a handwritten list of the names. Sculley scanned it, said nothing for a moment, and then asked about the other two issues about which the board had inquired: an investment in the venture and Steve's staying on the board of directors. Steve told him that they all felt uncomfortable about committing 10 percent of the company to Apple and that he had no intention of staying on the board. With that, they shook hands, and Sculley said he really hoped they could work together. Steve was heartened and felt that they could split up on a friendly basis.

Although Sculley didn't appear upset to Steve, he claims that he was "absolutely taken aback when Steve walked in and handed me the list." The company president felt that "the board had been deceived. He said he was going to take a few low-level people not involved in anything Apple considered important." Instead, there were two senior engineers: Page, an Apple Fellow, the company's highest honor for scientists; and Crow, the top engineer for power circuitry. Then two key managers were on the list as well: Tribble was the manager of software development for the company's Macintosh computer line in toto, and Lewin headed marketing to all schools and colleges, the only bright spot in Apple's woeful financial picture during that quarter. By the time Sculley came out of his executive staff meeting that morning, Apple's attitude had changed.

"The executive staff has been stunned and shocked that this has happened. I had no idea Steve was forming a company," said Bill Campbell, executive vice president in charge of marketing and sales. "Losing those people was a shock. But losing the chairman of the board was even more shocking. We've had a good quarter; the organization has come together after the reorganization. This seems to highlight turmoil at Apple, and nothing could be further from the truth."

Campbell's counterpart in operations, Del Yokam, was incensed and hinted at legal action. "I'm quite surprised that all this was being done while he was chairman, and furthermore, it would concern me if he gets into a business that's competitive with Apple." Jean-Louis Gassée, Sculley's chief of technology, was even more furious, and his Gallic temper couldn't be contained. Later in the afternoon, he blasted Steve and his group of conspirators in front of a meeting of the two hundred people in his Macintosh new product development group.

An aroused Sculley informed the board of Steve's plans by telephone and had the five "traitors," as they were referred to at Apple, escorted unceremoniously off the property by security guards, who sealed their offices that Friday. At the board meeting the previous day, Steve had indicated that it was still a nebulous venture, but by presenting names the very next morning, he had demonstrated otherwise. The attempt to home in on the company's strongest market, education, with the defection of Lewin, caused considerable grumbling. The company's position was that the appearance of unseemly plotting while Steve was still chairman of the board gave Apple strong legal grounds to use against him and the new business.

By noon of that day, Friday the 13th of September, the company was in an uproar. The news of Steve's new venture spread like wildfire around Cupertino, and Apple was stunned. Group meetings were held throughout the company, and the news was passed along to employees. Black Friday quickly joined Black Wednesday—the day of Scotty's mass firings four-and-a-half years earlier—in the company's folklore. There was shock and dismay that the company's visionary could have abandoned it. And in the Macintosh group, many of the original Mac team were disappointed that Steve had passed them over when selecting his new group. It wouldn't be long before most of them departed.

Emergency meetings of the board were held by telephone over the weekend, and the company was uncertain how to proceed. By Sunday, the news hit the front page of the *San Jose Mercury News*, and this time the story was also front-page news across the country.

Mike Markkula, the largest shareholder other than Steve, released a statement after a Monday board meeting: "The board interpreted this action to be in direct contradiction to his statements of the previous day and began the evaluation which is currently underway." The reticent vice chairman still refused to meet the press in person. "We are evaluating what possible actions should be taken to assure protection of Apple's technology and assets."

Steve was silent throughout the weekend. He didn't respond to reporters' phone calls until he heard about the statement Markkula had made. It was time to take control of the publicity apparatus that he'd learned to play so well over the years.

On Tuesday evening, September 17, 1985, as the sun set with a particularly dramatic flourish, Steve Jobs, thirty years old, founder and resident visionary of Apple Computer, for ten years the primary worldwide evangelist for the coming of the personal computer age, an all-around mythic American figure, turned in his letter of resignation to the company he had founded. Composed on the Macintosh computer that he had muscled and cajoled into existence, printed on the LaserPrinter that he had aggressively championed, he drove the three miles to fellow founder Armas Clifford (Mike) Markkula's nearby Woodside house to hand deliver it. It closed a remarkable chapter in U.S. popular history.

Dear Mike,

This morning's papers carried suggestions that Apple is considering removing me as Chairman. I don't know the source of these reports, but they are both misleading to the public and unfair to me.

You will recall that at last Thursday's Board meeting I stated I had decided to start a new venture, and I tendered my resignation as Chairman.

The Board declined to accept my resignation and asked me to defer it for a week. I agreed to do so in light of the encouragement the Board offered with regard to the proposed new venture and the indications that Apple would invest in it. On Friday, after I told John Sculley who would be joining me, he confirmed Apple's willingness to discuss areas of possible collaboration between Apple and my new venture.

Subsequently the Company appears to be adopting a hostile posture toward me and the new venture. Accordingly, I must insist upon the immediate acceptance of my resignation. I would hope that in any statement it feels it must issue, the Company will make it clear that the decision to resign as Chairman was mine.

I find myself both saddened and perplexed by the management's conduct in this matter which seems to me contrary to Apple's best interests. Those interests remain a matter of deep concern to me, both because of my past association with Apple and the substantial investment I retain in it.

I continue to hope that calmer voices within the Company may yet be heard. Some Company representatives have said they fear I will use proprietary Apple technology in my new venture. There is no basis for any such concern. If that concern is the real source of Apple's hostility to the venture, I can allay it.

As you know, the company's recent re-organization left me with no work to do and no access even to regular management reports. I am but 30 and want still to contribute and achieve.

After what we have accomplished together, I would wish our parting to be both amicable and dignified.

Yours sincerely,

Steven P. Jobs

Then, in front of the press gathered at his house, Steve burned all the bridges. The love affair was over. He faced the future with a kind of tough and brutal honesty that was immensely compelling.

He described the end in romantic, almost melodramatic terms that painted him as the aggrieved party. "My heart will always be there," he said, referring to Apple. "My relationship with the company is like a first love. I'll always remember Apple in the same way any man remembers the first woman he's fallen in love with.

"To me, Apple exists in the spirit of the people who work there and the philosophies and purpose by which they go about their business. If Apple becomes a place where computers are a commodity item, where the romance is gone, and where people forget that computers are the most incredible invention that man has ever invented, I'll feel I have lost Apple.

"But if I'm a million miles away, and all those people still feel those things and they're still working to make the next great personal computer, then I will feel that my genes are still there."

A few days later, Steve announced that he had settled on a name for the new venture. He named it NeXT and set about doing the paperwork to incorporate it. All week long, Apple and Steve's attorneys tried to come to some agreement to allow them all to part on, if not amicable, at least amenable terms. While Steve was willing to agree to a hiring freeze on Apple employees for a period of six months and not to use any proprietary Apple technology, he was unwilling to specify that his new products would not compete with Apple's present or future machines.

At the beginning of the following week, it looked like the company had done a little gene splicing of its own. On that day, September 23,

1985, Apple Computer filed suit in the Santa Clara County courts against Steve and Rich Page, contending that they had launched a "nefarious scheme" to use company research for a new venture, research that as chairman of the board Steve was privy to, and then deceived the company's board as to their intentions. With that legal action, the bridges were burned. Steve was incensed by the accusation and went back to the press, where once again he was treated royally.

"When somebody calls you a thief in public, you have to respond. I'm very surprised that Apple is suing me. We have spent an entire week talking with Apple lawyers, showing them that we have no intention of taking or using any Apple confidential information or proprietary technology in our new company.

"This sort of thing sure is hell and doesn't help Apple or its employees. We don't want to get involved with an unjustified lawsuit. We just want to build our company and invent something new." He went on to argue that Apple's suit appeared to assert that Steve would "not be able to practice my craft ever again in my life." That, he insisted reasonably, "seems odd."

He ended with a delightful capper: "It's hard to think that a $2 billion company with 4,300 plus people couldn't compete with six people in blue jeans." The press ate it up.

With that as Steve's parting shot, he and the new team headed across the country to visit universities, trying to find out what they should build into their new machine. The lawsuit degenerated into legal squabbles and one-upmanship over deposition scheduling and finally, in the wake of a record profit posted for the company during the final quarter of 1985, was quietly dropped. Apple was able to extract its pound of flesh, however. As part of the agreement NeXT was required to provide Apple with prerelease versions of its future products so that the company could ensure that they did not infringe on proprietary secrets and processes. But the relationship was over. Steve had sold most of his stock in the aftermath of his departure, and early in 1986 he completed the divestiture—retaining only a single share, which he said that he kept just so he would continue to receive the company's annual reports.

After so many battles won, Steve Jobs had lost a big one. This time it wasn't just a battle. This time he had lost the war.

PART TWO

New Beginnings

5

How much do you want?
—Ross Perot, offering Steve Jobs financing for his new company

The NeXT Step

Many adopted children who seek their heritage probably hope for the best but fear the worst. Steve Jobs had made intermittent efforts ever since his teens to trace his biological parents. He was almost ready to put it down as a hopeless cause when finally he unlocked the secret.

Steve discovered that he had a sister. Not a half- or step-, but a full sister. Mona Simpson was an aspiring novelist who had been working with writer, adventurer, and bon vivant George Plimpton at the esteemed literary journal *The Paris Review*. (Though the offices are in New York, the name is legitimate: the *Review* actually got its start in the French capital.)

Mona was born in Green Bay, Wisconsin, and says that her father was a political science professor and her mother a speech therapist. Elsewhere, her father is described as of Arab descent and a specialist in the Middle East. When Steve was born, his parents were not married. This was in the 1950s, before the changing social standards that blew in with the winds of the 1960s. Unmarried couples didn't live together, and unmarried young women didn't keep their babies. By the time Mona was born, two-and-a-half years later, the couple had married. When she was ten, her parents divorced. Her mother announced to Mona that they were moving to Los Angeles. Through their teens, Steve and the sister he didn't know he had were both coming of age in California.

Mona attended the now-infamous Beverly Hills High and remembers it as a place of "a lot of money, a lot of drugs, a lot of insanity." It was a public school in an almost lily-white community, but, she said, "So many people in Beverly Hills had domestic servants, so their kids went there, too." As if lamenting an age gone by, she added, "It was still a time when a middle-class kid like me could get in."

Steve was delighted with the discovery of a sister. The two were committed to building a relationship and became very close. He said, "We're family. She's one of my best friends in the world. I call her and talk to her every couple of days." Both are reticent to speak of their relationship or their family history, but Mona acknowledged strong feelings. "My brother and I are very close," she said. "I admire him enormously."

At the same time that he connected with his sister, Steve also located his mother, Joanne Simpson, and made his peace with her. From that time until her death, he remained in contact with her and included her as well as his sister in his family gatherings. Still, even today, he is apt to flare up if anyone refers to Paul and Clara Jobs as his "adoptive" parents; from infancy he knew them as mother and father, and though they are no longer alive, he continues to honor them with those terms. Use the taboo word and he's liable to snap, "They were my *parents*."

The start of NeXT in 1985 was an ugly beginning for a new venture, though the ruckus only solidified Steve's determination. NeXT was begun in haste and with little planning. Worse, Steve hadn't reflected on what his failures at Apple meant; he was blind to the lessons in the problems that had led to his firing.

He would launch an entirely new company, hire the best and the brightest—a crew of superstars from Apple—and show the world that it really was Steve who was the heart and soul of Apple. Better still, a computer specifically tailored to the educational establishment would reassure Apple's ruling junta that NeXT posed no ostensible threat.

At first, things seemed to be unfolding Steve's way. A financial supporter came forward for NeXT: Ross Perot, the maverick entrepreneur and later presidential candidate. NeXT had been featured in a television documentary called *The Entrepreneurs*. Perot happened to be in front of a television set, saw the show, and was impressed anew by Steve's initiative and imagination. He remembered the brash young man he had met when General Motors was vetting Apple as an investment and placed a phone call to Jobs the next day. He offered, "If you ever need an investor, call me."

Steve shrewdly waited a week so that he wouldn't look too anxious before calling Perot back. He adroitly side-stepped questions about NeXT revenue and profit projections and instead gave his usual compelling performance about vision, value, and the contribution to technology and society. Perot virtually offered Jobs a blank check. "How much do you want?" he asked. Steve offered a 16 percent share of NeXT for $20 million, and Perot accepted. To his critics, the diminutive Texas tycoon justified his seemingly emotion-based investment by insisting, "I'm investing in quality."

Aspiring novelist Mona Simpson became published novelist Mona Simpson when the New York publishing house Alfred Knopf brought out her first book, *Anywhere but Here*.

Just as there are people who are always eager to seek out the newest restaurant and art patrons always looking for the latest style, in the literary world there are people who seek out the work of first-time novelists. Partly, it's the appeal of hearing a fresh voice; partly, it's being in the know, keeping up with what the cognoscenti are reading—or if possible, keeping ahead of them. First-time authors with a special talent sometimes find themselves picked up and carried by a wave of unexpected praise. Mona was one of those.

The book was a gem, introduced to the world at a launch party in the literary capital of the United States, New York City, given by her former boss, the socialite and literary hero George Plimpton. Mona offered her own surprise that evening: she brought her mother and a young man she introduced to everyone as her brother, Steve Jobs.

Up until that moment, Steve Jobs's discovery that he had a sister was a closely guarded secret, shared with almost no one. Even Mona's literary agent, Amanda Urban, hadn't been told. Urban said, "I had known Mona for quite a while. She had said she had a brother who worked in the computer industry. But that party was the first time I learned that her brother was Steve Jobs."

Reviewers heaped praise on *Anywhere but Here*, one calling it "a wonder: big, complex, masterfully written," and "an achievement that lands her in the front ranks of our best novelists."

It's common for a novelist to fall back on her own life experiences in creating characters for fiction. Mona acknowledges that her work draws more than a little from the people and experiences in her life. So it's interesting to note one particular passage from the book. She has the central character describe another character, Adele, with these words: "And even if you hate her, can't stand her, even if she's ruining your life, there's something about her, some romance, some power. She's absolutely herself. No matter how hard you try, you'll never get to her." Later in the book, she writes that "it's always the people like [Adele], who start the noise and bang things, who make you feel the worst; they are the ones who get your love." Change the gender, and you have vivid descriptions of the way many people come to feel after they have worked a while for Steve Jobs.

Her connection to Steve was at the time guarded by the people who had been at that party and was entirely unknown to the public. The curiosity value could not have had any effect on sales. It was the quality of the writing alone that accounted for the book selling remarkably well for what in the trade is referred to as a "literary novel," a not really snide term for a book that doesn't deal with spies, serial killers, natural disasters, or the like, but succeeds because of the quality of the writing.

With her first book, Mona Simpson had established herself as a writer to be watched.

It had always been the box itself that drove Steve Jobs. The tiny, handheld blue box tone emitter that Woz created as their first product. The sexy, consumer electronics record player-cum-stereo by KLH, a fixture of most college dorm rooms, that was the guiding factor in the design of the Apple II. The oddly rectangular, vertical, and distinctive shape of the Macintosh—"no bigger than this phone book"—that was always part of the Mac's distinctiveness and appeal. Later, it would be the sleek, handsome shirt-pocket music player, the iPod. Fittingly, it would be the sleek black cube of the NeXT computer at the heart of the failure that changed him.

The site of Steve Jobs's personal Armageddon doesn't look like much today. A pair of two-story, off-white buildings with green glass, hard up against the bay in nondescript Redwood City, along the peninsula between San Francisco and San Jose. Today both buildings house dot-com start-ups, and few of the employees realize, as they climb the elegantly curving free-standing staircase in the heart of it, that they are walking on a million-dollar piece of architectural majesty crafted by I. M. Pei in an otherwise indistinctive Silicon Valley cookie-cutter building.

From the mid-1980s on, this was the corporate headquarters of the company that Steve created to show Apple and the world the genius that he knew he was. At that time, ensuring aesthetic perfection in everything he did was more important than substance—hence, the million-dollar staircase. Steve didn't want to break up the space with support beams. It was an apt metaphor not only for the organizing principle of the company, but for everything that was wrong with Steve at the time.

NeXT spent thousands of dollars with Paul Rand, a famous graphics designer, for a logo—a multicolored cube that resembled a child's building block, with an odd font treatment: NeXT. The irony was that the original NeXT machines were black and white only because of the complexity of the graphics they were designed to display. The machine was also housed in a sleek cubelike box—another vast design effort driven by Steve to his tune of cool. The money spent on design didn't do any good, however, because the computers were delayed, and even universities balked at buying specialized computers when cheaper alternatives were available from a company like Sun Microsystems.

The early years of NeXT were filled with glowing pronouncements from the young prince of technology. Another much-promoted issue was the NeXT factory, a state-of-the-art robot-driven factory that Steve built. It got an enormous amount of attention. Hundreds of NeXT computers could be built every day, with hardly any human intervention. It was a model of just-in-time manufacturing, designed to reduce costs by forcing suppliers to deliver components within hours of being needed. It was never used, however, because the demand never materialized. As Steve discovered during the Macintosh era, delivering real products was much harder than talking about them.

. . .

In the 1980s, Steve's head had been turned by the sophisticated, worldly women of New York. (On one occasion, a friend had set Steve up to have drinks with a woman named Diane. Steve called to arrange the date and was struck by how much the woman seemed to talk like a character in a Woody Allen movie. As they were about to hang up, Steve asked, "By the way, what's your last name?" She answered, "Keaton.")

Then he met a California graphic designer striking enough to be mistaken for a movie star. Except for her considerable intelligence and her beauty, Christina Redse, "Tina," wasn't a woman whom Steve's friends would have expected him to be drawn to. True, they tended to dress alike, in jeans and a black T-shirt or turtleneck. In some ways, they were both earthy: Steve with his Zen and his trip to India, Tina with her underplayed beauty that made her even more stunning when she went, as she most often did, without makeup. There was a sexual chemistry between them that was obvious—sometimes a little *too* obvious—to Steve's friends.

The surprising part had to do with the way they related to each other. Usually, Steve seemed to be comfortable around people who wouldn't challenge his authority. It was okay to challenge his *ideas*; as long as you could make a good case for your point of view, you could even argue with him. But when the dust settled, it would be his decision. With women, too, Steve wanted to be in charge.

Tina was strong-willed. She wasn't going to be pliant, yielding, or humble just so she could be seen on the arm of Steve Jobs. She moved in with him for a while, decided she didn't like it, and moved out again. But he kept seeing her. Tina Redse, it seemed, had found a place in Steve's heart.

In 1987, Steve attended a birthday party in Georgetown for Katharine Graham, the woman who had transformed the *Washington Post* into a newspaper of national stature and guided it through the crises of the Pentagon Papers and the debacle of Watergate that had ended in forcing Richard Nixon out of the White House.

Apparently because of his connection with Ross Perot, Steve had been invited to this Washington social event of the year. It's accepted in Washington that politicos get business done over drinks; Steve needed no encouragement to play that game, and he made two conquests before the end of the evening. He harangued King Juan Carlos of Spain, afterward claiming that he'd talked the gentleman into buying a computer. He had bullied a king into a sale! It was like meeting Michael Eisner at a party and selling him your screenplay. Or running into Britney Spears at a restaurant and convincing her to record your song.

Steve also met someone who for him was the incarnation of the archenemy. Not Bill Gates, but almost as bad: John Akers, the CEO of IBM. It wasn't as if they were facing each other over a conference table. Steve showed his gracious human side and dropped hints about a next-generation operating system that would surprise the industry.

The hints he dropped percolated through IBM, and one day Steve's administrative assistant buzzed him to say that an executive from IBM was on the phone. The company was interested in opening discussions about the operating system Mr. Jobs had mentioned to Mr. Akers.

Steve wasn't easily intimidated. Still, he had never had much taste for dealing with companies larger and more powerful than his own. IBM had always been a prominent member of that more-powerful group, but he agreed to negotiations. Quite possibly he was thinking along the same lines that Howard Hughes had been, years earlier. Hughes had been approached by a consortium interested in purchasing the cornerstone of his empire, the Hughes Tool Company. He agreed to entertain the proposal. The prospective buyers spent months on due diligence—examining the books, poring over the assets, evaluating the future prospects, and interviewing the executives. Finally, they returned to Hughes with an elaborate proposal. He thanked them warmly and said he would let them know. That was the last they ever heard of the matter, and they finally realized they had been played for fools. Hughes had just been interested in somebody else closely scrutinizing every aspect of the company—the assets, the financials, the processes, the quality of the executives—and telling him what they thought the whole business was worth.

Maybe Steve had something equally mischievous in mind. Whatever his true motives, IBM's examination of the operating system software, which Steve was now calling NeXTSTEP, convinced them that this was indeed powerful enough to enhance the IBM products. One day an IBM executive showed up at Steve's office for a meeting. The world's preeminent computer company was prepared to make a deal for the rights to use NeXTSTEP, and the details were spelled out in the one hundred–plus page contract that the IBM executive shoved across the table.

Steve picked it up and dropped it in the trash can. If IBM wanted to deal with him, he told the man, they would have to come up with the kind of contract that Steve liked—simple and short, something like five or six pages.

IBM went through some internal gyrations—you can just imagine. The company representatives got back in touch and suggested that Steve draw up a contract of his own liking. He did, and that got the deal back on track.

This was still early enough in the history of NeXT that Steve could think he would have the world beating a path to his door. Even so, he had to recognize that a deal with IBM would bring credibility like nothing else. It would crown him with a halo of approval, practically a guarantee of invincibility. Even rumors that the two companies were talking set the business reporters on fire, begging for confirmation of what was going on.

The negotiations continued. By 1989, with NeXT bruised and bleeding from lack of sales for the Cube, Steve's own executives were arguing that the company should get out of the hardware business and concentrate on making a run for it with the software. Then, seemingly just in time, IBM signed the deal with Steve, under terms that would pump in the millions that would rescue NeXT from sinking.

The story didn't have a happy ending. The IBM executive who had been the visionary driving the marriage, Bill Lowe, the man who had brought life to the IBM personal computer, left the company to take a position with Xerox, possibly not the best career decision he could have made. For NeXT, the loss of Lowe was practically a death knell. The project was left in the hands of people who didn't see the potential that Lowe had seen.

IBM paid the up-front amount required by the terms of the contract, then stopped returning the calls from NeXT and never did anything with NeXTSTEP. Only much later would Steve recognize the opportunity he had so narrowly missed out on. At the time, IBM and Microsoft were in the midst of a wrestling match over competing operating systems: Microsoft battling to establish dominance for its consumer-oriented Windows and IBM throwing its marketing muscle behind its more sophisticated program, OS/2. Both had been created by Microsoft, but Windows was better and simpler, and IBM felt that it had been played for a fool by the aggressive guys in Redmond.

Steve had the chance to push Bill Gates out of the picture and simply blew it. If he had been easier to deal with from the beginning, the negotiating could have moved much faster and the contract could have been signed long before Bill Lowe departed. Lowe would have seen to it that IBM began shipping PCs with NeXTSTEP, instead of Windows, as the operating system. Steve's software was vastly easier to learn and use. Other PC manufacturers would quickly have fallen into line.

It could have been Steve instead of Bill Gates who was sitting back and, virtually without effort, reaping a license fee for *every PC sold*.

Steve and his team of new pirates had quickly seen that creating a computer around a custom chip would be prohibitive, given their resources and manpower limitations. Instead, they turned once again to Motorola, settling on the 68030 microprocessor—the same family that the original Mac had used but a new generation.

Yet Motorola, after promising spectacular semiconductor achievement and a ship date in 1987 that slipped to 1988, and finally 1989, in the end seriously dropped the ball. The final chip had nowhere near the performance required to power the type of visual computing software the NeXT was promising.

If Motorola's delays in delivering a chip were frustrating, at least Steve was again successful in performing his magic with the exterior design. The NeXT computer was housed in a cube, a striking black box of eye-catching appearance. Unfortunately, the case was one of the machine's few admirable features.

Again, Steve had hamstrung the machine as he had the original Macintosh, with a series of decisions that made perfect sense to him but cursed the computer. NeXT had problems in spades. The design didn't call for a floppy disk drive but instead had a state-of-the-art optical magnetic drive that allowed data to be written onto special compact disks. It was the kind of aggressive, forward-looking technology decision that Steve loved to make—but it turned out instead to be a technological dead end. Magneto-optical drives never caught on, and the units installed in the NeXT machines were fraught with problems.

Essentially, Steve had managed to create another stylish computer that was more about flash than about substance and that aggressively thumbed its nose at the computing conventions of its market sector. Without the deep pockets of a public company, however, without a tradition of success and the style of a product like the Apple II or the Mac, the computer would have to enter the marketplace on its own merits.

Months before there could be any hope of NeXT computers rolling off the production line, the sales effort was already banging the drum. Steve's marketing team set up an important dinner for key buyers from a number of America's greatest universities, people who represented Steve's main target users for the NeXT machines—a gathering important enough that Steve himself came to the dinner. The meal got underway with appetizers. The plates were cleared, and salads were served. The salad plates were cleared, and the wait staff then came out—with dessert.

The senior NeXT executive at the dinner was bewildered, as obviously were the important customers. The explanation was that someone had slipped up and approved a menu that called for a main course of veal. At the last minute, Steve discovered that his vegan eating program had been overlooked; he gave an order to the staff that the entrée be skipped. Not even the vegetables were to be served.

Because the menu didn't suit *his* eating program, Steve had allowed a group of his best customers to leave not just hungry but wondering about his decision making.

The NeXT computer, the Cube, was finally released to great fanfare in 1989. Manufactured in that advanced factory, the machine garnered lots of attention from the press. What prospective buyers found, however, was an underpowered machine with a black-and-white display; crisp, yes, thanks to software called Display Postscript, which made onscreen fonts particularly sharp.

It made little headway in the market. The real battleground shaping up at the time was the operating system war—Microsoft's Windows battling IBM's OS/2. NeXT, with its unique, home-built operating system NeXTSTEP, seemed irrelevant.

. . .

With the Cube a reality and on sale, Canon, the Japanese printer giant, now came forward to join the Steve Jobs Money-Gathering Invitational as the major investor. (Canon's LaserWriter had been a strong addition to the Apple line-up. The eventual turnaround of Apple's fortunes with Macintosh would be due in part to this high-quality printer, championed by Steve along with the page layout program PageMaker that was created by Aldus and worked perfectly with it, despite the budget-breaking $7,000 price tag.) Canon would part with $100 million for a 16.7 percent share in NeXT. You have to wonder whether Canon ever learned that it had anted up five times as much as Perot for virtually the same-size stake in the company.

More funds were gathered from a group of universities, including Stanford and Carnegie Mellon. They ponied up $1 million each. All of this on top of $20 million of Steve's own money added up to a good deal more than had been invested in creating the original Macintosh. He was counting on this bankroll to be enough to fashion a new computer that would dazzle the world once again.

NeXT had product to sell, and Steve didn't mind rolling up his sleeves and going to work. Almost any CEO in the country would take a phone call from him. One of the prominent names on Steve's call list was Disney chief Michael Eisner. Steve got him on the phone and said he wanted to come in and show what his new computers could do for the Walt Disney Company. Eisner agreed, and Steve flew down on the appointed day with some of his executives, two technicians, and a couple of computers, one black-and-white, one capable of color.

Steve could be a compelling salesman, buoyed by his own conviction and enthusiasm, at times generating the same jaunty energy he did in front of a couple of thousand people at a product launch. This particular Disney visit, though, would be Steve's rude awakening to the world of gloves-off Hollywood kingpins.

The headliners of Steve's audience were Disney's number-two man, Frank Wells, and Jeffrey Katzenberg, the head of feature film production—a pair of the biggest names in Hollywood. Steve launched into a PowerPoint presentation that had been carefully crafted for the session.

According to one of the people who attended, "Steve said proactively that there was a change happening, and that Disney as a leader should be in the forefront of it. And that NeXT would be about that change."

The point of doing this dog-and-pony show with two computers was that Steve had planned to make the most of his rare opportunity. His plan was to convince the Disney powers that they needed NeXT computers for their routine business functions; he pitched the machine with the black-and-white monitor as one with myriad advantages for business uses that only NeXT technology could offer. It was a good pitch, and the elegance and coolness of the NeXT machine were well-suited to a Hollywood studio. The audience was receptive, if not rapturous.

Disney, of course, also meant animation. After a demo of the black-and-white machine, Steve switched to the computer with the color monitor, which he described as "the leading change agent for animation."

There's always a danger in talking without a script. You might get carried away with your own enthusiasm and veer into a landmined area. That's exactly what Steve did. He lost track of what he was there for and, in front of these two time-pressured executives, launched into an excited spiel about putting the ability to create computer animation into the hands of every computer owner. He spun a web of imagery and presented a vision of animation as the domain of the common man, powered by the personal computer, which he had been instrumental in creating.

In front of an audience, even without preparation, Steve's dynamic enthusiasm and built-in charisma could win the day. But not the audience he was playing to on this occasion.

Like a theatrical director at the rehearsal of a stage play, Jeffrey Katzenberg put his hand up. Steve wasn't used to being interrupted in the middle of a performance but stopped talking. Katzenberg the executive became Katzenberg the actor, delivering a performance Steve Jobs would never forget. Gesturing to the black-and-white machine, he announced, "This is commerce. Maybe we'll buy a thousand of these."

An order of a thousand units! For NeXT, that would be a *huge* sale, perhaps even enough to rescue the company.

Then Katzenberg gestured to the color machine. "This is *art*," he announced. He could have whispered the next words; it would still have felt like a bellow. "I *own* animation," he growled. "And *nobody's going to get it."* Then he capped his speech with language that seared: "It's as if someone comes to date my daughter. I have a shotgun. If someone tries to take [animation] away, I'll blow his balls off."

Any ordinary person would have been entirely thrown by an eruption like that—cowed, distraught, decimated, and probably unable to continue. Not Steve Jobs. He was familiar enough with that kind of passionate, intolerant outburst. He himself frequently exploded that way when someone made a "bozo" remark or, worse, when someone close to him was disloyal.

Steve paused for only a moment to let the air settle. Then he went right back to his sales pitch as if no one had said a word.

It didn't work. Disney remained a solidly Apple Macintosh account, as did most of the companies he pitched. The NeXT Cube sold in handfuls to some university computer departments, but software never materialized for it, even though its operating system was touted by Steve as having something called object-oriented programming. This was a way for programmers to create primitive or basic building blocks of software, then string them together to quickly generate programs.

As the eighties drew to a close, the NeXT machine, which had begun in such optimism, seemed relegated to a footnote in the history of modern technology.

Had Steve Jobs lost his magic touch?

6 When people saw [the Pixar computer graphics short] *Luxo Jr.*, they said, "Oh, *this* is what computer animation is all about!"
—Ed Catmull, president, Pixar

Show Business

How does anyone stumble into becoming a kingpin in an entirely different industry—*by accident*?

How did Steve Jobs, already a global poster boy for the computer business, manage to become a major Hollywood player—out of desperation? And just when his corporate empire was crumbling so rapidly that it looked quite possible he could be out on the street with most of his money gone.

Was the revival of Steve Jobs just plain luck, or payoff of that karma he had been storing through his practice of Zen for all those years. Or was it something more? An ideal combination of experience—Steve's history of leading and infuriating small groups working against the odds to create something "to make a dent in the universe"—with personal charisma, his ability to discover and challenge exceptional people to reach beyond their comfort zones —meeting opportunity: computer-based animation.

Had he tried to build another pure computer company—like NeXT—he would almost certainly have failed. When he turned his attention to computer animation, Steve realized that it wasn't the hardware or the software that really counted: it was the experience that the user, or audience, had that counted. It was the "content."

When Steve moved beyond the technology and rediscovered his strengths—after all, it was the Macintosh's user interface or "experience" that separated it from the universe of me-too PC clones and ignited a revolution in the way people used computers—he turned Pixar into another cultural phenomenon. In the process he discovered the secret that would let him ultimately revive Apple and remake his reputation.

Several years before Steve and his brat pack of young cubs saw the hidden treasures at Xerox PARC, another young fellow had his own extraordinary experience there.

Alvy Ray Smith, a powerfully built man with the looks of the guy on the Brawny paper towel wrapper, hailed from a thin pie-slice of the Southwest, where highway signs announce upcoming town names like Seminole and Muleshoe. The Texas–New Mexico border is not a region famed for spawning brilliant scholars. Alvy Ray was an exception. He had earned two bachelor's degrees and a Ph.D. from Stanford University. After an image from his dissertation landed on the cover of *Scientific American*, Alvy joined the faculty of New York University.

It's just possible that his worldview was slightly snake-bitten from the flatlands of his Tex-Mex upbringing. Whatever the reason, Alvy's early life path became as twisted as the notorious mescal worm. He found academic life in the Big Apple thin and anemic. Uninspired, he felt less and less like a professor because he had somehow morphed into what he described as a "wild-assed hippie." New York City had its share of hippie types, but the accepted mecca for this new mindset was California. So that's where he headed.

After kicking back for a while and running low on cash, Alvy smooth-talked his way into a teaching assignment at the University of California at Berkeley.

Alvy knew a computer scientist in Palo Alto named Dick Shoup, visited with him one day in 1974, and stayed over because Shoup seemed so fired up about the work he was doing at a place called Xerox PARC. Out of politeness, Alvy agreed to visit Shoup's workplace. What started as a sense of obligation turned into twelve awesome hours on-site, one of the most blood-stirring experiences he had ever known. Shoup demonstrated a computer with memory capable of storing graphic images and a software program designed to create pictures. When paired, these capabilities would herald the future of artists who would no longer need to rely on paintbrushes and canvas. Their works would not be limited to being sold one at a time in galleries but stored in computer memory and sold to as many people as wanted to buy them.

On that day, Alvy's destiny was set. He had discovered what he wanted to do with the rest of his life. PARC held the dream combination: computers, which fascinated him, and art, which cried out to his very nature.

He set himself the goal of being hired by PARC. Despite his enthusiasm and impressive credentials, the center had no job openings. That was a crushing blow, but some of the staffers recognized the contribution Alvy might be able to make, and an ingenious if not entirely ethical workaround was proposed: they wrote up a purchase order to pay for Alvy as if he were bottled water or blank computer paper being delivered every two weeks.

In hindsight, it's a blessing that the PARC bureaucracy soon discovered the ruse and put an abrupt end to it. Otherwise, Alvy might have stayed for years, developing great advances that would never become commercial products and never reshape an industry, much less contribute to the world's pleasure and laughter.

Alvy was out on the street. Like a vampire who had tasted blood and would be driven to pursue the taste eternally, Alvy now had the hunger for computer graphics coursing in his veins. Just as the vampire needs victims, he needed a computer, one powerful enough to support the work he wanted to do, and hardly any of those existed in the country.

His passionate search drove Alvy to the East Coast in search of a computer graphics guy he had heard about—Ed Catmull, another Ph.D. like himself. He found Ed on a lavish estate in Old Westbury, on Long Island, working with a small crew of computer graphics people recently hired by an eccentric millionaire named Alexander Schure, who had just purchased several million dollars' worth of DEC VAX computers. The machines, then among the fastest in the world, were suitable for doing graphics programming. Schure had installed them in what had originally been a garage on the rolling estate he had purchased as a home for a new educational institution they were starting, the New York Institute of Technology. For Dr. Schure, it was a spring-board to pursue a fanciful dream of becoming a modern-age Walt Disney, but to replace the inkers, the painters, and celluloid artwork with the bits and bytes of high-powered computers. Fortunately, he had the financial clout to back his dreams.

These days NYIT is an accredited institution with two campuses on Long Island, a building at Columbus Circle, a full-time faculty of 250, and schools of architecture, engineering, and management, among others. When you talk to Alex Schure today, it's clear that he still regards NYIT as one of the crowning achievements of his life.

After purchasing the computers, Alex Schure had gone on a scavenger hunt for people, discovering in the process that a leading center of computer-graphics research was located at, of all places, the University of Utah—not exactly on anyone's list of major U.S. high-tech centers. Nonetheless, Alex got in touch. Several people there mentioned the name of Edwin Catmull, a frustrated artist who had been smart enough to recognize he wasn't going to have much of a career at a drawing board or an easel, so instead he'd taken up physics and had just earned his doctorate. Alex Schure called the new Ph.D., painted a glowing picture of what he wanted to do and the world-class computer facility he was in the process of assembling, and convinced him to come to Long Island and take charge.

By the time Alvy arrived in New York, looking for Catmull, he discovered a lavish spread in the kind of rarefied community where you can live for years and never meet your next-door neighbors, the kind of place where you feel that at any time, you might come around the corner of a building and run into Gatsby himself. The one-time garage where the computer graphics operation was housed wasn't anything like the garage where Jobs and Wozniak had started Apple Computer. Instead, Alvy discovered it to be an elaborate building large enough for six Rolls-Royces.

Alvy and Ed became fast friends, as well as working partners, though in many ways they were the proverbial odd couple. Alan Deutschman, in *The Second Coming of Steve Jobs*, describes Alvy at that phase of his life as "long-haired . . . single and unfettered . . . a subversive renegade, talkative and gregarious" and "fiery if provoked." Today he's ruggedly handsome with a shock of white hair and a trim beard, looking as if he just stepped out of a Marlboro ad. In contrast, Ed is reserved to the point of being shy, a clean-living Mormon who went home at the end of the working day to his wife and children. He still looks the part today.

The pair shared a common dream, however: to create a full-length animated feature film that used computers to make an emotional connection with an audience. No cold-blooded slick graphics for them; they wanted to transcend the world of computer graphics and tap into human emotions.

The nearly unassailable mountain facing this pioneering crew of animators had to do with the question of light. Sure, you need a great many drawings to create the illusion of motion, but to accumulate a stack of flat, two-dimensional drawings like those for *Sleeping Beauty* involves creative animators doing the key sketches and hordes of people doing the "in-betweens"—the individual drawings to make the character appear to move from the position in one key sketch to the next. This was the traditional hierarchy of animation: the handful of "animators" and the much larger crew of "inkers and painters"—at Disney, mostly underpaid women who were kept in a separate building and given about as much praise and respect as the janitorial crew.

Now animation was struggling to move beyond the flatness of the 2-D style to the more vivid, real-world look of 3-D. What gives life to film animation, what gives it a sense of believability that the audience can connect with, has to do with the way light bounces off every surface of the objects in the frame. When we look at a Rembrandt or a Vermeer, we almost feel as if we are in the room with the subjects. In the history of painting, a great divide was crossed when artists came to understand the vital roles of light, reflection, and shadow and then discovered how to capture on canvas what the eye sees.

In film animation, trying to capture those subtleties of light on every object in the frame, in a movie that might have 100,000 or 150,000 separate frames, would spell financial suicide. That's where Ed and Alvy and their team came in. These clever Ph.D.s, working closely with artists, were attempting to define mathematical equations—algorithms—that would instruct the computer to calculate exactly the right light bounce automatically. If the light in the scene is coming from *here*, and this part of this particular object has just *this* curve, along with *this* color and reflectivity, then the strength, the direction, and the quality of the bounced light should be *that*.

Of course, all of that was purely technical mumbo-jumbo. The real magic was to create a story that could be told using computer animation. Doing that, and creating a film that was warm, funny, and emotionally satisfying, was much harder than all the computer animation work. When their benefactor, Alex Schure, took the group's early work and tried to create a film, it was an embarrassment. The team started to wonder if they would ever find a filmmaker who knew how to use what they could do to move an audience.

At the same time, filmmaker George Lucas was awakening to a recognition of his own. In *Star Wars*, one of the most memorable visual elements had been the duels with the light-sabers. To moviegoers, those sequences were magical; to filmmaker Lucas, they were a nightmare. The actors had to mimic a battle while holding nothing but the metal handles. Then, in postproduction, a battalion of special-effects animators had to paint in the light beams painstakingly, frame by frame—an exacting, time-consuming, excruciatingly expensive effort.

Then there was the problem of the spaceships. Hollywood special effects people had developed a high level of expertise in creating miniatures of skyscrapers, trains, ships, and spacecraft and making them look entirely believable on the screen. Lucas, though, had scenes that called for whole fleets of spaceships flying across the screen in every direction. Achieving that required taking the same pieces of film and putting them back through the animation cameras over and over again. A small mistake could ruin the negative, requiring that the entire scene be restarted from scratch.

As Steve Jobs later pointed out, "If you go buy a laser disk of any of the *Star Wars* films, [and] stop it on some of the frames, they are really grungy, incredibly noisy—very bad quality. George [Lucas], being the perfectionist he was, said, 'I'd like to do it perfectly.' He wanted do it digitally, and nobody had ever done that before."

Surely, someone must have a solution to these maddening problems. Why not find a way to do it with computers?

. . .

The years on Long Island were extraordinarily productive. Building on the work of earlier talented innovators at the University of Utah, the National Film Board of Canada, and elsewhere, Alex Schure's computer graphics group laid the groundwork for software that makes possible all of today's major animated feature films, from *Toy Story* to *The Lion King* to *Shrek*.

Alvy Ray Smith and Ed Catmull were slowly waking up to the reality of their situation: Alex Schure knew how to assemble equipment, technical talent, and animators, yet was dismal in selecting people who knew about story, character, or connecting with an audience. Their dreams of making great animated movies still seemed a distant reality.

Then an emissary from George Lucas came calling.

Reputation counts in life. So do achievements. So does keeping up contacts with the players in your field. The groundbreaking work by that irreverent gang of young innovators at the computer lab was being touted around the grapevine in Hollywood, thanks to visits that Alvy and Ed had secretly made to folks at Disney Studios. Now it was all paying off. The movie industry was beating a path to their door. Lucas was working on his *Star Wars* sequel, *The Empire Strikes Back*. When he offered the guys an opportunity, they had no problem deciding to go to work with him.

By 1980, the key members of the Long Island team had assembled at Lucasfilm across the Golden Gate Bridge from San Francisco. They were back together and settling in.

George Lucas quickly turned out to be a less-than-ideal godfather for the Ed and Alvy operation.

For one thing, Lucas was trying to keep too many balls in the air all at the same time. He describes it as finding himself "having to do a lot of design work on *Empire* and get the script done while I'm also starting a bunch of companies—ILM [Industrial Light and Magic], Skywalker Sound, and Lucasfilm. I was starting a video-game company. I was developing digital film editing. At the same time I was . . . launching digital animation and digital filmmaking. I was working on *Raiders of the Lost Ark*. And I was self-financing a movie." In classic egomaniacal micromanagement style, Lucas was trying to do it all himself. It helped that he could finance it all by himself, but that only exacerbated the problem.

The self-financing was made possible by Lucas's business foresight. He was blessed with an unusual combination of abilities, as a creator of stellar projects that had begun with *American Graffiti* and continued with *Star Wars*, and a businessman who could recognize opportunities others had not yet seen. On *Star Wars*, he had kept the merchandising rights for himself, and the enormous popularity of the film turned the sale of games, toys, and the rest into a gold mine. The actors had blithely signed away any claim to profit from toys based on their characters. Carrie Fisher, who played Princess Leia, recently joked, "These days, every time I look in the mirror, I have to send Lucas two bucks." The film became so successful that Lucas never again needed to take studio money: he was able to use the profits from one film to finance the next, while accumulating land and buildings for a whole movie studio in Marin County.

Taciturn and not given to schmoozing, Lucas nonetheless managed to communicate his goals. According to a Lucas insider, "As early as 1980, George had seen that films were going to go digital. He had three projects that he wanted serious work done on: digitizing the audio, digitizing editing, and digitizing special effects."

The cornerstone of his operation was an incredible special effects studio called Industrial Light and Magic. This was the domain of set builders, model makers, and camera operators who could single-frame extremely complicated scenes of unknown science fantasy worlds. It was all done on mock-ups and scale model sets, using multiple generations of film to composite the new universes. Using computers for special effects was something of an afterthought for Lucas, this insider said. "He didn't think 3-D computer graphics was far enough along yet to be worth putting a lot of effort into." But his newly acquired graphics group didn't see the subject in that light. Its members lived and breathed the same rarefied air as their original benefactor, Alex Schure—the all-too-pure oxygen that inspired dreams of an animated feature film created entirely on the computer. They would find the time to develop the software to make those dreams come true.

Lucas had installed the group in a building he owned in the charming, peaceful little town where he lived, San Anselmo. Their quarters, on the second floor above a laundromat, were no match for what they had left behind, but they would not have complained if they were being given challenging projects to strain their talents and sharpen their skills. Lucas needed them, but only for tasks that were hardly above the level of painting beacons of light onto light-sword handles.

The skies brightened when Lucas won an assignment from Paramount to do some scenes for a space epic, *Star Trek II: The Wrath of Khan*. Director Nicholas Meyer had specified that one particular scene was to be handled with computer graphics.

Alvy was ecstatic. Finally, at long last, he would be developing a scene for a major, big-time Hollywood production. That was only part of the reason for his glow. George Lucas hadn't been paying much attention. Here was the golden opportunity: Alvy would create a scene so dazzling that it would open George's eyes to the wondrous contribution that computer graphics could make to his movies.

Good wouldn't do. This would have to be *great*.

Ed Catmull, Rob Cook, and Loren Carpenter had been quietly at work on a program to create 3-D graphics. They conceived a system that would be tied into a specialized, very powerful computer and would be able to create animation blazingly fast. They were already far enough along with the software to use it on Alvy's *Star Trek* effort, which has come to be known as "the genesis scene," in which a dead planet comes to life.

Even after the concept had been approved, Alvy knew he still needed a capper, a slam-dunk that would drive home a message the withdrawn George Lucas could not possibly miss. He found it: he designed one elaborate camera movement, so intricate, so powerful, so wickedly clever that any filmmaker would be in awe, because it was a shot that would have been impossible to capture in real life. The camera flies above the flame-engulfed planetary surface, then pans to look back at the fire—while fleeing just fast enough to avoid being swallowed by the rapidly advancing wall of flame.

When the scene was finished, Alvy couldn't have been more pleased. But would it convey its special private message to Lucas? The day after the 1982 premiere, the taciturn Lucas stepped into Alvy's workspace, announced simply, "Great camera move," and disappeared.

Small praise, but that didn't matter. From then on, George Lucas began calling on Alvy Ray and Ed to spark scenes in his movies with their computer graphics wizardry.

.   .   .

While handling the computer graphics chores Lucas handed off to them, Ed, Alvy, and their team continued to develop new software tools and to hire the most talented animators around. The new hires and others were already at work creating 3-D still images. Sure, some of the images were artful, vivid, and breathtakingly real, but a single image could sometimes take months to complete. How could they dare to dream about creating even a very short film?

Then John Lasseter fell into their lives. A brilliant Disney animator who was considered a rising star among the young talents at the studio, John was one of those rare people who radiates energy and enthusiasm and is actually likable, to boot. On top of that, he was an animator with a keen sense of story and character—a rare and prized combination of abilities.

John had been captivated by animation at an early age. When the Disney studio inaugurated a character-animation curriculum at the California Institute of the Arts, he became the second student accepted into the program. To his delight, the arrangement included working summers as an apprentice at the studio.

Every year, the Academy of Motion Picture Arts and Sciences—the outfit that awards the Oscars—holds a separate national competition for student films. By the time he finished his studies, John had garnered two of these student Academy Awards. One of his winning films was called *Nitemare*; the other used a theme that he would return to a few years later with spectacular results. He called it *Lady and the Lamp*.

With that kind of success, it wasn't much of a surprise that Disney Studios hired John shortly after graduation. He worked on pictures such as the 1981 feature *The Fox and the Hound* and the 1984 short *Mickey's Christmas Carol*. In between those two projects, he did some work on the 1982 feature *Tron*, where he received his first taste of computer animation. He liked the flavor.

As it happened, John met the Lucas pair just at a time when his frustration at Disney was running high. He had done a demo clip showing how the popular children's book *Where the Wild Things Are*, by Maurice Sendak, could be brought to life with a clever composite technique that used hand-drawn traditional 2-D animation for the characters in front of vivid, colorful 3-D backgrounds created by computer.

John and his peers thought that they'd hit the bull's eye with this effort by capturing a new, sophisticated look, while keeping man-hours and costs in check. They had caught the original spirit of the classic Sendak book. The studio honchos, however, even with a proclaimed mandate to improve quality while cutting costs, showed no interest in the project. The idea of using computers for anything beyond word processing and accounting was simply too radical.

Ed and Alvy sensed John's unhappiness at Disney, and they had already adopted what Ed later described as a philosophy of "Hire people who are better than we are." In 1984, they enticed John up to Lucas-film to work with their computer graphics unit for a month. He didn't need much convincing to realize this was the place he belonged. Since they weren't supposed to have any artists in their technology part of the Lucas operation, Ed and Alvy gave John the job title of "interface designer." They were bending the terms of their arrangement with George, but, as things turned out, nobody complained. Hiring John proved to be a monumental decision, bearing on the lives of John himself, Ed and Alvy, and Steve Jobs as well. More than that, putting young John Lasseter together with computer graphic animation changed the course of the motion picture industry.

For all his success as a filmmaker, George Lucas was less successful in his relationships with people. He pours emotions into his films and can grab millions of people by the throat. Yet on a one-to-one level, he seems withdrawn, barely able to break through the emotional barrier that cuts him off from the rest of the world—even, to an extent, from those closest to him.

In mid-May 1983, George and his wife, Marcia, announced that they were filing for divorce. Soon after, George was squiring singer Linda Ronstadt, whose previous boyfriend had been the counterculture governor of California, Jerry Brown. It was hard to keep that kind of relationship out of the gossip columns. It didn't help divorce negotiations either.

Because California is a joint-custody state, the split meant that Marcia was entitled to half of everything George had acquired during their marriage. That presented a dreadful problem. The family assets were the movie companies themselves—Lucasfilm, Industrial Light and Magic, Ed and Alvy's computer graphics group, and the advanced postproduction facilities of Skywalker Ranch.

There was no cash to speak of, only a one-of-kind motion picture empire. Marcia was entitled to walk away with half the value, somewhere in the tens of millions of dollars. The idea of selling off a piece of the empire tore at George's soul.

The graphics experiment had made sense when it seemed like an inspired investment in the future, but Alvy Ray and Ed and their tribe of starry-eyed computer folks were one piece of the empire that didn't seem as close to George's heart as the rest. Reality now cast a harsh light on the fact that the group had managed to complete only an occasional project that brought in any money. Overall, they had been little more than a severe cash drain. Should he sacrifice the computer graphics operation?

In 1985, Steve Jobs had an extra $150 million from the termination deal with Apple and had gathered a small group of people who were already at work on what would become the NeXT computer. A former Xerox PARC wunderkind, then an Apple scientist with the exalted title of Apple Fellow, Alan Kay, told Steve he should "go visit these crazy guys up in San Rafael, California," who were working at Lucasfilm. It was, Steve heard, a computer operation that George Lucas had put together and now wanted to sell. Steve seemed interested.

He made the trip north up the coast to where Lucasfilm and ILM were housed in warehouselike buildings in the un-chardonnay part of San Rafael, while Lucas himself continued to dwell like a member of the landed gentry in expansive splendor on his property called Skywalker Ranch. It was, in one viewer's phrase, "an almost feudal arrangement: the lord in his manor, his serfs in the squalid town."

Steve Jobs was stunned by what he saw that day. The computer graphics enthusiasts showed him the incredibly vivid digital pictures they had created and film clips like nothing he had ever seen. It was another Xerox PARC moment.

These were the greatest talents in computer graphics, gathered in one place and creating groundbreaking stuff on a daily basis. The computer systems they had assembled, the software they had created—all of it was incredible. And George Lucas was willing to let it go!

Steve was lusting for it, the whole package—the people, the computers, the software—everything. But George had saddled the operation with a price tag of $30 million.

On the other hand, Steve read the smoke signals. George Lucas was clearly in a hurry to sell. Not in such a hurry that he was ready to bargain because he thought he had another buyer, but Steve smelled the odor of smoldering panic. He knew how these things went. He would bide his time.

Alvy Ray and Ed Catmull approached Disney about taking over their unit. They found a Disney executive who saw how this could make sense for the studio, and presented a deal for Disney to buy a one-half interest from Lucas for $15 million. When the executive tried to get approval for the deal, Jeffrey Katzenberg announced that he had more pressing issues to deal with and this would be a waste of his time. He nixed the investment. That path was dead, but another opportunity opened up.

In 1985, industrialist Ross Perot, having sold his company, EDS, to General Motors and became a member of the GM board of directors, was looking for new worlds to conquer. His eyes lighted on George Lucas's computer graphics operation. (Perhaps Steve had also been too enthusiastic about it during the negotiations over NeXT.) Over a period of months, Perot corralled Philips, the giant Dutch electronics firm, into joining him, and made an offer with a bottom-line figure very close to Lucas's asking price of $30 million. After a deal had been worked out in detail by both sides, on the very day that Perot was supposed to sign the paperwork, the newspapers carried an announcement that Perot had been bounced from the GM board. He was no longer in a position to make any commitments on behalf of General Motors.

Suddenly, George Lucas found himself without the buyer he had counted on.

This was the opportunity Steve Jobs had been waiting for. He began negotiations in earnest with Lucas. Negotiations between Steve and George should have been smooth. Both very much wanted the sale, and both shared a dedication to a way of life that emphasizes tranquility. Lucas describes his religious affiliation by commenting, "Let's say I'm spiritual." He explains that he was raised Methodist, but "It's Marin

County. We're all Buddhists up here." He and Steve should have been on the same wavelength.

Steve was stinging from the wounds of the Apple embarrassment and wanted this plum as a demonstration to the world—and especially the business reporters—that he was still a player.

Nonetheless, Steve can be a painfully difficult negotiator, and the discussions dragged on. At one point Lucas, though desperate for the cash, could no longer stand the ordeal of haggling with Steve and announced he was withdrawing from further negotiations. Steve wasn't willing to give up, keeping after Lucas until he finally agreed to come back to the table.

Finally, Lucas and Steve came to terms. Steve would buy the entire operation—staff, computers, software—for just under $10 million. Accepting that figure, barely one-third of the amount he had originally aimed for, was a bitter pill for Lucas. It wouldn't come close to providing the sum he owed Marcia in the divorce settlement. Still, it would take care of the immediate pressure, and he was out of time and other options. Lucas was at least able to walk away with one concession that was important to him: all advances that the new company made on the computer graphics software would be provided to Lucasfilm free of charge.

Steve's waiting for the price to come down and then applying a heavy dose of Stevian determination won the day. The computer graphics group had shifted its patronage once again, from the quirky Alex Schure, to *Star Wars* commander Lucas, to the pirate king himself.

Oddly, in Steve's view he was buying a hardware and software company—adding another computer firm to his roster—while Alvy and Ed still had their dreams pinned to creating an animated feature, a goal that had become all the more realistic with John Lasseter and the animators he had brought in to join him.

Alvy Ray Smith and Ed Catmull would become cofounders of a new company, each with 4 percent of the stock, the other 92 percent going to their angel investor, Steve Jobs.

Alvy, Steve, and Ed all wanted a company name with a high-tech flavor. Not long before, Alvy had dubbed one of their computers "Pixer," which he felt carried the suggestion of *pixel* changed into a verb. Then, drawing on his heritage of growing up in a Tex-Mex region, he amended that to a name with a Spanish sound: Pixar. (Another source claims that Alvy made the change because the last two letters became Alvy Ray's initials.) "Pixar" carried a flavor of technology and a spirit of creative imagination—just the right combination for the new company.

Pixar it would be.

The Pixar staff was a bit squirrelly. Nonconformist, to say the least. Among the forty or so people in the new company, it wasn't at all uncommon for many to straggle in about lunchtime and then stay late, perhaps working until somewhere around midnight. Steve Jobs, when he showed for one of his very rare appearances, came in his standard uniform of ragged jeans, T-shirt (usually black), and New Balance running shoes—casual enough that he couldn't have been dismayed to discover some of the Pixar crowd wandering around in bare feet. According to one report, a few of them didn't bathe very often—another Jobs trait from his earlier days.

This was a crowd whose members sensed that they were on a new frontier of filmmaking, not simply pushing an envelope others had defined but creating the outer limits of the envelope themselves.

Steve later claimed that he was tuned in to the Pixar mission from the first. "Pixar's vision was to tell stories—to make real films," he said. "Our vision was to make the world's first animated feature film—completely computer synthetic, sets, characters, everything." In fact, that wasn't Steve's vision when he bought the group from Lucas, and it wasn't the direction he first set the company on.

He had never really understood software. The programming that came so easily to some remained a dark mystery to Steve Jobs. He was basically a hardware guy with a talented amateur's knowledge of software. With hardware, he had proved to be a visionary. Of course, he had marred one effort after another by being too much of a visionary, demanding achievements that were not yet possible. He had stumbled often by being too much of a perfectionist, beginning way back with the insistence on those perfect solder lines in the Apple II that few purchasers would ever see or care about.

Despite all that, he clearly understood and had a unique connection with aspects of the computer business that involved things you could see, touch, and hold. He had demonstrated a true genius in picking designers of imagination and brilliance and then driving them hard until he was finally satisfied. He truly cared, deep down where he lived and breathed, about design.

The Macintosh project had deepened Steve's appreciation for software, if not his understanding of what was involved with it. With the Mac user interface the combination of hardware and software had created a new way of working with computers; although it might have been derived from the work at Xerox PARC, it was all Macintosh now. As a result, Steve had grown to value the combination of operating system and hardware that defined the essence of a computer. By the time he started NeXT, he understood that it was also the application programs—the software that let users do something with the computer—that mattered. Now he had bought a company that was all about using software to create state-of-the-art images. In a certain sense, Pixar was only a software company and the hardware was incidental. The computer graphics stars had built a specialty piece of hardware—a supercomputer for the day—to handle their needs. But it was what they did with it that made all the difference.

Steve wasn't quite ready to hear that message yet, however.

In Palo Alto, Steve had a gang of earnest youngsters working to design the NeXT as a next-generation computer, an effort just getting started and not likely to generate any income for a couple of years at the earliest. In Marin County, though, he had just bought an outfit with a serious computer that had the potential of being turned into a commercial product. The computer that the Pixar team had created was unique, and Steve was determined to find a way to market it. He was blinded by his love for the hardware, hardware that made such an impression on him.

True, it was a specialized machine, tailored specifically for the computer graphics industry, built with the capacity to store a huge number of extremely detailed images. But Steve, always captivated by being on the forefront of technology, launched the effort to turn the prototype into a marketable product. The result was a machine that they dubbed, unimaginatively, the Pixar Image Computer.

It was obscenely expensive for any ordinary use, with a price tag of $135,000 in 1980 dollars, plus another $60,000 or so for the software and peripherals such as tape drives—items that were essential but not included in the base price. What's more, Steve found Ed and Alvy Ray woefully inadequate at running a business, calling them "babes in the woods." He thought he could plug the holes in time to keep the ship from sinking. "I think I can help turn Alvy and Ed into businessmen," he said.

The principal challenge was to find a larger market for the Pixar Image Computer.

They set their sights on the medical community, because of the need to store vast numbers of images. A radiology lab, for example— large files, floppy images on every patient who has ever stepped in front of its X-ray machines. How much better if all those pictures were on a computer, instantly available to the doctor? With all the new technologies coming along—MRI and the rest—the image-storing needs were growing exponentially.

On top of the money he had already spent to buy the company, Steve was willing to provide additional streams of money to get sales rolling. Pixar opened sales offices in seven U.S. cities and fielded a sales force of some twenty people.

Despite the mammoth effort, it was doomed to fail. The truth was that the Pixar computer had been designed by specialists to be operated by specialists. Medical technicians and doctors didn't get it. Nor did anybody, for that matter, who wasn't a well-experienced technology wonk. It was just too complicated. The professional leaders of hospitals, clinics, medical centers, and medical research institutes sat down to listen to the sales pitch and took the time to see the system for themselves, then decided that the learning curve was way too steep. With all the time pressures on doctors and their staffs, nobody wanted to dedicate the days that would be needed to master the Pixar Image Computer.

To keep Steve Jobs out of the lion's den, away from the Pixar employees, unable to harass, intimidate, cajole, or otherwise discomfit the hardworking and highly motivated troops, Ed and Alvy regularly made trips to the NeXT headquarters in Palo Alto to sit down with their benefactor and update him.

After a while, these trips started to become more and more uncomfortable. How often can you say, "The money is flowing out at an extraordinarily fast rate, and damned little is coming in, but you're doing the right thing by continuing to back us and trust us," and still be believed? So that they wouldn't appear tongue-tied and shuffle-footed, the two men would hammer out a carefully orchestrated list of discussion topics designed to provide a candid appraisal, while at the same time, they hoped, distract Steve enough that he wouldn't ask difficult questions.

The strategy was solid but almost totally unsuccessful. They discovered from the first that Steve's engaging, captivating personality could overwhelm the best-laid plans. This wasn't some clever, manipulative tactic; it was just Steve Jobs being himself. No matter how well rehearsed Ed and Alvy were, no matter how determined to stick to their agenda, no matter how many times they had been through the sessions with Steve before, the same thing almost invariably happened: they would sit down with Steve, get through a few pleasantries, and launch into their presentation. Steve would have something else he wanted to ask about or talk about. He would interrupt in mid-sentence and bring up whatever was on his mind abruptly. Alvy or Ed would head off in whatever direction Steve wanted and get further from whatever they had come to discuss. Meanwhile, the other guy would sit there far enough removed from the scene that he was wise to what was happening but unable to stop it.

Eventually, Alvy says, the two worked out a signal. If Ed was getting seduced by Steve and led someplace they didn't want to go, Alvy would tug an ear. And vice versa. That didn't necessarily mean they would be successful in steering Steve back to their own agenda. But at least, like a virgin being romanced until her brother arrives in time to bring her to her senses, the one being seduced would be awakened to what was going on.

The whole point of hiring Disney animator John Lasseter while the group was still part of the Lucas operation had been so that he could design short demo films that would show off the capabilities of the team's computer graphics software and hardware. In 1984, the Pixar group showed up at the annual conference of the computer graphics organization Siggraph. The group brought with it an animated short conceived and directed by Alvy Ray and animated by Lasseter and his team. Called *Andre and Wally B* and only a minute and a half in length, the little picture was the runaway hit of the convention. In part, this was because it displayed techniques that went beyond what other computer graphics systems were capable of, and in part because it told a story and captured emotions. In ninety seconds, that's quite a feat.

Now that the group was under the Pixar umbrella and concerned about generating income, its members felt ever more urgently the desire to show off the company's technology. When they came back to Siggraph, it was with a much more impressive short, *Luxo Jr.*, which has become a landmark in the history of animation. The six thousand technicians and animators who had gathered at the convention in Dallas were dazzled at the technical brilliance of the piece and rewarded it with "prolonged and enthusiastic applause." Steve Jobs, sitting in the audience, took it all in, knowing that but for his rescue of the company, this wouldn't have been happening.

The applause wasn't only for the technical achievement, impressive as that was. John Lasseter, this time directing as well as animating, had achieved something startling: the only characters in the bit of film were two *lamps*—two ordinary-looking desk lamps, one full size and one much smaller. Adult and child. Lasseter had actually captured human emotion with no humans or even animals in the scene. Viewers sensed that they knew what these inanimate objects were thinking and feeling. (You can relive the experience by watching the picture as that first audience saw it, on the Web site www.pixar.com/shorts/ljr/theater/ index.html.)

Luxo Jr. captivated audiences everywhere it was shown. The picture won a Golden Eagle at the CINE film festival in Washington, D.C., which qualified it for submission to overseas festivals as an official U.S. entry; it also qualified the picture to be considered for an Oscar by the Academy of Motion Picture Arts and Sciences. The Pixar guys decided that it was worth submitting and entered it in the animated short category. John Lasseter and William Reeves were listed as producers. The whole Pixar crew was elated to learn that *Luxo* had earned an Oscar nomination. It didn't win, but the nomination alone was enough to spotlight the work that the Pixar crew was doing. Ed Catmull offered the viewpoint that "it was really the milestone. When people saw this, they said, 'Oh, *this* is what computer animation is all about.'"

· · ·

Steve's monthly review sessions with the Pixar management were sometimes held on Steve's own turf and occasionally at Pixar. He reviewed business and operational matters and went over the finances. After each meeting, he ordered a wire transfer of the cash needed to cover the upcoming month's expenses; the funds would show up within a few days in the company's bank account.

Four men gathered to meet with Steve for one of these meetings in early spring of 1988—Alvy and Ed, vice president of finance Rick Wood, and vice president of sales and marketing Bill Adams. For this meeting, Steve drove up, and the group met in an upstairs conference room at Pixar.

It proved to be one of their most painful meetings ever. None of the Pixar people had anticipated the disturbing news that Steve had for them. By now feeling considerable strain over the monthly expenses at both NeXT and Pixar, Steve had come to the session determined that big cutbacks needed to be made. Every workgroup at Pixar would have to let a significant number of people go. The executives discussed each group of the entire company, often weighing the pros and cons of specific individuals.

The distress level in the room was almost palpable. These men had chosen their employees with extraordinary care, selecting the best— people not only extraordinarily qualified but who would also fit into the nonconventional, rather anticorporate culture that made the company not only highly productive but a laid-back, fun place to work. Pixar people were loyal to the company, and the company was loyal to them. Now the executives had to come to terms with breaking that bond of loyalty. They understood Steve's reasons. From a business standpoint, it was a logical move. That didn't make it any easier.

The session went on for hours; "the hardest meeting we ever had," one of the participants called it. It was like a knife in the gut for each of them.

When they were through, Steve asked, "Is that all?" and put his hands on the table, ready to get up and walk out. There *was* one other topic: funding was badly needed for an animated short to show at the next Siggraph conference, only five months away.

Ever since the days at Lucasfilm, what was now the Pixar team had done a short for Siggraph's annual convention. It was always a high point of the gathering. It had become a kind of tradition; everyone expected to see a few minutes of footage that cleverly showed off the group's latest technological wizardry. Within Pixar, an R&D team was now hard at work turning the software that Ed, Alvy, and the others had been evolving since the Long Island days into a commercial software product. Many people in the computer graphics field eagerly awaited the product, and Steve had high hopes that it would begin to generate a significant revenue stream. That income, added to the revenue from sales of the computer, could ease the cash strain Steve now suffered. Prospective buyers at Siggraph expected to see another short that would once again dazzle them with breakthrough technology. If the Pixar group showed up empty-handed, it might be taken as a sign that the company was in trouble and would throw a cloud of suspicion over the software, undercutting sales before the product even reached the market.

Yet after the painful discussions that had just taken place with Steve, which resulted in cutting several hundred thousand dollars from the budget, how could they ask him to come up with an almost equivalent amount to produce another short? Everyone sat still, looking at his lap, choked up at the idea of having to ask for money at this very awkward moment. Finally, Bill Adams spoke up. He explained about the short, said, "Steve, we need to do this," and listed the reason why it was essential for the sales of the forthcoming software product.

The company would have fifteen to twenty people working on the short, over a period of months. For Steve, it meant adding hundreds of thousands back to his cash outlay.

Steve sat silently, thinking about this difficult request, analyzing the consequences of a yes and the consequences of a no. Finally, he asked, "Are there storyboards?" Told that there were, he asked to see them. The group got up and trooped downstairs. John Lasseter had done his usual stellar job of creating a storyboard that captured not just the look but the emotions of the piece. Impressed, Steve agreed to dig into his pocket and fund the short, which would be called *Tin Toy*.

"If nobody had spoken up and Steve had walked out of the room," Bill Adams said, "or if he hadn't agreed to spend money, *Tin Toy* would not have been made. And without *Tin Toy*, I don't believe Disney would ever have come to the table" to fund Pixar movie productions.

Steve, despite feeling so pinched that a significant number of staff people had to be fired, was willing to spend a large chunk of money on what was essentially a promotional film. It was a pivotal moment in Pixar's history.

Months later, Lasseter and Reeves were back at the Oscars with their nominated short, *Tin Toy*. As if the earlier challenges hadn't been diffi-cult enough, this time they had set themselves the hurdle of animating a person—or, more accurately, a crawling, stumbling toddler. They had given sales and marketing vice president Bill Adams a screen credit for his role in bringing up the subject of funding the picture with Steve; "Ralph Guggenheim brought me a piece of 35mm film from the movie with my screen credit on it," Adams said. (As a Hollywood inside joke, another credit was for "Best Boy." And another credit, caught only by that small percentage of people who actually read movie credits, listed five women identified as "Babes John Looked at a Lot.")

Funny credit titles aside, you didn't have to be an animator or a software engineer to appreciate the achievement that this little picture represented. The members of the Motion Picture Academy clearly felt that way: they awarded the Oscar for animated short to *Tin Toy*—the first time the award had ever gone to a film made entirely by computer animation.

While continuing the effort to find markets for Pixar computers, the company had managed to present the animation world with a new product in 1988—a software package called "RenderMan." In simplest terms, it represented putting into a box the fruit of the team's labors from its earliest days on Long Island. RenderMan became a crutch for Steve, providing the little company with much-needed cash flow.

The process of rendering is best understood by analogy. Think of Rembrandt standing at a canvas, ready to begin a painting. Seated in front of him is a model whom the artist has cloaked in an elaborate gown and provided with sparkling earrings and a glittering necklace. The artist has arranged the furniture that will appear in the picture, and he has posed the model so that light flowing into the room strikes the model at just the right angle. The artist does not start by painting the face or the contours of the figure; instead, he starts by visualizing the anatomy, the bones and the muscles. In a sense, he begins with the basic structure and works toward the surface.

The process of creating a scene for an animated film begins in a similar way. "Modelers" start by defining the room or other setting—for an interior, this will include where and how far apart the walls are, the furniture pieces, their shape and location, and so on. Other specialists add the color and the texture details for each item. Shaders add the lighting information—where the light is coming from and how it is reflected by every part of every object. Because the camera will show the scene from several different angles, this detail must be defined for 360 degrees of the entire setting.

All of this together is what animators mean when they talk of "rendering." Pixar's RenderMan software provided the tools for many of these steps. When introduced, it was by far the most advanced product of its kind and has remained the most widely used rendering product in the industry.

In an entirely just world, the greatest creative talents would reap fabulous praise and fantastic rewards, and companies exhibiting the greatest creativity would be successful beyond the dreams of their leaders. Real life is more cruel.

John Lasseter's demo films were supposed to impress the world with the terrific capabilities of the Pixar computer systems. The films did draw the attention of prospective computer buyers, but not much else. Pixar could barely give its computers away. They were simply too complicated to use and far too expensive. A handful were sold to universities, and a number were purchased by the intelligence community for use in analyzing satellite images.

In connection with the intelligence sales, the government demanded that every company executive be cleared for Top Secret; everyone in the computer group who would work with satellite photos needed an even higher clearance. These were mostly Marin County superliberals, and the whole idea didn't sit well at first. Worse, the intelligence community referred to this as a "black project," which gave the work a sinister connotation. Still, once they got up to speed, many found the work fascinating.

One Pixar executive was sitting in Steve's office discussing some current issue when a call came in for Steve from a government security investigator. "For five or ten minutes," the executive said, "Steve sat there answering questions, a lot of them about his drug use." He seemed annoyed by the call but answered "candidly and straight-forwardly," without ever asking the executive to leave. "The caller would ask a question and Steve would answer, 'The last time I used that was about . . .' and then he'd give a date or say how long ago." Once or twice he answered that no, he had never used whatever it was the caller had just asked about.

The executive explained that "you're supposed to list information about your drug use on the application form for the security clearance. Apparently Steve hadn't done that, so now they were asking him over the telephone." If you're honest about your drug use, the executive said, then you're probably okay—lying about it suggests you're hiding something that might leave you open to blackmail and giving away secrets.

When Steve finished the call, he looked at the executive with a wry smile and asked, "Did I do okay?" The executive answered, "I guess so," and they laughed together. Steve was willing to go through that embarrassment, the executive believes, because he knew how important the security clearances would be: the intelligence agencies promised to be a big customer for Pixar. In the end, the intelligence community bought well over a million dollars' worth of Pixar Image Computers.

Even so, by 1988, not many more than a hundred of the machines had been purchased.

The company was tearing through money at an alarming rate—nearly $1 million a month. Yet despite money being extremely tight, Steve could be his old irascible, unreliable self in dealings with potential customers. On one occasion, a leading firm in the computer industry took an interest in the RenderMan software, which it wanted to adapt for a consumer version and sell to the general public. High-level executives of the two companies flew back and forth for three months hammering out the deal. They reached an accord, one that would have been very lucrative for Pixar. Steve had been kept in the loop all through the negotiations. But when it came time to sign, he announced that he had changed his mind. He didn't want to do the deal after all. According to one insider, the executives of the other company were livid.

Steve didn't care. What's more, he didn't bother giving any reasons or excuses. He didn't have to. He was Steve Jobs.

The year 1989 proved to be a painful time for Steve. Despite the glitz and glamour of introducing his groundbreaking, sexy-looking NeXT computer, accompanied by the trumpet blare and applause of reviews from the computer press and lavish fair-haired-boy-makes-a-comeback coverage in the popular press, the NeXT computer was doomed.

The situations at NeXT and Pixar were curiously parallel. At NeXT, the computer product was a bomb set to explode, and at Pixar, the computer was similarly doomed. Steve had always wanted to be seen as a cool hardware impresario but was striking out badly every time at bat.

Meanwhile, ironically, both companies had broken new ground on the software front. Steve had originally conceived of NeXT as a company that would produce software "tools"—products used by developers in creating new software applications. On a visit to Carnegie Mellon, a university with one of the best reputations in the country for its computer research, Steve learned about a new type of "kernel," the software element at the heart of a computer operating system. Even for someone lacking in an understanding of software, Steve was excited by the potential of this arcane mass of programming code, which had been dubbed "Mach." One of the most important parts of the Mach approach was called object-oriented programming—this was a way to encapsulate the programming code for often-used items, or objects, in such a way that they could be used over and over by many programs. It supposedly simplified the brutal "black art" of writing software.

Steve was still always looking for new ideas that would show him to be in the forefront of technology, and he was convinced that Mach fit the description. In the aftermath of that Carnegie Mellon visit, he made a decision that would have long-reaching impact: NeXT would not develop software tools but would be a company that built computers differentiated by running an advanced operating system that NeXT would create—an OS based on Mach. To make it happen, he recruited Avie Tevanian, a key member of the Mach team.

While the NeXT computers in the end never generated enough sales to grab a permanent place in the market, the sharp, capable software team Avie assembled laid the groundwork that eventually surprised them all and led the company out of the wilderness.

The unexpected parallel in Steve's other life, at Pixar, was stunning. On the software side, RenderMan became a solid money earner. Software, of course, is a very high-margin product; a printed user manual, if one is even provided, costs more to produce than does the CD or other media that contain the product. For that matter, in many cases even the box costs more than the actual software medium. With software like RenderMan carrying a price tag of thousands of dollars, you don't have to sell vast quantities to experience revenues that make executives and owners smile.

On the hardware side of Pixar, Steve had taken a battering ever since the product was announced. The grand plan of sales offices scattered across the country and a beefed-up army of sales reps out knocking on doors had done little more than burn money. Hardly anyone was answering the knocks. Incredibly, for months Steve had threatened to fire John Lasseter and his animators because the little films they turned out were a luxury the company couldn't afford.

Steve's personal financial adviser had given Steve messages that he didn't want to hear. NeXT had burned through a huge amount of money, but at least it wasn't all Steve's. There was Perot's $20 million and Canon's whopping $100 million. Steve himself had kicked in only (only!) $12 million. But the cost of developing and marketing a computer that everyone admired but few wanted to pay for had by this time nearly cleaned out the piggy bank.

Yet NeXT actually looked good when compared to the truly ugly financial picture at Pixar. Layoffs continued. Finally, Steve had to face a painful reality. The two companies were bleeding him dry. From being one of the richest men in the United States, richer by far at the time than Bill Gates, Steve now had a dwindling fortune of a mere (for him) $25 million. If he continued to keep the two companies afloat out of his own pocket, he'd soon be selling off his precious German sports cars and the (still unfurnished) mansion that had been his home for years.

Steve finally made a decision that he'd dreaded and resisted for too long. The Pixar computer had achieved some notable sales but almost exclusively in niche markets, mainly to university and medical customers and the intelligence community. Bill Adams's hardworking sales force had even managed to achieve sales overseas, in Europe, Australia, Japan, and China, but these weren't enough to justify the product. Steve finally admitted to himself that the Pixar computer wasn't going to sell widely enough to justify continuing the effort. He had been chasing a fantasy.

By this time, Adams had just left Pixar; today he remembers Steve as "the smartest man I ever met" and acknowledges that he would "work for him again happily." Steve asked Bill to take on a short-term job as a consultant. The task: find a purchaser for Pixar's computer business. Adams located an outfit called Vicom, which bought the business and hired a number of the staff people, paying Steve several million dollars.

No one finds it easy to admit defeat. It's hard enough to do this in private, sharing only with people closest to you. When your defeat is meat for the daily press, it can be humiliating. For someone like Steve Jobs, there's no place to hide. He could have said no to requests for interviews, but he couldn't stop reporters from writing embarrassing stories.

Over the next few months, the company shrank to half its previous size. Yet in the carnage, one group remained intact. For over a year, Steve had been pressing Ed Catmull and Alvy Ray Smith to close down the animation group. Each time he had been ignored or convinced to hold out a little longer. Now, even though the ax was falling on all sides, Steve didn't need any pressure about holding on to John Lasseter and his animators. Their Oscar had made all the difference.

Steve showed himself to be talented at picking brilliant technologists, but gaining the brilliant creative force that was John Lasseter when Steve acquired Pixar wasn't talent; it was sheer luck. John was the latest in Steve's string of superstars.

Doing business with Hollywood appealed to Steve. Yes, the company leaders could be ruthless bastards, but they were *smart* ruthless bastards, some of the best businessmen and negotiators anywhere. He had seen only a little of it, but he had heard the stories. They were people who would intimidate you if they could, people you had to stand up to as if you held a royal flush every time.

That was a game Steve thought he knew how to play.

Steve Jobs as a senior
at Homestead High
School in 1972.

Steve Jobs introduces the new Apple II in Cupertino, California, in 1977.
(AP/Wide World Photos)

Steve Jobs sits in his first home, in Los Gatos, California, on
December 15, 1982. *(Diana Walker/Getty Images)*

The twelve-bedroom, 17,000-square-foot mansion in Woodside, California,
that Steve Jobs lived in through most of his thirties, and has continued to
own. Built in 1926 for copper magnate Daniel C. Jackling, the house was
designed by renowned architect George Washington Smith. *(Courtesy of the
Woodside History Committee)*

Steve Jobs and Stephen Wozniak with the Apple IIc computer at the unveiling in San Francisco, spring 1984. *(Jim Wilson/Woodfin Camp)*

Steve Jobs sits with Apple president John Sculley on January 30, 1984, in Manhattan's Central Park, a few days after the official release of the Macintosh; the bag contains a Macintosh. *(Diana Walker/Getty Images)*

The team at NeXT. From left: Dan'l Lewin, Rich Page, Bud Tribble, Steve Jobs, Susan Kelly Barnes, and George Crow. *(Ed Kashi/Corbis)*

Steve Jobs and Ross Perot announcing the Texas billionaire's investment in NeXT. *(Ed Kashi/Corbis)*

Steve Jobs receives his Presidential Citation from Ronald Reagan at the White House, on February 19, 1985. *(Courtesy Ronald Reagan Library)*

Steve Jobs with daughter Lisa at the former headquarters of NeXT in Redwood City, California, February 1989. *(Ed Kashi/Corbis)*

Steve Jobs and his wife, Laurene, share a lighthearted moment in their backyard. *(Diana Walker/Time-Life Pictures/Getty Images)*

Apple Computer Inc. chairman Gil Amelio with cofounder and former chairman Steve Jobs at the MacWorld exposition in San Francisco in January 1997. *(AP/Wide World Photos)*

Disney chairman Michael Eisner; Pixar's John Lasseter, who produced and directed *Toy Story*; and Steve Jobs at the premiere of Disney/Pixar's *Monsters, Inc.* in 2001. *(Frank Trapper/Corbis)*

177

Laurene Jobs at the opening of the San Francisco Apple store, February 2004. *(Courtesy of
Gary Allen, www.ifoAppleStore.com)*

Bono, of the music group U2, and Steve Jobs show off the "U2 Special
Edition" iPod at a launch event in October 2004. *(Mark Richards)*

The unique style of the Steve Jobs signature reflects his creativity and his unwillingness to follow the usual ways of doing things.

Steve Jobs addresses the cheering crowd at MacWorld Expo, 2004.
(John Green/ZUMA Press)

Steve Wozniak and Steve Jobs at MacWorld Keynote in San Francisco, on January 11, 2005. *(Alan Luckow)*

Steve Jobs unveils the new Mac Mini while wearing the new iPod Shuffle around his neck after giving the keynote address during the MacWorld Conference and Expo in San Francisco on January 11, 2005. (*AP/Wide World Photos*)

7

We've found that when the technology is strong, it inspires the artists. And when the artists are strong, they challenge the technology.

—Ed Catmull

Master of Ceremonies

For someone who had attended only one year of college—and without actually showing up in a classroom very often, at that—the idea of being invited to lecture at one of the nation's great universities had unmatched appeal to Steve Jobs. Whenever an invitation arrived, he always accepted if he could. He was on the Stanford University campus in the fall of 1989 for another of these appearances, this time at the invitation of a group of students from the business school.

Partway through his remarks, he lost his train of thought, stumbled, and seemed unable to get back on track. He seemed curiously muddled and unfocused. This remarkable guy who could stand before a packed auditorium of one or two thousand people, talk impromptu for an hour, and hold listeners enthralled suddenly couldn't seem to concentrate. People in the audience who knew him were baffled.

The explanation was simple. Steve was *smitten.*

His gaze had settled on a young woman so irresistible that just looking at her distracted him. She had an attractive face, a bright, intelligent look, a dancer's long legs and slim waist, and flowing blond hair, and was endowed with curves just where most women want them.

Her name was Laurene Powell, as Steve learned when he spoke to her after the session. He asked for her phone number and gave her his own, the private home line he shared only with his closest friends and business associates. He thought of asking her to dinner but already had plans, so he left.

Then he felt an emotional tug too powerful to resist, one of those "this may be a door to the rest of my life" moments. He said, "I was in the parking lot, with the key in the car, and I thought to myself, 'If this is my last night on earth, would I rather spend it at a business meeting or with this woman?' I ran across the parking lot [and] asked her if she'd have dinner with me. She said, 'Yes.' We walked into town and we've been together ever since."

Laurene came equipped with impressive credentials. Raised in a well-to-do Pennsylvania family, she had earned dual undergraduate degrees—a B.A. from the University of Pennsylvania and a B.S. from Wharton. From campus she went straight to Wall Street, first at Merrill Lynch Asset Management, then switching to Goldman Sachs in training as a fixed-income trading strategist.

Like Steve, she was a vegetarian; unlike him, she had broad interests much beyond her career. When she received her acceptance from the Stanford Business School, she quit her job and flew to Italy. Settling in Milan, she spent months studying art history, soaking up the life of a city that is one of the glories of Europe. She remained in that stunning environment until it was time to return to the States and join her new classmates.

Before long, according to *Forbes*, Laurene had moved into Steve's Palo Alto home, sometimes driving to class in his silver BMW with "NEXT" on the license plate. After the long succession of women in Steve's life, it might better have read "NEXT AND LAST."

Steve wasn't yet over his passion for Tina Redse, which had lasted for five years. Not long before, he had asked her to marry him. Tina declined. It was one thing to have him for a friend and a lover, but to make a commitment to live with him for years didn't suit her vision of life. Friends say he told her about the new girl he had met, though, and kept her supplied with details.

When school broke for the summer, Laurene had succeeded in surviving her first year of business school, despite the distractions.

Steve took her to Europe for a week, and Laurene showed him around her Italy.

While things were going well in the romance department, Steve's outlook in business was also about to get a welcome shot in the arm. On a Tuesday in mid-September 1990, Steve once again took the trip to San Francisco for a launch session to announce the product that he believed would turn his fortunes around. This was the new NeXT computer, called the NeXTStation and designed to address the shortcomings that had made the original machine celebrated and admired but not purchased.

The new NeXT gleamed with the same shiny black magnesium case, this time not in the distinctive cube shape that had been so costly to manufacture; instead, the shape was more conventional but still distinctive enough to be referred to as "the pizza box."

Many would-be buyers had been put off by the black-and-white display, in a world of computers going color. The NeXTStation boasted a color display, which Steve showed off at the launch meeting with the kind of dramatics he loved. He had had his staff license a scene from *The Wizard of Oz*, in which the image turns from black-and-white to color. The audience roared its enthusiastic approval.

The unbridled enthusiasm died as soon as the show was over. The new computer was less expensive than the original NeXT but still cost thousands of dollars more than the machines it had to compete with. It became painfully evident that Steve had blindly run down the same path that had led him into the thorn bushes in the past. Great design, even world-class design, isn't enough to sell a computer. Maybe design is enough to sell sunglasses, lamps, or top-caliber fountain pens—but not computers.

It's easy to admire the latest breathtakingly gorgeous young starlet even if her brainpower doesn't measure up, but that doesn't mean you want her to help you get your work done for the next few years. Most buyers don't pick computers solely on good looks, either. If Steve Jobs was such a brilliant guy, such a world-class marketer, why did he still keep making the same obvious mistake?

When the NeXTStation proved to be yet another disaster, Steve finally faced up to the truth: the Holy Stevian Empire was collapsing.

He considered closing the doors on both companies and getting out of business altogether, but he had been in business since his part-time job at the electronic parts shop as a teen. Waking up in the morning without a company to run or challenging business decisions to make seemed like a bleak, miserable, uninviting way to live.

Under the circumstances, shutting down the businesses was undeniably the only real choice, yet it seemed unthinkable. Steve closed his eyes to logic and common sense. Instead, he tightened his belt and crossed his fingers. In this case, belt-tightening meant slashing the workforce at Pixar again. He ordered nearly one-third of the staff to be laid off. Going against standard business practice, he refused the idea of severance pay. The employees being fired—even people who had been with the team for years—would be paid the money they were due but nothing more. It was cruel and cold-hearted, but Steve wasn't in a position to be generous.

One group at Pixar was again spared the chopping block. John Lasseter's animation team had not just an Oscar in their favor; they were now producing big-time television commercials for major clients, generating a revenue stream that more than covered their expenses. Once again, the animators squeaked past a cutback.

As it would turn out, luck was once again very much on Steve's side.

Steve Jobs liked people who had the guts to stand up to him—but with a very demanding limitation: this applied only to people he respected, people who had a real contribution to make and whom he could look on in some respects as his equals. For anyone else who tried to talk back to Steve, his time at the company would probably come to an abrupt end. (There was some flexibility here, however. Apple engineer Alex Fielding once sent Steve a strongly worded e-mail complaining about the firing of another engineer whose work was crucial. Steve sent back a reply, "If you feel that way, you should probably leave the company." But he didn't insist, and Alex lasted another six months.)

Alvy Ray Smith was one of the people whom Steve would take gaff from. Since they had started working together, Alvy never had a problem looking Steve in the eye and telling him he was wrong about something. Steve might not change his mind, but he wouldn't blow a gasket. He at least listened and possibly even considered the point of view.

All of that changed in a blinding flash at one Pixar meeting. Steve has certain territorial imperatives, like having the right kind of bottled water laid out for a meeting. And ownership of the whiteboard is a strange quirk of his, a part of his need for total control.

At this particular Pixar meeting, Alvy disagreed with what Steve had said and was writing on the whiteboard. Alvy thought Steve was wrong. He stood up, walked to the whiteboard, picked up a marker, and began to explain his disagreement while writing on the board.

Everyone in the room watched in fascinated horror as Steve Jobs imploded. "You can't do that!" Steve screeched. Alvy was stunned and speechless as Steve leaned into him until their noses almost touched and hurled insults meant to demean, belittle, and wound.

Then Steve stormed out of the room.

"It was ugly," Alvy said afterward. "Steve turned on me with everything he had." Even today, Alvy remains sensitive about reopening the wounds from Steve's irrational, undisciplined, little-boy-with-a-big-temper outburst and from what followed. Alvy now says, "I'm rather pleased to have gotten over my animus against Steve and am not interested in reviving it."

Alvy handed in his resignation. He was one of the two cofounders of Pixar, one of the two towering giants who had led the innovations that had seen computer graphic animation graduate from a university lab to the movie screen. He had given it fifteen years of his life, but he was willing to give it all up rather than continue to have Steve Jobs in his life.

Ed Catmull must have been torn by Alvy's departure—on one hand, regretful at the breakup of a partnership that had defined the frontiers of their field but, on the other, aware that Alvy's departure left Catmull king of the mountain, the sole commander calling the shots creatively and technologically for the leading company in its field. He eased Alvy's departure by working out arrangements that opened the door for Alvy's next venture, which was to prove highly lucrative.

Steve Jobs didn't lift a finger to stop Alvy Ray Smith from leaving or to make his departure any less painful.

Worse, Steve has mounted an active campaign to rewrite history. In speeches and interviews, as well as on the Pixar Web site, all mentions of Alvy Ray Smith have been expunged. It is as if he never existed, never contributed any of the underlying technology, never cofounded Pixar with Ed Catmull. As far as Pixar is concerned, it's "Alvy *who*?"

For Alvy's usurping of the whiteboard, Steve Jobs has exacted an ultimate form of revenge.

The idea of doing animation with computers wasn't new around Disney, but the first major project had done little beyond provide ammunition for the studio old-liners who wanted to stick with what they did better than anyone else in the world: the traditional ink-and-paint 2-D animation of *Sleeping Beauty* and *Snow White and the Seven Dwarfs*.

The studio's first swing at computer-based animation had been *Tron*. Originally conceived as a six-minute animated short by an independent East Coast animator, Steve Lisberger, it was reincarnated into a one-hour animated television special that would be part of NBC's extensive coverage of the 1980 Olympic games in Moscow. When President Jimmy Carter, in a fit of pique at the Soviets, decided that the United States would not participate in the games, the project was without a home.

Disney animation at the time was living under a black cloud from a string of box-office disappointments. *Tron* would be a gamble, but it offered the appeal of trying to break the run of dismal pictures by turning to computer graphic animation.

When the picture opened in 1982, it combined live actors with computer animation in a way that was quite striking for the time. The studio later described it as "a masterpiece of breakthrough [computer graphics] ingenuity, a dazzling film at the flashpoint of a continuing revolution in its genre." Whatever degree of truth that description may have contained, the movie bombed. The production managed to garner two Oscar nominations, for costumes and sound, but moviegoers stayed away in droves.

It would be years before Disney leadership could be convinced to try computer graphics again in any important way.

Meanwhile, interest in computer graphics was stirring elsewhere around Hollywood. One of its chief proponents was the enormously prolific writer-director James Cameron. He had already made his reputation with *The Terminator* in 1984 (memorable in part for starring Arnold Schwarzenegger in a role that became part of his legend) and *Aliens* in 1986, which earned seven Oscar nominations.

Cameron next went to work on an underwater science fiction thriller, *The Abyss*. Cameron and his screenwriting partner and sometime wife, Gale Anne Hurd, conceived one character that Cameron the director would have a hard time filming—a creature composed of seawater. Cameron understood enough about current technology to recognize that computer graphics offered the solution. The project was given to Lucasfilm's Industrial Light and Magic, and "magic" is a good term to describe their success. *The Abyss* was the first major Hollywood film with a character created entirely on the computer, and it earned an Oscar for visual effects.

Cameron's contribution to the use of computer graphics took a quantum leap ahead with his next film, *Terminator 2*. For this one, he set an even more difficult task in calling for a character who appears throughout the film and seems to be made of liquid metal. The effect was captivating to moviegoers and absolutely convincing to just about everyone involved with special visual effects who hadn't yet been convinced. Computer graphics had won a permanent place in filmmaking.

After *Tin Toy* received an Oscar, John Lasseter found enough confidence in the technology from the film industry to enable him to plan more challenging projects. Disney's Jeffrey Katzenberg, he who *owned* animation, was already a big fan of Lasseter's—he had tried to tempt John into coming back to the Disney fold and had been rebuffed. When approached, Katzenberg readily agreed to a meeting. Lasseter took the big leap of proposing that Pixar, which had never done a picture longer than about five minutes, produce a half-hour computer-animated TV special, possibly a Christmas special, which Disney would fund. Katzenberg was encouraging but noncommittal.

Disney still hadn't come up with a blockbuster computer-animated movie, and James Cameron had shown Hollywood that computer graphics was no toy but a powerful weapon to tell stories in a way never before possible.

After conferring with studio boss Michael Eisner, Katzenberg contacted Lasseter to make a remarkable counteroffer: Disney was opening the door for Pixar to produce a full-length animated feature, which Disney would fund, promote, and distribute.

For Steve Jobs, the news came as a lifesaver. A feature film! For

Disney! With the studio pouring in enough money to keep Pixar solvent! Not a measly television production but a full-length film, to be distributed by Disney and shown at your local neighborhood theater, around the world. Amazing!

For Steve Jobs, the news couldn't have been better, but he wasn't one to share his gloom and sense of doom when things were darkest, and now that some light had broken through the clouds, he wasn't about to dance down the corridors of Pixar or clap Ed or John in affectionate, thankful hugs. Yet even if he didn't show it outwardly, he knew that they had just brought home his salvation, gift-wrapped by Katzenberg and the Disney organization. There weren't any specifics yet, but a deal with Disney would mean tens of millions of dollars flowing into the Pixar coffers.

Steve wouldn't face the public humiliation of having to close down the company. He began the wait for the call from Disney.

Earlier, Steve had seen the deal with IBM come to nothing as a result of his own delays. Now the Pixar deal with Disney was dragging on with nothing happening. If the much-needed Disney cash didn't show up soon, Steve might have to shut the doors not just on Pixar but on NeXT as well.

Snatching spare time from work on the television commercials that provided some measure of cash flow, John Lasseter was jotting story notes and filling drawing pads with character and scene ideas. But Disney hadn't agreed to a story concept yet. Worse, the Disney people weren't even setting up meetings to hammer out the deal terms.

The word coming from John's old contacts at Disney couldn't have been more discouraging. Katzenberg's desire to go outside the studio and have another company produce an entire Disney animated film on its own flew in the face of Mouseworks tradition. In business for more than half a century, the company had never done this.

With the studio seemingly unable to break its string of mediocre animated films, Katzenberg was willing to go against tradition and roll the dice with outsiders. Pixar had John Lasseter, which lent strength to the project on the artistic front. And Pixar knew how to make an animated film using computers, which meant that it could be done for vastly less money than in the traditional Disney way, which often involved hundreds of people in the creation of a single film. To Katzenberg, it just made good business sense to try.

The story that got back to Pixar made it sound as if Katzenberg's number-two man, Peter Schneider, might be holding to a "stick with tradition" viewpoint, and his foot-dragging or counterarguments might be winning the day. Schneider now says it isn't true—that he never opposed the arrangement—but a source within the company contradicts this, saying that he thought Schneider was conflicted. "He wasn't sure that Lasseter wouldn't make him look bad in the end because Peter would have everyone believe he was the only one capable of making great animated films, and here was somebody else who was making great animated films." A Pixar executive who was privy to the negotiations said, "Peter was very opposed to the whole thing, but Jeffrey said, 'Let's give it a try—this [3-D computer-based animation] may be the future.' Katzenberg, this executive said, "had the vision."

Up north at Pixar, it began to look as if doing a feature film for Disney might never happen. Finally, the Pixar powers decided on a strategy that combined the hopeful with the manipulative. They began to have meetings with other studios in town. If any of these studio executives were willing to take time to have lunch at a place that "above-the-line" industry types favored, like the Polo Lounge, the Bel Air Hotel, or the Ivy, being seen with them would make it all the better.

The plot apparently worked. Jeffrey Katzenberg sent word that he wanted to meet with Steve Jobs. Steve came, attended by Ed Catmull and two others. They were shown into Jeffrey's conference room adjoining his office, where they found a very long conference table. Steve sized up the situation intuitively: if he sat along one side, Jeffrey would take his customary seat at the end and everyone else, Steve included, would be subservient.

Steve sat himself down at the far end of the table. The two royals would face each other as equals.

The Pixar contingent must have been laughing inside when Jeffrey came in and announced that if Pixar's animators wanted to do a project for Disney, they were to talk only to Disney. Pixar had managed to pull Jeffrey Katzenberg's chain!

It's the Steve Jobs style to negotiate as if he holds a position of strength. He negotiates that way even when the cards are stacked against him. Katzenberg didn't know just how weak Steve's position was—that he could no longer afford to keep financing his two companies and had essentially run out of options for producing income at either of them. At least, not enough income to make the companies viable for the long term. Yet Steve intuitively understood that he needed to speak up to Jeffrey Katzenberg as if they were bargaining from equally strong positions.

Steve insisted that Disney would be funding production work only; the deal would not involve Pixar selling the rights to any technology. Jeffrey acted as if Disney "was the be-all and end-all, and Pixar just a gnat," said former Pixar executive Pam Kerwin. All the revenue from video sales would go to Disney, he told Steve. Pixar would not participate. Still, he wasn't just talking about one film, he was talking about *three.*

Jeffrey now led Steve onto the main battlefield, the discussion of the production budget and how the pie of profits would be sliced. Pixar would receive 12.5 percent of the net, Jeffrey said. It's doubtful that Steve or Ed Catmull even knew what a reasonable number was. This was Hollywood insider stuff, information you couldn't find in any book. Only a handful of people at the top of the studio structure, and their lawyers, knew whether 12.5 percent represented a royal screwing.

Steve must have been holding his breath. The size of the production budget was key. Big enough, and it would mean the survival of Pixar. Steve, Ed, and John had gone over the numbers thoroughly, but it's not like a math problem on the SAT: "If 15 people can create a 5-minute animated film in 3 months, how many people will it take to create a 90-minute film in 3 years?" There are so many intangibles.

Worse, whole elements of filmmaking were complete unknowns to these nervous neophytes. How much do you need to budget for a musical score, orchestration, and recording sessions? How much for each of the A-list movie stars to record the voices? How much for the completion bond—the insurance policy that protects against some indispensable member of the production team falling victim to a terrible ailment partway through?

One published account describes how Jeffrey forced Steve to announce a production budget figure, then said Disney wouldn't spend that, and seduced Steve into accepting a much lower figure, when all the time the original figure Steve had named was significantly under what the studio had been spending per picture.

It's a good story, but not the way the cards were played, according to Pam Kerwin. Disney understood that the Pixar guys didn't know how to budget an animated feature, she said. "We figured out the costs in collaboration with Disney." It was in the common interest of both sides to arrive at a budget that made sense all around.

For Steve, the important part was that Disney would put up the full cost of production. *If* Pixar stayed within budget, Steve would not have to reach into his own pocket. If the picture went over budget, he would be on the line for as much as $3 million. He would remain on edge about that $3 million commitment during most of the time it took to produce the film, demanding reports and assurances at frequent intervals that the costs remained in line.

But that was all ahead. On the day of the Katzenberg meeting, Steve walked out with a handshake commitment for a three-picture deal with the most prestigious company in the history of animated film, a deal that would save him and his company. A deal that would eventually lead to his becoming successful even beyond his dreams.

Now all he had to do was wait for the Disney minions to work out the nitty-gritty details and call to say they were ready to negotiate the specifics.

While Disney and Pixar were just beginning to dance together at the executive level, the two companies had been busy for some time in other areas that had already borne fruit.

Before Alvy Ray's painful departure, he and Lem Davis of Disney had come up with the idea of doing a joint research project, which eventually led to a software package called Computer Animation Production System or CAPS.

Traditionally, animators drew their images on paper. Each image was then transferred to celluloid sheets (cels) and given to ink-and-paint workers in white gloves who added the edge lines and painted in the color. With CAPS, the computer takes over this work: the paper images are scanned into the computer, then digitally inked and painted onscreen. From there, the art can be digitally composited, using as many layers as desired.

According to Dylan Kohler, one of the software engineers who worked on the development, the CAPS project was considered highly confidential. The studio was obsessive about not wanting anyone to know that some of the Disney animation was being done with computers instead of all by hand. "They were afraid if word got out, the luster of the Disney name would be tarnished. Everyone involved with the project had to sign a nondisclosure agreement," Kohler said. "I didn't even tell my family about CAPS. We developed this great thing, we got through the hell of getting *Rescuers Down Under* out, and then we were still under these very strict [nondisclosure agreements] so we couldn't even celebrate what we had done with other people. *Rescuers Down Under* came into the theaters, and we couldn't say to anybody, 'This is the first feature in history to be produced entirely in the digital realm, from fade in to fade out.'"

The secret came out after *Beauty and the Beast* reached theater screens, with a ballroom scene that to the trained eye had clearly required the use of computers. At that point, "Jeffrey Katzenberg started bragging to the press that computers were now in fact part of *every* sequence," and the developers of the software were at last free to talk about their work. CAPS was used on every Disney 2-D animated feature from that time on, including *Beauty and the Beast*, *Aladdin*, *The Lion King*, and *Pocahontas*.

This early collaboration between Pixar and Disney built confidence among the folks in Burbank toward their brethren up north. As Ed Catmull described it, Pixar had "performed on time and on budget and gave them more than they bargained for," and as a result, "Disney realized they had something special."

The project paid off handsomely, not only in establishing the Pixar bona fides with Katzenberg, but in another important way as well. The 1992 Academy Awards included a technical award to Pixar for CAPS. As a belated irony, Alvy Ray Smith, who had already made his painful departure from Steve Jobs's company, was one of the recipients sharing in the award.

The following year, the same lightning struck again: another Oscar to Pixar, this time for the RenderMan software. Pixar's only marketed software product, RenderMan has continued to provide a revenue stream through the years and even today is the most widely used rendering software, not only on animated films, but also on computer-based visual effects for live-action features. (In fact, as of 2004, RenderMan had been used in thirty-five of the last thirty-nine films nominated for an Oscar in the best visual effects category.)

On March 18, 1991, Steve Jobs gave up his bachelorhood.

A whole army of people thought they would receive an invitation to the wedding, but it wasn't going to be that kind of function. Steve and Laurene invited almost no one. Maybe it was because Steve was feeling the financial pinch so severely that even for this cornerstone event in their lives—the first marriage for both of them—he wasn't willing to spend the money for a large, splashy *People* magazine sort of function.

Or maybe it was just the minimalist, laid-back Steve Jobs doing things his way. It certainly wasn't any young woman's lifelong dream of a ceremony.

The wedding was to be at Yosemite National Park. The small group didn't fly there but climbed into one of those lavish private-party buses Steve had rented for the drive from Silicon Valley. Laurene's parents sat together, trying to get comfortable with Steve's side of the family—his mother, Joanne Simpson, and his novelist sister, Mona. Steve must have sorely missed his adoptive parents, Paul and Clara Jobs, to whom he owed so much.

The ceremony itself could not have been simpler or more austere. Zen had meant so much to Steve over the years, and now it dictated the style of the ceremony. Incense was burning as the guests and the bridal group entered the room, and the Buddhist monk whom Steve had worked with for years—Kobin Chino—presided. Instead of wedding bells, the small group heard the boing of a Buddhist gong, as thirty-six-year-old Steve married twenty-seven-year-old Laurene.

The usually reliable *Forbes* carried an item saying that Steve had opposed the idea of exchanging wedding bands. "But just days before the ceremony," the magazine reported, "he was spotted at Tiffany's in San Francisco shopping for a ring in the half-million-dollar neighborhood."

To all appearances, Steve and Laurene have since had a stable, satisfying marriage. But the wedding almost didn't happen. Their first child, a son named Reed, was born on September 22, six months after the ceremony. When Laurene told Steve she was pregnant, his back went up, just as it had years earlier when Chris-Ann became pregnant. Laurene, naturally enough, wanted to get married. Steve refused. It was the same scene being played out all over again, with a different female lead.

This time the outcome was different. One of America's most prominent bachelors had renounced his bachelorhood, but the celebrating was brief. Laurene had to get back to the classroom and her studies, and Steve, who had still not heard from Jeffrey Katzenberg about moving ahead, went back to looking for some way to dig himself out of the worst financial hole he had ever been in—with the business press ready to write about his ultimate disgrace.

Finally, Disney got in touch to say it was ready to move ahead with the contract negotiations. Steve went on a hunt for an appropriate entertainment attorney to advise him in the deal-making. After considering leading talents like the esteemed Ira Epstein, a founding partner of Cooper, Epstein, Hurwitz, he decided on Harry Brittenham, whose client roster included people like Harrison Ford and the leading independent film producers in Hollywood, Bob and Harvey Weinstein of Miramax. Brittenham, known as Skip, is a short, thin man described as "low-key" by people who know him personally and as having "an outsized personality" by others. In a town filled with big-ticket attorneys, he's ranked among the fifty highest earners and is considered one of the top two or three powerhouses among entertainment lawyers.

It turned out that Disney hadn't been ignoring Pixar but had been busy all along, with the legal department drafting terms and key executives reviewing and calling for changes. Because this was breaking new ground for the studio as the first-ever animation production to be "outsourced," proceeding with due caution made sense. For Steve, Ed, and John, though, it would have been a less antsy, less anxious time if the Disney people had kept them posted with progress reports.

Now that negotiations were moving ahead, Steve flew to Burbank from time to time to sit down with Jeffrey Katzenberg and go over details of the contract. On a chartered aircraft? No way; he wasn't spending money frivolously at this point. He flew Southwest, standing in line like any tourist or businessman on a budget. Pam Kerwin says the Pixar people rode Southwest from Oakland to Burbank so often that they nicknamed it "the Southwest bus." She recalls one later occasion when Steve decided after their meetings that he wanted to experience the fun of the Jurassic Park ride on the Universal Studios tour. He made a phone call that got them to the front of the line and onto the ride. "We went to the airport soaking wet," she recalls.

In the deal that was finally put on the table, Disney, in addition to picking up the production cost, would also fund the promotion and the distribution. Pixar would develop all the creative aspects—characters, character appearance, screenplay, dialogue, casting of actors for the voices, and so on. Disney would, of course, retain approval power over all creative decisions, but that was fine with the Pixar team. Who would complain about having the expertise and the creative sensitivity of seventy years of animation heritage as a sounding board?

The overall terms followed the lines that had been laid down by Katzenberg in the initial meeting, along with two items that hadn't yet come up. John Lasseter would have to sign a long-term contract, binding him to stay on board for all three of the pictures covered by the agreement. Katzenberg was adamant. After the *Tin Toy* Oscar, he had tried to entice John back to Disney, promising creative freedom on his own productions; John had replied that at Disney he could make movies, at Pixar he could make history. If Katzenberg couldn't have John, this deal was at least a guaranteed way to acquire his talent. So a commitment from John was a deal-breaker: he would commit to stay the course or the deal was off.

John agreed. If it's nice to be wanted, it's even nicer to be fought over.

The second new term said that Disney would keep the income from merchandising royalties—toys, games, fast-food tie-ins, and all the rest. When Steve later saw how much this added up to, he figured out a way to cut Pixar in on subsequent films.

With John Lasseter in the controlling role as director and head writer and Ralph Guggenheim (a colleague from the original New York Computer Graphics Lab days) as producer, Pixar launched into the daunting, totally unfamiliar task of developing a feature-length motion picture that came to be called *Toy Story*. John had always been drawn to buddy pictures, and he had won an Oscar for his three-minute short featuring a small baby and its toys. Those themes came together in the concept of two toys in a youngster's collection struggling with their own competitiveness until they must join together against an outside adversary. Typical buddy-film stuff, of course, but never done before with toys as the heroes.

Over a period of months, they developed the story to the point that John felt it was ready to be presented to Disney. Members of the Pixar team assembled the pencil sketches they had prepared and transferred them to video. John took the video to Burbank, where he ran it for Jeffrey Katzenberg while providing a live narration and a soundtrack by acting out all the roles. (Lasseter can captivate an audience so effectively in this kind of session that some claim he could have had a successful career as an actor.) After John left, Katzenberg told another Disney executive that it was "wonderful, terrific—the best pitch I ever heard." (A while later, he went around telling everyone how much work was needed to fix problems in the story.)

From that germ of an idea, John and his writing associates spent the better part of a full year developing a script. John took one long weekend to learn the basic tools of the Hollywood screenwriter's craft by signing up for a cram course in Los Angeles—the same one that's parodied in the movie *Adaptation*. Though some people ridicule the course for its set of hidebound rules and proscriptive do's and don'ts, Lasseter's writing clearly did not suffer from the experience.

John chose one scene from the story with the two central characters, astronaut Buzz Lightyear and Woody, a cowboy, and set the animators and the technical crews to work on producing a thirty-second demo intended to capture the brilliantly realistic look that the finished film would have. All of the top Disney executives knew what 3-D animation looked like, but none of them had seen it before in footage being developed for a picture that would carry the studio's name. Peter Schneider, who had prevailed in his drive to have the project under his control, watched the clip and was astonished. In mid-January 1993, Pixar finally received a thumbs-up from Jeffrey Katzenberg on the plot concept.

While the rest of Pixar—the folks not working on the movie, the software developers, the business types, and so on—suffered from penny-pinching and bean counting, the production side of the house grew from a handful of people to more than a hundred, eventually including thirty technical directors and nearly as many animators.

. . .

Screenwriters often turn to file cards when they work out a story's structure, writing a brief description of each scene on a card, pinning up all the cards on a pegboard, and then moving them around to find a better order. Film animators often do the same but use sketches instead of file cards. If you had visited Pixar in the early 1990s, you would have found hallways enlivened by an impromptu art show of sketches for successive moments in a scene, with story editors and animators tossing out ideas on how to make the scene flow.

As you stood in the hallway examining those rough but engaging hand-drawn art pieces, you might have seen John Lasseter hurrying past. As director of the film, John was commander in chief, in charge of every creative aspect. Every day he worked his way through the large bullpen where the animators had their individual carrels. Meticulously detailed, the drawings allowed John to look at a series of images and envision every aspect of the action, then rattle off a string of suggestions, from which way a character's toes are pointed or how he's gripping the object in his hand, to how quickly he turns, where his eyes are focused, and how he shows a reaction to what he sees.

John had sensed early in his career that it takes more than drawing skill to be a superior animator. For Pixar, he insisted on animators who would be "more actor than artist." Creating animated characters that spring to life onscreen, he said, requires acting ability more than anything else. Later on, the company would help develop that ability by requiring incoming animators, modelers, and shaders to attend "Pixar University," a course of several weeks that even includes sessions in the art of improv.

When a scene involved dialogue, the animators initially worked to a "scratch track" recorded by various Pixar employees, no acting experience required. Later in the process, the big-name actors and their lesser-known brethren showed up at a recording studio in Los Angeles, where Lasseter guided them through the performance, line by line. For *Toy Story,* John had his heart set on Tom Hanks for the voice of Woody, because, John said, Tom has "the ability to take emotions and make them appealing." Before Hanks came in to discuss the project, Lasseter prepared a thirty-second reel showing a bit of action with the Woody character, to a soundtrack of Hanks's voice from the movie *Turner & Hooch*. Hanks, watching the clip, threw back his head, roared with laughter, and then asked, "When do we start?"

Others in the voice cast were Wallace Shawn, comedian Don Rickles, and magician Penn Jillette of Penn & Teller. The role of Buzz Lightyear was voiced by Tim Allen. (Billy Crystal had originally been offered the role but turned it down—a decision he later regretted. "It was the biggest mistake I ever made in my life," he said. "Only thing I ever turned down that I felt bad about." He managed to make up for it by taking a voice role in a later Pixar film, the 2001 production *Monsters, Inc.*)

As animators worked on a character for a particular scene, they not only listened to the dialogue track but also watched videos of the voice talent reading the dialogue, reviewing the footage and the dialogue repeatedly until they had command of every nuance. Starting to work on the scene, they animated the movements of the character's body first, then added the facial animation and movements of the mouth and the lips in sync with the recording. Facial animation makes use of "pull points" that the animator creates for the facial muscles; the Woody character had eight controls for his eyebrows alone.

"John has a working knowledge of everything," said visual effects supervisor Tom Porter, who also worked as a shader. "He well knows when you can do something better" and isn't the least bit hesitant about calling on people to try again. Yet he invariably manages to give these orders in a way that makes people feel challenged instead of scolded or put down.

After Lasseter's morning visit to the animators' bullpen, he usually hustled to a screening session with the lighting team, where they scrutinized scenes that were ready—or almost ready—for final approval and transfer to film. Here, John the director became John the perfectionist at his most ardent. Changing the character of the lighting, even subtly, could reshape the mood of the entire scene, redirect the viewers' attention, or convey a different message. What did John originally want the scene to express—what story point or character revelation? Would that goal be better achieved by shifting the key light of the scene to come from *here* instead of there? Or by adding a fill light from the side? Or could the scene make an even stronger point than the one he originally had in mind?

There is no need to rebuild a set and reassemble the actors in this new world. It's one of the continuing miracles of computer-based filmmaking that these changes can be achieved with hardly more effort than the wave of a magician's wand even if there is a lot of computer horsepower behind it. The director has so many more options that he becomes a Merlin, able to reshape reality with a simple command.

A visitor to one of these sessions watched as Lasseter and his lighting team studied a scene in which the viewer looks out a window covered with raindrops. "Each drop is a lens," John coached, "and should reflect everything that's going on outside. Let's add fifty more so people won't miss the effect."

Lasseter feels that an animated film needs to convey the same sense of believability to the eye as a live-action film. That extends to the smallest details; his teams created a dozen different "filth libraries," for things such as giving baseboards in a bedroom marks that made it look scuffed by kicks from children's shoes.

Few people would ever notice, but this kind of thinking extended to camera moves as well. Layout supervisor Craig Good explained, "We tried to do what we could do on a set with real tripods and cranes. We deliberately borrowed shots from live-action directors."

All of this was done by calling on equations and algorithms stored in the computer, mathematical statements that were developed and refined over the years, some tracing their roots all the way back to the Alex Schure days and earlier, becoming more powerful but also more complex. As an example, technical director Bill Reeves explains that "It's amazing how big our shaders are. They used to be a few lines of code. Now some of them are ten to twelve pages." (A shader is a block of software that describes a surface and defines how the surface reflects and bounces light.)

Once a scene received John's final benediction, it was sent off to the "renderfarm," a factory of three hundred Sun Microsystems workstations, where the complex information for each scene is rendered into pixels, frame by frame, ready to be translated onto motion picture film. Thirty-five-millimeter film speeds through the projector of your local multiplex at the rate of 24 frames per second, and there were some 116,000 frames in the completed *Toy Story*. The rendering process can take as much as five hours for each frame of film, which explains why the Pixar renderfarm has so many computers.

While Steve had plenty of reasons to be happy about the progress being made at Pixar, his other company, NeXT, was on a roller-coaster. Steve thought he might have a solution to the problems when he managed to entice away from Microsoft Mike Slade, a marketing whiz with a spectacular success record, to pump some life into NeXT's sales as its new director of marketing. With the hard-driving Slade onboard, employee morale picked up dramatically, and so did sales, multiplying fourfold.

It's incredible to think that a fourfold leap in sales wouldn't be enough, but it wasn't. In all of 1992, NeXT sold only twenty thousand computers. If Pixar had ever sold that many, everyone would have been popping champagne corks. For NeXT, it was pathetic. Apple was selling more computers than that *every week*.

Steve wasn't in a position to pour in any more money of his own—not without jeopardizing his entire future.

By January, though, the picture was more encouraging. NeXT had reported annual sales of $140 million, and Steve was making aggressive statements: "We entered the commercial workstation market several years ago, and our market share is about half of Sun's and growing. Watch for us to continue taking market share away from Sun." In fact, the picture was only a little brighter. Steve's prediction came more from his blind, self-deceiving optimism than it did from the realities of the marketplace. The people at Canon, however, impressed by the sales increase at NeXT and not eager to see their hundred-million-dollar investment go down the drain, decided to put in another $30 million to keep the company afloat.

The promise of new money came with a demand. Canon was by now convinced that Steve was a large part of the problem and made it a condition of the new contribution that he hand over a large measure of control to a new executive of Canon's choosing. For Steve, it was a painful choice. This was almost like a replay of John Sculley taking Apple Computer away from him, but the alternative was closing the doors, throwing a lot of people out of work, and suffering humiliation from the ridicule the press would heap on him. He agreed.

No one would ever argue that Steve Jobs wasn't a nightmare to work for, from time to time. Yet his remarkable charisma, the mysterious attraction that drew people to him even when they knew he might attack at any moment, created a degree of loyalty that few executives ever match. Having a new co-chief of NeXT might have looked like a good idea on paper, from a management perspective, but it wasn't exactly a winner with the staff. Key people began to hand in their resignations. The vice president of marketing left, then the vice president of sales, then the chief of hardware—the last remaining cofounder of the company.

This ranked among Steve's darkest moments, but it was to get even worse.

Canon's $30 million was soon gone. The Japanese company poured in still more, possibly as much as another $70 million, for a total of $200 million, according to *Wired*. By 1993, Steve had to face the reality: the only way to keep NeXT afloat any longer was by shutting down the hardware business. A reporter who interviewed him when the decision became public found him "fragile, depressed, and withdrawn." Ross Perot became disillusioned with Steve's management style, bailed out, and wrote off his investment.

Steve could hardly have known at this dark moment that what remained of NeXT—the impressive NeXTStation operating system software based on the Mach kernel from Carnegie Mellon—would prove to be the springboard for his greatest triumph.

John Lasseter knew he was blessed to have the Disney tradition and experience behind him. He was good—great, even—and the Disney animated pictures had been faltering lately, but Disney was still unquestionably the industry giant, with an acquired sense of what audiences would respond to.

Still, the attitude of some of the Disney people toward their northern partner wasn't so much paternalistic as patronizing. That was reflected in remarks by animation president Peter Schneider. "We act like partners are supposed to act," Schneider said. "We look every day at what they're doing, we demand, we push, we talk," which, he insisted, led to a better product. Being Peter Schneider, he couldn't resist a dig: "Who gets the credit really is never the issue for us, although I know sometimes it is for Steve [Jobs]."

One of his fellow executives thought that Schneider was now

conflicted over a new concern about *Toy Story* and Pixar. If he had originally opposed the project and it turned out to be a success, it would make him look like a poor judge of people and of material. If it failed, he'd be just another Disney animation executive backing projects that reached the screen and couldn't find an audience.

Toy Story was John Lasseter's baby, but John knew he had to keep Schneider and Katzenberg happy. At regular intervals, John and his team assembled the rough art sketches for an upcoming scene and put them under the camera to create a crude filmed storyboard. John would hop on a flight to Burbank and play the footage for Katzenberg and Schneider, while acting out the roles and providing a running description of the action.

John respected Katzenberg for his experience and insight; Katzenberg respected Lasseter for his obvious talent and creative genius. With Steve, too, the relationship was solid, and it went beyond merely professional. Katzenberg had even developed enough respect and admiration for the Pixar CEO that he invited Steve to his home for dinner.

But now Jeffrey Katzenberg was troubled. Something about the story simply wasn't working for him. He knew what he didn't like, just not how to fix it. On a small point, when the story was dragging, Jeffrey had remarkable antennae for sensing something was wrong, and he'd spring one of his favorite lines: "They're going for popcorn"—meaning "you're boring them."

Yet what they now struggled with wasn't something small. Lasseter knew the Pixar animators were breaking new ground, achieving things no one in the field had thought possible. The work looked great. It *glowed*. He was excited about what they were achieving. But Jeffrey Katzenberg was unhappy, and it wasn't just a little popcorn problem.

The problem was one that Katzenberg couldn't put his finger on and Lasseter couldn't yet recognize, because it was so fundamental. The concept for the entire story had sprung from Lasseter's fascination with the idea of bringing toys to life through animation, a theme that had run through his award-winning demo reels at Pixar, beginning with the lamps in *Luxo Jr.*, which he had treated as playthings. Starting from there, John and his writing team had originally fashioned a story about a tin soldier left behind at a highway rest stop, and the hazards and the adventures he faced in trying to find his way home.

Screenwriter Andrew Stanton, one of the writers on the film, said that over a period of months, the writers conceived Buzz and Woody as the two main characters—Woody, the old-fashioned cowboy, and Buzz, the with-it astronaut with the spaceman's gadgets. "They would fight over who would be the favorite," Stanton said. "Then the two would get lost and have to learn to work together to get back home."

But the writing team had gone astray on the character development. Woody and Buzz needed different personalities; good drama demanded that. Their personalities or goals would have to clash—again, as required for dramatic conflict but even more as a basic element of the formula for buddy films—before they joined forces to overcome a common threat or enemy. In trying to meet those essentials, though, the writers had been too influenced by movies like *Lethal Weapon*, with its screw-you attitude of the Mel Gibson character—not exactly the right inspiration for Woody and Buzz. The script didn't convey a fun mood for an audience of children, even if their parents might enjoy the sharp-edged humor and Woody's bloated ego.

It had been an exciting landmark when Jeffrey Katzenberg allowed the picture to advance from script to production in mid-1993, but now, months later, he still wasn't happy. John kept coming back with new ideas, but none of them offered a solution to what bothered Jeffrey. Like the early Hollywood moguls, Jeffrey was incredibly astute about what audiences would connect with and warm to. He could tell you in an instant if there was a problem. The difficulty was that he couldn't tell you how to fix it.

On November 17, a date that the Pixar team came to call "Black Friday," Pixar was officially notified that the Walt Disney Company was shutting down production on *Toy Story*. The studio had decided that the script was too "juvenile," Lasseter said, and had pushed to make it "more edgy, more adult." Tom Schumacher, Disney's executive vice president of animation, accepted some of the blame on behalf of the studio. "We pushed them too far," he said. "They interpreted us wrong and made the film too abrasive. It lost a lot of its charm." Accepting some of the blame didn't help; the production was at a standstill.

Steve Jobs, once the cover boy of the computer industry, was being lambasted in the press over the problems at NeXT. Fallen heroes make great copy. Steve could expect the business press to heap ridicule on him, but that wasn't the worst part. The demise of *Toy Story* was secret and hidden in private communications, but once it was public, all pretense would be over. Steve was a failure.

The empire of Steve Jobs was in tatters and seemed unlikely ever to recover.

Ten years after the launch of the Macintosh and the dazzling *1984* Super Bowl commercial, 1994 was the year from hell for Eisner and Disney, as well as for Steve and Pixar.

An Easter ski vacation came to an abrupt and deadly ending in April with the crash of a helicopter. Frank Wells, Eisner's number two and the president of Disney, was one of the four who perished. The giant loss to Disney's leadership would not be recovered by any stopgap replacement. Frank Wells had been the quintessential go-to guy for Eisner who had given Eisner the luxury of sharing a giant portion of the burden in running the increasingly complex combination of Disney enterprises. Wells was the filter and the interpreter who allowed Eisner's raw business sense to become practical reality. Many Hollywood armchair quarterbacks believe that had Frank "the Rock" Wells survived—as some of the others had in that fateful crash—the waters of the Disney ocean would have remained calm; the company would have avoided the myriad problems that created such turmoil in the following years.

The task of finding the right man to take Frank Wells's place would prove to be far more lengthy, costly, and complex than anyone could have imagined—least of all Michael Eisner.

For months after Frank Wells's death, Eisner struggled to manage the company on his own, all the while casting about for someone with the intelligence, the drive, the knowledge, the experience, and the ability with people that Wells had had in such abundance.

One person he *didn't* consider at first was, curiously enough, a close friend: Michael Ovitz, head of the talent firm Creative Artists Agency, and one of the most powerful men in Hollywood. Ovitz had a different set of qualifications, chief among them his close ties to almost everyone of importance in town and his determined, almost cutthroat drive to put deals together to benefit his clients. He was at the top of the pyramid of agents in town.

Once Eisner started to think about Ovitz as a Wells replacement, however, he had to be subtle about negotiations. The infamous industry gossip mill could spoil any deal before it ever got to the table. In a curious sense, the dealings that Michael Eisner now entered into with Ovitz would be like a rehearsal for his later dealings with Steve Jobs. Both relationships would be badly marred by a giant clash of personalities.

In their first conversation on the subject, Ovitz responded with, "I'm ready for a change" and "We would make an unbeatable team." Eisner sensed that they'd passed a threshold. Then Ovitz floated his version of the arrangement between them: "We should be co-CEOs." Eisner immediately understood that his vision of Ovitz as a replacement of Frank Wells, as a number two instead of a co-equal, wasn't the same role that Ovitz saw for himself.

Shortly after, Eisner began to have pains that landed him in the hospital, facing immediate heart surgery. He told his wife, Jane, who should succeed him as CEO of Disney in case he wasn't able to continue after the operation. He named two men: Barry Diller, who had been chairman of Fox when Eisner was president, or Michael Ovitz. He also said that he wanted to be interred aboveground. The fear was real.

Jane called Ovitz, as a close family friend, told him about the impending surgery, and asked him to come to the hospital—Cedars Sinai in Los Angeles—to take charge and give orders as might be needed, which was understandable enough, given the emotional strain any wife would be under at such a time. After the quadruple bypass, completed without a problem, Ovitz ordered that no one be allowed at Eisner's bedside with the exception of his immediate family, his psychotherapist, and his lawyer. When Disney general counsel Sanford Litvack arrived to have a press release approved by the recovering Eisner, Ovitz—though he was not a Disney employee and had no authority to make corporate decisions—infuriated Litvack by refusing him access to Eisner. Instead, Ovitz took it upon himself to approve the release. His takeover was a help to Jane but had already sown seeds of dissent among the Disney executives that would come back to haunt him in the near future.

Steve Jobs didn't want to believe that *Toy Story* was dead. He had a contract. Disney had poured millions into the production.

In Hollywood, Steve was learning, studios from time to time shut down a troubled production. Often, they would start it back up again when the kinks were worked out. Disney wasn't happy with the script? Lean on the writers to come up with a solution.

It wasn't as if the writers weren't already trying. As usual with such things, when they found the answer, it seemed obvious. The challenge was that they couldn't change Woody's character so much that it would take away all the edginess. But they finally realized that they didn't have to. They wrote some new scenes for the early part of the picture, setting up Woody as a good guy, helpful to the other toys, generous with his efforts, and not self-absorbed. Once audiences had this positive, favorable view of Woody, they would accept his personality changes under the pressure of competing with Buzz Lightyear, who appears and challenges his leadership.

Steve was figuring out that executive blowups in Hollywood shouldn't be taken to heart. The town was filled with high-strung executives. Nothing surprising in that, when the products they dealt with cost millions of dollars, yet carried such a high chance of failure, and when they spent much of their day in conversation with temperamental directors and actors and demanding, hard-nosed attorneys, agents, and managers.

Encouraged by their new approach, the Pixar team went back to Katzenberg, who loved the new solution, gave his blessings, and lifted the production freeze. *Toy Story* was back on track—perhaps to make the reputations of the creators and the animators at Pixar or else leave them looking like a bunch of beginners and fools. They would not know which for another year and a half.

When Eisner was well enough to return to the office, searching for a number-two man stood near the top of his priority list. One name was very briefly tossed in and quickly pulled out of the hat: Jeffrey Katzenberg. During his seven years as Disney's president of production and boss of animation, he had been largely responsible for keeping the studio alive, extremely visible, and close to solvent with a series of animated masterstrokes: *The Little Mermaid, Beauty and the Beast, Aladdin,* and soon *The Lion King.* His personality style seemed to brim with self-confidence, and he was sure that he was a shoo-in for the number-two slot.

But the chemistry between Eisner and Katzenberg was wrong. Friction had been building for months between them, dating back to immediately after the helicopter accident that took Frank Wells's life. Within two days, even while funeral arrangements were still being made, Katzenberg had put the pressure on, asking for a face-to-face as soon as possible. Eisner set up a private lunch.

Katzenberg didn't bother with social niceties. As soon as the two sat down, Katzenberg unleashed an attack. "I can't believe you didn't offer me the job as president as soon as you found out about Frank's death," he said. "After eighteen years together, I've earned the right to be your partner."

Aside from Katzenberg's appalling gaffe in bringing up the topic at this point, Eisner had great reservations about his qualifications for the position, finding him "secretive" and "pursuing [his] own agenda" instead of acting for the overall good of the company. Worse, Katzenberg didn't have the support of the Disney board. Roy Disney, the only family member represented on the board, had specifically cautioned Eisner that he didn't believe Jeffrey Katzenberg to be ready for the job, and other board members had apparently expressed similar opinions.

By the end of lunch, Katzenberg had stated his outright intention to quit his job and leave the company unless he was given Frank Wells's position as president of the Walt Disney Company.

That put Michael Eisner into an extremely uncomfortable corner. He later wrote, "For Jeffrey to quit immediately after Frank's death would only prompt more media attention, compound the company's trauma, and exacerbate the sense of anxiety that our employees were already feeling." There were practical issues, as well. Over the next weeks, Disney would be opening *Beauty and the Beast* on Broadway, followed by *The Lion King* in movie theaters. "I was especially loath to lose Jeffrey before these projects were launched," Eisner wrote.

The hard-edged Jeffrey Katzenberg felt that he had earned his bones. He *deserved* the number-two slot. And he was certain that he had Michael Eisner up against the wall. Eisner, meanwhile, felt torn. "I was fed up, angry, and absolutely convinced that the only solution was to let Jeffrey quit. On another level, I still valued his strengths running our movie division."

But Eisner understood that he needed to assume the worst, and he was correct. When Katzenberg learned that he'd been passed over, he paid Eisner back by leaving in a blaze of media stories. First, there was the question of whether he quit or was fired. Then journalists delighted over the idea that Katzenberg had found a way to poke a stick in Eisner's ribs: he joined with David Geffen and Steven Spielberg to form the highest-profile new studio to open its doors in Hollywood for decades: DreamWorks SKG.

Eisner was left not only short a top executive, but with a major new competitor to bid against for "above-the-line" talent—producers, writers, directors, and actors—and a new studio to juggle against for release dates and theater screens.

Then Katzenberg demanded $250 million that he said was owed him by Disney under his contract, based on the turnaround he had achieved in the success of Disney pictures. Eisner refused. The lawsuit would drag through the courts for years. At one point, the two sides agreed on some $90 million as a compromise, but Eisner nixed the deal. That proved to be a costly decision; when the matter was finally settled, Disney paid even more than the $250 million Katzenberg had originally claimed, on top of a fortune from three years of legal fees.

Pixar's agreement with Disney had been set in place in 1991, for a picture to be released four years later. By 1994, with production back on track and only one more year to go before release, Steve Jobs should have been bursting with confidence and enthusiasm.

He wasn't. Closing down the NeXT hardware manufacturing and sales operations had relieved much of the financial pressure on that end but brought only temporary relief. By 1995, the company was in far deeper trouble. Staff bailed out, and all of the original team of NeXT founders, as well as most of the early hires, were gone. Steve surrounded himself with a new crowd of executives who were willing to be taken in by his aura and believe in his compelling visions, but none of it was enough. NeXTSTEP was dead in the water. The company had created versions that ran on the Intel 486 chip and on Sun's SPARCstations, so there was a broad target market for the NeXT software. But for all the ease of programming that object orientation promised, few customers stepped forward. The picture was growing darker and darker. Nonetheless, Steve refused to throw in the towel.

Meanwhile, Pixar was now taking in millions annually from the sale of RenderMan software, as well as the regular infusions of production funding from Disney.

Although the cash-flow crunch had eased, it was still a never-ending source of pain. Steve groused to *Fortune*'s Brent Schlender, "If I knew in 1986 how much it was going to cost to keep Pixar going, I doubt if I would have bought the company." He had done the calculations. *Toy Story* would have to bring in more money at the box office than any recent Disney film just to be a wash. Only if the film earned at least $100 million would Pixar actually make any money. Lasseter and Catmull were spectacular, but could these first-timers really turn out a picture that would out-Disney Disney?

Steve had come to understand what he so blithely had agreed to when Katzenberg insisted on keeping the merchandising revenues. If *Toy Story* were only a modest success, Steve would see barely a trickle of income from the profits, while Disney might rake in handsome revenues from the sales of toys, games, T-shirts, chocolate bars, and the rest. He was such a great negotiator, and Katzenberg had snookered him. Just thinking about it rankled Steve.

He was so distressed by Pixar's financial plight that he began to look for an out, actually making inquiries to several companies, reportedly even to Microsoft, hoping that someone would put an offer on the table so that he could at least have the option of selling out and walking away with his head held high.

He stopped looking when Michael Eisner made what was, for Steve, a monumental decision. With Eisner proclaiming it "both a spectacular movie and a lovable movie," the studio advised Steve that *Toy Story*'s release would be postponed . . . because it would be Disney's 1995 holiday release. It would not just be dropped into the fall/winter release schedule but would reap all the benefits of the Christmas holiday season, when parents become enthusiastic about discovering any movie they can take the whole family to.

Steve had won a reprieve.

8

Steve was onstage by himself and Silicon
Valley was there to pay him homage.
—Julie Pitta, *Forbes*

Icon

As the release date for *Toy Story* approached, the Pixar team tried to ignore the pressure of expectations from the drum-beating Disney promotion machine. Peter Schneider was declaiming, "In my heart, I know it's a great movie. It is really, really, really funny. And it looks so different." Eisner promised, "The technology is brilliant, the casting is inspired, and I think the story will touch a nerve." Steve was singing from the same songbook: "You've got to believe there's some truth to Disney's reputation for being hard to deal with, but we haven't experienced that. We have found that we share the same values."

In his business life, Steve Jobs was facing two doors and had no idea which one he'd be walking through. One of them led into darkness: continued failure at NeXT, the possibility of a disastrous failure for *Toy Story*, public humiliation, and quietly spending the rest of his life as—what? A venture capitalist nervously parceling out fractions of his remaining nest egg? A Zen master? A stay-at-home father?

The other door led to sunshine and cloudless skies—a world where *Toy Story* would be a smash hit, Steve would take Laurene to the Oscars, Pixar would be written about as a wonder company, and Steve could sell Pixar shares through an initial public offering that would leave him never again having to worry about money.

His business life, in other words, meant facing possible outcomes that were nothing short of extreme.

Fortunately, his private life provided solace. Steve the husband and father was a Steve no one had ever seen before—calmer and more at peace with the world. He seemed to thrive on playing with his son, Reed, and could occasionally be seen inline skating around the neighborhood with his daughter, Lisa, now a high schooler, whom he had accepted into his life. The joys of parenthood had finally softened Steve's rejection of his first child. Friends credited Laurene with the change. They welcomed the teenager into their life, and their home. At Halloween, Palo Alto neighbor Bud Bromley, escorting a covey of trick-or-treaters, watched as the kids rang the bell at the Jobs residence. The door was answered by Steve himself, carrying a child in one arm and handing out goodies to the costumed children with the other. Not candy, of course; forever the vegetarian and health-food addict, Steve had a small bottle of carrot juice for each visitor.

Laurene, while still at Stanford University working on her MBA, had started a business with a classmate, and it was thriving. Because she, too, was a vegetarian (or, at least, had been since first meeting Steve), the business was dedicated to providing gourmet natural foods to local markets. They called the company Terra Vera (supposedly for "green earth," though "true earth" is closer in the Italian that Laurene was familiar with from her time spent in Milan) and eventually managed to cadge arrangements to provide their organic salads and other healthful offerings through the neighborhood outlets of major food chains.

Laurene had put up with Steve's quirky eleven-bedroom house in Woodside when she was just a live-in girlfriend. After the wedding, she asked for something less of a nightmare to look after (who even wants to supervise the help needed to keep a 17,000-square-foot pad tidy, never mind that most of the rooms were never used?). They settled on a modest ranch-style home on Waverly Street in Palo Alto, a mile from the Stanford campus. It's the kind of community where people know the others living on their street, and where neighborhood kids are free to drop in. Many of the homes, originally built for Stanford faculty, have small yards and only two bedrooms.

Under Laurene's influence, the Jobses had begun to live like "just another family." They continue living in the same home today, despite their changes in circumstances, financially and in terms of family size.

In December 1994, Laurene found that she was pregnant again.

In 1995, Apple was in desperate straits. With the business world flocking to the latest generation of IBM PCs, enhanced with the much-improved Microsoft Windows software, Apple had continued to fall further and further behind. The company seemed trapped in a proprietary cul-de-sac, with hardware it couldn't or wouldn't price to compete with the IBM-compatible market. Apple was floundering.

John Sculley had been forced out in 1993 after Apple's market share had shrunk on his watch from 20 percent down to a feeble 8 percent. Michael Spindler, a German who had also lived in France and had done an impressive job as the head of Apple Europe, had been brought to corporate headquarters by Sculley and looked to the board members like the man of the hour when they decided that Sculley's leadership had failed. But Spindler had been the wrong man for the post.

Quiet, taciturn, a fine operational analyst, and a hard worker who frequently put in eighteen-hour days (for which he earned the nickname "the Diesel"), Spindler proved uninspired when it came to catching the consumer spirit. He wanted to direct Apple toward the big, beckoning PC market, hoping to go mano-a-mano with Microsoft for the large office and business market that Microsoft understood to perfection. In this space, only price and performance mattered. Style was almost entirely irrelevant—especially when the style didn't have an advocate like Steve, whose unique personal history and silver tongue beguiled almost everyone.

Increasingly desperate as sales stalled in 1994, Spindler put out feelers to several companies, thinking that Apple could be saved only by a white knight. Philips and Sun were intrigued, and, as sales slowed in 1995, the interest from Sun grew even stronger. While that company's main strength was the workstation business, Sun found it hard to make much money in such a specialized area. The Internet was only starting to get attention, and this new technology would ultimately energize Sun's fortunes for a time. If Sun could manage to acquire Apple, the move would instantly put the struggling firm into the public spotlight.

By the beginning of 1996, just as negotiations for selling the company to Sun had reached a delicate point, the ever-alert business reporters covering Silicon Valley picked up hints about a deal in the making. This came at the same time that Apple released a revenue report showing the company to be in terrible shape. It was all too much. CEO Scott McNealy announced that Sun was dropping its interest in Apple.

At that point, Apple looked doomed. The Apple board had seen enough of Spindler, and board members conversed among themselves about candidates for replacement. Two possibilities were already sitting at the table as board members. One was Jurgen Hintz, executive vice president of Procter & Gamble, but the thought of installing another German who might prove equally inept in the all-important area of marketing to American buyers didn't win much support among the rest of the board.

The other was Gil Amelio. A brilliant Ph.D. physicist who showed remarkable skill as a business manager, Gil at the time was the author of a new business book, *Profit from Experience*, that had just become a national best seller and been nominated in the National Business Book Awards competition.

Amelio had climbed the ladder rapidly at Rockwell International and then been named president and CEO of National Semiconductor while still in his forties, at a time when the company burned through half a billion dollars and was struggling to survive. Three years later, Amelio had shuffled the executive staff, chucked unprofitable product lines, and become a Wall Street hero by bringing the company to record-breaking profitability.

Gil had been an Apple fan from way back. In his first executive position, rescuing a troubled division of Rockwell, he'd installed Macintoshes in the executive suite while the rest of the employees were condemned to using Windows machines. When an invitation came to join the Apple board, Gil was delighted and jumped at the opportunity. Once on the board, he received a call from Steve Jobs, asking for an appointment. Steve at that point had been out of Apple for years, of course, and Gil couldn't picture what Steve would want to talk to him about. When Steve arrived, dressed in his usual scruffy clothing, he didn't take long in getting to the point: Apple needed a new CEO, and he was the company's cofounder and understood its culture and its capabilities better than anyone. "There's only one person who can rally the Apple troops," he said, "only one person who can straighten out the company." He wanted Gil to champion his cause and convince the board to award him the crown that had so far escaped his grasp, naming him CEO.

Gil was more than a little surprised at the suggestion but was willing to listen. He said, "Okay, suppose you were CEO tomorrow. What would you do? What would be the first decision you would make and why?" Steve suggested that "the world has changed, the Macintosh has outlived its usefulness, it's time to go on to something else." But when challenged about what the "something else" might be, Steve clearly had no answer. Gil decided that Steve didn't have a plan for Apple; all he had was the desire to be its leader.

In the intervening months since that go-nowhere meeting, the picture had changed dramatically. Then, Steve had been asking for the CEO's job when the job was already taken; now, the board was looking for a new CEO, and Gil Amelio was sitting right in their midst, a board member who'd already had the guts to argue that the company's problems could be solved, when almost every other board member was focused on which of the corporate suitors Apple should sell out to. With the quarterly report sitting on the table, the situation seemed too drastic to wait any longer, not even long enough for an executive search. The board asked Gil to take the job as Spindler's replacement.

For Gil, the decision wasn't easy. At National Semi, the hardest part of the turnaround had already been accomplished, and the stock options that would vest if he stayed would set him up for life. At Apple, he'd be faced with launching a turnaround from scratch, in an industry he didn't really know, of one of America's most popular and most visible companies. And the financial deal he was being offered left many uncertainties.

Yet what CEO could turn down the opportunity to run Apple Computer? At a board meeting in New York, Gil was formally offered the job, and he accepted. He served as CEO for about three months before the terms were finally settled, giving him a pay package of more than $3 million a year, a $5 million loan, and payments for the use of his own private jet that amounted to about $1,000 an hour. As generous as the

terms sound, they were in fact considerably less than he had been ver-
bally promised by the board when he agreed to take the job.

He proved to be a great business manager but an uncomfortable fit
with the renegade Apple culture, a culture that had been molded by
Steve Jobs and that, in hindsight, no other Apple CEO has ever been
able to corral successfully. Gil would hold a meeting of his top management on some pressing issue, such as two highly expensive development projects, working in competition, with no communication
between the groups and each trying to undercut the other. A decision
would be reached, and Gil would give the order—one of the groups to
be closed down, the two groups merged, or some other sensible solution. Months later, he would discover that the responsible executive had
ignored his order—the two groups would still be at work, still savaging
one another, still churning through money the same way they had in
the Apple II days when there had been money to burn. Chaos reigned
in the product-development teams and in the group developing the
company's much-needed new operating system.

Gil tried to wrest control by installing some top aides from his
National Semiconductor days; they only made matters worse by bringing authoritative, old-style, command-and-control management attitudes and making the natives more restless.

It didn't help that Gil had no experience selling to the consumer
marketplace and never found a viable advertising campaign or a successful marketing approach.

Amelio did bring in Fred Anderson, a no-nonsense chief financial
officer from ADP, the payroll company. The times called for tough
measures. The two took big charges for inventory write-downs and
restructuring and announced a painful layoff of 15 percent of the workforce; these would not be the only layoffs on Gil's abbreviated watch.

By taking hard-nosed professional management steps, Amelio
seemed to have stanched the flow of red ink. Now he could get on with
more intractable issues: getting Apple's products back on track. Meanwhile, sales continued to fall and software developers continued to press
for specifics about the long-promised next-generation operating system.

While Gil was making enormous strides in solving Apple's cash
crisis, inside the company he couldn't seem to bridge the gulf between
himself and the all-important new-product-development teams, most

of whom were young turks trying to prove their brilliance. Worse, even his top managers were routinely disloyal; when Gil decided that the inside story of the struggle to save a major company would make an invaluable business history lesson and arranged to start accumulating data for the project, his public relations people concluded that they didn't like the idea and leaked word to a *Business Week* reporter, who dutifully published the item—successfully killing the project but at the expense of publicly embarrassing their own CEO.

For Steve Jobs as well, 1995 promised to be filled with dramatic events. Laurene would give birth to their second child, *Toy Story* would open in November (God willing), and Steve was girding himself for the effort of making a Pixar IPO happen.

Steve wanted to launch the company just after the opening of *Toy Story*. He was desperate to get off the hook for endlessly bankrolling the company, and a public offering would also give him the cash he needed to resurrect his finances. If the movie proved to be a success—or even only a moderate success but generated a lot of media attention, which Steve could bank on with the power of the Disney promotion machine behind the film—the publicity for the film would draw attention to the IPO as well. He'd be riding a wave of free press worth millions of dollars. The timing seemed propitious. The people who refuse to accept conventional wisdom are more often the ones who provide the most stunning breakthroughs.

Steve, with his usual chutzpah, chose to ignore the downside. Pixar was a highly unlikely candidate for an IPO. What sensible investor would want to put money into a company that had been in business for nearly a decade but had yet to turn a profit? (Sure, in the go-go years of Internet investing that lay just ahead, pouring money into a start-up based on little more than its future expectations would be commonplace—but this was still 1995, at the very beginning of the wave.) Steve had been living with the deadening pain of failure; if nothing else, you might have thought that his Stanford M.B.A. wife would have been able to convince him that trying to arrange an IPO for a cash-starved, unprofitable company was folly.

Steve had always lived on determination and audacity. If he was often hit in the face with a wet fish for daring things that more cautious men knew better than to try, this same determination and audacity kept him afloat, still in there swinging, while more cautious types had already dropped off and crawled out of sight.

He started to look for investment bankers, knowing that he needed people who would be on the same wavelength, which meant people he could cast his spell over. He was eager to see some qualified financial worker bees start to draw up the ton of paperwork that would be needed to file an intention to sell securities to the public. And there were so many decisions to be made about how the income would be split.

Meanwhile, his home life became even more of a pleasure. To many who had watched him in his bachelor days, Steve as a family man and a devoted father seemed almost unthinkable. But to see him with Reed was to recognize a truly dedicated and loving father.

Now the family was expanding. As if he didn't already have enough on his plate, Steve and Laurene became the parents of a baby girl on August 19. They named her Erin Siena.

Steve was now forty-one, still young by most standards but no longer so trim around the middle, with a receding hairline and eyes that needed help from glasses. He should have been able to slow down. But for type A personalities, that's not in the cards. Steve was as driven as ever.

Everyone in the computer industry is familiar with product launch events that conjure up words like *lavish*, *memorable*, and *spectacular*. And annual meetings with professional actors, troupes of dancers, and laser light shows worthy of a rock concert. Steve Jobs had splurged on plenty of elaborate shows in his time.

He wasn't prepared for the spectacle Disney put on under a tent in New York's Central Park as advance work for its own upcoming *Pocahontas*, as well as *Toy Story*. Mayor Rudolph Giuliani gave the opening introductions. Michael Eisner was there, and Roy Disney, and most of the top entertainment journalists. Steve was dazzled and star-struck. He had always craved the approval of others and felt incomplete without the praise and admiration that an adoring press corps had heaped on him in earlier times. Now, suddenly, he was like an invalid who had survived a successful operation and could throw away his crutches. *Toy Story* was going to be a rousing success: the Disney people believed in it, they were talking about a big-scale promotion effort, and Steve was ecstatic.

He returned to California with new resolve. He had always let the Pixar guys run Pixar, while he focused on NeXT, where at least he understood the language, knew the players, and had a certain command of the technology. And he was still revered by the engineers and the techno-wonks at NeXT, even though they were afraid of him, terrified of encountering him in a hallway and being challenged with one of his standard attacks, like "What do you do here and why are you worth what I'm paying you?"

At Pixar he had always felt like an outsider, like some arm's-length investor who puts up the money, comes around only once in a great while to ask foolish questions that embarrass everyone, and quietly slinks away again. But no longer. Buoyed with enthusiasm from the endorsement implied by the promotional spectacle in New York, he resolved to step in and take charge.

Steve notified Ed Catmull of a change in status. Ed would still continue with all his functions but would no longer be president of Pixar. Steve was taking that title for himself, as well as chairman of the board that was being formed for the IPO. Instead of putting in appearances maybe once a month, he started to spend two or three days a week at Pixar. He commanded the presence of the top Pixar management at weekly executive sessions; this was bad enough, but he insisted that John Lasseter be there, too, which took him away from his mounting pressures as director of the movie and its chief creative force, with release of the film only months away.

Steve Jobs walks around his companies as if an invisible shield surrounds him, a shield that deflects any vibes of dislike and any symptoms of the friction he's causing. One former Pixar executive describes him tactfully as "not socially adept." John Lasseter had set the tone at Pixar, making it a place where people worked hard but felt good about themselves, the work, their coworkers, and the company.

John Lasseter is *fun* to be around. He truly likes people and cares about their feelings. Steve lashes out, sometimes even at his closest associates and friends. John gives hugs and compliments. Steve commands loyalty; John earns it.

Strangely, you almost can't help feeling sorry for Steve. He craves respect, perhaps even affection, yet is able to walk down a corridor and leave turmoil and ill will in his wake. His efforts to take charge of Pixar proved a disaster, and worse was yet to come.

A year had passed since Michael Eisner's initial testing of the waters with Michael Ovitz. The strength of the friendship between the two families had allowed doors of possibility to remain open, and the subject of Ovitz joining the House of Mouse found its way into numerous conversations. Eisner's need for help in running the giant business had become even more pressing. The previous year had seen Eisner's mammoth effort to purchase the ABC television network pay off. That acquisition alone had more than doubled the size of Disney operations, and Eisner was still handling all of Frank Wells's former responsibilities, heaped on top of his own. The pressures on him were way beyond enormous, and he felt the strain.

In August, Eisner decided to heave caution to the hurricane, follow his gut, and make an offer to Ovitz before the insidious rumor mill spoiled the chances of it happening at all. For his part, Ovitz was apprehensive about his own company getting wind of his imminent departure and causing a panic before he had a chance to tell people in his own way. Eisner had decided to offer a $1 million salary, a figure he knew Ovitz would consider chump change compared to the nearly $20 million he had been drawing from his agency. But Ovitz would, Eisner hoped, be lured by the promise of stock options based on profit performance, the same arrangement Eisner himself had. This could be vastly lucrative, enough to make up for the ownership stake in CAA that Ovitz would be walking away from, a pile of gold that Eisner understood to be valued at more than $100 million.

Eisner's main concern was whether Ovitz would be more willing than he had been the year before to take a position as second in command instead of as a co-head sharing equal power. "If the answer was a sufficiently enthusiastic yes," Eisner wrote, "I was strongly inclined to go with him."

They met in Aspen, where the two spent an entire day going over salary and stock options, duties and responsibilities, and myriad other details. Ovitz asked for time to speak to his wife. He called Eisner a short while later and said, "I'm putting myself in your hands. Let's go forward."

Eisner hung up and almost immediately put in an unfathomable call to Tony Schwartz, the writer who at the time was actively engaged in coauthoring Eisner's autobiography. The choice of confidant seems curious, but Eisner had unburdened himself to Schwartz about so many personal things that one more was perhaps understandable. Reaching the writer on the phone, Eisner blurted out, "I think I just made the biggest mistake of my career."

Later the same evening, Ovitz, done in from the day's overdose of deal-making, arrived to join his wife at their Aspen home. She asked how the day had gone. Incredibly, his response was, "I just made the biggest mistake of my career."

This was an exceedingly important decision for the two men and for the Walt Disney Company and all its stockholders, and both men, immediately after the decision was made, concluded that it was disastrously wrong. Yet both felt bound by the strength of their personal friendship and their business values to honor the commitment they had made to each other.

"I just made the biggest mistake of my career" was the smartest thing they had both said all day.

Any Steve Jobs friend or employee who violate the principal of loyalty, Steve Jobs version, may find himself excluded from Steve's circle and his companionship for a very long time. He has been known to relent, though the healing process may take years.

Steve's sister, Mona Simpson, continued to live in Beverly Hills with her husband and child, while teaching one term a year at Bard College, on the Hudson River about two hours' drive north of New York City. In October 1996, Random House brought out her latest novel, *A Regular Guy*. In this one, she posed new challenges for herself: she had written in a more traditional narrative style, third person instead of first. Where the previous two works had been heavily autobiographical, this one was based on her view of someone else.

The central character is Tom Owens, a college dropout who gets a girlfriend pregnant and then refuses to acknowledge the child as his. He starts a biotech company that turns into a roaring, multimillion-dollar success but won't help the ex-girlfriend who is struggling to raise his daughter. He's ultimately pushed out of his own company by business types whom he himself brought in. Emotionally, he's trapped in his own narrow concerns and largely closed off from the people around him. And he lives in a couple of rooms of a nearly barren mansion. When his daughter shows up on his doorstep one day, he admits her into his life. As the girl builds relationships with some of the people around him, he becomes more open and accepting, and he eventually marries and builds a family life.

The opening line is a grabber: "He was a man too busy to flush toilets."

For many people who knew Steve Jobs well, the book read like a painful exposé of Mona's brother. Journalist Steve Lohr sat down a few months later to interview Steve for a profile in the *New York Times Magazine*. This was a period in his life when Steve had been extremely uncomfortable about media interviews. Toughened journalists quaked at asking him questions, having heard stories of how he had blown up or gone to pieces in front of one of their peers. Nonetheless, Lohr dived in. He later described the moment in his article, first pointing out that "given the similarities between Tom Owens and Steve Jobs, most of the book's reviewers have mentioned the Simpson-Jobs family tie. . . . It would be hard not to notice."

Lohr asked the difficult question: how much of himself did Steve see in the character in his sister's book? "About 25 percent of it is totally me, right down to the mannerisms," Steve admitted. He quickly added, "And I'm certainly not telling you which 25 percent."

The journalist followed up by asking whether Jobs felt "exploited or betrayed."

Steve gave a dismissive wave. "Of course not," he said. "It's a novel."

According to Alan Deutschman in *The Second Coming of Steve Jobs*, a writer working on a story contacted Mona, who said that although Steve continued to call now and then, he had almost completely broken off the relationship with her because of the book. Whether or not that source was reliable, Mona Simpson now denies she ever said this. She insists that the report that Steve had broken off with her because of the book "is totally wrong and untrue." This is backed up by her editor at Knopf, Gary Fisketjon, who says he "has never heard such a statement."

. . .

Gil Amelio saw a new, updated operating system as a key element to Apple regaining market share against Windows machines, but he finally gave up hope that the in-house development group would ever arrive at a finished product. In desperation, he and his chief technology officer, Ellen Hancock, started to make overtures to Sun in hopes of licensing its software as the basis for a new generation of Apple machines.

Then a different suggestion was brought to Gil. If Apple had to go outside the company for an operating system, at least he should talk to Jean-Louis Gassée. Under Sculley, Gassée moved from being marketing director to become head of Macintosh development. Gassée was a perfectionist, however, unable to let go of a project until he was fully satisfied, which on one project after another had begun to seem to Sculley like "never." The usually soft-spoken Sculley and this hot-tempered Frenchman clashed often and loudly in battles that became Silicon Valley legend.

Sculley finally showed Gassée the door. Jean-Louis may have thought that a blessing. Using the $1.7 million severance that Sculley arranged and bringing in outside investors, Jean-Louis was able to start his own software company, Be, Inc., which focused on developing an alternative operating system to run on Macintosh hardware. Fitted out with several innovative features, it was the darling of the cognoscenti but, like Jean-Louis's projects at Apple, never seemed to reach a state where the company was able to launch it as a major product. In the six years he had been running the company, he had shipped very little and taken in only a pittance of sales revenue. Even so, his software was far enough along to serve as the basis for a project that could be brought into Apple and finished quickly.

Gil was under pressure to sign a deal before the upcoming 1997 MacWorld Expo in January, so that he would have a realistic answer—and, he hoped, a realistic release date—to offer to shareholders and the Apple faithful.

Meanwhile, Bill Gates had thrown his hat into the ring. He besieged Gil with daily phone calls, arguing that Windows NT could be converted to become the new Apple operating system and insisting that "I'll put hundreds of people on the project" to get it done quickly. Of course, Gates wanted something in return—not just cash but something much bigger. "Apple is really good at the human interface. Much better than we are," he admitted. Gates hoped to use the promise of an operating system solution that Gil so desperately needed as a wedge to coerce Gil into signing the intellectual property agreement Gates had been angling for. In Gil's phrase that would "give Microsoft Windows the same charm that the Macintosh operating system had."

The offer from Gates made a certain kind of sense, yet Gil knew that any deal with Microsoft would inflame the passions of Apple loyalists and employees, as well as of many shareholders; Microsoft was the enemy, and a deal with Gates would be seen as a sell-out.

One day Ellen Hancock received a phone call. She remembers that the caller said, "I hear you're looking for an operating system." The guy on the other end of the phone was an engineer working for Steve Jobs at NeXT. Ellen chose a team of her engineers and sent them over. They made several trips, and the reports were favorable. In fact, Gil had been wanting to talk to Steve about whether his NeXTSTEP software might be a viable option for Apple but had been unsure about reaching out to him.

Finally, the NeXT engineers broke the news to their boss, Steve Jobs, that they were in conversations with Apple. For Steve, this had to be stunning news. His mind must have been spinning with the possibilities.

The idea of licensing the Sun software was still on the table, while negotiations with Be, Inc. dragged on through October and November. At one point, Jean-Louis flew to Hawaii where Gil was attending an Apple sales force meeting, just to be able to sit down with Gil and plead his case. Gil was leaning toward Jean-Louis's software, called "BeOS," as the best technological solution. When Gil asked about price, Jean-Louis replied, "Money doesn't matter to me. I don't get involved with price," and suggested that he would accept whatever price was deemed fair.

The story of Gassée's meeting with Gil was leaked to the press. Gil was sure that Jean-Louis was the source of the leak, suspecting it to be an attempt to force his hand. But it did something else. There was no one in the technology business Steve Jobs hated more than Jean-Louis Gassée, the man who had ratted on his plans to Sculley. If ever Steve needed a reason to swallow his pride, Apple's impending purchase of BeOS was it.

By the time he showed up in the first week of December, Steve had prepared his ammunition. Meeting with Gil and Ellen, he launched into a pitch that was Steve Jobs at his best. At some of the most challenging moments in his business life, he gives the impression that he has done no preparation and has not bothered with any rehearsals because he simply doesn't need them. He speaks with the fluency of someone in total command of his subject, the passion of someone totally committed, and exactly the right control over his listeners' emotions. It's a remarkable performance, so convincing that you could listen for an hour without interrupting, so compelling that you wonder whether he might not have had an amazingly successful career as another Jack Nicholson or Jeff Bridges.

That day, he started out by giving the reasons why the Be operating system would be a disaster for Apple and then, almost as an afterthought, slipped into his main theme: "If you think there's something for you in NeXT, I'll structure any kind of deal you want—license the software, sell you the company, whatever you want." Then came the main pitch: "When you take a close look, you'll decide you want more than my software. You'll want to buy the whole company and take all the people." Gil promised to have an Apple technical team get together with counterparts at NeXT.

The truth was that the companies of both Steve and Jean-Louis had good software but were sinking fast. Both men were desperately hoping that Gil Amelio and Apple would throw them a lifeline and save them from drowning.

Nonetheless, Jean-Louis, who had proclaimed no interest in the money, sent in an offer to sell his company in exchange for shares representing 15 percent of Apple. Gil did a little mental arithmetic: the figure came to about $500 million. He called Jean-Louis and said, "You have zero sales, you've got an operating system that's three years away from any reality, and you want 15 percent of the company. That's not in the cards. That's not even within the realm of possibilities." Jean-Louis eventually came down to $275 million, still more than Gil was willing to pay for BeOS. The Frenchman's holdout was calculated. Ellen said that Jean-Louis had told her, "I don't think you have any other options."

Gil had Ellen assemble panels of in-house experts to evaluate the pluses and minuses of using software from each of the four contenders—Microsoft, Sun, Be, and NeXT. One team member, an

Apple senior software engineer, said that the process was confused. "Doug Solomon [senior vice president of corporate development] thought he was in charge, Ellen Hancock thought she was, Gil was playing a role, different people were calling meetings. The whole process was a little bizarre." That doesn't seem surprising, given the pressure Amelio was applying to get a decision made quickly.

The evaluation teams drew up two sets of parameters for measuring each solution. Their analyses showed that while Jean-Louis's software was already capable of running on the Macintosh, it had a number of shortcomings. For one thing, every time the software needed to be updated, every third-party developer would have to update its applications simultaneously, which would be unacceptable to the developers; for another, the operating system had no provisions for supporting complex language systems such as Japanese, Chinese, or Korean—a basic requirement, given Apple's sales in the Far East. On the scoring system the technical teams had devised, Steve Jobs's NeXTSTEP won handily, by a score of 184 to 146. Gil's own evaluation had brought him to the same conclusion.

The final decision was too important and involved too much money for Gil to be comfortable making it alone. He invited Steve and Jean-Louis each to appear before the entire Apple executive team and make their case. The sessions were held on December 10 at the Garden Court hotel in Palo Alto, in hopes of avoiding the reporters, who had been having a field day with the story.

Steve Jobs went first, and again was brilliant and compelling. "Pragmatic, specific, and precise," Gil later called it. Then he handed off to Avie Tevanian, his top technical guru. Tevanian had brought along a laptop to demonstrate that NeXTSTEP was not just an idea in progress but a functioning operating system. The two of them put on a gold-star presentation.

They were followed by Jean-Louis, who either misunderstood that this was a shoot-out and his final opportunity or was so certain of a decision in his favor that he didn't think he had to do anything more than show up. He arrived alone, empty-handed, and not prepared to do anything much more than answer questions. Gil wrote later that "everything pointed toward Steve Jobs and NeXT, but Jean-Louis had made it a no-contest. The vote for NeXT was almost a foregone conclusion." (Some insiders thought that Gassée's software would have been the better solution. Looking back from the perspective of all these years, Jean-Louis disagrees, insisting that Gil's final decision was the correct one. But this may be the seasoned judgment of a man sensibly unwilling to flagellate himself for past actions. "I'm way past being critical," Jean-Louis says.)

Gil needed to talk numbers with Steve but had to do it out of sight of enquiring eyes. They met at Steve's home, and Steve made tea for them. The first number Steve put on the table was $12 a share. Gil wrote later, "That was high, but I was figuring, 'We're picking up an existing operating system, we're picking up $50 million a year in additional revenues from NeXT sales, we're picking up WebObjects, *and* I'm getting a team of about 300 very talented people. All of these were things I wouldn't have gotten in a deal with Jean-Louis; this was obviously worth more—but how *much* more?'"

The due-diligence calculations had been run; Gil knew what they showed the company was worth, but in a strategic situation like this, when the acquisition is critical to the future of the company, "the price is largely irrelevant." He had in mind that even an additional $100 million "would represent only three days of sales for Apple."

He told Steve, "I think I have a shot at convincing the board to take $10. I don't think I can get a penny more than that." Steve agreed.

Within a week, the board approved the purchase of NeXT for $377.5 million in cash and 1.5 million Apple shares. The cash went to pay back investors. The shares were all Steve's. Gil designated Steve as a "special adviser" and, in hopes of restoring some of the pizzazz, glory, and enthusiasm of the company's earliest days, convinced Woz to accept a similar honorary position at the same time.

But while Amelio breathed a sigh of relief and thought that he had crafted a way to give Apple momentum again, the story was much more complicated.

By December 1996, Michael Ovitz had been the number-two executive of the Walt Disney Company for fourteen months. Fourteen *ugly* months. Perhaps there would have been some solace for Eisner if he could have seen his struggles with Ovitz as an opportunity to learn lessons he could use profitably in the struggles he would soon face with

Steve Jobs. But that would have required uncommon foresight. As it was, Eisner was too busy running Disney and contending with the Ovitz wars to look for lessons in it all.

Michael Ovitz's well-deserved and undisputed reputation as a power titan in Hollywood, which had initially seemed such an attraction, carried with it the seeds of a growing aggravation. Here was a man who had spent twelve years getting used to being in charge as the CEO of his own immensely successful company. He was completely unaccustomed to the political gamesmanship and etiquette needed to work beneath a top man. His proven track record was built on his ability to get things done, and it was universally known that he had his own distinct way of going about that.

Early on, Eisner praised Ovitz as being "professional, attractive, and competent." In a 1995 letter to board members and stockholders, Eisner wrote, "His coming to Disney was a great coup for us and a saving grace for me. Everybody is excited being with him, enjoying his energy and knowledge, sense of humor and enthusiasm." Less than a year later, an e-mail to a studio public relations chief found Eisner labeling Ovitz a "psychopath," "totally incompetent," and "untrustworthy to everybody." What happened?

The love-hate relationship grew out of control exponentially as Eisner and Ovitz turned high-level executive misunderstanding into a new Olympic event. From the start, other executives at Disney saw Ovitz as an out-of-control locomotive and tried to avoid being run over. Eisner invited Steve Bollenbach, Disney's chief financial officer, and general counsel Sandy Litvack over to his house to meet Ovitz on the eve of Ovitz's starting day. Bollenbach offered his congratulations and then shook Ovitz to the core by saying, "And by the way, I'm not reporting to you. I'm reporting to Michael Eisner." Litvack chimed in with his agreement to that surprising sentiment. Ovitz was stunned—Eisner had made it clear that both of these men would report to him. Now they had refused, and Eisner wasn't insisting. He was letting them rebel. The explanation was simple: both cherished their working relationship directly with Eisner and knew of Ovitz's reputation for being difficult. Eisner clearly considered them too valuable to risk losing.

Ovitz was seemingly on a steroid pump from the starting gate. On his first day at Disney, he suggested building a private staircase to allow easier access from his offices to Eisner's. The stair-building notion was vetoed by Eisner. Ovitz next threw a $90,000 meet-and-greet soiree to impress the Hollywood community and to flaunt the Hollywood muscle he would be bringing to the Disney table. Ovitz defended the outrageous party cost as "a bargain." He launched construction of a new multimillion-dollar office for himself and his staff. According to *Variety*, in little over a year he ran through "roughly $6 million in random expenses," which represents a fairly liberal attitude toward petty cash.

Outlandish gift-giving, rumors of possible Disney stock information told out of school, no-shows to appointments, and arriving late at scheduled company meetings of the top executive staff—and that was just in the first few weeks.

Ovitz made internal Disney enemies at an alarming rate. One by one, all of these new enemies reported the infractions of company policy and the perceived insults to Eisner. As his best friend, Eisner went the extra mile to watch Ovitz's back, but that job very quickly became an overbearing task. He wrote later, "Every day was managing Michael Ovitz. I did nothing else."

Eisner thought he saw a solution to his pain and frustration. Ovitz was involved in negotiations with Sony, and the Sony people were obviously impressed with him. Eisner tried to convince Ovitz that he should offer himself to run Sony's U.S. operations. Ovitz, of course, recognized this was just a gambit to get rid of him, and didn't fall for it.

At last, desperately employing the fine arts of avoidance and delegation simultaneously, Eisner sent Sanford Litvack to inform Ovitz that he was being terminated. Ovitz refused to believe the hapless messenger and told him, "Sandy, you're going to have to *pull* me out of here. I'm not leaving."

On December 12, in New York for the holidays, Eisner handed a press release to Ovitz. It announced Ovitz's departure from Disney "by mutual consent." In the original contract terms, Eisner had recognized that Ovitz would be walking away from that $20 million annual income he'd received from his agency business and had included a "what if" provision in case the job at Disney didn't work out. No one ever expected the provision to be of consequence, but now it was.

It provided that if Ovitz left Disney, except if being terminated "for cause"—fraud, embezzlement, or the like—Ovitz would be entitled to a severance payment of $140 million. That's a vast sum of money, especially when paid for *not* working. But that was the agreement, and Disney paid up.

These former best friends never dreamed that the gory details of their business fracas would end up in lengthy tell-all sessions documented in thousands of pages of a court reporter's transcript of a trial held in 2004 in a Delaware courtroom, 2,500 miles from Tinseltown.

In Steve's own phrase, having handed Apple to "a bozo once before," now that he was back, he was determined to make his presence felt and rescue the company from the brink of disaster where it had been teetering.

Looking back years later, he would describe his life view not in business terms but as a creator, the vision he wanted to hold of himself. "One of my role models is Bob Dylan. As I grew up, I learned the lyrics to all his songs and watched him never stand still. If you look at the artists, if they get really good, it always occurs to them at some point that they can do this one thing for the rest of their lives, and they can be really successful to the outside world."

But the young man as artist is always in some ways at war with the young man inside. The moment of recognizing that he can be successful is also "the moment that an artist really decides who he or she is. If they keep on risking failure, they're still artists. Dylan and Picasso were always risking failure."

That lesson was now rooted deep within Steve. "The Apple thing is that way for me. I don't want to fail, of course. But even though I didn't know how bad things really were, I still had a lot to think about before I said 'yes' [to becoming part of Apple again, even only as a 'special adviser']. I had to consider the implications for my family, for my reputation. I decided that I didn't really care, because this is what I want to do. If I try my best and fail, well, I tried my best."

From a young age, Steve had recognized his own uncanny flair for computer design. Whenever he looked at other people's computers, he saw clunky square boxes with unappealing colors and massive monitors. Driven to break away from those boring, distressing, styleless shapes, Steve had made the Apple II a wedge, with the box molded out of high-quality plastic and distinctive. The Macintosh was the next product stamped with his indelible sense of design—an amalgam of cool, surprise, elegance, and wit. Ditto for the NeXT cube. They might not have been as functional as they should have been, they might have been aggressively nonconformist, but they always had a distinctive, spectacular look.

"We don't have a way to talk about this kind of thing," Steve said. "In most people's vocabularies, 'design' means veneer. It is interior decorating. It's the fabric of the curtains and the sofa. But to me, nothing could be further from the meaning of design. Design is the fundamental soul of a man-made creation that ends up expressing itself in successive outer layers of the product or service."

Still, it was vastly more than design that he sensed lacking at the Apple he had returned to. The fire had gone out. "It was much worse than I could imagine. The people had been told they were losers for so long, they were on the verge of giving up. The first six months were very bleak, and at times I got close to throwing in the towel, too."

Through various CEOs, Apple had attempted an on-again, off-again quest to gain a foothold in the business market, envious of what looked like Microsoft's easy success, where one sale could mean hundreds or even thousands of products.

Apple couldn't compete when the bottom line was price and performance and when style was irrelevant—as it was in the standard office market. Apple could sell when a consumer was willing to pay a bit more to be different, to look cool, to feel the thrill of belonging to an elite with a certain status, or to gain the advantage of ease of use. Apple was a company with two superb, serious business sectors: graphics and desktop publishing, where the LaserPrinter (which Steve had championed over nearly everyone's objections) and page-layout software from Aldus had turned the Mac's fortunes around in the years after he was ousted. But its other market was the consumer, and there the firm had lost its way.

Within a month of his return, Steve's key lieutenants from NeXT were in charge of software—in the hands of NeXTSTEP architect Avie Tevanian—as well as hardware.

As the NeXT crew carried out its putsch—that's what it was, though few people at Apple yet recognized the handwriting on the wall, least of all Gil Amelio—things grew worse. Gil had allowed himself to remain surrounded by executives who were part of the problem and a board of directors with very little consumer computing experience.

When revenue numbers were toted up for the 1997 fiscal year in the summer of that year, sales had fallen to $7 billion and losses were over $1 billion. It was just the opening Steve had been waiting for. So many times in the past he had coldly refused to show loyalty to his closest friends; why should he now show any loyalty to Gil Amelio, merely because Gil had brought him back into the company he loved?

Steve Jobs has maintained an arm's-length relationship with most reporters. Basically, he seems to mistrust anyone who uses words for a living, an attitude that was shaped in the crucible of experience. Yes, the press has often been extremely laudatory; it's the media that made Steve into the rock star of high tech. But the press has been painfully unkind as well. It's easy to say that this is the price of being a public figure; just because the statement carries a great deal of truth doesn't make it any less difficult to bear the stinging words.

So Steve responded by giving interviews and stories only on his own terms and even walking out of an interview or a TV appearance when his ground rules were broken. A few reporters, though—a very few—earned Steve's trust and respect, and one of these was Brent Schlender of *Fortune*, who has built his success in part on being able to form strong connections with industry leaders such as John Chambers, Michael Dell, Bill Gates, and Andy Grove.

Gil Amelio never formed the degree of connection with Schlender that Steve Jobs had. When Schlender wrote a major story on Apple for the February 1997 issue of *Fortune*, he didn't see Gil's successes in cleaning up past mistakes, writing off unsalable inventory, and arranging loans to keep the company operating—necessary steps on the rocky road to recovery. What Schlender focused on were the problems.

The title alone told the story: "Something's Rotten in Cupertino." The article was more than a litany of complaints against Gil and his management style. Schlender told *Fortune* readers that there was salvation for Apple: Steve Jobs was waiting in the wings.

Steve couldn't have asked for better ammunition. The article laid the groundwork; Steve knew how to make the most of the opportunity. An ailment that might be called "board of director's impatience" also came into play. Ellen Hancock—Gil's chief technology officer, who now serves on the board of major companies such as Colgate-Palmolive and EDS—finds that boards of troubled companies have a tendency not to give the CEOs enough time to solve the problems. "Even when most signs point to the company being on its way back to good health, the board may be impatient and turn out the CEO."

Both of these factors probably helped fan the flames. The arsonist in the case, though, was Steve himself, and the kindling he used was board member Ed Woolard, who was then the chairman of DuPont and had earlier served on the board of IBM. That Gil had personally recruited Woolard to the Apple board made little difference now. According to a source close to the situation, "Steve went to work on Ed Woolard and convinced him to lead a revolt, which he did. He convinced a majority of the board that they were all going to be sued if they didn't make the change." Apparently, the Damocles sword of a lawsuit wasn't an idle threat; the same source believes that Steve had already obtained an agreement from his billionaire friend Larry Ellison to sue the board and its members if they didn't turn Gil out. Ellison dropped hints to a reporter that he was considering a hostile takeover bid for Apple. The strategy, and Woolard's wooing of his fellow members, won the day. Mike Markkula and Del Lewis held out for letting Gil finish the job he had started, the insider says, but three other outside members agreed to cast their votes with Woolard.

In July 1997, Gil received a call from Woolard, who said he was calling "with bad news." Woolard went on, "You've done a lot to help the company, but the sales haven't rebounded. We think you need to step down." Gil sensed that a discussion was futile but pointed out that the company had "just finished a quarter with results that were better than the analysts' predictions." He asked, "You want me to step down just when things are beginning to look better!?"

Woolard answered, "We want to find a CEO who can be a great marketing and sales leader for the company." But, of course, they had already "found" him; the description was tailor-made to fit Steve Jobs.

Steve was the first person who called when Gil returned from his July Fourth holiday. Was he offering condolences or gloating? Gil was never sure.

When Gil had taken the job as Apple CEO, he told the board that he would need three years to bring the company back to health. Now the board had fired him after a year and a half. Gil later regretted that he had not put a three-year "no fire" clause into the terms of his contract.

Many people inside the company and out were glad to see Gil leave Apple. Some in the press derided the national best seller *On the Firing Line* that he wrote about his Apple experience, attacking it as representing only Gil's own point of view—as if any autobiography could be expected to do anything else. Few people seem to take note of the most significant fact of Gil Amelio's reign at Apple: when he took over, the company had enough money in the bank to survive for three months; when he departed, he left a legacy of $3 billion dollars in cash—a bankroll that allowed Steve to keep the company in business while he tinkered.

Now applying his own loyalty principle in the opposite direction, Steve apparently recognized how his gigantic disloyalty had damaged the reputation and the stature of the very man who had rescued NeXT from oblivion, made Steve wealthy again, and given him the foothold within Apple that had allowed him the platform to position himself for the takeover. Recognizing how disloyal he had been toward Gil, Steve became cool and distant, as if afraid that Gil's own sense of loyalty would make him vengeful. Sometimes Steve could show an uncanny reading of other people; sometimes he could be blind.

Deep down, even from the very beginning, Steve had felt certain that he could run Apple as the company's CEO. No one could argue that he had no claim to justify the desire—he had been the driving force that got the company started. Steve Wozniak had been essential, but he was no entrepreneur.

Finally, thirteen years after being summarily thrown out of his own company, Steve Jobs was back—and not just back, but with a vengeance, as chief executive. His first suggestion was to re-price stock options so that staff morale would improve; his second, to make everyone in the company work to a bonus that was stock-related so the whole crew would pull together.

One of Steve's first calls was to Bill Gates, who had been negotiating with Gil for months. Only an alliance with the most important company in the technology world could quickly shore up Apple's fortunes. Steve knew just what Gates and Microsoft wanted: an agreement that would allow Microsoft to design a user interface like Apple's—the very item Gates had been harassing Gil about for eighteen months, that Gil recognized would be a giveaway and would deprive Apple of its most significant differentiation from the clumsy Microsoft operating system. Steve signed away Apple's most precious intellectual property, without blinking, so that he would be able to appear onstage in early August at another MacWorld Expo with Gates at his side, garnering praise from the media for settling an old dispute. But at what cost! The deal called for Microsoft to invest $150 million in Apple, and to continue to update and sell Microsoft Office productivity programs for the Macintosh platform for the foreseeable future. It also called for Apple to adopt the Microsoft Internet Explorer Web browser as its default program for accessing the Web, installing it on all Macintosh machines sold. Steve had a deeper understanding of the realities of the situation than almost anyone: without Microsoft's support, Apple would be a cul-de-sac with no way to operate in a Microsoft-dominated world. He had to bide his time by keeping Gates on his side.

The crowd at the Boston MacWorld in the summer of 1997 booed the announcement.

Steve understood the power of ownership. He had no interest in being on the payroll; in fact, the grown-up Steve Jobs rarely accepted paychecks from any of his companies. His salary at Apple would be $1 a year, and his title was "Interim CEO," while the board half-heartedly engaged a search firm to hunt for a permanent replacement.

For years, the company had been run by a series of outsiders, none of them ever able to get control of the Apple culture. The one person who might be able to was the one person most responsible for the company's dysfunctional culture: its cofounder, Steve Jobs.

He set out on an egalitarian remake of Apple. No more business-class travel. No more sabbaticals. No more special severance deals for executives. Everybody in the company (except Steve, of course) was going to be in the same boat.

He found that the board wouldn't go along with his ideas. No problem—he was chairman of the board, he could remedy the problem easily. Steve was able to get most of the board of directors to resign within weeks, even the oldest hand who'd been around from the very beginning, Mike Markkula. As replacements, Steve brought in a couple of old friends: Larry Ellison and his one-time vice president of sales, "the coach" Bill Campbell.

Steve's business life was now undergoing a resurgence. With his return to Apple the previous year as its interim CEO, he was busy remaking the company. Gil Amelio, before his ouster, had been busy slashing products and product lines as part of the effort to return the company to profitability. Steve slashed even more vigorously. On another front, he tackled the culture.

People who are called to Washington by the president to join his cabinet as the Secretary of Whatever discover that one of their biggest challenges lies in trying to goose the bureaucracy into action. The civil servants have outlasted a series of secretaries of their department, they know they'll still be there when this one leaves, and there's a compelling tendency to think that they have a clearer long-term vision than the boss does. Apple CEOs had struggled with a similar kind of "we know better than you" unwillingness to cooperate. The Apple executives, managers, and troops in the trenches had made a fine art of the press leak. Don't like that the CEO is going to chop off your project? Slip some confidential details to that pal who's been cultivating you—Julie at *USA Today* or Peter at *Business Week* or Brent at *Fortune*—and maybe they'll put something in print that embarrasses the CEO and makes him change his mind.

Steve quickly saw lots of things he didn't like. His predecessors in the CEO's office had never figured out how to take the reins in a commanding manner. When Steve Jobs sets his mind to a task, you had better join him or get out of the way. He set about changing the culture of Apple. Some of the changes were small (no dogs at work, no smoking), and some were whoppers, such as an absolute ban on talking to anyone outside the company who uses words as a tool of his trade. (The one exception: it was okay as long as you had a public relations dog-watcher sitting at your side and yanking your leash whenever she wanted you to stop talking.)

These new edicts were laid on top of the aura of fear Steve carried with him like a dark cloud. You didn't want to be called in front of him to do a product presentation because he might decide to lop off the product, and you with it. You didn't want to encounter him in a hallway because he might not like an answer you gave and would say something so demeaning that it could undermine your confidence for weeks. And you sure as hell didn't want to get trapped on an elevator with him because by the time the doors opened, you might not have a job. Some Apple-ites took to walking the stairs to avoid the possibility of an elevator encounter.

It would be easy to call this a reign of terror, but the fact is that the company began to turn around. Steve's two most trusted technologists from NeXT were holding down top positions—Avie Tevanian running software and the brilliant Cornell engineer Jon Rubinstein running hardware. The new Apple billboards, spare and stunning, with a simple message of "Think Different," sprang up everywhere, even painted on the sides of buildings, announcing a fresh start for the company. They boosted employee morale. It didn't matter that the phrase was gratingly ungrammatical; maybe that was even part of its charm.

Steve was back. He seemed to know what was going on in every corner of the company. He was getting Apple back on track.

Five months after his coup, Steve appeared at the January 1998 MacWorld in San Francisco to give his traditional lengthy but absorbing keynote speech. At the very end, pretending he was finished but then returning to the microphone, he added as if just a footnote, "I almost forgot. We're profitable."

The MacWorld audience had never adored Steve more than they adored him at this triumphal moment. Back only months and already he had made their beloved Apple profitable again!

In truth, of course, no one turns a giant company around in half a year. Almost all of the credit for the recovery belonged to Gil Amelio, but he would get none of the praise, not from this audience and not from the press. He was already forgotten. His accomplishments in rescuing the company would be buried deep, covered over, and ignored. Steve was once again basking in someone else's sunshine.

These days Steve shows no embarrassment for his double-dealing with Gil. But then, Steve has never been famous for showing warmth even to his close friends.

·   ·   ·

A gambling man would have been driven mad by the signs and the countersigns pointing in opposite directions about how *Toy Story* would fare with audiences. Michael Ovitz was bad-mouthing the picture all around town and to every Disney exec who would listen, predicting disastrous box office. On the other hand, it had been a pet project of Jeffrey Katzenberg's and Katzenberg was in disgrace at Disney, so to many people Ovitz's dire predictions sounded biased and petty.

Then a near-final version of the picture was run for a random, sneak-preview audience, and the reaction started a small panic. Maybe Ovitz was right, after all. While the viewers had warmed to the picture as the story unfolded, the first big laugh moment was greeted with silence. A chagrined John Lasseter set his writing crew to work on figuring out something that would captivate the audience from the start.

Still, within the Disney hierarchy there were a few who thought *Toy Story* would win the hearts of audiences, among them Dick Cook, the studio's marketing chief. He put together a promotion budget that astounded Steve, John, and Ed Catmull—reportedly, a whopping $100 million.

A hundred million! More than three times what it had cost to produce the picture!

But with the studio sending out distinctly conflicting messages, it was hard to know whom to believe or what to expect.

All the uncertainty was soon to be resolved. The *Toy Story* premiere was held on a Wednesday, the day before Thanksgiving in 1995, at the lavish 1920s movie palace the El Capitan Theater on Hollywood Boulevard. A Hollywood premiere—even one held at midday—is a thing of legend, like stepping into the pages of *Vanity Fair*. Yet this one was a remarkably casual affair. Tom Hanks, the voice of Woody, looking almost overdressed compared to the rest of the crowd, came in a sports jacket over a plain white T-shirt. Buzz Lightyear's Tim Allen wore the Hollywood uniform of black leather jacket over a black shirt. Michael Eisner looked as if he had specially dressed down for the occasion as he sauntered by looking just a bit rumpled, the ultimate in nonchalance, in a blue-gray golfing shirt, his hands thrust in his pockets.

At the end of the picture, as the credits started to roll, the audience applauded enthusiastically. But what did that really mean? This was an industry audience, by nature inclined to be polite and encouraging even if everyone hated the movie.

The Pixar team walked around in a daze until the reviews started to appear. The *Washington Post* Style section piled on the praise: "Must-see, must-talk-about, must-plan-to-see-again." It doesn't get much better than that. *Variety*, the industry newspaper that's so important because it's read by everyone in Hollywood and therefore shapes opinions that can affect people's careers, offered a prediction that made pulses race in Emeryville: "The film sports a provocative and appealing story that's every bit the equal of this technical achievement. It's a hard-to-beat combination that will translate into bountiful box office returns and provide [Disney] with a whole new stream of animated product with mass-market appeal."

By the time those reviews appeared, Steve Jobs had held his own premiere. For the occasion, he rented the Regency, a San Francisco movie theater that was a throwback to the elaborate movie palaces of the thirties and forties. He invited old friends, associates, and a who's-who of high-tech movers, shakers, and CEOs. In what seemed like a reversal of roles for the infamously casual Steve, the invitations said "creative black tie." Quite a few people dressed formally, but some took the phrase as an invitation to show their in-your-face response to the suggestion that Steve, who hardly ever showed up anywhere in anything but his standard uniform of black T-shirt, jeans, and New Balance running shoes, could expect them to get dressed up.

Steve surprised them all by putting on a tuxedo, offset by what one observer described as "a beige silk waistcoat." In fact, he and Laurene looked like the kind of Hollywood beautiful people whom the paparazzi stalk. She was magnificent in a classic, simple black evening dress, her blond hair hanging down her back, her skin tanned and glowing, as radiant as any supermodel. She's brilliant besides. It was enough to make any of the high-tech billionaires in the crowd sick with envy.

Ed Catmull took the risk of inviting his one-time closest companion, the man who had been his sidekick in laying the groundwork that made *Toy Story* possible: Alvy Ray Smith, who came to share in the moment despite his still painful animosity toward Steve Jobs.

Along with the rest of the audience, Alvy got a full dose of the Jobsian behavior that had made him flee the company. When the screening was over, Steve took the stage. A reporter who was there, Julie Pitta of *Forbes*, described the moment to author Alan Deutschman: "This was Steve's return to center stage and, my, did he hog it. Steve was onstage by himself, and Silicon Valley was there to pay him homage. He was not going to share the stage with John Lasseter, who was kept very much in the background."

It was easy to ridicule Steve. But at that moment, he became what he had always imagined for himself, what he had once been, in his cover-boy days, but had lost.

Steve Jobs was an *icon*.

PART THREE

Defining the Future

9

I think Pixar has the opportunity to be the
next Disney—not replace Disney—but be
the next Disney.
—Steve Jobs

Mogul

In the late fall of 1995, as the Pixar IPO approached, Steve had
once again helped to set a pattern, even though he couldn't
have known it at the time. Pixar was about to become part of the initial wave that would turn into a flood of speculative investing that we
now look back on—in most cases, with regret—as the dot-com boom.

When Steve had first gone knocking on doors looking for an investment firm to lead his IPO, the bankers all but laughed in his face.
Investors only want companies that are making money, he was told.
You first have to show a record of successful profit-making years and
stable management.

All very sensible, the accepted wisdom of every reputable investment banker.

Except that just a few months earlier, a company called Netscape
Communications had managed to break the rules. (In one of those
small-world coincidences that seem to occur with unaccountable
frequency, the company founder, Jim Clark, had worked briefly for
Alvy Ray Smith and Ed Catmull as part of the original pre-Pixar computer graphics team on Long Island.) Netscape had been in business
for a year, offering a software product that allowed people to connect to

the still-not-much-understood universe of the Internet. It had never shown a profit, yet in that overheated environment somehow the business press saw a unique potential. Writers vied with one another to describe an ever brighter potential future for the company, which caused a clamor for the stock. Trading opened at $28, and by the time the exchanges closed at the end of the first day, the price had doubled. Jim Clark's holding was worth half a billion dollars.

Numbers like those caused some of the more aggressive investment bankers to see an opportunity. Steve's instinct led him to shift his focus. Instead of going with one of the prestigious, big-name New York City firms, ever the hands-on manager he decided to work with a local outfit that would allow him to keep a close eye on the progress. He asked around and chose the San Francisco–based Robertson Stephens, which describes itself as "a boutique investment firm."

The success of this IPO could shape Steve's whole future. He didn't want to make a bad choice, so he talked to some institutional investors, asking them whether they'd be wary of becoming involved in the IPO if the lead firm were Robertson Stephens instead of, say, Goldman Sachs & Co. He was reassured. "All of them said the West Coast guys would be as good. And half preferred it, because [the California firms] treat them better," he said. Robertson Stephens was delighted to get the business, with company chairman Sanford Robertson noting that "the New York firms have always come in and just skimmed the cream off the top, taking only the very best offerings." Not this time.

Steve made their work easier, in no small part because of his instinct about the timing. By scheduling the IPO just a week after the *Toy Story* opening, Steve wouldn't have to rely on the usual dog-and-pony show, in which the executives of the company travel to major cities across the United States in hopes of convincing local stockbrokers and investment firms to talk up the company to their customers. Instead, he would be riding on the coattails of the massive Disney publicity campaign. Every investor in the country would be bombarded with the Pixar name just at the opportune moment.

The IPO took place on the last Tuesday of November 1995, one week to the day after the *Toy Story* opening. In the early hours of the morning a select few of the top Pixar team showed up at the offices of Robertson

Stephens in downtown San Francisco. Trading was due to begin in Pixar—symbol PIXR—on NASDAQ at 7:00 A.M. West Coast time. The firm had set up arrangements in their trading room so that the Pixar visitors could witness the scene firsthand.

Former Pixar executive Pam Kerwin says, "Robertson Stephens was in a magnificent building on Market Street." She recalls that the group included Ed Catmull, chief financial officer Larry Levy, John Lasseter, Ralph Guggenheim, and Bill Reeves. "Steve was late but he raced in just in time."

The stock had been set to begin trading at $22. Steve's financial advisers had argued for the $12 to $14 range. Steve knew that the lower price would mean less money to Pixar—once the initial shares have been sold, any further price increases put money in the pockets of the traders and the speculators, and the company wouldn't directly benefit. He insisted on the higher price, and when Steve makes up his mind, he sucks the air out of the room and arguing is futile if not dangerous. Twenty-two dollars it was.

The higher price represented a significant risk. Maybe investors would figure that a no-profit company just wasn't worth that much. If any shares being offered remained unsold by the end of the day, Steve would be faced with humiliation and a small catastrophe. The failure to sell all the shares would scare investors, who would start to sell, driving the price down.

Steve Jobs certainly had a mixed record in judging the market; the failure of the NeXT computers was all the proof anyone needed. This time, though, he was dead right. Exactly at seven o'clock, the ticker showed active trading in PIXR.

The Pixar group sat watching the rows of traders at their computers. "There were some who were specifically handling our early stock sales," Pam says, "and they would gesture to each other as soon as each offer came in. So we could see and hear everything as the stock rose in price."

Those moments are still vivid in her memory: "The Pixar team, who had been struggling to survive for over ten years by then, was euphoric—everyone privately multiplying their stock options by the current price to determine their net worth. We all had a toast with Steve's favorite Odwalla carrot juice to celebrate."

By the end of the first half hour the stock was trading at $49. PIXR had more than doubled its opening price.

Suddenly Steve Jobs had, on paper, what entrepreneurs and executives—at least, those in Silicon Valley—affectionately call f—k-you money: enough that you never have to worry about what anybody else thinks. Not that Steve had ever spent much time worrying about that, except in the case of the few people he envied for their financial muscle, like Bill Gates, Warren Buffett, and Larry Ellison.

By the end of the day, the price had settled back to a slightly less impressive but still fantastic $39.

Steve Jobs was a billionaire.

Attorney Lawrence Levy, who had joined Pixar as its CFO and had helped to lead the way to the initial public offering, had a paper profit of $62 million at the end of the first day. He was thirty-six years old.

Attorney Larry Sonsini had become a buddy of Steve's and had accepted a place on Pixar's board. His firm was Wilson, Sonsini, a preeminent law firm in Silicon Valley and favored by high-tech start-up entrepreneurs through the go-go years. Steve's Los Angeles entertainment attorney Skip Brittenham, who had also become a friend, was another who accepted a seat on the board. Both held stock options that became worth more than $1.1 million as a result of the single day's trading.

Within the company, four men were blessed by the IPO but not through Steve's willing generosity. Disney had originally insisted that these four be harnessed to long-term arrangements with Pixar, so that if *Toy Story* proved to be successful, the creative team would be locked in to work on the other pictures covered by the Disney contract. In exchange for their commitment, each of the four—Ed Catmull, John Lasseter, Ralph Guggenheim, and technical director Bill Reeves—had been given a participation deal that cut them in on a small share of profits from the movies. But in making arrangements for the IPO, Steve learned that the participation deals wouldn't fly—investors don't accept the idea that employees are dipping into profits that should go to stockholders.

Steve was burned up at the idea, but he had to find something that would induce the four to waive their profit participation. The worst part was that he didn't have much of a negotiating position. He *had* to get their agreement. When the deal was finally worked out, Steve, with thirty million shares, still owned a whopping 75 percent of the company's stock, but he had been forced to give up control over a good many more shares than he had wanted to. John Lasseter alone was worth $31 million at the end of that first day.

Still, the four suffered from conflicting emotions. Steve had been less than generous with the rest of the company, and there were long faces, accompanied by plenty of grousing, in the hallways. A few people were suddenly, unaccountably rich, and everyone else, even people who had been with the company for years, felt left out in the cold. Steve has been criticized harshly for being tight-fisted about this, when he could so easily have shown appreciation for his employees' loyalty and incredibly long hours.

One former executive, who had left well before anyone started talking about an IPO, disagreed. "Steve was writing checks out of his personal checkbook to keep everybody employed. So it seems to me a little shallow [for employees] to say, 'I didn't get my share.' I don't know that anybody was led to believe they were going to get more stock than they did." As with any other company, he said, you knew when you were hired whether you were getting any options, how many, and when they would vest. It was all spelled out in writing in your employment agreement.

He said, "We live in a world where everybody says, 'It's unfair— somebody gotten more than me.'"

Sure, some other CEO might have been more generous, but, as this ex-executive pointed out, "Steve had been pouring money into Pixar every month. Even long after there had seemed any hope of ever recovering his investment." On two different occasions, Fortune 500 companies had stepped up, checkbooks in hand, offering to buy Pixar. Neither offered as much as Steve had already invested. He can be painfully stubborn, so stubborn that he will go against his own best interests. A more reasonable man would have cut his losses, been glad to get what he could, and gotten out while he still had some money left. Both times, Steve had refused.

Now his stubbornness had paid off. "He gambled," the former executive said. "He put $50 or $60 million into Pixar. The gamble paid off. Some of those employees had options worth in the hundreds of thousands of dollars.

"Can you really blame Steve if he didn't feel like giving them more stock than they had agreed on when they were hired?"

On Pixar's initial day of trading, 11.7 million of its shares had changed hands, making it the second most active IPO in NASDAQ history. Together, the Netscape and Pixar IPOs helped to launch a new way of thinking, an attitude that said, Don't look at profits, look at potential. During the roughly five years of the dot-com boom, from 1995 to 2000, stock prices raged out of control, fueled by venture capital firms and stock brokerage houses that created this pipe dream and sold it to the investing public.

The go-go philosophy wasn't yet entrenched at the time of the Pixar IPO. Within a week, Pixar's stock price dropped back to $28.50 a share, only a tad above the opening price and well below what most investors had paid. The market rogues who call themselves the Motley Fools in 1998 described the situation in plain terms: "Getting up early to make a purchase in the first hour of the first day of trading could guarantee a bad day, or even a couple of bad years. Three years ago, Pixar Animation Studios . . . had its IPO during the week following the release of *Toy Story*. . . . Pixar shares were trading at $25 within a week, and sank to $12 within a year. It took more than two years and the recent smash release of *A Bug's Life* for Pixar shares to return to the price at which they traded on their first day."

Steve wasn't a billionaire then, though the "almost" category is close enough for most purposes. In any case, he had been one long enough to make a point with Larry Ellison and Bill Gates: Larry, the long-time friend who looked up to Steve and who yearned to have his stage presence and charisma, but whom Steve had envied for his riches, and Bill Gates, his long-time rival. Steve had seemed to hold the attitude that Gates didn't deserve all that success. Now it didn't matter so much any more. Or did it?

The harsh reality of the motion picture business is the unpredictability of the product. Unlike, say, a new piece of furniture, the next generation of personal computer, or a new line of cookware, each new movie is like reinventing the wheel. It doesn't matter who the stars are or the track record of the writer and the director; it doesn't matter that the sneak preview audiences loved the film (or didn't like some aspect, which was subsequently fixed by last-minute reshooting). None of that provides any guarantees. Screenwriter William Goldman summed it all up with a line that has become famous in Hollywood: "Nobody knows anything."

Steve Jobs soon had plenty to smile about. It was as if he had put one bet on the roulette table and been paid off twice. Not only had he joined the ranks of the super-rich from the IPO, but *Toy Story* was a stunning success—the kind of success that in Hollywood turns players into princes. On the opening weekend, theater box offices across the United States took in $29 million, virtually equal to the cost of producing the movie. The picture went on to become the highest-grossing release of the year, eventually bringing in more than $350 million worldwide, plus another $100 million in video rentals.

Steve Jobs had always been a tough-as-nails negotiator, capable of being ruthless, at times almost vicious, in his determination to win. When he had originally sat down with Jeffrey Katzenberg to hammer out the terms of the Disney-Pixar deal, he had dressed in a cloak of bravado but was hanging on to his companies by his fingernails. He was an M&M negotiator—tough on the outside but soft and yielding underneath the shell.

Yet Steve never considered a deal set in stone, no matter how intricate the contract was or how many signatures were affixed to the last page. Chipmaker Rick Shriner and his venture capitalist Gordy Campbell at VLSI had found that out when Apple summarily canceled their company's multimillion-dollar contract to develop high-speed chips for the Macintosh; it had cost them a fortune in legal fees to force Apple to relent and pay up. Now Steve was ready to throw another contract into the wastebasket: the one with Disney.

From his perspective, the cards had been shuffled and redealt. With *Toy Story* a box-office smash, he now held a winning hand. In addition, he was now CEO and chairman of a company with a capitalization of a billion and a half dollars and was personally sitting on hundreds of millions of dollars in Pixar stock. The bargaining positions had changed.

Steve called Michael Eisner and said that they needed to talk. When Eisner found out what Steve wanted to talk about, he was stunned. They had a contract! The terms were set! And who was this young man, this Hollywood outsider, this novice in the movie business in which Eisner had worked all his years, who seemed to want to be treated as an *equal?*

Steve Jobs held the upper hand: he owned the rough-cut but brilliant diamond called John Lasseter. Eisner knew what a treasure that was. Barring some catastrophe, John's talent would only grow, and the movies he would create would bring in hundreds of millions of dollars. Billions, even.

Jobs and Eisner, though from very different worlds, are remarkably alike. Both scraped their way to the top of the heap, both are blessed with great intelligence and unusual insight, both have an instinct for business and for handling people that borders on the extraordinary, both value loyalty as one of the most treasured character traits of the people around them, both have on occasion been incredibly vindictive to people they felt had proven themselves unworthy of continued trust, both are capable of ruthlessly cutting off a long-term associate whom they decide has proven himself or herself unworthy. (Once, when one of his executives came in to tell Eisner that he was leaving to take another position, the Disney CEO said, "I'll never speak to you again." He was not kidding. Encountering the man in a restaurant, Eisner looked right through him as if he were invisible. Of course, it didn't help that the executive had been recruited by archenemy Katzenberg.)

Now, emboldened by the success of *Toy Story*, Steve laid three demands on the table. First, Pixar was to have sole creative control over the movies it produced for Disney—no more running to Burbank for reviews of concepts, characters, story, scenes, and petty details.

The next point turned on Steve's vision of the Pixar name as a brand that could support the sale of a wide range of consumer items, similar to the Disney retail stores—and Disney was selling consumer products to the tune of some $10 billion a year. Imagine if Pixar could do even half of that. A third of it. More money than they would ever make from movie ticket sales.

So Steve's second point was a stab at making the public more conscious of the Pixar brand. He insisted that on all movies, DVD packages, fast-food chain tie-ins, toys, and other products, the Pixar logo be the same size as the Disney logo. This may seem like a small item—how often are any of us consciously aware of the branding on a toy, a game, or a taco wrapper? But with millions upon millions of exposures per year, the name begins to sear itself into the public consciousness. Steve, with his innate business acumen, had looked into the distant future and saw billions of dollars flowing into Pixar from a *side business.*

If those first two demands were difficult for Eisner, the third was a stunner: Steve wanted all revenues from Pixar movies to be shared fifty-fifty between Disney and Pixar.

Steve Jobs and Michael Eisner are both capable of giving way to anger. Both are master negotiators who know how to spot the other guy's weaknesses and take advantage of them. The entire culture of the Walt Disney Company was founded on the notion that if you wanted to do business with Disney, you were agreeing to do things the Disney way, with no discussions about what was "fair."

Yet Michael Eisner capitulated. One of the most powerful men in Hollywood gave in, not because of Steve Jobs and his bargaining power but because of John Lasseter. Taking a smaller share of the Pixar revenues would be better than pissing off Steve and having him run out his contract and then go find another studio to distribute his movies. The hated Jeffrey Katzenberg would surely offer a tempting deal to get Pixar away from Michael Eisner. That was too painful a possibility for Eisner to contemplate.

The new contract covered seven films in total: *Toy Story*, *Toy Story 2*, *A Bug's Life*, and four more films to be determined. Disney would still control the rights to make sequels, but Pixar would start to participate in the merchandising money. In an industry where many A-list producers settle for a meager 15 percent share of box office revenues, Steve would get 50 percent. Onetime Pixar marketing executive and close Steve Jobs associate Pam Kerwin says that Steve "enabled us to negotiate as equals." She credits this bargaining triumph to Steve's "brains, energy, and chutzpah."

Even before the *Toy Story* premiere, animators who finished work on their part of the project had been pulled off and set to work on the initial phases for the sequel, *Toy Story 2*. It seems curious now, looking back, but this was planned to be a direct-to-video production, a decision governed strictly by financial motives. That rubbed against the culture of Pixar. Ed Catmull explains, "*Toy Story 2* was the defining moment for the studio. We had started off making the movie for video instead of theatrical release, but realized halfway into it that we'd created a two-tier studio. And that," he acknowledged, "was not good for our souls.

"Nine months before it was to be delivered, we basically threw it away. We redid the whole movie even though we were told it was too late, but we did it anyway because it wasn't good enough. [Because of the intense time pressure] we had people who had repetitive stress injuries, one permanently. After that, I thought to myself, 'We can't run a company this way.'"

Instead, Pixar shifted gears and moved up the next film on the schedule, *A Bug's Life*. It was finished in time for the 1998 holiday season, and once again Disney opened the picture just before Thanksgiving. To everyone's great relief, *Bug's* gave the much-hoped-for proof that *Toy Story* hadn't been a fluke. The picture broke the box-office record for the Thanksgiving holiday, earning some $46.5 million and knocking off the pedestal the previous record-holder for that period: Pixar's own *Toy Story*.

In the short time between its opening and the end of the year, *A Bug's Life* became the highest-earning animated film of 1998. *Toy Story* had won two Oscar nominations for music and one for the screenplay, and the Academy had presented John Lasseter with a well-deserved special achievement award for "his inspired leadership of the Pixar *Toy Story* team, resulting in the first feature-length computer-animated film." *A Bug's Life* added to the studio's list with one more Oscar nomination in the music category.

Helped once again by hype for the movie and with two other films already in the works, Pixar's stock soared throughout the year, at one point breaking through $60 a share. Steve's 73 percent stake put him back among the exalted again. His holdings were worth $1.4 billion. And in May, his third child with Laurene was born; they named her Eve.

Yet Steve's detractors never seem to disappear. At the same time that *A Bug's Life* was opening and everything in Steve's life seemed so rosy, *Business Week* ran a story by Peter Burrows and Ronald Grover crediting Steve with being sweeping, bold, and audacious, but saying that "many in Hollywood think Jobs is living in Fantasyland. The industry's cognoscenti consider the computer exec another movie-industry wannabe, and Pixar, they say, acts as little more than a well-paid subcontractor to Disney." They denigrated Pixar's achievements: "While Disney has built its reputation over 70 years with gobs of talent and billions of dollars, Pixar has made all of two feature films so far."

Just as newspapers prepare obituaries in advance so that they can be ready for the death of anyone great or famous, it sounded as if *Business Week* was preparing its obit that would run to commemorate (or celebrate?) the end of Steve's business life.

When does a manager's insistence on attention to detail cross the line to become a compulsive focus on minutia?

Time magazine writer Michael Krantz, who followed Steve around Pixar one day, began his article this way: "It's 3:00 P.M. in Richmond, Calif., and Steve Jobs is micromanaging." Scrutinizing "the endless promotional arcana" for *Toy Story 2* and "perusing the timeline like a rabbi studying Talmud," Steve rattled off challenges about when the TV ads would start, what the plans were for theme-park events, when he would be able to review the billboards, and which television news-magazine shows they should aim for.

If the movie has an incredibly big opening weekend, he wanted to know, would Disney consider delaying the date when their retail stores will replace the *Toy Story* displays with items for Christmas? A Disney senior vice president sitting nearby tactfully explained that Snow White and Winnie the Pooh drew such big business that they would help sell Buzz and Woody. With a sigh, Steve acknowledged the reality of that marketing wisdom. "Yeah," he agreed. "Pooh is huge."

Without a way of exercising Jobsian control over the creative activities, at least he could benefit his own company with his proven talents in marketing.

In the late 1990s, the women of the Jobs family were acquitting themselves admirably. Steve's daughter with Chris-Ann, who was now using the name Lisa Brennan-Jobs, was growing into an impressively accomplished young woman, despite her fatherless early years. The Jobs intellectual genes seem to have been passed along. Lisa spent her college days in Cambridge, Massachusetts, earning her undergraduate degree at Harvard.

Steve's love of music had obviously been passed along as well, which added to his pleasure in her. Lisa tried her hand at songwriting and also did some singing. At one Silicon Valley charity concert, she fronted a band that included Merl Saunders, legendary among Deadheads for the album he recorded with Jerry Garcia. Slender, with long blond hair, Lisa didn't bear any particular resemblance to Steve, but her name alone was enough to cause a stir in the crowd of people with high-tech connections. Her song selection for the event could have been a headline for what her father was now accomplishing: Tracy Chapman's "Talkin' 'bout a Revolution." It was an amateur's performance, but well enough received.

Steve's wife, Laurene, was winning applause of a different kind. She had turned out to be the sort of woman whom other women like to be around but tend to be jealous of. Besides her attractive looks and athletic build (even after bearing three children), she has keen intelligence and wide interests and, as the wife of Steve Jobs, is, of course, obscenely rich. More than that, she's one of those admirable mothers who doesn't believe that being a good mom means you have to be a stay-at-home mom.

With no need to work for money and having already proved her ability to get a start-up off the ground with the natural foods business, Laurene was following the notion that some of America's founding fathers had sought to instill in their children: once a family's money needs have been taken care of, donate your time, skills, and energy to serving the public good. In 1997, she founded College Track, a non-profit that set up afterschool programs to prepare at-risk high school students for college. Later, she took over as its president.

Laurene put her business school knowledge to work in accepting a friend's request to join the board of a San Mateo company called Achieva, which provided online tools to help middle school and high school students improve their study skills. She remained a valuable board member until Achieva was sold a few years later to Kaplan Inc., an educational provider owned by the Washington Post Company.

The Jobses also threw their backing behind various Democratic candidates and causes and became friendly with the Clintons. In October 1997, they received one of those dream invitations that every socialite, social climber, and hanger-on aspires to: after a sizable contribution to the Democratic Party, they were invited to a state dinner at the White House in honor of Chinese president Jiang Zemin, and were guests of the Clintons overnight, reportedly staying in the Lincoln bedroom.

"You must come have dinner with us some time" isn't quite reciprocal in exchange for a state dinner at the White House, but the Jobses did their best a couple of years later with a dinner party at their Woodside home for the president and Hillary. Laurene corraled Michael Chiarello, owner and chef of the renowned Napa Valley restaurant Tra Vigne, but threw him a difficult challenge: he had to prepare a gourmet meal with an all-vegan menu, and was instructed to cook the vegetables as little as possible. (One prominent industrialist who had eaten a characteristically vegan, mostly raw, dinner at Steve's home said afterward that it was fine as long as you left early enough to find a restaurant still open.)

When Chelsea Clinton was a student at Stanford University, President Bill Clinton and the First Lady had a standing invitation to use the Jobs's unoccupied Woodside mansion, which they did on occasion. The political connections and handsome donations to the party led to Laurene becoming a delegate to the Democratic National Convention in 2000, the one at which Al Gore became the party's nominee. Later, when Arnold Schwarzenegger ran for election to become governor of California as a Republican, Laurene threw a luncheon political reception for Steve Westly, the Democrat who was running simultaneously to become the state's controller. A former vice chairman of the Democratic Central Committee for California, Westly is seen as a likely future candidate for state governor and for high national elective office. While Schwarzenegger's movie-star popularity was enough to provide an easy election, it wasn't enough to carry the whole Republican slate into office. Steve Westly won his bid to be controller.

Steve Jobs has a history of picking winners. On this round, Laurene showed she could do it, too.

By this time, Jeffrey Katzenberg was well ensconced at DreamWorks, where he was fiercely determined to establish an animation kingdom that would clearly outshine not just Pixar but Disney in particular.

A Disney executive who has worked closely with Katzenberg said, "The first thing you need to know about Jeffrey is that he knows very little about anything. He's a quick learner and he's learned a lot about motion pictures from experience, but he doesn't seem to be in touch with a broad range of knowledge. It always amazed me that he would approach subjects so naively." He is a man of enormous self-esteem, this executive said, and "one of the people I least understood in life." In meetings with the top Disney people, Katzenberg would say things like, "If the people in this room ran General Motors, think how much better it would be." The statements were so outlandish that "they would drive Eisner slightly crazy and he'd say something like 'Jeffrey—*please!*'"

John Lasseter felt that he had developed a friendship with Katzenberg, remembering how Jeffrey had championed *Toy Story*. "He's the one who had believed in us when we wanted to be up here [near San Francisco] making movies for Disney," Lasseter recalls. So Lasseter wanted to keep in touch after Katzenberg left Disney for DreamWorks.

At one point in the fall of 1995, when John was in the early stages of thinking about *A Bug's Life*, he and screenwriter Andrew Stanton dropped in on Jeffrey and regaled him with some of the story ideas. "We told him all about *Bug's*," says Lasseter.

Jeffrey proved to be an enthusiastic listener, encouraging John with questions and drawing him out. He asked about the release date. John told him the picture was scheduled to be another holiday release, to open just before Thanksgiving.

John Lasseter's conversation was, to say the least, ill advised. It wasn't that Jeffrey didn't return John's feelings of friendship; he probably did view John as a friend. But there was another, stronger element at work that John could not have been aware of. According to the ex-Disney executive, Michael Eisner had taught Jeffrey Katzenberg the daunting power of information, and Jeffrey had learned the lessons well. Information, Eisner believes, is a weapon to discover opportunities and identify weaknesses in what your competitors are doing and then use the knowledge to beat the competition at its own game.

Once Eisner sat in on a weekly meeting of the Disney Sunday Movie team. A public relations staffer related that she had a friend, an executive at another studio, who had mentioned that he was working on a similar project. Eisner asked her a question about the other project. The woman said that her friend hadn't shared that information. Eisner looked at her and said, "Have you slept with him yet?" He told her, "I don't care how you do it, you've got to get that information." The woman did not seem offended by Eisner's admonition, but the moment underscored his attitude that information is king.

On another occasion, Eisner generated gales of laughter from a group of his executives with a tale of how he and a colleague had once climbed over the fence onto the Universal lot to do some scouting. They were spotted and chased by guard dogs, narrowly escaping back over the fence in the nick of time.

These two stories, each from the source who heard it firsthand, illustrate the ruthless thirst for information that Jeffrey Katzenberg had learned at Michael Eisner's knee. So, to Katzenberg, what he did after pumping Lasseter about *A Bug's Life* wasn't violating a friendship; it was simply doing business.

For a few years, an idea had been bouncing around Hollywood for an animated film that would be a twist on Aesop's fable about the ant and the grasshopper.

Not long after the John Lasseter visit, DreamWorks purchased a 40 percent interest in Pacific Data Images (PDI), a pioneering animation house in San Francisco that was struggling.

The story came out later that Katzenberg told PDI he would do a deal with them that would include an infusion of cash and a contract to produce an animated film only on condition that they could complete the film and get it into release before *A Bug's Life* came out. The PDI film was to be developed from the ant-and-grasshopper idea: Katzenberg was undercutting his friend Lasseter by pitting one insect film against another—and making sure that *his* would be the first to reach theater screens.

An industry executive who worked with Katzenberg over a number of years doesn't see anything particularly unexpected or even malicious in this behavior. "Jeffrey was very strategic about those kinds of things," the executive says. "He could look at two competing projects with the same idea, and he would absolutely, religiously not be willing to be the second one to enter the marketplace. He would make that strategy perfectly clear to everybody [working on his project]: 'It is absolutely essential to us in doing this film that we be first.'

"And that was the case with *Antz*. His decision to make *Antz* was that he would make it *only* if he could make it before *Bug's Life*. That kind of strategic thinking is one of the things Jeffrey was very good at." The executive added, "He probably has a history of sour relationships [from how he has played this game]."

This time around, Katzenberg capped his beat-the-competition strategy by assembling an all-star cast for the voices. The list included Jennifer Lopez, Sharon Stone, Danny Glover, Gene Hackman, Dan Aykroyd, and Anne Bancroft. Katzenberg even talked one of the industry's most hard-to-get talents into taking part. The voice of the lead ant, Z, was voiced by the inimitable Woody Allen.

Antz opened on October 2, 1998, a full six weeks before Pixar's *A Bug's Life*. By the time *Bug's* reached theaters, *Antz* had already taken in $84 million.

John Lasseter and Steve Jobs had the last laugh. John had once again performed incredible magic. When the box office records were assembled at the end of the year, *Antz* had grossed $87 million, a paltry sum when compared to the Pixar film's gross of $114 million. By the end of January, an industry newsletter noted that *A Bug's Life* had already crossed the $150 million mark to become the fourth-biggest-grossing animated feature of all time.

A year later, the revised *Toy Story 2* was ready. Ed Catmull bragged, "We made *Toy Story 2* in nine months, when it usually takes four years to create an animated feature. I'm very proud of that." But moviegoers wouldn't care about record-breaking production time. Working on such a compressed timetable, had Pixar stumbled at last and turned out a bomb?

No way. Audiences couldn't wait to spend more time with Woody and Buzz Lightyear and the rest of the toys. People lined up on the sidewalks and filled every seat. On its opening weekend, *Antz* made $17 million, *Toy Story 2* an astounding $57 million on the single weekend and $80 million in the initial five days, breaking the previous records for an animated film that had been set only a year earlier by *A Bug's Life*. The numbers put it into a rarefied class with the fourth-biggest opening weekend of any film ever, following *Star Wars*, *Jurassic Park*, and *Independence Day*.

It's accepted wisdom in Hollywood that sequels don't do as much business as the original. *Toy Story 2* became the first animated sequel ever to outdraw its predecessor. Children begged to see it again and again.

Pixar had turned out three hugely successful movies in a row—one a year for three years. To some people, that put Jobs in a class with George Lucas and Steven Spielberg. With success comes leverage; Steve had acquired a big stick.

In Hollywood, awards go to the filmmakers; acclaim goes to the director and also to the producer and the head of the studio. Steve Jobs had acquired the mantle of a movie industry giant. He was a veritable mogul.

Tinseltown buzzed with anticipation about how he might use his new leverage.

Steve had taken no salary from NeXT through the early years, until after his marriage. At Pixar, he had taken $50 in some years; in others, nothing at all. Even at Apple, after it returned to profitability and the company could have afforded a handsome stipend for its CEO, he explained his salary by saying it was only so that he would qualify for the medical plan. The board regularly pressed him to accept a large bundle of Apple shares; he always refused. One writer calculated that with the gain in Apple's stock price, Steve had walked away from as much as $1 billion in profit.

"Steve Jobs, Capitalist"? The label doesn't seem to fit. In fact, it's laughable. Yet Steve had clearly made the distinction between being on salary and being an owner. It was almost as if accepting a salary was distasteful to him, something his adopted father, Paul Jobs, had had to do that Steve did not want to repeat.

In January 2000, the Apple board finally won Steve over. This was following nine successive profitable quarters, and the board felt generous. Apple board member Ed Woolard said in a statement, "Apple's market [capitalization] has risen from less than $2 billion to over $16 billion under Steve's leadership since his return to the company two and a half years ago." Woolard's statement went on to announce that the board was bestowing two items on Steve in gratitude. The first was options on ten million shares of Apple stock, with a value at the time of $870 million. The other was worth a tenth as much in dollar value but much more in the delightful sense of being so practical: a Gulfstream V corporate jet aircraft, a plane that can carry up to twenty passengers (though it's usually equipped to carry only eight), cruises at Mach 0.8—80 percent of the speed of sound, about 500 knots—and carries enough fuel to fly from San Francisco to London nonstop. This was not a company airplane that would be provided for his use but a personal gift to Steve. Apple also picked up the tab for the personal income tax that Steve would otherwise have had to pay for this elaborate present. In all, the price tag to the company added up to about $90 million.

Some observers saw this shift—from continually declining the board's offers to suddenly accepting not just options and salary but the phenomenally generous gift of the airplane—as a fundamental change in Steve's attitude. It was said that he moved from the unassuming small office he had chosen for himself to the CEO's suite with a view of the mountains that Gil Amelio had used, and that he resumed his practice of parking in a handicapped parking space. And that in interviews with journalists he again became petulant, arrogant, and insulting. He was a creature of contradiction.

With the release of *Monsters, Inc.* in 2001, Pixar entered a new mode and a new era. For the first time, John Lasseter passed the role of director on to other hands—Peter Docter, David Silverman, and Lee Unkrich—leaving the probably correct impression that it took three people to do what John had been doing single-handedly. The Hollywood rumor mill was buzzing over the question of whether Pixar might have become too much, too soon—overextending itself and undermining the quality of the product.

The doubters were silenced at the beginning of November. *Monsters, Inc.* broke through $100 million at the box office in its first nine days, the fastest ever for an animated film. The picture earned three Oscar nominations, including best animated feature, on its way to become the third-highest-grossing animated feature ever.

Four in a row, four huge, record-setting winners at the box office, acclaimed by critics and audiences. Jeffrey Katzenberg had laid claim to "owning" animation. If anyone merited the title of owning animation, it wasn't Jeffrey Katzenberg.

Steve Jobs said, "I think Pixar has the opportunity to be the next Disney." A few years earlier, it would have sounded like more Stevian smoke and mirrors.

Yet perhaps "the next Disney" was too modest. The media would soon report that Pixar, breaking through $2.5 billion in earnings, had become the most successful Hollywood studio of all time.

Steve Jobs had stamped his mark on two of the world's most prominent industries. And he wasn't done yet.

10

Breaking New Ground

Casting about for a new role that would set Apple apart, Steve came to see that getting an Internet angle for the Macintosh needed to be a top priority. As he surveyed the ruins of Apple, he realized that he had to catch the Internet wave among consumers. Since the beginning, Apple had touted its ease of use; it wasn't much of a leap to combine that ease of use with the Internet. The company had to deliver a new kind of consumer computer.

He envisioned a product that would catch the currents of public interest and captivate people with radical design. "Computers are still awful," he groused. "They're too complicated and don't do what you really want them to do—or do those things as well as they could. We have a long way to go. People are still making automobiles after nearly 100 years. Telephones have been around a long time, but even so, the cellular revolution was pretty exciting." Steve didn't see enough innovation in his industry. "My purpose in coming back to Apple was that our industry was in a coma. It reminded me of Detroit in the '70s, when American cars were boats on wheels." He was absolutely sure that Apple had a good chance to be a serious player again if only he could graft the ease of use and the elegance of the Macintosh to the freedom of the Internet.

. . .

Steve took up Gil Amelio's drive to fix the waste in development, neglecting to mention that the effort wasn't one that he himself had started. "We've reviewed the road map of new products and axed more than 70 percent of them," he said, "keeping the 30 percent that were gems." In fact, Amelio had laid out a plan to cut 80 percent of the development projects and was already well along with cleaning the house when Steve took over.

An all-out program to create a new low-end consumer Mac was another effort Steve also took credit for, explaining that "we have a lot of customers, and we have a lot of research into our installed base. We also watch industry trends pretty carefully. But in the end, for something this complicated, it's really hard to design products by focus groups. A lot of times, people don't know what they want until you show it to them." Another whopper of reality distortion. Together with Ellen Hancock, Gil had launched a low-end computer project early in his reign, and the product was "within three or four months of being finished when Steve took over," Amelio says. "[Steve] gave it the name iMac and took all the credit." One engineering executive of Amelio's regime said, "Most of the products that came out in the first three years after Steve took over were started under Gil."

It was the old Steve, but with a fair number of his good ideas from the early days still intact. He was going to trust his instincts, drive a small group to outdo themselves, and capture the consumer mindshare with panache, style, and a handful of innovations, not revolutions.

The new Steve had been through three different companies. Now, in his second term at Apple, he understood some basic issues of organization and high-tech evangelism. A crucial step was to create single-marketing, sales, manufacturing, and finance groups that operated across the company, as a remedy for the balkanized duchies, the warring teams, and the lack of communication that had been the norm since the early days. He fired John Sculley's ad agency, BBDO, and rehired Chiat/Day, the firm that had created the famous *1984* spot. Steve made developers a priority, assigning each a single evangelist whose job it was to handle all of their needs. He knew that stopping the flight of developers to Windows was essential to the future of the Macintosh line.

One of Steve's strongest suits had always been his operational management. From the days of his high school job at Haltek to his aggressive bargain shopping for parts for the Apple II, and on to the Mac, he was obsessed with details. Not just the details of design and software-user interface, but the details of manufacturing efficiency. So, while he was reshaping Apple on the aesthetic side, he was also revamping Apple's manufacturing and inventory picture. In the quarter after he arrived, Gil had reduced Apple's inventories down to $400 million. Nine months later, when the company reported fiscal year 1998 revenues, Steve had successfully continued the effort, and the inventories were down to $75 million.

Steve later said that managing inventories was one of the most valuable things he learned from Gil, in particular the way Gil had taken $2 billion of inventory inherited from Michael Spindler and turned it into $1.5 billion cash. The power of this kind of discipline impressed Steve, and he embraced the lesson. "Fred Anderson," Gil said, sharing the credit, "also schooled Steve on this."

It was the kind of hidden, fiscally conservative move that wasn't usually associated with Steve Jobs, but it made a big difference. For fiscal 1998, Apple's sales fell to $5.9 billion, but the company nonetheless managed to eke out a profit. When Steve hosted the analyst call that year, he had what he called his "Schwarzenegger announcement," playing off the famous line from *Terminator II*, "We will be back."

Magic was starting. Apple had recaptured momentum and consumer buzz. Most of that was on the back of the iMac—a little computer with clear colored plastic side panels that, at $1,300, was also a very shrewd deal. Included in the computer's box was a complete set of the features that a consumer needed to go online. The introduction of the iMac on May 6, 1998—kept so secret that few even inside Apple knew it was coming—was classic Steve showmanship. So was the look of the computer. By integrating the monitor into the same box as all the circuits, modems, and plugs, he had gone back to the days of the early Macintosh and created a consumer-computing appliance in one unit. Plug and play had been an old Apple battle cry, now being reapplied in a new era. Open the box, plug it in, and get surfing.

This was not so much revolutionary as evolutionary. Every personal computer company in the world had been stuck in the separate monitor and CPU design since the IBM PC had done it in 1981 and the Apple II even earlier. The Mac, with its toaster concept, had tried to break out of the mold in the mid-eighties, but technology and components weren't advanced enough back then. The original machine was too small. In the interim, Apple had lost its way and introduced a series of computers that fixed the glaring problems of the original Mac but showed no innovation in design—they had separate CPUs and monitors and were hardly distinguishable from the rest of the marketplace.

The iMac took the best idea of the Macintosh and reapplied it to the new era—but it was also just plain classic Steve. There was no floppy disk in the iMac—it included a CD-ROM drive, with a much higher capacity, but there was no way to write files to a disk and carry them around. In Steve's view, the way to transfer files was over the Internet and through e-mail—forget floppy disks, those were from a previous generation. He was criticized mercilessly for this, but this time he had the upper hand. "Look, you've got to do the right thing. Just take the floppy: people aren't thinking clearly. Nobody's going to back up a four-gigabyte drive onto one-megabyte floppies. They'll use a Zip drive if they want to do it, but those are too expensive to build into a consumer product. Besides, hardly anybody backs up anyway, so why build the cost into every system? The second reason for a floppy is software distribution, but a lot of software now comes on CD-ROMs because it's better and cheaper."

This was the same Steve who thought he knew better than the market gurus—only this time he really did know better. He was 110 percent right. The floppy drive was an anachronism and unnecessary, and the iMac took off in the market without one. Years earlier, the marketing manager of the Mac team had described their market research as consisting of "Steve looking in the mirror every morning and asking himself what he wanted." That was still the case, but now it wasn't just Steve—he was asking the rest of the crew at Apple to look into the mirror too, and listening to them as well.

The iMac was only one element in an accelerating stream of products that started to come out of the newly invigorated company. New operating system upgrades appeared every few months. Then there was the iBook, an iMac-inspired portable. When introduced, it also offered "Airport"—a wireless networking option to free the iBook from wires in a home or an office. Not revolutionary, but an evolutionary step that many consumers appreciated. And Apple made the most noise about it, even though Dell, Compaq, and other companies already offered it.

In a little over a year, Apple sold over two million iMacs, and the momentum accelerated. It was enough to launch the company into a string of profitable quarters.

A few of the initiatives didn't pan out. In 1998 Steve determined to buy the Palm Pilot line from 3Com, as a way of offering a handheld product without having to wait for its development. When Palm executive Donna Dubinski broke away with some other top management to start a rival product, Handspring, Steve tried to buy that company instead. No dice with Handspring, either. One of the principals called negotiating with Steve "the worst experience of my life," and Dubinski had worked for Jobs in the early Mac days: "Never again," she vowed.

When Steve was asked by an interviewer about the new commotion over the technology called the Internet, his answer reflected the family man he had become and a thoughtfulness the new status had brought: "The rewarding thing isn't merely to start a company or to take it public. It's like when you're a parent. Although the birth experience is a miracle, what's truly rewarding is living with your child and helping him grow up. The problem with the Internet start-up craze isn't that too many people are starting companies; it's that too many people aren't sticking with it. That's somewhat understandable, because there are many moments filled with despair and agony, when you have to fire people and cancel things and deal with very difficult situations. That's when you find out who you are and what your values are."

Steve had seen plenty of people become "fabulously rich" from their startups, but felt that they were "gypping themselves out of one of the potentially most rewarding experiences" and might never discover their own values or "how to keep their newfound wealth in perspective."

This was Steve Jobs reflecting on his years in the wilderness, the years of self-imposed exile caused by his childlike arrogance and pride. Offered the perfect job by John Sculley—to head Apple's internal R&D lab—he had turned it down in a fit of pique. It was only then, in failing when he went out on his own, that he learned just what he had walked away from. Even the gods get their comeuppance. But sometimes you get to return home.

. . .

Where a run-of-the-mill CEO who led his company into a new product area might consider it a crowning achievement, for Steve Jobs it had become routine. Now he was about to do it again and, in the process, shake up one of America's—and the world's—most visible, most incendiary industries; not just shake it up, but save a dinosaur of an industry from the threat of extinction.

When Steve had been installed as Apple's interim CEO, among the products he axed was the Newton, the world's first practical PDA. It had been released prematurely but was finally coming to maturity as a product and was just about at break-even, with a hugely promising future ahead. Its handwriting-recognition feature, though clumsy and unreliable at first, had been improved to a surprisingly accurate state that was not matched by any other product for years. Gaston Bastien, the Belgian who was the vice president managing the Newton, had much to be proud of. John Sculley had spun the Newton group off, setting it up as a separate, external business. Steve had first brought the unit back into Apple and then, having second thoughts, closed it down. For him, the Newton apparently bore one great flaw: it had not been created by him. Worse, it had been John Sculley's baby. All the more reason for Steve to cancel it.

It was the same with the computer called the 20th Anniversary Macintosh. Gil Amelio had discovered a small development project tucked away in a dark corner of R&D and had fallen in love with it. Today the concept sounds familiar: a computer screen with the entire computer works built into a small space behind the display. That's a description of the G5 iMac introduced by Steve Jobs in 2004. It's also a description of the computer project that a small team of hardware engineers dreamed into reality in the mid-1990s. Though it would carry a hefty price tag, Gil saw it as a handsome machine with a forward-looking appearance that computer-resistant CEOs would be glad to have on their desks. Introduced in 1997, it was another victim of the Jobs massacre after his return.

Ever a contradiction, Steve continued to show signs of growing more settled and mature, while at the same time actions like these gave testimony that the Old Steve was still very much alive. Although he was gunning down perfectly viable products with Billy-the-Kid abandon, he also recognized the need for something stunningly new to revitalize Apple and the new digital frontier. Additions to the Macintosh line, taking advantage of the latest improvements in technology and the Internet—sure. But this wasn't enough. Beyond it, he was looking for something else, something big, something that held the explosive promise of becoming "the next new thing." The goal, he said, was to "revitalize," and with an optimism that might not have been justified at the time but turned out to be prescient, he added, "If there were opportunities, we'd see them."

Eventually, his eye lit on the music scene. Why music, when everybody and his brother were launching a crash project to create some new kind of PDA? In a 2001 interview with *Fortune* magazine's Brent Schlender, Steve explained, "You can't imagine how many people think we're crazy for not doing a Palm [a handheld PDA]. I won't lie; we thought about that a lot. But I started asking myself, How useful are they, really? How many people at a given meeting show up with one? Whether I was here or at Disney or at Pixar, the percentage peaked about a year ago at 50 percent, and it's now dwindled to less than 10 percent. It kind of went up really fast and then went down.

"I don't mean to be disrespectful to those guys at Palm at all. I'm just saying I don't think early cultures had organizers, but I do know they had music. It's in our DNA. Everybody loves it. This isn't a speculative market." Steve's public relations people must have been tearing their hair that his language wasn't more graceful. But for any businessperson, ideas weigh more than elegance of language, and in this case the ideas were very much on target.

With so many projects shot down, Steve was desperate to find something revolutionary. His industry scouts turned up a music software product called SoundJam MP that was being marketed by some friends of the Apple family, a small company called Casady and Greene (C&G).

One day in 1992, a young programmer named Jeff Robbin dropped by C&G, hoping to sell the company a software utility he had developed, and met with Terry Kunysz, the firm's president. Terry didn't think the product was strong enough to stand on its own but thought that the programmer showed promise. He offered Jeff the chance to work on a product idea that C&G had developed. Jeff went away to think about it and came back to say he was interested. The result was a utility called ConflictCatcher, which fixed incompatibilities, that quickly caught on with Mac users and won "best utility" awards three years in a row.

C&G also developed a number of Macintosh games, including the first game in color for the Mac, Crystal Quest. (In the summers, the company would hire thirty or forty eighth-graders as product testers for the games. "What did you do last summer?" "I played computer games and got paid for it.")

Soon Jeff took a job with Apple, then left because he had an idea for a software program that he wanted to work on. He dropped by C&G once again and told them about his idea: to develop better MP3 player software. This was software that could play digital sound files on a computer, before anyone made portable devices. The results of his efforts, guided by input from C&G on the feature set and design criteria, was a program called SoundJam MP. The Apple engineering staff jumped in to help with advice and guidance on the development. "They really liked what we were doing; it really showed off the Mac's math co-processor," Terry said. SoundJam became the most popular MP3 player on the market, quickly grabbing a 90 percent share of the Macintosh market, and was soon pouring substantial revenues into the company's coffers. Journalist Adam Engst gushed that SoundJam was a "one-stop solution" that offered "a compelling alternative to the mishmash of programs for converting, encoding, and playing MP3s."

In a short time, the three-man company grew to a staff of about forty, taking in as much as $5.5 million annually, with the lion's share coming from SoundJam. Things were looking rosy for C&G, and the company poured money back into the development of new products. Jeff stayed involved, turning out new, improved versions of SoundJam every three or four months and doing the upgrades of ConflictCatcher at the same time.

Then one day, "Apple comes to us like an 800-pound gorilla." The company wanted to buy the rights to SoundJam, and the offer wasn't very subtle. The basic message, Terry said, was "sell the rights, or we'll develop a competitive product and put you out of business." The truth was that given what Apple had in hand, there wasn't enough time to develop a competitive product, especially not in the face of the delivery requirement Steve had secretly imposed on his people: have it ready for sale in time for the Christmas buying season. C&G had no way of knowing all this.

The good news was that Apple didn't have a problem with C&G continuing to sell SoundJam for the time being. So, in addition to being paid by Apple for rights to the product code, the company would still have a healthy cash flow from its own sales of the product. As the cards were being played, however, there was a serious downside to the deal. Apple wasn't raiding the company just for the software but also for warm bodies. They wanted Jeff Robbin to become a key part of the in-house software team, modifying SoundJam to become the Apple-branded music software product. Jeff, Terry said, hadn't liked the atmosphere at Apple in his earlier experience there, but the company made him an offer he couldn't refuse. (He must like conditions better since his return: as of this writing, Jeff is still at Apple.)

Jeff wasn't the only windfall from Apple's personnel raid. C&G was known for the quality of its products, with a lot of the credit going to the small quality assurance testing team. Apple stole two of the top QA people and hired away C&G's head of development as well. For Terry, that last bit left a bad taste: the development guy had been one of two people on the C&G side of the table negotiating the contract with Apple. Terry returned from a vacation to find that the deal had already been signed. Apple had won not just a single hand of the card game but the whole jackpot.

C&G was left with a decimated staff, contractual limits on what development it could do, and an uncertainty about how long Apple would permit it to continue selling SoundJam.

On top of that, C&G couldn't even talk about the Apple deal. Other major companies were also getting interested in the digital music arena, and in order to avoid tipping off competitors about Apple's intentions, C&G was forbidden to mention its arrangement with Apple.

What at first had sounded to Terry like the happy news of a settled contract with Apple turned out to be C&G's death knell. Apple was killing off one of the developer companies that is so vital to any computer firm's continued success. In Terry's colorful phrase, "Apple was eating their young again."

One day the word came from Apple: You will stop selling SoundJam in sixty days. Two years later, C&G closed its doors.

A different thread of this intricate tale began a long way from California, with a college student bored by his entry-level courses and vexed by a roommate grousing about how painful it was to download music from the Internet, forever complaining about all the addresses that no longer worked and the music indexes that were rarely updated. This student did something about it.

Shawn Fanning loves music. Out of that love, in 1999 the then eighteen-year-old Northeastern University freshman brought panic to the music industry. Shawn and other youngsters like him launched a movement that would change the industry forever. A year later he was testifying before the Senate Judiciary Committee. His effort had become a matter of national concern.

Shawn had come late to an interest in computers. In high school he had been the typical jock, avid for baseball, basketball, and tennis, but then became so captivated by computers and the Internet that he gave up sports and spent his spare time learning the science and art of programming. When his roommate's complaints about the nuisance of downloading Internet music began to get on his nerves, Shawn had an idea about how to ease his friend's pain.

It hadn't taken music lovers long to figure out that the Internet was a great way to cobble together a collection of all their favorite songs by their most cherished artists without having to shell out a fortune. Convert your music from a CD into a digital file—called "ripping" a song, in the vernacular of hackerdom—then send it to your friends. It quickly turned into a vast potluck dinner for melodies: you presented an armload of your own favorites and got to load up with savories that others had brought. At first, it was something of a nightmare because of all the competing software packages; too often, you'd find a site that had the songs you were looking for, but you had to download yet another software application before you could get the music and play it.

The technology called MP3, which provided a standard for the compression of music files, soon rose to the top of the pack. (For anyone interested in the nitty-gritty, "MP" is shortened from "MPEG," which stands for the Motion Picture Experts Group, a gathering of "experts" who originally assembled to agree on a standard for compressing video signals to a size that, they hoped, would make it possible to fit a full-length motion picture onto a CD. An institute in Germany developed three algorithms for this type of compression, of which the third one was deemed the most satisfactory. Hence, MP3. While the Experts Group never met the goal of cramming high-quality video information for a 90- or 120-minute movie onto a CD, DVD technology with vastly more storage space came along just in time to rescue them from failure.)

If MP3 wasn't powerful enough to fit a movie onto a CD, it turned out to be just the ticket for music, reducing the digital tracks to about one-tenth their original size with minimal loss of quality. At a time when most people were still connecting to the Internet over dial-up modems, MP3 compression made downloading music from the Web a practical reality.

When a San Diego University graduate jumped into the fray with a company he called MP3.com, offering a well-organized service for storing and swapping music files, more than ten thousand users tapped into the site in the first thirty-six hours alone. Before long, millions of music tracks were available for the taking. In the go-go frenzy of the Internet boom years, the company went public only sixteen months later, in July 1999. At that point, the founders had already managed to burn through $1.4 million. The stock opened at $28 and went up to $105 before settling back to $63. By the end of the day, investors had snatched up company shares to the tune of over $340 million.

For all the enthusiasm of the obsessive fans of rap, hip-hop, country, Christian, easy listening, and other flavors of popular music, the company's storage site, my.mp3.com, was unstable and inconsistent, a major source of the frustration suffered by Shawn Fanning's roommate. Fanning began to write computer code for a real-time system that would locate music files on the hard drives of other users on the Internet but soon discovered that he didn't have all the computer-programming skills required. He bought a programming book on Amazon and charged ahead, captivated by the project and, according to what has already become legend, working sixteen hours a day. His uncle John, who was his mentor and backer, said, "I just couldn't have been happier. He had finally developed the work ethic to be successful on the Internet."

With help from two others, Shawn finished a working version of his music-download software package at the beginning of June 1999, which he then shipped off to thirty people for testing, mostly youngsters he had met through chat rooms. His request was, in effect, "Try this and let me know about any problems or suggestions, and please keep it to yourself because I don't want people to know about it yet."

A few days later, the software had been downloaded by 10,000 to 15,000 people. At that point, John says, "We all knew from the beginning that this would be huge."

By the time snow started falling in Boston, Shawn had dropped out of college to devote himself full time to what had started out as an amusing sideline. John rounded up money from angel investors. When it came time to incorporate, Shawn stuck with the name he had been using as an online handle and an e-mail address based on the nickname he had acquired from his nappy hairstyle. He called it "Napster."

In September 1999, Shawn turned his back on the severe Boston winters and opened an office in California. Despite the skepticism of friends who doubted whether people would be willing to share their files, by October of the following year Napster had thirty-two million users and was adding another million every week. Shawn's software was simply better than what users found at MP3.com or other competitive sites.

Both services, of course, faced deep trouble: by allowing people to download music free that they would otherwise have to buy, the services denied music publishers their due profit and artists their royalties. Simply put, Napster and mp3.com were breaking the law. The music industry was up in arms and scared silly about a future in which they might find themselves redundant, perhaps ceasing to exist altogether.

The Macintosh faithful and FOS (Friends of Steve) stand in long lines when Jobs gives a public speech. On January 9, 2001, more than five thousand people braved the San Francisco weather and packed into the auditorium at the vast Moscone Center to hear him deliver the keynote address for the first of that year's MacWorld Expo events. Another audience of an estimated thirty-five thousand people listened or watched the worldwide live Webcast.

A Steve Jobs speech is an event to behold. On the floor of the U.S. Senate, it might be mistaken for the beginning of a filibuster. At many of these appearances, he has talked for an hour and a half; on this particular Tuesday, he was onstage for some two hours. Almost anyone but a professional lecturer or a self-help guru would put an audience to sleep. Not Steve Jobs. He is a captivating speaker who exudes as much charisma to an audience of thousands as he does one-on-one (when on his best behavior).

The performance is all the more breathtaking when you know what goes on behind the scenes. His staff schedules rehearsals, but Steve rarely shows up for them. A speech might be written for him, but he probably won't even look at it. He will, though, work with the technical team on how he wants to show the product and what he wants to do in the demo. It's one of those areas he truly cares about. Call it superficial, if you will, but to Steve it's as important as the design of a new Apple computer or a giant billboard ad. He will lean on the show's producer and the technical crew so that the timing is exactly right, the lighting precisely the way he wants it, the overall effect achieving the maximum impact. From wherever such talent comes, Steve Jobs has the same uncanny instinct for achieving dramatic flair that will produce maximum audience impact as the legendary moguls of Hollywood's early days.

Working with the technical crew is often as far as he goes to prepare. He knows the product, he knows the details, and he knows which features will make the eyes of the Macintosh faithful light up. While his public relations people stand in the wings, panicked because they have no idea what to expect, Steve takes the stage with the aura of Mick Jagger. He is a sensational speaker, gripping, magnetic. To know that he does this without notes, without a TelePrompTer, without rehearsal, is to know you are witnessing a magic act. Steve Jobs, magician extraordinaire, pulls the rabbit out of the hat every time.

Once, when introducing a blockbuster product, Apple's first Laser-Writer, he reached the climactic moment—he sent a print command from the computer onstage—and nothing happened. Some technical glitch. The LaserWriter sat there like a hunk of iron, lifeless. Steve didn't even flinch. He went right on talking, holding the rapt attention of the audience while several white-jacketed techies appeared from backstage and began checking connections, cabling, power, software. In a few moments they had found the problem and fixed it, then vanished. Steve transitioned smoothly back into his demo just as if the whole thing had been planned. It was an absolutely incredible performance, the kind you never forget.

This MacWorld occasion at the beginning of 2001 marked a turning point for Apple, a major entry in what Steve had taken to calling Apple's new "Digital Hub" focus that would extend the company's computer franchise to include other digital elements such as music and photography. The new product he was announcing, the result of the Steve-inspired crash program to drive the company into the world of music, was being called "iTunes." It certainly wasn't the first in the field, and it offered many of the same features as the SoundJam MP application it was based on. In fact, in Apple's hurry to get the program finished, it had dropped a number of SoundJam features, so that SoundJam from C&G offered the advantage of being more feature-rich than iTunes.

The difference was unmistakable. In every project Steve had been connected with, he pounded on the themes of elegance, ease of use, and artistry of design. iTunes was no exception. As Steve made clear in his pitch and demo in the MacWorld launch announcement, iTunes was suddenly *the* product of the category.

With it, Macintosh users could copy tracks from a CD onto their computer, from where they could select and play any desired one in an instant. They could also download MP3 music files from the Internet. (Mac users only; there would be a Windows version later on, but initially, the product brought its advantages only to Apple loyalists.) Even better, owners of portable MP3 players such as the popular Rio could use iTunes to download songs to the player. An Australian reporter who roused himself to watch the live Webcast that aired at 3 A.M. Australian time was especially impressed by one feature of the software program that Apple offered. "The best news of all," he wrote, was that "iTunes is a free download."

Steve told the enthusiastic audience, "Apple has done what Apple does best—make complex applications easy, and make them even more powerful in the process. iTunes is miles ahead of every other jukebox application, and we hope its dramatically simpler user interface will bring even more people into the digital music revolution."

With iTunes, Apple had joined the revolution. It was another step in Steve's creation of Internet services to go along with Apple products, his vision of the Apple experience from cradle to grave. But the world would soon learn that Steve Jobs wasn't just joining the revolution; he was about to reshape it.

11

Somebody finally got it right.
—Dr. Dre

iPod, iTunes, Therefore I Am

Only after Apple had come up for air from the hurry-up project to stake out a place in the digital music files area did Steve and his team start to look more closely at the music field. While some people downloaded music to play on their computers, others loaded the songs onto their Rios and listened while driving, shopping, or jogging. The portable players offered a Walkman shrunk down to pocket size. Users could listen to music from more than just a single CD and more pleasurably than from a radio station, where you had to suffer through the pain of commercials and talk for every song played.

It looked like a ready-made market, yet consumers hadn't taken to the idea. Steve's people showed him the numbers: sales of the devices were anemic. Why weren't they selling better? Apple vice president Greg Joswiak boiled it down to the basics: "The products stank." Steve said that there was "plenty of evidence from the MP3 players already out there that consumer electronics makers don't know diddly about software."

Steve had shot down a number of Apple development efforts because they weren't aimed at creating products that matched the company's core focus. Neither did an MP3 player. Now that reasoning didn't seem to matter anymore. He saw the new frontier, recognized the market potential, and seized it. This wasn't even a matter of playing catch-up. It looked to Steve as if the other companies in the field weren't offering any kind of tough competition. The entire playing field was his for the taking.

Apple already had iTunes, a track record for great industrial design, and a heritage all the way back to Steve Wozniak for miniaturization. The cards seemed heavily stacked in favor of a music player over a PDA.

That, of course, turned out to be a brilliant decision.

Steve gives himself credit for being the one who started the ball rolling, seeing the possibilities in a lightning bolt of inspiration: "Wouldn't it be awesome if people could buy high-quality audio tracks via the Internet and load them directly into iTunes instead of going to the store to buy CDs to rip?"

Apple already had an electronic pushcart, the Apple Store, that was racking up $1 billion in sales every year on computers and software. Why not add music? Establishing a beachhead in the music business would land him in a world he had long held in awe, though mostly from a distance. Sure, he could get U2's Bono on the phone; he could extract an enthusiastic quote about the Macintosh from rock superstars and show off his products to the likes of Mick Jagger. Yet for the most part he was like a visitor to the Oscars who has to sit behind the ropes on the sidewalk bleachers and watch the glitterati parade past.

How would Apple get started? In fact, a practical approach for creating a music player had been handed to Apple on a platter.

Even Steve doesn't always know where the next big thing will come from. One day a young itinerant high-tech consultant came to work at Apple with the rudiments of a design in his head for a handheld music player. It was, as some now say, a marriage made in high-tech heaven. But it could only have worked with the new Steve; the old one never would have accepted an idea that he hadn't championed originally.

The hardware guy, Tony Fadell (he pronounces it Fuh-dell) had worked on developing a number of devices at General Magic (a company started by some of the original Mac team members) and later at Philips. After Philips, he set out on his own and tried to shop around the idea for a business that would combine a hardware element—an MP3 player—with a major sales element, a Napsterlike music source. He tried it out on several companies, with no success, but it turned out to be just what Apple was looking for.

Steve gave the assignment of overseeing the project to Apple's head hardware honcho, Jon Rubinstein, known as "Ruby"—the smart, hard-driving business manager Steve had brought along with him from NeXT.

This wasn't a project Ruby could afford to botch. He saw that working with Tony made all kinds of sense because the development work that Tony had already done would give the project a jump start. But when Ruby said he wanted to meet with Tony, the Apple folks who had been in touch with him had a hard time tracking him down: Tony was on a ski slope.

Contact was made, and Ruby offered him a position as an Apple employee in a team that grew to be about thirty people strong. But the job came with expectations that would give anyone pause: he would have to design a product distinctive enough and intuitive enough to use that it would meet Steve Jobs's exacting standards. To make the assignment all the tougher, Steve set the same kind of deadline he had set for turning SoundJam into iTunes: the product would have to be ready in time for the Christmas buying season, less than twelve months away.

Of course, trying to live up to Steve Jobs's near impossible and frequently changing expectations had crushed many strong men. Tony accepted Ruby's offer anyway. For him, this was a dream job doing what he had spent months trying to talk some company into letting him do.

Fadell decided to base the new design on an existing product, PortalPlayer, from a company in nearby Santa Clara, California. Some people considered the decision "unique and risky," perhaps because PortalPlayer itself had been in business less than two years at the time. Still, the company had a stellar leadership team and was backed in part by venture capitalist Gordon Campbell, who had dealt with Steve at VLSI many years before. He seemed to pop up everywhere around the valley and had a handsome reputation for choosing likely winners.

Tony had done his homework and knew that PortalPlayer was working on designs for at least two MP3 players, one of them not much bigger than a pack of cigarettes. A senior manager at the company told wired.com journalist Leander Kahney that Apple sparked enthusiasm among the PortalPlayer people by telling them, "This is the project that's going to remold Apple. Ten years from now, [we're] going to be a music business, not a computer business."

The design challenge was to figure out how to achieve superior performance and shrink the goods into a small package, but not draw so much power that the batteries run down quickly. This is a little like pedaling a bicycle across Niagara Falls on a high wire while performing a juggling act. Despite the hurdles, Tony found that PortalPlayer's electronic designs were well advanced, though by no means finished. The prototypes were "fairly ugly," according to company manager Ben Knauss. One in particular was "typical of an interface done by hardware guys. It looked like an FM radio with a bunch of buttons."

Knauss figured that the company's work "was attractive to Apple because we had an operating system. That was a real selling point. We had the software and the hardware already done." All the more important because Steve Jobs and Jon Rubinstein were in such a hurry to bring the product to market.

By the time that Apple came on the scene, PortalPlayer was already recognized as a leader in the field of MP3 design. IBM was a customer, along with some dozen other companies, mostly Asian. The IBM concept called for a sleek, black pocket-sized player designed to work with Bluetooth headphones—a feature that today's iPod users are still waiting for. But Steve Jobs holds an unusually proprietary view of intellectual property. One condition demanded of PortalPlayer was that it renounce its other customers. This couldn't have been easy, but Tony Fadell's prediction that this project would remold Apple may have been enough of a carrot to help the decision along. For most of that year, the entire engineering force of PortalPlayer, in the United States and in India, worked only on the new Apple MP3 device.

Steve Jobs stayed close to the project all the way, his brilliance as a marketer and his flawless taste in design shining through in his rigorous-as-ever demands for the highest standards. In his interview for the wired.com piece, PortalPlayer's Ben Knauss recalled, "Steve would be horribly offended he couldn't get to the song he wanted in less than three pushes of a button." On other occasions, the team was told, "Steve doesn't think it's loud enough." "The sharps aren't sharp enough." "The menu's not coming up fast enough." Every day, Knauss said, there were comments from Steve saying what improvements he wanted. About the order to boost sound volume, Knauss said that the maximum volume was louder than almost any other MP3 player. His explanation is that Steve is partly deaf, though this is a contention that close friends of Steve's vehemently deny.

Because of the impossibly short schedule, there wasn't any time to custom-design computer chips. As it turned out, that was just as well. Perhaps the music quality could have been a tad better, the unit a little lighter, or the batteries longer lasting if the designers had started from scratch, but they were stuck with off-the-shelf components, and they made it work.

Here was another sign that Steve had matured, adjusting to the realities of the world as it is instead of the world as he wants it to be. At Apple in the early days, he would go outside the company for creative aspects like product design and advertising. For everything else, Steve blindly followed the corrupt "NIH" philosophy—"not invented here." The technology had to be done within Apple; if his technical wizards didn't know how to do something, they would just hire someone who did. Going outside the company simply wasn't acceptable.

He who can't change his ideas is a prisoner of his past. Steve was breaking out of that prison.

In the hands of Rubinstein and Fadell, Apple's design chain relied on off-the-shelf components integrated in an especially elegant way. Even critical pieces such as the digital-to-analog converters were selected from a manufacturer's catalog. The supercritical, nearly microscopic hard drive that the team chose was another available-to-anyone item, a standard Toshiba piece of hardware, although Apple cornered the market for the first year by buying all the production. (If you go to the Settings menu of the iPod and select "Legal," you'll find copyright credits for PortalPlayer, Inc., and other companies that Apple tapped for needed components.)

Steve's passion (or was it mania?) for craftsmanship even where it couldn't be seen was just as intense as it had been back in the days of the demand for straight, precise solder lines on the Apple II. After the unit had reached the market, a team of experts took one apart for *DesignChain* magazine and heaped praise on it, calling the internal design "elegant."

The creative genius behind the external look and feel of the iPod was Jonathan Ive, vice president of Apple's Industrial Design Group. An affable Brit who had arrived at Apple nearly a decade earlier after paying his dues designing products that ranged from electronic devices to toilets, Jonathan had already earned much praise from his peers and the appreciation of consumers with his creation of the futuristic look that became the iMac's signature style. Meanwhile, he had ruffled feathers by declaring that "the computer industry is creatively bankrupt."

Jonathan considered Apple Computer a stellar place to work because the boss shared his love of excellent design. He considers Steve "an exceptional designer."

When Jonathan Ive had earlier created the look of Apple's first elegant laptop, the PowerBook, he commented, "Expectation is extraordinarily high—it's a bit scary." In 2001, he faced even higher expectations—only this time they weren't from the public but from his boss, Steve Jobs.

"From early on, we wanted a product that would seem so natural and so inevitable and so simple, you almost wouldn't think of it as having been designed," he said.

"Like everyone else on the project, I knocked myself out, not so much because it was a challenge—which it was—but because I wanted to have one," he said. "Only later, as it came together, did the broader significance of what we were working on become apparent."

How many companies could tackle a project in a brand-new category, create a groundbreaking widget that looked great and worked better than anyone else's—and do it all in under a year? It happened only because Steve Jobs cracked the whip in his usual roles of slave driver, taskmaster, and ringmaster. His odd, unlikely, incomprehensible charisma drew people into his spell, yet this magnetism was interspersed with daily tantrums that made employees cringe and want to crawl under the table.

Many creative people become tongue-tied and virtually incoherent when they try to explain their art. Steve, the college dropout, could have been forgiven if he belonged to that fraternity. Instead, he is often surprisingly perceptive. In a 1996 interview, Steve said, "Design is a funny word. Some people think design means how it looks. But, of course, if you dig deeper, it's really how it *works*. To design something really well, you have to 'get it.' You have to really grok what it's all about." (A geek's word, *to grok* is a coinage of science-fiction writer R. A. Heinlein, meaning to understand something thoroughly by having empathy with it.)

Steve went on, "It takes a passionate commitment to really thoroughly understand something. . . . Most people don't take the time to do that." He then proceeded to tell a story that both sheds light on his private life and gives some insight into the decision-making process that often turns life into a hell for people who work with him. Making the point that design isn't just an issue for "fancy new gadgets," he described how his whole family became involved in, of all things, the selection of a new washing machine and dryer. This is a little hard to picture: the billionaire Jobs family didn't have very good machines. Selecting new ones became a project for the whole family. The big decision came down to whether to purchase a European machine or an American-made one. The European machine, according to Steve, does a much better job, uses about one-quarter as much water, and treats the clothes more gently so that they last longer. But the American machines take about half as long to wash the clothes.

"We spent some time in our family talking about what's the trade-off we want to make. We spent about two weeks talking about this. Every night at the dinner table"—imagine dinner-table conversation about washing machines *every night!*—"we'd get around to that old washer-dryer discussion. And the talk was about design." In the end, they opted for European machines, which Steve described as "too expensive, but that's just because nobody buys them in this country."

Of course, this wasn't really about washing machines; it was about passing along the concern for design to his children and perhaps to Laurene. The decision clearly gave him more pleasure than you would expect. He called the new machines "one of the few products we've bought over the last few years that we're all really happy about. These guys [had] really thought the process through. They did such a great job designing these washers and dryers."

Steve's surprising tagline on the story says a great deal about how much design really means to him: "I got more thrill out of them than I have out of any piece of high tech in years."

. . .

Despite what seemed to be an unrealistic deadline reminiscent of Steve's earlier hopelessly inaccurate promises for the first Macintosh, the iPod was actually tracking on schedule. In August, several prototypes were ready for testing with focus groups. The designs were still very much under wraps, and Steve was manic about leaks, so each unit was sealed in a separate reinforced plastic box, much larger than the actual unit—closer to the size of a shoebox. Wires for the controls were strung to random spots on the exterior of the box. On some, the scroll wheel was on the side, for example, and the screen on the top; anyone looking at the box would have no idea how the controls were placed on the actual unit. It was all part of keeping the competition off balance until the veil was lifted at the official introduction, and part of the increasing paranoia about leaks that afflicts Steve.

For Steve, the iPod provided an excuse to hang out with prominent artists of the music world. Several of them were so blown away by the product that they gladly allowed themselves to be filmed for clips in the video to be shown at the product launch. Moby, the electronica musician, enthused, "I've had three MP3 players, and I haven't figured out how to use any of them. And, this one, I held it and 45 seconds later, I knew how to use it." Seal, a British soul vocalist who was then working on his third album, offered, "You can see the thought, and the time, and the love that's gone into it. It's just wonderful. I want it now!"

Smash Mouth frontman Steve Harwell expressed a sentiment that many iPod owners later shared: "I'll take two of 'em! One for me and one for my girlfriend, 'cuz I'm not sharin' this with nobody!" He also expressed a sentiment that ever-irreverent Steve Jobs must have particularly enjoyed: "This kicks every other product's ass right here."

Even members of the Apple team who worked on the project were getting pumped. Design group leader Ive commented, "As a design team, I cannot remember the last time where we were collectively lusting after a product as badly as we are after an iPod."

No project ever goes smoothly from start to finish. Late in the game, when the parameters of the electronic design were already locked in, routine testing revealed an alarming flaw. When the iPod was turned off, it continued to draw battery power. Turn it off at bedtime, and by morning the unit would be dead. Actually, it was even worse than that—three hours in the off state was enough to drain the battery all the way down. According to PortalPlayer's Ben Knauss, "The production lines had already been set up. That was a tense part of the project. For eight weeks they thought they had a three-hour MP3 player."

By the time the problem was fixed, Ben had lost confidence. He quit shortly before the release date, suspicious that the product would flop. "It was probably a mistake, but then you have to go with what you think at the time."

As the days ticked off toward the splashy October launch event, a routine item in the business news cast a shadow across the path of everyone involved in the project. Leading chip manufacturer Intel, located just down the road from Apple in Santa Clara, announced that it was closing the doors on its consumer electronics division. Intel, with all of its brilliant engineering and marketing savvy, was admitting that it couldn't figure out how to survive in consumer electronics. And one of the division's products had been a portable MP3 player.

Then there was an even bigger shadow. Barely a month before the launch date, a stunned nation watched in horror as television stations played over and over the destruction of the twin towers of the World Trade Center.

That was the situation as the launch date approached: the technology bubble had burst and the high-tech industry was in a shambles, Intel had admitted it couldn't make a go of consumer electronics, lawsuits over the rights to music and music royalties were swamping the courts, and Americans were still numb from the shock of a terrorist attack on their own soil.

In that dark climate, the time had come to introduce iPod to the world.

Steve Jobs was at his mesmerizing best. Even better, in fact. As he explained to the crowd that had gathered at Apple corporate headquarters in Cupertino, "Why music? Well, we love music, and it's always good to do something you love."

The company had once been a leaky sieve in which no secret remained secret for very long, whether it was word of an executive soon to be fired or details of a hot new computer. Steve's crackdown on that behavior had been hard enough that it changed a culture pattern ingrained since the earliest days. Whispering into the ear of a friendly reporter became grounds for being escorted out of the building by an armed guard, never to return. It may have been Draconian, but it was successful. One press report of the launch referred to the occasion as "a surprise announcement."

On this Thursday, October 23, 2001, Apple was introducing what would turn out to be its most successful product ever. Successful enough, in fact, that it appears to be changing the character of Apple from a computer company into, well, time will tell.

The iPod first introduced that day had struggled past the battery problem to offer as much as ten hours of playing time between charges. It was white, and not just everyday white but a stunning, luminous, brilliant, attention-getting white. Inside, it carried 32 megabytes of chip memory, far more than almost any Palm Pilot. By being built around a 5-gigabyte hard drive instead of the widely used flash memory, the iPod offered enough storage for 1,000 songs. "Apple has invented a whole new category of digital music player that lets you put your entire music collection in your pocket and listen to it wherever you go," Steve bragged.

"Isn't this cool?" Steve asked the assembled crowd. Demonstrating how quick and painless the designers had made it to transfer songs, he said, "iTunes knows all about iPod, and iPod knows all about iTunes." The high convenience was another of the great features: the software and the hardware were so well integrated that the user didn't need to do anything more than plug the iPod into the computer, and any new songs stored on the computer would automatically download. But then, Steve Jobs had practically defined the standards for ease of use, and he had personally cracked the whip over iPod's design team and engineers. No one who understood Steve could have expected anything less. This product once again raised the bar by being a device that had no need for a thick user manual.

He said, "With iPod, listening to music will never be the same again." The statement proved to be truer than Steve Jobs could ever have imagined.

.   .   .

Some industry observers made snide remarks about the iPod, especially about the $399 price, significantly higher than most competitive products. There were small MP3 players around at the time, as well as others that could hold a lot of music. But the iPod answered both demands in a single package: small size, big capacity. Yet initial reaction from the marketplace was mixed: the thing cost so much more than existing digital players that it prompted one online skeptic to suggest that the name might be an acronym for "Idiots Price Our Devices." At first, it called to mind the Newton, Apple's pen-based personal organizer that was years ahead of its time, yet priced out of easy reach.

But Steve continued to operate along Churchillian lines: "Never, never, never, never give up."

Early sales were encouraging but not exactly breakaway. Steve and Ruby kept a stream of new versions coming out—a 2,000-song version in March 2002, followed in July by a version for "everybody else," the legions of Windows users.

Sales began to take off. In the fall of 2002, 140,000 units were sold; more than 200,000 were purchased in the Christmas quarter. The following July, Steve's chief financial officer Fred Anderson (who had the unique distinction of being the only senior executive Jobs had retained from the previous administration) announced that Apple was the only computer company other than Dell to be earning a profit on operations.

The little pocket music player was vastly outselling Apple's core product, the Macintosh, and Steve began to predict that the iPod and the iTunes Music Store would account for half the company's revenue. Adjusting to what now looked like a shift in the nature of the company, Steve created a separate iPod division and asked Jon Rubinstein to give up his key position as head of hardware to take over masterminding the iPod and music operations.

Whether by extraordinary good luck, the sheer love of music, or astounding foresight, Steve Jobs had found a gold mine.

Few things in life are pure blessing or pure curse. Steve had never thought that getting into the music business would be without tribulations.

Steve Jobs has been described as "the kind of obsessive Beatles fan who can talk your ear off about why Ringo is an underappreciated drummer." That, and counting Bob Dylan as one of his all-time favorites, suggests retro tastes. But retro tastes didn't keep him from extending an invitation to a musician whose style must have appealed more to his children than to Steve himself. The dude was Dr. Dre, a hip-hop producer and a one-time gangsta rapper, a former partner with the notorious Suge Knight in a company they called Death Row Records. Dre mentored newcomers like Snoop Dogg and Eminem, then produced them and helped make them headliners.

Steve had a specific business goal when he extended the invitation to Dre: he wanted the rights to Dre's music, including the Death Row catalog, for Internet downloading. According to music impresario and producer Steven Machat, when Dre and Suge Knight broke up Death Row Records, Dre understood that it had to be a clean break so that Suge would have no reason to be unhappy with him later. Dre recognized that having Suge angry with you could be bad for your health. To make the break as clean as possible, Dre actually signed away his rights to all of the Death Row music that the two of them had recorded and released together.

Some time later, Machat was engaged by a company called music-maker.com to broker the Internet download rights to Death Row's music. He traveled from Los Angeles to the place where Suge was then living, at government expense: a California prison outside Sacramento. Suge gave the visitor a hard time—who was this white guy trying to make a deal with him? Machat kept his cool, talked straight, and won the producer's confidence. Suge relaxed enough to brag of a hold he had over Dr. Dre.

When Suge heard that at least a million dollars was on the line, however, it was enough to break down his barrier. He signed the agreement, and the money went into the designated bank account.

Here was Suge receiving a million dollars for music that Dre had jointly had a hand in creating. Dre may have hoped to carve himself a piece of that million. His lawyers sent a letter asserting that when Dre signed over the Death Row rights to Suge, it didn't include the right to download Death Row music on the Internet. They argued that this technology had not existed when the agreement was signed. Dre felt safe in throwing this curveball, Machat said, because a Suge Knight behind bars was a Suge Knight unable to bring harm to his old partner.

When Dre flew up to Cupertino, Steve Jobs was determined to obtain the rights to download not just Dre's new music, which included some of the Eminem songs, but everything in the earlier Death Row catalog as well.

Dre had already said publicly that never, over his dead body, would he ever sign away Internet rights to any of his music, offering as explanation the same reason the record companies gave: that downloading posed a threat to the entire music industry, as well as to his own pocketbook. Machat believes that he probably had another reason as well: if Suge pocketed a million dollars from the Death Row catalog, why should Dre settle for a few cents every time a piece of music was downloaded?

Steve's charm and charisma had swayed many people and had even brought audiences of hard-nosed press people to their feet, applauding him with a standing ovation. Press people! Now here he was sitting down with Dr. Dre, one-time gangsta rapper, the unlikely pair huddled together in an hours-long session. After the session Dr. Dre announced, "Man, somebody finally got it right."

In the end, Dre signed the agreement, giving Apple the rights to his new music.

The product that Dre was enthusing over was the third piece of the Apple music equation: the iTunes Music Store. Steve and his team had spent months putting this together, and the toughest part hadn't been the technology but the cooperation of the other players: Sony, Warner, Universal, EMI, and BMG—the five big music companies. By the time of the Dr. Dre demo, Steve had in his pocket signed agreements from all five companies, agreements that made possible the new project that Apple was preparing to launch.

The iTunes Music Store would be the first great download music service, the first one to have the blessing of the music industry. Steve knew deep down that his digital service would forever change the way music is sold and distributed. As usual, he had his finger on the pulse of the future.

Steve's solution couldn't have arrived at a better time. The music industry was suffering, with total revenues down more than 8 percent in the previous year. In part, this was the result of growing resistance from consumers, who couldn't help but notice that instead of plucking a new CD from the rack at the local Target and paying $15 or $20, they could walk to a different aisle and for the same price, or even less, pick up a DVD of a recent movie, complete with half a dozen entertaining extra features plus some interactive content.

Even more significantly, the music business had suffered a loss of revenue from vast hordes of people illegally swapping music files over the Internet. Napster had been reined in and largely defanged by lawsuits but had been replaced by something much worse and, from the perspective of 2003, virtually uncontrollable. Napster serves as a vast storage vault of songs, but the service called Kazaa and its brethren operate more like an Internet dating outfit, helping one interested party get in touch with another for what amounts to an electronic one-night stand. What's more, the servers were in Denmark, the software was in Estonia, the Web site had an Australian registration—and that was just for starters.

When the heat got turned on, the people behind Kazaa added several more layers intended to further confuse anyone trying to track them down, especially people with guns and badges who might come bearing a search warrant or an arrest warrant. The interface was turned over to a company called Sharman Networks, formed days earlier on the South Pacific island nation of Vanuatu, which proudly boasts of its strict secrecy laws. Ownership of the domain landed in the hands of LEF Interactive (LEF supposedly means *liberté, égalité, fraternité*, the slogan of the French Revolution). Sharman, it seems, has no employees—they're all contracted through LEF, a company with offices in Sydney. The woman in charge, with the title of CEO, is a blond thirty-something British stunner with a direct gaze and only a little embarrassment at the corporate skullduggery she's hiding behind. Or rather, that the whole operation is hiding behind.

If you had trouble following that, you can imagine what the leaders of the music industry and their attorneys have been up against.

While Steve Jobs was smiling over the best Apple profits in years and the prospect of a continuing healthy boost in revenues, the big music companies were busy laying off thousands of employees and crying "piracy" over all those millions of songs being swapped and downloaded on the Internet, an illegal never-ending tidal wave, day and night, around the world. Steve Jobs knew about pirates; hadn't he been the pirate king, in the early Macintosh days nearly twenty years ago?

Steve had foreseen that he would be wading into crocodile-infested waters. Music piracy would be a radical issue with the Music Store, far more than with iTunes and the iPod. It was an issue Steve had deep feelings about. He was well aware of the blood, sweat, and tears that go into any creative endeavor and so had a higher degree of sensitivity than most people do about the value of a musician's work. "Apple is one of the few companies in our industry that owns any intellectual property," he says. "We know how expensive it is to develop it, and so we really believe in protecting it."

Protections had been built into the iPod to deter piracy. Not the rigid, customer-be-damned kind of restrictions that the music industry favored; certainly not the anything-goes freedom of the college campuses and song-swappers; but a sensible, carefully thought-out plan that would collect appropriate royalty payments on a scale that music lovers could live with. He believed that most people, given a reasonable choice, would choose to do the right thing. "Stealing music is a behavioral problem more than a technological problem," he said. "We believe most people are honest and want to pay for their music." Part of the challenge, he believes, is making sure that being dishonest isn't too easy.

With the iPod, Steve had driven his people to devise a scheme that would meet his demanding standards for ease of use while at the same time throw up barriers for people who tried to use their iPods to share music files with others. You can transfer music from your computer to your iPod in a breeze, but don't expect to be able to load those songs onto someone else's computer. Or to download songs from someone else's computer onto your iPod.

Steve explained that if you tried to sync your iPod with someone else's Mac, a message would warn you that continuing the operation would load the new tunes but would also erase all the music you already had stored. And then, when you got back to your own Mac, the same thing would happen. (In fact, it turned out that there was a fairly easy workaround, but it's unlikely that more than a small number of hard-core users ever learned the trick. Did Steve know the protection could be defeated so easily? After all, this was the man who once loved to circumvent AT&T's billing systems.)

For the iTunes Music Store, Apple developed a whole new set of piracy protections, including a home-grown music file format, AAC—created because none of the available formats had the capability to build in sufficient defenses. It was also intended to keep iPod users tied to Apple, which refused to license the format to others. Buy a song from the iTunes Music Store, then try to upload it to Kazaa or another of the illegal swap sites, and you'll find your path blocked. The AAC song file is encrypted with a digital key that prevents it from being transferred online.

A lot of frustrated song pirates probably tried to burn the tunes onto a CD and then reload them onto their computer in MP3 format. The method works. There's just one problem: by design, the sound quality of the resulting files is lousy, so bad that no one would want to listen.

If impossible tasks are the catnip of overachievers, then Steve Jobs was rolling in catnip.

On the last Monday in April 2003, Steve was back at the Moscone Center, an hour's drive north of Apple headquarters in the heart of Silicon Valley. Looking radiant, pumped as usual in front of an audience, his charisma turned up to the max, he launched into his announcement of the iTunes Music Store. Steve the outsider had done what observers would have predicted was impossible: getting signatures on agreements with the top music companies.

He'd wanted those agreements so badly that he'd done the negotiating personally. Ordinarily, on an issue with as many strategic implications as this, the CEOs would have agreed in principle and then left their underlings to see whether an agreement could be worked out. Steve got each CEO to say, "We'll consider it," and then had been willing to do the horse-trading himself.

Even for Steve Jobs, breaking the logjam of the music industry was no pushover. Hilary Rosen, who was then chief executive of RIAA (the Recording Industry Association of America), explained that top executives of major music companies were wary of people from the computer industry, who in the past had shown little grasp of music industry issues. "The [music] industry was very focused on how to create a simple push/play kind of environment because that's what consumers were used to. The IT industry had never operated with those sorts of standards before." So when Steve first approached the record companies, "there was skepticism that he could pull it off."

Steve won them over for two reasons, Hilary believes. The first is mundane and almost laughable: "Apple had such a small market share that it made their risk fairly low." The other reason isn't unexpected: "The shift came about above all because of the sheer willpower of Steve. His sheer charisma and his intensity absolutely made a difference."

Then there's Steve's attention to detail. Hilary came to appreciate that aspect from personal observation: "The first time he showed me a prototype of the [Apple Music] Store, we were sitting in a conference room with a couple of members of his team. They had just come back with yet another version based on feedback that they had gotten. Steve spent about twenty minutes back and forth with the engineers about the best place within a three-square-inch section to put three words. He was *that* focused on the details of the design."

Sheer enthusiasm also helped to win over the music industry executives. "To lots of folks in the tech world," Hilary said, "music was just software. Steve is an incredible music fan. For people in the music industry, that was very special."

Many people, Hilary said, believe that Universal first signed up for Steve's vision. In fact, "Steve developed a relationship at the outset with Roger Ames, at Warner. Roger was really the first one to jump on board."

One executive who was closely involved in the negotiations for a top-five music firm saw the action from an inside perspective. The music companies, he said, had been wary about the idea of downloading, dragging their feet, unwilling to move ahead until completely satisfied with every detail of the terms. Then Steve Jobs showed up on the scene. Suddenly, the source said, "the industry folded at his feet, acquiescing to whatever he wanted. There was a train about to leave, and everybody wanted to be damned sure their company was on it. For the first time, the leverage [in negotiating download deals] shifted to the other side." It was the same at all five of the companies, he said.

Speaking on condition of anonymity, he described one of the most visible executive vice presidents in the music industry, who was that company's point man in dealing with Steve, the target for every bit of Steve's overpowering charisma. Every time our informant saw the vice president during this period, the man was full of talk about Steve this and Steve that. He was completely taken in, glowing as if he had just found his true love or at least a lifelong friend. If the vice president had been asked, the informant said, he would have knelt down and shined Steve's shoes and would have been willing to do it in front of a conference room of other people.

Other executives quickly fell in line because what Steve was proposing made so much sense. Andrew Lack, CEO of Sony Music Entertainment, was one of those. "I don't think it was more than a fifteen-second decision in my mind [to license music to Apple] once Steve started talking," he said.

Steve the billionaire, Steve the pooh-bah of a global company, sat at his conference table while a parade of executive vice presidents and CEOs marched up to Cupertino to be serenaded by him.

The agreements Steve gave them didn't deter the five companies from pursuing their own competitive ventures. Not just competitive with Apple, but with one another. Universal and Sony teamed up in an online project called Pressplay, while the parent companies of Warner and BMG joined forces with EMI and RealNetworks to form Music-Net. Forget about everyone jointly looking for solutions to the very real problems that rattled the industry—the only thing that the two rival groups could agree on was that Pressplay would not license any of its music to MusicNet, and MusicNet would not license any of its music to Pressplay.

Worse, both operations set up rules that catered to the interests of the businesspeople and the musicians, leaving consumers pretty much out in the cold. One allowed users to download songs to a single computer on a monthly subscription basis; stop paying your monthly fee, and the music all goes *poof!*—erased. And you could listen only on that one computer. The other operation allowed CD burning, but only for a small portion of its catalog. Neither provided anything for the millions of owners of portable music players. These restrictions weren't part of iTunes Music Store.

Standing on the stage at the Music Store launch, Steve was able to let the world know he had the agreements. That was the important thing. That was what allowed him to pronounce "a new era for digital music consumption." The Music Store was opening its doors with a library of

200,000 songs, available for purchase individually for 99 cents, or as albums for around $10. Ninety-nine cents—an impulse item.

Even better, the list of available tunes included previously unreleased material from artists like Missy Elliott, Sheryl Crow, Bob Dylan, and U2. Steve announced that users would immediately be able to download music from the Eagles, who had never before allowed their songs to be sold for download. He also told the enthusiastic audience that he was personally lobbying big-name holdouts like the Rolling Stones.

He spent a few moments taking swipes at some of the other download options. The illegal, peer-to-peer operations like Kazaa prove that "the Net was built for music distribution," he said, but "it's stealing." And, as if this were a reason that might sway the hardest heart, he added as a kicker: "It's best not to mess with karma."

As for subscription-based online services like the ones that the music industry attempted, Steve ridiculed them: their rigid rules "treat you like a criminal," he said, when "people want to buy downloads like they buy CDs."

Those music company executives who thought they had made such a great new friend found themselves being severely criticized. Within two weeks, *Fortune* went to press with a long interview in which Steve said that no one from the music companies ever went out and asked users, "Would you like to keep paying us every month for music that you thought you already bought?" Instead, he insisted, "The record companies got this crazy idea from some finance person looking at AOL, and then rubbing his hands together and saying, 'I'd sure like to get some of that recurring subscription revenue.'"

Steve said, "This will go down in history as a turning point for the music industry. This is landmark stuff. I can't overestimate it!"

If Steve Jobs has too often been overly enthusiastic in promoting the prospects of his products, this time he was on the mark. Steve was indeed, as journalist Peter Lewis put it, "almost single-handedly dragging the music industry, kicking and screaming, toward a better future."

In short order, the iTunes Music Store had taken over 70 percent of the legitimate download music business. A year later, the store had sold an incredible 85 million songs and been named *Fortune* magazine's Product of the Year for 2003.

. . .

A rare magic can transform a product from familiar item to cultural icon. Attempting to predict which items will reach iconic status is hazardous. Recognizing when it's happening is easier.

Steve Jobs was riding down Madison Avenue in New York in mid-2004 and noticed that on every block, there was someone with white headphones. He remarked later, "I thought, 'Oh, my God, it's starting to happen.'" Journalists reported sightings all over the map. One told of the University of Michigan professor who said, "When you walk across campus, the ratio [of people wearing the iPod headphones] seems as high as two out of three people." And the professor himself was part of the flock: "When my students see me on campus with my iPod, they smile. It's sort of a bonding."

iPod designer Jonathan Ive found the same thing in London. "On the streets and coming out of the tubes, you'd see people fiddling with it." Ive himself had become something of a British cultural icon. For his design work on the iPod and products like the iMac, he was named "the most influential person in British culture" for 2004, beating out contenders who included Ewan McGregor and J. K. Rowling. A computer designer had won out over the creator of Harry Potter!

Music Store shoppers can also purchase audio books, although, odd as it seems, the audio title is in some cases more expensive than the hardback, even though the cost of delivering the digital title is close to zero. But the convenience of carrying your reading in digital form, instead of lugging a heavy volume, has won avid fans. When former president Bill Clinton's autobiography went on sale at 3 A.M. one day, despite the ungodly hour, thousands of digital copies were downloaded within the first few minutes. In the courtroom, in the case of *Apple v. Apple*—the Beatles' record company disputing the computer firm's use of its trademarked name—the judge wondered aloud from the bench whether he should recuse himself because he is an iPod fan. (He decided he could be impartial anyway. The dispute remains in litigation.)

PortalPlayer, the company that Apple contracted to supply the MP3 decoder chips for the iPod, went public in November 2004. Investors had been warned that a company with only one major client could get into trouble in a hurry, but that didn't put much of a damper on the

IPO. The stock, initially set to enter trading with a price in the $11 to $13 range, actually opened at $17 and rose as high as $27 on the first day, closing the day with a gain of more than 50 percent. The iPod connection had paid off in yet another way. Another company, Synaptics, rode the same wave: the company created the scroll wheel that is one of the iPod's key features. A rumor that Apple was going to make them itself cut the stock price in half. Audible, the company that sells recorded book content for the iPod, saw its stock also skyrocket. Sigmatel, a tiny maker of audio chips which supplied the early Apple players, had a stock market run, too. This is iPod country.

About the same time, Apple announced its financials for the summer quarter: profits up 37 percent and iPod sales up an astounding *500 percent* from the same quarter a year earlier. The company is making almost as much profit on each iPod as on an iMac, but the iPod costs a fraction to manufacture. With the fashionable music player leading the way, Apple had rung up its best fourth-quarter revenue in nearly a decade. Steve Jobs acknowledged that he was "thrilled."

He kept pulling new goodies out of the iPod bag. At what was deemed a "news conference/rock concert" in San Jose, Steve stood alongside rock star Bono of the Irish band U2. As each of them held up a new, limited-edition black-and-red version of the iPod, Steve announced an industry first: the iTunes Music Store would be selling a complete set of four hundred U2 songs that would include music from a not-yet-released album and two dozen rare or unreleased tracks. Bono called it "mind-blowing." This was the Bob Dylan Bootleg Tapes gone digital and mainstream.

A TV commercial for the product pulsed to the beat of a new U2 single, "Vertigo," under theme visuals that featured silhouettes of shimmying dancers against brilliant solid-color backgrounds, an arresting design that defined the look of iPod TV commercials and billboards for that period. While U2 will garner royalties from the sale of its eponymous iPod, Bono said that the band wasn't charging Apple a penny to be in the ad, though the group had supposedly turned down offers of $20 million for the use of its music in other commercials. The band, Bono said, would get as much value as Apple does from the commercial, by promoting its music and the U2 iPod. This kind of reality distortion field is beyond comprehension, except to those who've experienced the Steve Jobs effect.

Steve had set himself a goal of roping in some of the music greats, especially artists and groups that had previously withheld material. The incredible Jobs persuasiveness had won the day yet again.

Steve Jobs touted the iPod as "the Walkman of the twenty-first century." Bill Gates was aiming to make it more like another major Sony product: the Betamax, with VCR technology that, although superior, lost out to VHS and died.

Steve was happy to contemplate moving Apple from computer hardware into the entertainment arena, where the company gloried in higher margins, vastly improved revenues, and a resurgence of its stock price. The problem was that Bill Gates and his CEO Steve Ballmer were pursuing a similar goal. Not that they had any intention of slighting the company's phenomenal software sales, but they had also spotted the impressive sales in various corners of the entertainment market.

The iPod makes an attractive target. Microsoft wasn't alone, merely the elephant leading the pack and hoping for a replay of history. Neither Steve nor Bill ever forgets the days when Apple was king of the hill in the computer business with the Apple II, while Microsoft was just another small company looking on with envy. Mike Murray, Steve's marketing manager for the Macintosh, used to say that Steve would "beat up Gates every once in a while" during the years before the Mac was released and Apple was the most important personal computer company in the world on the basis of the Apple II. Gates turned the tables on Apple once before and doesn't see any reason why he can't do the same this time around. "This story has played out on the PC and worked very well for the choice approach there," he said. But the consumer market is fundamentally different from the humorless business environment. Microsoft, even with Gates's billions, may well be outclassed, outgunned, and outmaneuvered by Steve Jobs.

What happens when rivals enter the marketplace with music players designed to match the most prized features of the iPod? Even the best of these entries probably won't have the snazzy, with-it allure of the Apple device, but some are certainly lower priced. What's more, the iPod works only with music from Apple's Music Store; competitive models will give users a much wider choice of music sources. This is not a space that Apple will own forever. Some erosion is already occurring; early in 2005 Apple announced price cuts for its iPods. But the big issue is, how much is cool worth? In a world of undifferentiated products and Wal-Mart retailers, wouldn't most consumers be willing to pay $50 more to have an undeniably cool product? Maybe they wouldn't pay thousands more, but less than $100 is probably safe, especially when the "user experience" of the iPod, the part of the product that Steve focuses on and at which he is almost preternaturally excellent, is so very good. Years of Apple work stand behind the combination of hardware, software, and online machinery that makes having an iPod such a satisfying experience. No other company on earth has this combination.

No other company has Steve Jobs, either. Whether Steve and his team will figure out ingenious solutions for remaining among the dominant players will be fascinating to watch. Don't bet against them.

With the entry into the music business, the Steve Jobs scorecard racked up a stunning win. Steve's palpable envy at the success of Steve Wozniak's Apple II fired the drive to prove himself as capable of the same kind of achievement. First it was the Macintosh, then the NeXT cube. Neither calmed the demons.

In the music business, Steve Jobs was finally having his day. He had achieved the truly extraordinary, taking on one of the most entrenched, "my way or the highway" industries in the United States, and actually *reshaping* it, bending it to his will. He came along at a time when the industry was in a paroxysm of shrinking revenues, downsizing work forces, and the threat of extinction from an apparently unstoppable force called downloading. An outsider and not even a fan of today's music, Steve had done the almost unthinkable: he had changed the face of a second industry.

And he *still* wasn't done. Not by a long shot.

[Steve Jobs] gets his face on *Time* magazine, he's loved by Wall Street. He'd be a perfect guy to take over Disney.

—A Disney executive

12

Clash of the Titans

The essence of the clash between Steve Jobs and Michael Eisner was revealed in one moment of the Pixar-Disney partnership. Shortly before *Finding Nemo* was released in 2003, Eisner met with the Disney board of directors and offered a prediction: Pixar was headed for a "reality check." Early clips of the clown fish movie had failed to impress him, he said. The movie paled in comparison to *Toy Story* or *Monsters, Inc.* and would not sell as many tickets.

It was as if Eisner were reveling in the idea of a Pixar dud. Such a stark reality check would give him bargaining power in the upcoming contract-renewal negotiations with Steve Jobs. If *Finding Nemo* flopped at the box office, Steve would lose the leverage he had gained from previous Pixar blockbusters. Unlike the last negotiation, he would not be able to push for more favorable terms. Eisner desperately needed to protect every dime of Disney profits, which had slipped an incredible 41 percent in the first quarter of 2003. Though Disney would lose profits in the short term with a *Nemo* flop, it would win in the long term with a favorable Pixar-Disney contract.

Finding Nemo is the story of a clown fish dad who sees his precious only son carried away by a diver, and has to overcome his own fears and anxieties on a lengthy search to be reunited with his offspring.

Even as a summer release, *Nemo* was a resounding success. Earning some $70 million at the box office on its opening weekend, the picture had by the end of the year taken almost $370 million. Once again Pixar had broken all records: *Nemo* became the highest-earning animated feature of all time, and the ninth highest-grossing film in Hollywood history. It wasn't just audiences who fell in love with the movie: *Nemo* garnered Oscar nominations for screenplay, sound editing, and original score, and won the Oscar as the best animated film of the year.

All of this is even more impressive in light of the production arrangements. John Lasseter remained in charge of the overall creative aspects of all productions, but he was showing himself willing to help other talented animators move up the ranks by putting the day-to-day duties as producer into other hands. This time it was Andrew Stanton who carried the creative burden and who accepted the golden statue on Academy Awards night. Lasseter was demonstrating his strengths not just as an animator but as a team player and a leader.

In the process, Steve had earned more than better leverage; he had stolen the ace right out of Eisner's hand. "The impact of *Nemo*," said David Davis, senior vice president and box office analyst at Houlihan, Lokey, Howard & Zukin, "is like a baseball player hitting sixty home runs in the final season of his contract."

Pixar stock jumped up by 4 percent.

Other suitors swooped in. Warner Bros. stopped by the Pixar studio. So did Sony Pictures. "Who wouldn't want to be in business with Pixar?" said a spokeswoman for Sony. Disney executives fumed about Steve's ego. "He's strutting around like a rooster right now," one said. "Only time will tell if he gets his feathers plucked."

If Steve was a crowing rooster, Eisner was a wounded peacock. "This is all personal," one former Disney executive complained. Some people said that Eisner felt threatened by Steve's seemingly effortless success—and his celebrity. Steve "gets his face on *Time* magazine, he's loved by Wall Street. He'd be a perfect guy to take over Disney."

Steve joked once about stealing Disney from Eisner, hinting in May 2003—just before *Nemo*'s release—that he could purchase Disney outright. He immediately realized that reporters were treating his taunt as if he'd been serious. When asked, he replied, "I'll just leave that alone"—

as if the decision belonged to him, an emperor toying with land treaties.

Eisner knew exactly how to kick Steve down a few rungs. "What Pixar has that we don't have," said the Disney chairman, "is John Lasseter." John—not Steve—propelled Pixar to critical acclaim and box office success, and Eisner knew it. He also knew that he could use it as a club to batter Steve in the media.

Still, Eisner made some friendly overtures, inviting Steve to a springtime dinner at an Indian restaurant in the Bay Area. When asked whether curry and naan had warmed the relations between the two CEOs, Steve quipped, "I'd say we had dinner." They also went to a World Series game in the fall of 2003. When reporters asked Steve if it meant the two had a rapprochement, he was equally dismissive: "Sometimes a baseball game is just a baseball game," he retorted.

It makes a certain poetic sense that Steve would seek a deal similar to the one George Lucas had worked out with Fox. Financing and producing his own films, Lucas owns them in toto, merely paying Fox a fee for handling his distribution. By industry standards, it's a lousy deal for Fox, but the company does make some money from the arrangement and also benefits from the connection to one of the most powerful franchises in the motion picture business.

For his upcoming round of negotiations with Eisner, Steve signed on former Lucasfilm president Gordon Radley as a teammate, who advised him to be firm: "Draw a line in the sand" in order to force Eisner's hand. Otherwise, Radley warned, the talks could drag on indefinitely with no favorable agreement.

"The line in the sand that we drew," Steve said, "was that we want to own our own films going forward, and we wanted to own *The Incredibles* and *Cars.*" These were the two remaining films in the renegotiated Disney-Pixar pact.

According to Steve, he offered Disney a deal "less favorable to us than we could get from several other studios—for example, with much higher distribution fees, a much longer-term commitment, and free use of our characters in their theme parks." That was his public statement; in fact, he was demanding 92 percent of the profits. Describing the kind of distribution deal he was after, he said, "You rent a system." He wanted to rent the Disney marketing machine, not partner with it.

Steve must have known what Eisner's answer would be. The Walt

Disney Company stood to lose hundreds of millions of dollars by signing away the rights, shutting itself out of not only money from ticket sales but also merchandise franchises, tie-ins, and sequels. No CEO would have willingly sacrificed so much, even to save a valuable partnership.

"We're not for rent for anybody," Eisner said. He wanted a partnership, and in his mind it was Disney who brought the most to the table.

Negotiations devolved to the point that Al Gore attempted an intervention. Former vice president Gore joined Apple Computer's board of directors in 2003 and offered to see if he could broker a peace between Pixar and Disney, where he felt he had some connections, though these were on the feeble side. The company had donated *Beauty and the Beast* costumes to him and his wife for a Halloween party, and Gore, while still serving as vice president, had discussed legislation with Eisner. He called Disney board member George Mitchell, a former Democratic senator, and encouraged him to press forward in talks. Mitchell in turn called Eisner.

Gore's efforts only raised Eisner's hackles. Not even a former vice president could convince him to make nice.

The problems were personal. As early as 2003 Steve had been buttonholing various Disney execs to warn them that he and Michael Eisner couldn't work together: "I don't see how the relationship can continue as long as Eisner is there," he told one executive. This dovetailed with a boardroom battle brewing in the Magic Kingdom. Roy Disney, Walt's nephew, had decided that Eisner had to go. After a dinner at Steve's home in Palo Alto to sound out his feelings, Roy was alarmed. It seemed as though Steve was willing to take Pixar out of the Disney fold, and that would be disastrous for the company's ailing profits.

Roy had reson to be concerned. The ax was about to swing, and the woodsman was Steve Jobs.

In January 2004, Pixar abruptly ended negotiations. "After ten frustrating months, we ended our talks with Disney," Steve said. "Frustrating" was no slip of the tongue. With that one word, Steve made his position clear: the talks were not friendly. Pixar played the victim of Eisner's tyranny.

Justified or not, Steve acted as if Disney and Eisner had broken a solemn oath of loyalty to Pixar. He never fired a single public warning shot before making his announcement about the walkout. Not even Dick Cook, the Disney studio chief, knew that Steve planned to pack up his tent and move on—and Steve actually *liked* Cook.

Steve couldn't stand the thought of Disney holding beloved Pixar characters and movie titles captive. It made him resent their current agreement all the more. "We feel sick about Disney doing sequels," he said. "Because if you look at the quality of their sequels, like *The Lion King 1½* and their *Peter Pan* sequels, it's pretty embarrassing."

In his view, Disney had never contributed to Pixar's creative process. "The truth is that there has been little creative collaboration with Disney for years," he said. "The collaboration we do have with Disney is centered around the marketing of the films, not the making of them."

He even denigrated Disney's marketing efforts. He paid a compliment to "Dick Cook and his talented marketing team" but then alluded to the Disney flops and added, "But no amount of marketing will turn a dud into a hit." In other words, Disney couldn't even market its own productions into blockbusters.

His final insult, however, was also the most pointed. "We think the Pixar brand is now the most powerful and trusted brand in animation," Steve said. He mentioned Disney's own research showing that Pixar had transcended Disney as a brand. Pixar was now more persuasive and meaningful to movie fans than Disney was. Steve wanted a deal that would reflect it.

Disney licked its wounds and bit back. Zenia Mucha, the Disney senior vice president of corporate communications, called it "sad and unfortunate that he has resorted to insults and name-calling in the wake of the disagreement. We expected better of him."

The Stevian snipes at Disney animation reeked of ego. *The Lion King 2: Simba's Pride* holds a DVD sales record. Most of the Disney sequels have been runaway DVD hits. *The Lady and the Tramp II: Scamp's Adventure* sold more than three million copies within its first six days on the shelves.

Steve meant failure in another sense, something more intangible than profits or awards. To him, Disney failed at *creating*. "You can compare the creative quality of Pixar's last three films with the creative quality of Disney's last three films and judge each company's creative ability for yourself," he said.

. . .

In part, Steve still smarted from previous wrestling matches with Eisner. A year earlier, in the spring of 2003, Eisner had testified before the Senate Commerce Committee that Apple's "Rip, Mix, Burn" marketing campaign practically gave consumers permission to "create a theft if they buy [his] computer."

Eisner and other entertainment executives worried about digital duplication and Internet file sharing, resenting what they saw as Apple's complicity in consumer theft. Digital piracy threatened to severely cut profits and damage brands. Swapping pirated digital versions of movies on the Internet posed no lethal threat yet—the quality of most of the Hollywood movies then available online ranged from poor to dismal, and downloading a high-quality digital movie could take hours of online time. Even so, technology improves at a rapid pace; it was no wonder that Eisner and other Hollywood czars were looking nervously over their shoulders. Napster had shaken the music business, almost bringing the entire industry to its knees. The same could happen to the film business.

The testimony against the "Rip, Mix, Burn" campaign was galling to Steve. It made no sense. Disney was, after all, Steve's partner in the movie business; why would Eisner attack his own partner, even in another area?

Steve later commented, "'Rip' in that phrase means 'take the bits off the CD and put 'em on your hard drive.' Rip the bits off your CD—as if you're physically ripping them off and putting them on your hard drive. Michael Eisner, . . . because he didn't have any teenage kids living at home, and he didn't have any teenage kids working at Disney that he talked to, thought 'rip' meant 'rip off.' And when somebody actually clued him in to what it meant, he did apologize."

Pixar also clung to bitter memories of *Toy Story 2*, when Eisner whipped out the contract and interpreted every comma, period, and dotted i in his favor, insisting that the sequel could not count in the multifilm deal. Then he did the unforgivable. According to the *Los Angeles Times*, he "publicly bragged about the leverage he had over Pixar."

Now, Steve could brag just as loudly.

Steve's view of the negotiations seemed to hold sway with stockholders. On news that he had walked out of talks, Pixar's stock climbed, while Disney's fell. Stockholders appeared—for a moment, at least—to stand firmly on Pixar's side.

"It makes it look like Eisner did something wrong again, but we shouldn't jump to conclusions," said Patrick McKeigue, an analyst at Independence Investment—not exactly a vote of confidence for Eisner, but not an indictment, either.

The *Wall Street Journal* noted that Disney stood poised to profit even more now that its studio could produce Pixar sequels without sharing half the take. Media analyst Jeffrey Logsdon said that Disney's earnings wouldn't be "that dramatically different in terms of dollars." In addition, Pixar would be forced to pony up its own production funds and possibly open films head-to-head against Disney releases and against Katzenberg's releases from DreamWorks and PDI, as well.

Eisner had said earlier about the possibility of a Disney-Pixar divorce, "We're Martin and Lewis. We're Abbott and Costello. We're a better team together than separate. I know it. I hope he knows it." Abbott and Costello? Did Eisner mean to allude to one of the most famous feuds in entertainment history? Perhaps so, because Abbott and Costello knew better than to split, despite their differences.

"I have always felt from Day One," Eisner said, "that it is in Pixar's best interests to continue with the Disney company . . . but we can only make half the deal."

Dennis McAlpine, of the research firm McAlpine Associates, summed up the catch-22. "The Pixar folks would be foolish to go somewhere else, because this deal has worked. Disney, on the other hand, would be foolish to let them go, because this deal has worked."

Still, Pixar had, incredibly, accounted for more than 45 percent of the Disney film studio's operating income between 1998 and 2001. Merrill Lynch puts that at 35 percent of Disney's studio profits. The *Wall Street Journal* summed up Eisner's dilemma: "The move is a high-profile setback for Disney Chairman and Chief Executive Michael Eisner, whose company often has relied heavily on Pixar smashes like *Finding Nemo* to generate the profit Disney's own animated films couldn't produce in recent years."

Financials aside, the Pixar walkout smelled distinctly personal. Dennis McAlpine said about Steve and Eisner that "if you put them in a room together, the chances of them coming out unscathed was impossible." Indeed, the clash between Steve Jobs and Michael Eisner seemed almost destined, fated in the Shakespearean sense.

On one side sits Steve, who spent his childhood and adolescence in California, the epicenter of two cultural quakes: technology and 1960s psychedelic music. He loved Bob Dylan and computers. He hated television; he still does. "When you're young, you look at television and think there's a conspiracy. The networks have conspired to dumb us down." For Steve, television is the "most corrosive technology" ever. He prefers technology that spurs him to interact and think, and he has spent his life giving the world computers that enhance exactly that.

When he saw music and technology at odds with each other due to Internet file sharing, he set about making peace. The Apple iTunes Music Store was nothing less than the culmination of all his creative dreams. "This will go down in history as a turning point for the music industry," Steve said. He had proved yet again that his ideas could, in fact, change the world. Just as with Pixar, technology and art had converged into one. He made a dent in the universe.

On the other side sits Eisner, who grew up in Manhattan, America's capital city for live theater and entertainment. He had started his college education as a pre-med student but switched to literature. A summer job as an NBC page sparked a desire to work in the entertainment industry. He loved television.

Eisner said that his father required him "to read two hours for every hour of television" that he wanted to watch. "I came from Manhattan, and when you're made to read so you can watch this new technology called television . . . honestly, to me it was kind of a chore."

Eisner was dazzled by the promise of technology, just as Steve was. The key difference is that Eisner never created his own company or, for that matter, his own show. Steve had already cofounded Apple Computer by age twenty-one. Eisner managed creative ventures; Steve created.

This difference did not escape notice of the press. "Eisner might be the single largest stockholder in Disney," Claude Brodesser wrote in *Variety*, "but that isn't the same as being its parent." When Steve played rough, the public indulged him. After all, he had built his companies. Eisner was not afforded that luxury.

Perhaps if Eisner's image hadn't already been damaged by his clash with the other titan, Michael Ovitz, as well as a string of other issues—low ratings at ABC, flat stock prices, poor performance of the movies, troubles at Euro Disney, and problems with dissident board members—he would have been praised for turning down a decidedly unfavorable deal from Pixar. Everything Eisner did seemed darkened by the clouds hovering over him. David Shore, director of the Trust Initiative at the Harvard School of Public Health and a corporate brand expert, said, "In most industries, the CEO is the steward of the company, the face of the brand. That face is now tarnished, and with it, the reputation and sales of the company often follow."

It didn't help that Disney pays Michael Eisner some $7 million annually; the value of the salary, the bonuses, and the stock he has received from the company over the span of his years there is said to be a stunning figure: around $1 billion. Stockholders haven't fared as well. According to Richard Barrett, president of Stonebridge Capital in Los Angeles, anyone who had a $10,000 stake in the company when Eisner arrived and had held on to the shares would have an asset worth over $210,000 today. But in the ten years since 1994—perhaps not so coincidentally, the year Frank Wells died—Disney stock has returned only 84 percent, while the stocks of the S&P 500 Index have returned nearly double that figure.

The break with Pixar could hardly have come at a worse time. Eisner faced hostility from within his own ranks, most notably from former board members Stanley Gold and Roy Disney, the only family member still in the company. Eisner, apparently chafing under Disney's criticisms, had arranged for the board to enforce its existing limitation on the age of board members. His goal was splendidly clear: only one member was affected. Roy Disney was seventy-three. His sidekick and business partner, board member Stanley Gold, resigned in protest and left the board with Roy.

For Roy Disney, the squeeze play that forced him out symbolized a corporate culture in decline. In his letter of resignation as chairman of the Feature Animation Division and from the board of directors, he wrote that the Walt Disney Company had "lost its focus, its creative energy, and its heritage." He listed as one of his complaints "the perception by all of our stakeholders—consumers, investors, employees, distributors and suppliers—that the company is rapacious, soul-less, and always looking for the quick buck." Other items on his list included "the failure to bring back ABC prime time from the ratings abyss," "timidity of investments" in theme parks, a "creative brain drain" in the company, and Eisner's "failure to establish and build constructive relationships with creative partners," including Pixar. The entire letter was less a resignation than a cannon shot aimed directly at Eisner.

In happier times, Roy had been called the "Jiminy Cricket" of Disney. Now he was ready to play a different role: Terminator. Disney and Gold launched a campaign to oust Eisner, opening a Web site they called SaveDisney.com. The name told their story: if you're a stockholder in the Walt Disney Company, if you're a fan of Disney, or if you just care about the heritage of *Sleeping Beauty* and *Snow White*, join in the effort to save the company by getting rid of its wicked usurper.

According to Roy, the Walt Disney Company suffered for years under the reign of Eisner's authoritarian regime. "Nobody is empowered to do anything on their own," he said. "Everything goes up to Michael if it costs more than a dime."

"At Disney," SaveDisney.com proclaims, "The System is King; Management Theory is tantamount. Those who can't play the game or obey the rules can't survive." Other essays sing the praises of Pixar.

Roy went so far as to file an SEC complaint, alleging that Disney executives were overcompensated in the extreme, taking home more than $68 million in total compensation packages over the previous three years, even as share prices dropped by 50 percent. The complaint also alleged that the "daring, dynamic, creative and businesslike management of the post-1984 years has given way to a staid and inbred group under the singular imperial rule of an Emperor (Michael Eisner) and his enabling Court (the board of directors)."

Eisner and the board, Roy charged, produced "schemers, who rather than supporting the creative soul, dictate to the artists what must be done (and won't tolerate differing views)."

This stands in stark contrast to conditions at Pixar, where the corporate culture is close-knit, intensely personal, and egalitarian—in large part due to the freewheeling style of John Lasseter, tempered only slightly by the mostly hands-off stance of Steve. High-tech meets

Hollywood in a successful, happy embrace. Even moving into a larger Emeryville building didn't break the family bonds. The building is a renovated $88 million brick warehouse, filled with light and elegance—there's an indoor badminton court, catered high-quality (vegetarian, of course) food, sandblasted steel bridges, a brick pizza oven, and a swimming pool. There's also a helicopter pad for Steve's use on his quick trips jetting between Palo Alto, Cupertino, and Emeryville. In the center of the whole place is an atrium, a gathering place for the entire company. Off in one corner is a waist-high passageway into the Love Lounge, a stainless-steel lounge for on-the-job relaxing that embodies the unique spirit of the place.

In one of the bonus features on the *Finding Nemo* DVD, Pixar creatives dressed up for an Ugly Contest, an event designed to encourage interaction and collaboration during the awkward early days in the new, vast space. Men grew mustaches (and sometimes half-mustaches), while women slathered garish, frosty blue shadow from their eyelids to their brows. Costumes became more and more outrageous every day. The Ugly Contest worked, bringing back the feelings of cohesion and let's-help-each-other cooperation.

Steve faults other companies for mishmashing creative innovation and marketing, noting how they lose their edge when "the product people aren't the ones that drive the company forward anymore." As a result, Pixar animators work free from micromanagement by a decidedly unartistic CEO.

At Disney, Michael Eisner has been labeled a micromanager, a charge that the media repeats over and over. The accusation is largely unfair, insists a former Disney animation executive, who says that in his view, "Michael didn't micromanage more than any other executive." But at times he could be excessively hands-on. The same executive tells the story of an experience with the pilot for a television series starring Ellen Burstyn. After screening the pilot, Eisner announced that he wanted to give his notes to the writer/producer in person. (In Hollywood, "notes" refers to the comments, criticisms, and demands made by a studio or a network for changes and is a standard part of the development process almost universally hated by producers and writers.)

Usually, the head of a network or a studio passes his notes to the appropriate executive, to be relayed. Not this time. When the producer came in, Eisner began as usual in "a friendly, congenial way and then offered praise and compliments." After that, he got down to business. The ending troubled him, specifically the part about the mother and the daughter being drawn together when the family cat is discovered in the closet, where it has given birth to kittens. A cat, Eisner explained, was the wrong choice. More Americans owned dogs than cats. "Everybody loves dogs," he insisted. "Dogs are more human, more emotional." The ending would be wonderful, he said, if the tiny newborn creatures were not kittens but puppies. The head of a multibillion-dollar business was taking his time to change the pets in a TV pilot from cats to dogs!

On another occasion he intruded into a story conference and demanded that writers and animators change the protagonist in *Chicken Little*, a forthcoming Disney animated feature, from a girl to a boy. No explanation. No reason. Animators were simply expected to make the change.

Incidents like that help explain the friction between Eisner and Roy Disney, who besides being a board member also held the post of chairman of the Feature Animation Division. Only a few weeks before the board forced him out, Roy discovered that a screening had been scheduled for a new animated picture—a screening about which Roy had not been informed, even though it was in his division of the company. He called Eisner to complain. Eisner made it clear that not inviting him wasn't an oversight: Roy was not welcome at the screening. Roy insisted he was coming anyway. Eisner offered no apology. "I guess I can't put a guard by the door," he said.

During the messy negotiations with Pixar, Eisner sabotaged friendships, commanding that no one—not even Roy—visit the Pixar studio. Presumably, he didn't want his position weakened by unauthorized conversations or information leaks, and he certainly didn't want Steve or John sweet-talking anyone on Disney's side of the Maginot Line. "I was asked, not so politely, to stay out of that," Roy said.

This explains why, immediately after Steve announced an end to negotiations, Roy sided with Pixar. "We had this relationship with some bright and creative people," he said. "It devolved into arguments over whether they could make a *Toy Story 3*. John Lasseter had a great idea for it, and they wouldn't make it."

The way Roy described it, though, the Save Disney movement aspired to more than simply salvaging Disney's creative partnerships or liberating the company from a totalitarian regime. Roy never could stand to use the words *brand* and *Disney* in the same sentence. Brand "means all the things that we're not," he said. "We're Snow White and Mickey Mouse and Donald Duck and Goofy and all those guys and gals."

Still, beneath all this righteousness hid a calculated strategy. Roy and Stanley's departures were sequels to an old drama; resigning in disgust was the battle plan the two had used in 1984, when they helped oust then-CEO Ron Miller. Stepping down was not a retreat but rather a negotiation tactic.

Some analysts believed that Pixar was working the same angle. Claude Brodesser of *Variety* thought Steve was simply taking a different tack: "give 'em enough rope." With Eisner in so much hot water, "there might not be a different studio in Pixar's future, just a different CEO."

While Disney shareholders moaned about underperforming stock and dwindling profits, and Roy launched the first grenades in his war, Steve planned the tactical equivalent of hovering over the Magic Kingdom with an atomic bomb. Eisner might be forced to save face and back down on *The Incredibles* and *Cars*. Better yet, he could be forced out altogether—in complete and total surrender. The situation devolved into a lose-lose for Eisner: if he flubbed the deal with Pixar, he faced stockholder attacks for losing *another* creative partner, but if he signed the deal Steve wanted, Wall Street might decry the potential losses.

Fate twisted the knife deeper into Eisner's side. The Disney annual general meeting loomed in March 2004, and Roy and Stanley rallied their troops.

The duo sent a letter to shareholders large and small. "We are seeking a NO vote on Michael Eisner," they wrote. "And also a NO vote on George Mitchell, Judith Estrin and John Bryson [the Eisner-loyalist board members] because they symbolize, respectively, the poor management, poor governance, poor compensation practices and a lack of board independence that are impeding the development of a long-term shareholder value at The Walt Disney Co."

At the meeting in Philadelphia, Roy and Stanley bunkered down at the Loews hotel, across the street from the Marriott where Disney was holding its meeting. Roy's language, though meant symbolically, carried a threatening taunt: "I used to say . . . if I had enough rifles we could have this thing over with."

Shifting gears to the mundane, he went on, "I've had e-mails asking me when we stopped cleaning the restrooms. Whoever takes over is going to need to change a lot of lightbulbs, both literally and figuratively," implying that Eisner's ouster was a done deal.

It ran counter to the charges in his resignation letter. Could Roy actually blame Eisner for dirty toilets?

A strictly logical analysis would miss the point. This was drumbeating, a buildup to what Roy saw as the CEO's worst failure of all: flushing creative partnerships down the toilet. Eisner was such an oppressive force that creative talents felt muzzled, according to Roy. "Right now, the second anyone tries to stick their little head out of the rabbit hole, they get smacked right back down."

In the end, shareholders delivered a stunning 43 percent No Confidence vote against Eisner. As a result, the board voted unanimously to split the two positions—chairman and CEO—into two separate posts. This forced Eisner out of his post as chairman but retained him as CEO. Suddenly, his future at Disney seemed uncertain. Could he ever renew his contract as CEO, or would he finally announce his resignation from that post, too?

To many investors it was pure déjà vu, but Eisner recognized no similarities between the current climate at the Walt Disney Company and the state of the Magic Kingdom when he came to its rescue in 1984. "The only relationship between 2004 and 1984," he said, "is that they both have fours in them."

To Steve Jobs, however, the Roy Disney–Michael Eisner titans clash couldn't have been more welcome. It put Eisner under very public pressure to come to terms on the Pixar deal. Steve's chances of prevailing looked ever more promising, even if he would have to wait for an Eisner-free Disney Company to see it happen.

Meanwhile, Pixar was about to release its riskiest film yet: *The Incredibles*.

Prior to starting *The Incredibles*, Pixar worked like a hermetically sealed laboratory, with in-house talents creating and directing every feature: John Lasseter, the creative force behind all of Pixar's films; Andrew Stanton, writer and director of *A Bug's Life* and *Finding Nemo*; and Peter Docter, director of *Monsters, Inc.* Indeed, the company policy clearly stated that the studio would "create all stories and ideas in-house." No unsolicited stories were accepted—period.

"We have spent the last ten years," Steve said, "growing our creative talent base and our technical talent base. These are skills that you cannot go out and acquire on the outside. There are not people out there that know how to do these things that you can go hire. So you have to grow them." Pixar liked its little family.

Risks do lurk when a studio constructs a moat to keep outsiders at bay. Many people thought that the inbred nature of Disney's top ranks explained the problems the studio had with turning out movies that audiences wanted to see. Some blamed the "nine old men" philosophy: the remaining old-timers who were with Walt in the early days had been in their twenties or thirties when they had helped create the studio's most enduring classics, but now they resisted fresh voices. To them, animators in their twenties needed to put in several decades before they would do anything worthwhile. An attitude like that simply stifles innovation.

Could Pixar become complacent? Could it lose its innovative edge and churn out soggy clones of its early successes, á la Disney? It's easy to imagine how such wild success could inflate egos and make even the most rigorous process vulnerable. Still high from Pixar's blockbuster success with *Toy Story* and *Finding Nemo*, John Lasseter wanted to keep the free-flowing creativity from freezing into a hard, cold, unbreakable tundra.

Talking about Apple, Steve said, "The system is that there is no system." Then he added, "That doesn't mean we don't have a process." Making the distinction between process and system allows for a certain amount of fluidity, spontaneity, and risk, while at the same time it acknowledges the importance of defined roles and discipline.

In 2000, it was time to take the leap and prevent the Pixar process from becoming a system. Enter the outsider: Brad Bird.

John Lasseter had actually talked to Brad about joining Pixar back in the *Bug's Life* days, but at the time Brad was busy finishing what would turn out to be a masterpiece, *The Iron Giant*, for Warner Bros. A critically acclaimed though underappreciated animated feature, it hinted at intriguing possibilities for a collaboration with Pixar. Brad had not worked with computer-based animation, but it made no difference. He had what it took to succeed at Pixar, the quality that John Lasseter most valued: a passion for good stories. In many ways, he was the obvious choice.

Brad had landed his first job in animation when he was hired by Disney at the tender age of fifteen to work under Milt Kahl—the man behind iconic movies like *Bambi* and *101 Dalmatians*. "He was my hero," said Brad. "It was like being an actor and getting coached by Brando."

"But once Walt died," Brad said, "watching Disney films get made, as Mike Barrier said in *Funnyworld*, was like watching master chefs cook hot dogs." The films still stunned with their visual brilliance, but they were based on what Brad called "lame ideas." He ended up studying animation at CalArts on a Disney scholarship, where he first met John Lasseter. After graduation, he had to decide between returning to Disney or accepting an offer to work on *The Simpsons*, where the ideas were amazing but the animation less than stellar. Though devoted to animation, he chose ideas and went to work on *The Simpsons*.

Given the same circumstances, John Lasseter would undoubtedly have made the same decision. Brad had proved himself to be a living, breathing example of exactly the kind of character Pixar so loved. He committed himself to ideas above profit margins, artistry over formula.

When John Lasseter called and said the door was open, Brad came in and pitched a story called *The Incredibles*. It would be a computer graphic animation feature with—gasp—an entire family of human superheroes. Human beings are notoriously difficult to depict in CG animation, which is why so many films feature animals or monsters, with as few human characters as possible. To propose a feature of all-human characters to a CG animation studio would be tantamount to creative suicide—if you were pitching to any other leading animation studio.

But John was happy with the idea of a challenge that would throw the studio "off balance," pushing his animators and technical wizards to the limits. It was just the kind of challenge he had thrown at his animators all along, but this time scaled up to the near impossible. Pixar said yes to *The Incredibles* and to the company's first outsider. "In all respects," said Ed Catmull, "we are looking for people who are better than we are, who do things that we don't do. You aren't looking for somebody who echoes what you're going to say."

Brad found it refreshing to be accepted precisely *because* of the trouble he might stir. "I have been fired for shaking things up, but I have never actually been hired for it, and this was with the full complicity of the heads of the company, John Lasseter, Ed Catmull, and Steve Jobs." (A former Pixar exec said of Catmull, "Because he's quiet, he doesn't get much attention. But he selected the team, and he's the person who makes the place run. He doesn't get nearly enough credit.")

Shake things up he did. *The Incredibles* was Pixar's first PG-rated release after a series of G-rated blockbusters. Nobody knew whether a movie like this could sell tickets, especially at a length of 115 minutes. Would it appeal to both adults and children? Would parents be offended? Pixar decided to leave it up to the audience. Brad explained, "Some kids were mildly traumatized by *Raiders of the Lost Ark*, and they probably shouldn't have seen it, but I don't think you would ever say take all that stuff out. . . . *Raiders* is the movie it set out to be."

Brad's movie pushed Pixar to its technical limits. "I had the knees of that place trembling under the weight of this thing," Brad said. Supervising technical director Rich Sayre agreed. "The hardest thing about *The Incredibles* was there was no hardest thing. Brad ordered a heaping helping of every expensive item on the menu."

The movie was make-or-break for Pixar, as its first studio release since the blowup with Disney. Steve Jobs needed another huge hit to maintain the Pixar leverage as he negotiated with new suitors. He also needed blockbuster profits to provide the bankroll to fund a continuing stream of movies.

By this time, one titan was folding under pressure. Under attack from several directions simultaneously, Michael Eisner in September announced his plans to step down as Disney CEO when his contract expired in 2006. He had never recovered from losing his post as chairman of the board.

Meanwhile, a pack of New York lawyers filing class action suits accusing companies of malfeasance, impropriety, or actions not in the best interest of stockholders set their sights on Eisner. The lawyers signed up willing stockholders and filed suit against the Walt Disney Company over the $140 million Ovitz received in his severance package. After seven years of skirmishing, the Court of Chancery in Georgetown, Delaware—the state where Disney was incorporated—slotted the case on its docket.

The trial opened in front of Chancellor William B. Chandler III in October 2004. The years of pretrial discovery uncovered a massive pile of evidence, mostly supporting the accusations Roy Disney and Stanley Gold had hurled at Eisner and his cohorts in the company. University of Miami law professor Elliott Manning called this "yet another exhibit in the problem of the imperial CEO."

Of all the headline-making stories that sprung from the trial, perhaps the most stunning was this: the root of the action grew out of hiring Ovitz (on the grounds that he was unsuited to the position) and firing Ovitz (on the grounds that the $140 million severance package was unjustified and unnecessary). Ovitz and Eisner both needed to defend the severance package and rebut the plaintiffs' case. So Ovitz and Eisner, whose conflict constituted the heart of the action, found themselves on *the same side*. Talk about strange bedfellows!

At one point, the court unsealed a letter Eisner had written to his former friend Ovitz. It revealed a side to the clash that few had ever seen. Here were two of the most powerful men in the entertainment biz engaged in a game of king-of-the-hill. Eisner summed it all up in simple, direct terms. "You do not like being number two in a company," he wrote. "And I do not think you really understand or like or are capable of managing a public company in the Disney style."

What a perfect bit of dramatic irony: Eisner, the accused anti-Disney, accusing Ovitz of not being Disney enough.

Ovitz, for his part, never experienced the magic of the "magic kingdom." On the witness stand, he said the company was "not particularly sensitive to human beings." He detailed how executives called each other on the telephone, rather than walk a few feet to the office next door.

The trial brought out how Eisner had rejected one Ovitz plan after another—including a plan to buy a 50 percent stake in Yahoo! for $100 million, a slice of the Internet pie that would have been worth $24 billion at the time of the trial.

On one occasion, actor Tim Allen walked off the set of the mega-hit

TV show *Home Improvement*. Ovitz testified that he invited the actor to dinner at his home and presented him with a $1,200 Roy Lichtenstein print as a gift. The star soon got over his pique and returned to the set. Instead of the company expressing gratitude for his heroic rescue of the television show, Ovitz testified, a "senior Disney executive" scolded him that the gift violated Disney policy and lectured him about corporate governance.

According to Ovitz, the Disney legal chief walked behind him "with a knife" and Michael Eisner "had the final say on everything."

Through all of this, Steve Jobs must have been secretly cheering. Michael Eisner had worked his way onto the Stevian "bozo" list, and now here was Ovitz doing his best to prove Steve's point. If Jobs had hired an entire squad of professional verbal abusers, they couldn't have done any more damage than Ovitz had single-handedly achieved.

Documents entered into evidence proved embarrassing to both. Eisner had written in a 1996 memo that Ovitz's "strength of personality together with his erratic behavior and pathological problems (and I hate saying that) is a mixture leading to disaster for this company. The biggest problem is that nobody trusts him, for he cannot tell the truth."

The two were on the same side in the trial, both desperate to establish that the $140 million paid to Ovitz was proper and justified, yet each was doing an admirable job of cutting the other off at the knees.

Eisner wrote a number of the Ovitz-related memos himself, in longhand or pecked out on the keyboard, presumably to prevent Mindy, his personal assistant, from knowing the details. His rampant spelling errors and grammatical gaffes betrayed his feelings—one imagines his trembling fingers and flushed face as the words flowed out.

In a final letter, Eisner recapped the Ovitz tenure at Disney. "We started having differences right from the beginning," Eisner wrote. "Which I attributed to some misguided over-enthusiasm. . . . You started off slowly with which I believe you would agree. You were nervous and wanted to impress everybody. Any you [sic] would agree that this was a mistake. I tried to support you, was frustrated by you, and wanted to help, inform and possibly guide you. By January, I was really concerned about our relationship."

The most revealing part of Eisner's Dear John letter comes at the end. "You may think that so much of what I have written in this letter is petty," he confessed. Did the highly literate Eisner recognize a Shakespearean quality to this debacle—two men bound by a lengthy friendship, both brilliant in their own right, destroying one another over a misfit of working styles?

"I would like to remain friends," Eisner concluded. "To end this so it looks like you decided it, and to be positive and supportive. . . . I hope we can work together now to accomplish what has to be done. I am ready to work as hard as necessary and as long." As hard and as long as necessary, that is, to get Ovitz out of Disney with the minimum amount of public spectacle.

Despite Eisner's attempts to smooth over the firing, Ovitz felt betrayed by his one-time friend. "I was cut out like a cancer," he testified in court. "I guess you could say I got pushed out [my office's] sixth-floor window."

In a 1995 memo Eisner wrote to Ovitz, he said, "The higher the position of the person making the mistake, the more interesting the fall, and the further the fall." The note was eerily prophetic and maybe even sad, because here were two old friends in the highest positions, whose biggest mistakes were *each other*.

While Eisner endured these embarrassing revelations in court, *The Incredibles* had become another box-office smash, taking in $45.5 million in its first weekend—the biggest single international weekend in history. Pixar had proved beyond any doubt that it didn't need a formula, and that the Pixar magic wasn't limited to one or two brilliant in-house talents but that Pixar could spot brilliant A-level talent like Brad Bird on the outside and put that talent to work. *The Incredibles* broke all the rules—an all-human computer-animated film, rated PG, aimed at adults, and succeeding with both audiences and critics alike.

For Steve, it meant something more: Pixar could produce and finance future movies *without* Disney. Independent financing is extremely important, given the distribution deal the studio seeks. Steve articulated his vision: "If our next two films do as well at the box office as we hope, we project that Pixar will have between $800 million and $1 billion of cash in the bank in 2006, and that's net of funding 100 percent of our future productions."

Once again, it was time to ask Michael Eisner to reopen negotiations and rewrite the agreement. And once again, Steve was cruelly perfect in his timing.

In the aftermath of Steve's January break-off of negotiations with Disney, reported in the colorful lingo of the trade journal *Variety* as his having "ankled the Magic Kingdom," he had walked away following ten months of sometimes heated talks. Steve needled with a statement that said, "It's a shame that Disney won't be participating in Pixar's future successes."

The statement from Eisner was more gracious, admiring "the wonderfully creative team [at Pixar], led by John Lasseter" and wishing them "much success in the future." Disney would have "enjoyed continuing our successful collaboration under mutually acceptable terms," the statement said, while acknowledging that "Pixar understandably has chosen to go its own way to grow as an independent company." Even Eisner critics had to acknowledge that the use of the word *understandably* showed that he recognized the good sense behind Steve's decision.

At that point, Pixar's five films had earned more than $2.5 billion at the worldwide box office and sold over 150 million DVDs and videos. While it might be difficult to sustain, especially if moving ahead without the Disney partnership, the company had achieved a remarkable 30 percent annual growth in revenues.

Yet in this clash of the titans, both were winners and both were losers. Disney loses a huge amount of income. Steve loses what may be the best marketing partner of all time.

The clash was hardly worth the costs on both sides. Despite Eisner's conciliatory parting words, Jobs and Eisner had behaved like Eisner and Ovitz, shooting poison-tipped arrows, slinging rocks, and hurling insults. It was as if the two men needed a fight.

"Pixar put a deal on the table that was almost insulting to Disney," said Jordan Rohan of Schwab Soundview Capital Markets. Steve had been insulted so many times that he could not resist a declaration of war.

Still, Steve's victory stance had its bittersweet component. He, John Lasseter, and the entire Pixar team will suffer the indignity of watching Buzz Lightyear and Woody and the rest of the *Toy Story* characters parade through a *Toy Story 3* made by the Disney studio, taking advantage of the contract provision that all rights to produce sequels of the Pixar films belong to Disney. To make it all the worse, Eisner—as if looking for a way to drive in the knife as deeply as possible— announced in January 2005 that a competition had been conducted for a *TS3* story concept, and the writer with the winning script was a novice from the Disney writing program. A novice.

It was all eerily reminiscent of the Ovitz-Eisner feud: two men, each brilliant in his own right, clashing like Norse gods in a Wagnerian opera. Roy Disney weighed in, taking the opportunity for another attack on Eisner. "More than a year ago," he said, "we warned the Disney board that we believed Michael Eisner was mismanaging the Pixar partnership and expressed our concern that the relationship was in jeopardy."

In the end, Steve won a crucial battle. Eisner will step down a year earlier than planned, and new CEO Bob Iger will have a better chance of getting the Pixar-Disney relationship back on track. Meanwhile, Pixar has enough money in the bank to fund its next several productions—without Disney. Whatever happens in the future, whether Pixar resumes its dance with Disney or chooses another dance partner, it will be Steve Jobs who makes the call. He who runs Disney runs a giant complex of businesses, but that does not make him the king of animation. That title belongs to Steve Jobs. Never mind that he could never have attained such an exalted post except on the shoulders of John Lasseter.

Steve is a certified movie mogul.

Even on Mount Olympus, the gods of Greek legend were not invulnerable. Mere mortals fare no better. Wealth, success, and celebrity do not bring protection from the same plagues that strike ordinary people.

On Sunday, August 1, 2004, Steve Jobs sent an e-mail to friends, associates, and employees. It read like this:

Team,

I have some personal news that I need to share with you, and I wanted you to hear it directly from me.

This weekend I underwent a successful surgery to remove a cancerous tumor from my pancreas. I had a very rare form of pancreatic cancer called an islet cell neuroendocrine tumor, which represents about 1 percent of the total cases of pancreatic cancer diagnosed each year, and can be cured by surgical removal if diagnosed in time (mine was). I will not require any chemotherapy or radiation treatments.

The far more common form of pancreatic cancer is called adenocarcinoma, which is currently not curable and usually carries a life expectancy of around one year after diagnosis. I mention this because when one hears "pancreatic cancer" (or Googles it), one immediately encounters this far more common and deadly form, which, thank god, is not what I had.

I will be recuperating during the month of August, and expect to return to work in September. While I'm out, I've asked Tim Cook to be responsible for Apple's day to day operations, so we shouldn't miss a beat. I'm sure I'll be calling some of you way too much in August, and I look forward to seeing you in September.

Steve

He added a P.S. that showed he hadn't lost his sense of salesmanship or his sense of humor.

P.S.: I'm sending this from my hospital bed using my 17-inch PowerBook and an Airport Express.

While some thirty-two thousand cases of pancreatic cancer are diagnosed in the United States every year, only a few hundred of those are the kind that Steve had. Dr. Robert Howard, an oncologist with the Medical Center of the University of California at Los Angeles, said, "The pancreas has been described as being like a loaf of raisin bread." In this analogy, the bread part makes enzymes for digestion and other functions. "The islets are the raisins, and they make hormones." The tumor may not produce any symptoms while still small. It's often detected when the patient has an MRI or a CAT scan for some other reason or begins to exhibit symptoms such as abdominal pain.

An oncologist can determine with outpatient procedures what type of tumor is present and whether it's benign. In a case like Steve's, the results come as a great relief because the patient learns that the tumor is the slow-growing type and is "resectable"—removable by surgery.

The surgery doesn't need to be scheduled on an emergency basis. Even so, Dr. Howard says, the patient would ordinarily be wheeled into the operating room within a couple of weeks or a month.

When the tumor is caught early and removed completely, the patient is likely to go back to enjoying a normal life, but there are no guarantees, Dr. Howard emphasized. "You can say what the typical prognosis is for a hundred people, but you can't say what it is for any particular individual. There are too many variables." The odds? Fifty percent of patients survive for five years.

Steve's prediction of an early return to work wasn't just a pipe dream. He began to show up for a few meetings in early September, barely more than a month after the operation, appearing enthusiastic and making no mention of what he had just been through.

Though his rift with company cofounder Steve Wozniak has never been completely healed, at least the two are in touch these days, and Woz was able to report that his old buddy "was in excellent spirits."

The reason for Steve's returning to work so quickly after surgery became clear in a few months: Apple was building a collection of new products that was designed to play off the success of the iPod, chasing after an outlandish Stevian dream: to take back the computer business from Microsoft.

Of course, anyone familiar with the history of Steve Jobs knows that he has a way of making outlandish dreams come true.

13

Showtime

As 2005 began, Steve was riding on top of the world. Sales figures for the iPod were way ahead of expectations, a fact that he would reveal at the annual MacWorld Expo in San Francisco. He had apparently beaten back pancreatic cancer, which, ironically, would claim his original adversary over the Macintosh—Jef Raskin—only a month later. Pixar was having another big success with *The Incredibles*, on its way to winning an Academy Award for the best animated film of the year. At the show that year Steve displayed his new-found humility by letting writer-director Brad Bird bask in the spotlight by accepting the award by himself. Steve was at the apex of his popularity.

The mark of a master showman is that he can dazzle a crowd, deliver a magical experience, send them off buzzing about what he has produced, and create a word-of-mouth tsunami that will keep crowds flocking to his tent for months to come. The evangelist, an Elmer Gantry, does one more thing: he can convince his faithful to go out and proselytize for his religion.

Steve Jobs is the master evangelist of the digital age. The Mac faithful go forth and do his bidding, convincing the unwashed, the unbelievers, that there is truth in Macintosh. But to do so, they have to be given the right tools.

Finally, in January 2005, Steve Jobs was no longer just waving his hands, selling the dream of the Macintosh as the "computer for the rest of us" with nothing to back it up, dazzling with slick marketing and *1984*-style advertising, compelling the committed to follow his Pied Piper act through the streets of the Digital City with his extraordinary oratory alone. For the first time since the Macintosh had been released in 1984, Apple really did have the goods.

The story began back in the Internet era, when Steve's best friend, Larry Ellison, pointed out that the Internet made complicated personal computers, with expensive processors and complicated operating systems, dinosaurs. Eventually, all that was needed to do most of the tasks people want to do was what was called a "thin client": a simple, Internet-capable computer equipped with a browser and a big hard drive to store material downloaded from the Web.

Of course, this flew in the face of everything that Macintosh stood for—up to that point the BMW of computers, with high-powered microprocessors, video capabilities, and the best page-layout and graphics capabilities of any computer on the market. For years, Apple's only successful business segment had been high-end graphics and publishing, and it had exploited that niche shamelessly, never reducing prices and always extending features and capabilities. Video was only the latest of these.

If Larry was in fact correct, most future capabilities that people were going to use would be delivered across a high-speed- (or broadband-) enabled Internet. Packaged software would disappear, to be replaced by on-demand programs. The most important "applications" would be delivered by Internet portals such as Yahoo! or Google. If Apple was to succeed, it would have to find a way to build thin clients that delivered the Apple experience.

The first step was to create a true Internet portal owned by Apple. iTunes was one step in this development, but iMovies, iCards, and iPhotos came first. These were all applications that could be accessed over the Internet, from any Mac, and they created the sense of community that most Mac faithful craved. When iTunes came along, it was the next stage of development, because it supported not just Macs, but also PCs, welcoming iPod owners from any operating environment into the Apple experience. As part of this Steve struck a deal with Hewlett Packard—venerable staid HP, undergoing a transformation under Carleton Fiorina that would soon fizzle out when she was fired—to sell iPods for the Windows platform with the HP logo. Although HP never made much headway, it showed that Steve was covering all the bases.

It was a modest development and hardly stirred any attention in Redmond as Microsoft rolled out its own MSN network and a couple of other end-user initiatives. There was one giant difference, however: Apple's services were consumer-oriented and built around fun things to do; Microsoft's lacked fun appeal and were utilitarian. Quietly and without drawing attention to itself, Apple had set up the structure of its future. Soon Safari, a Web browser from Apple, was released, and Mac machines were no longer dependent on Microsoft's Internet Explorer to browse the Web. The deal that Steve had struck when he returned to Apple was no longer so important.

All of this was collected into something called .Mac (dot Mac), a membership portal that offered a suite of services (including online hard drive storage, backup, and automatic software upgrades) for the Mac community.

Then came iPod Nation. The success of the inexpensive music-playing device changed the way Steve thought about everything. While Apple didn't make as much money on each one sold as it did on its high-end G5 computers, the volume of sales meant that by the end of the company's first fiscal quarter in 2005 (Apple, idiosyncratic to the end, has a fiscal year that runs from September to August), the iPod was generating as much cash as the company's computers. Steve started to think about what it all meant.

"We live in an era where more and more of our activities depend on technology," he said in an interview early in 2005. "We take our photos without film and have to do something with them to make them usable. We get our music over the Internet and carry it around in digital music players. It's in your automobile and your kitchen. Apple's core strength is to bring very high technology to mere mortals in a way that surprises and delights them and that they can figure out how to use. Software is the key to that. In fact, software is the user experience."

For all that Steve wanted to be a broadscale purveyor of digital technology, however, traditional PCs were still much cheaper, and Microsoft was the king of software. How was he going to change that?

The first step had been the eMac, an integrated Mac that included the computer with a monitor in one package. Add a keyboard and a mouse, and there was no longer any computer box. The success of that idea—a stylish evolution of what constituted a personal computer— led to the iMac G5 line. These were flat-panel all-in-one computers that used the fastest processors that Apple had and integrated everything into one unit. They were very successful, but all of this was only the preamble. After all, these Macs were still more expensive than comparable PCs, and they required that the buyers be motivated enough to pay the price of joining the Apple universe.

How could Apple combine the startling succecss of the iPod with the ubiquity of the Internet in a way that brought people who had been introduced to Apple through the small music player into the fold? This was the issue that securities analysts focused on with laserlike intensity: could the iPod drive sales of Macintosh computers? And how could the company break through in the business market?

One week before Steve walked onstage at the MacWorld Expo in January 2005, the company quietly introduced two crucial pieces of its new strategy: an upgrade to the Xserve high-powered Mac server that added a dual-processor configuration and the XSAN, a storage-area network system. The former provides a high-powered corporate server for businesses, and the latter a disk storage system for businesses that is priced extremely aggressively compared to Microsoft-capable systems from companies like Dell, EMC, and Network Appliance. With these two products, Apple had set the stage for a corporate CIO (chief information officer) to choose Apple. When the products were introduced, however, there was no inkling in the world at large that Apple would try to change the face of business computing. The products were touted as perfect for providing Linux-based computing power—the Mac has long been the gold standard for people who favor Linux, the open-source operating system, because Apple's OS-X operating system is Unix-based and therefore a close fit for Linux—and it offers the kind of vast storage that's necessary for video editing.

But Steve had something more in mind.

Twenty-one years after Steve introduced the Macintosh to a friendly crowd at Cupertino's De Anza College in January 1984, he slipped onstage a few minutes after 9 A.M. on January 11, 2005. Twenty-one years earlier, he had worn a double-breasted, pin-striped suit, and his intensity was palpable. Now he wore a black T-shirt and jeans. The intensity was still there, but his mood was very different. He was almost light-hearted, and he smiled a lot more.

Four thousand people were in the audience, many in overflow rooms where they had to watch him on giant projection screens, a kind of hip version of Big Brother. The buzz that Apple was going to introduce a new version of the iPod had been all over the media and the blogs (Web logs) in previous weeks. The crowd wouldn't be disappointed.

"Good morning."

The applause lasted just under a minute. The voice was still reedy, thin, and strangely insubstantial. For someone with such a commanding presence, Steve is shorter, at about 5'10", and slighter than one would expect.

"We've got a lot of firsts for you today. Among them is that this is the first time we've used HD, high-definition projection. You might wonder why."

With that, he launched into a one-man show that lasted for nearly two hours. He started out with a brief discussion of Apple retail stores and then the iMac. From there, he headed into the new Mac OS 10, "Panther," and he described the next version of the operating system, called "Tiger." It includes a kind of search capability called "Spotlight," which is Apple's Google killer—it enables a user to find anything stored on his hard drives. "Of course, it is from Apple so its user interface is a lot nicer," he quipped, receiving a great deal of applause. In the middle of the demo, the software crashed. "I've got a little bug here," he explained. Problems like this in front of an audience had never fazed him in the past, and didn't faze him now. "Well, that's why we have backup systems here," he quipped, as he restarted the program and went right on.

From there, he covered a number of features that had been improved in the newest version of the operating system. "It's pretty doggone cool. . . . We are on track to deliver it this year, and that is long before Longhorn [Microsoft's next version of Windows]," a jab at Bill Gates.

But it was in iMovies that Steve unveiled Apple's latest magic. For years, Apple had been the leader in online digital video editing and assembly. "This is the year of high-definition video," Steve said several times during his presentation. When he launched into his explanation of how the company was expanding iMovies to handle HD video as a native format, he showed off the latest Sony HD camcorder. A $3,499 product, and "you've just got to go get one of these." Then he brought out the president of Sony—Kunitako Ondo—who talked for a few minutes about Sony-Apple cooperation.

It was as if the company was answering Steve's complaint about "old generation" media companies that he'd expressed in an interview. "You or I move into a new house, and the first thing we do is call the phone company to get our land line turned on. Kids, they just move in with their cell phones. Stereos are the same: kids aren't getting stereos; they're getting speakers for their iPods. That's become the audio market. People are buying iPods and Bose speakers instead of a JVC or Sony stereo system. And those guys have never come to us and said, 'Could we work with you on the iPod?' Some companies are prisoners of their point of view."

Next came iWorks, his salvo over the bows of Microsoft. First he showed Keynote, Apple's slide show and presentation program that competes with Microsoft's PowerPoint. For the first time, PowerPoint would have serious competition as software for creating slide-show presentations. But the next program was the important one: Pages. Pages is Apple's version of Microsoft Word, a new word processing program that combines the basics of word processing with the page-layout capabilities that Apple pioneered years earlier when it destroyed the lithography and typesetting business with the LaserWriter and Post-Script fonts and where it still leads the market. "Word processing with an incredible sense of style." By bringing back a business-oriented word processing program, the company had thrown down the gauntlet to Microsoft, which has had the Macintosh and the PC word manipulation market to itself for years, and to Adobe, with its Pagemaker program for page layout. When Steve returned to Apple in 1997 he invited the executives of Adobe over and asked them to help him create a version of their video editing software for the Mac. Even though it had been Steve and Apple that put the company on the map twenty years before, they now refused. It galvanized his decision to beef up Apple's internal software development efforts. Now Apple had combined Word and PageMaker together, adding the company's ineffable sense of style and raising the ante. One more reason not to use Macs as business machines has disappeared.

There is only one missing piece: a spreadsheet to compete with Excel. While Steve didn't announce it at the MacWorld show, it won't be long before it is unveiled.

"What's next?" Steve went on. "I wish I had a nickel for every time somebody asked me why Apple doesn't build a stripped-down Mac. So today we're introducing it: it's called the Mac Mini." Eighty-two minutes into his presentation he unveiled the most important product of the day. He pulled one out from behind a counter. It was tiny, and it didn't include a keyboard, a mouse, or a display. That was the genius of it.

"This is a very robust computer, but it is very, very tiny. We supply the computer. You supply the rest. The great thing about Mac Mini is that you can hook it up to any industry-standard display, keyboard, and mouse. We want to price this Mac so that people who are thinking of switching won't have any excuses."

The audience was enraptured. The applause spilled over as he announced the prices: $499 and $599—"the cheapest, most affordable Mac Apple has ever offered." It was a challenge to the hegemony of the Microsoft Intel world.

Combining corporate servers and storage networks with cheap devices that could populate every desk, a suite of applications that challenged Microsoft's tired productivity applications, and an online environment that provided a pleasant and pleasurable user experience was a strong challenge. Certainly in the consumer world, where the iPod had already dominated the market and Apple was the king of cool (a recent top five brand study showed Apple as the world's leading brand—interestingly, Disney had fallen off the list, and Pixar was number five), the new Mac Minis were likely to be a big success. But it is the business desktops of the world where the quantities of sales are huge. Could Apple compete?

When Steve returned to Apple he shut down the clone Macs that his predecessors had reluctantly licensed. He claimed that they only stole sales from Apple with their low prices, never penetrating the Windows and IBM PC market. Now he was going one step better. With the falling prices of components, and his experience with Far Eastern contract manufacturing for the iPod, Apple was outcloning the PC clonemakers.

Steve has put together all the pieces—Bill Gates is a tough competitor. The battle should be intense. Will cool beat copycat?

Steve wasn't done. It was time to move to iTunes and finally the iPod.

"In the last quarter I am pleased to report that we have sold over four and a half million iPods. That is a 50 percent growth year over year. We have sold over 10 million iPods to date and over 8 million of them in 2004. The digital music era is upon us, and we are leading the charge.

"Thank *you*." It was a remarkably heartfelt thanks, given directly to his audience. Steve seemed to have learned that the real key to his success were his customers. This was the new Steve Jobs.

With that, he described some of the over four hundred secondary products for the iPod—iPod Nation—and described a series of cars with iPod adapters. "Even Alfa Romeo and Ferrari." But that wasn't all. He told about the Motorola iTunes deal and showed one of the cell phones that will soon play music. "These two things and many more are why we believe that we have just begun the world of digital media.

"But there is one more thing we want to tell you about. It's pretty great."

After describing the iPod market share as having doubled versus the flash memory–based players in one year—from 31 percent a year ago to 65 percent in 2004—he launched into his new player. (The original iPods contain a tiny hard disk drive—flash memory players store songs on so-called "flash" memory chips.) Apple's newest offering was a flash-based player called the iPod Shuffle. It was tiny, "no bigger than most packs of gum," stored about one hundred songs, and was simpler to use than the original iPods. It was not met with the enthusiasm of the rest of the presentation, but he still had the audience in his hands after ninety minutes.

A tag line popped up on the screen: "The iPod Shuffle. Because life is random." For a man who had battled cancer and seemed to have conquered it, this was a fitting epigraph.

To finish the presentation off, he invited John Mayer onstage to sing his Grammy-winning song, "Daughters." For a man who had neglected his own firstborn daughter for years, it was an ironic choice. But maybe not. "Fathers, be good to your daughters," sang Mayer. "Daughters will love like you do."

Steve Jobs had returned, to all appearances as fit as before and even better.

A couple of days later, Apple announced its best quarter ever. Revenue was $3.49 billion, up 74 percent from the same quarter a year earlier. Profits were 70 cents a share, compared with 17 cents a year earlier—and 21 cents above analysts' consensus. While iPod sales had skyrocketed—five times as many as a year earlier—Macintosh sales had also risen by 26 percent year over year, to more than a million Macs.

Steve Jobs, at age fifty, had made himself into an icon of three different industries.

Yet at times it seems as if he is only just getting started. He hasn't changed fundamentally. He's still the same aggressive, opinionated, driven creator who inspires people around him to reach unimaginable heights and destroys the fragile egos of those whose skin is too thin to handle his abrupt barbs and relentless questioning. Yet now he's a middle-aged man, with three kids at home and a world of experience behind him. He is warmer, richer, more forgiving, and more understanding, but on reaching fifty, he's still the same man he always was.

"[Turning fifty] makes us look further ahead, but it doesn't make us more patient," he said. "You know better what questions to ask. There aren't enough good people to do everything you want to do. So now we chew on things for a while before we decide to have the A-team go after something. That's not the same as being more patient."

Patience is a quality that no one will see in Steve. A legion of admirers, a world of investors, a universe of music lovers, an audience of moviegoers, and a generation of digital kids are impatient to see what worlds he will conquer next.

So is he.

Epilogue

Every one of us is a walking set of contradictions. The great among us are no different, except that their contradictions tend to run to extremes. Steve Jobs today in some ways suffers from the same need to be in control as when he forced his parents to move so that he could go to a different high school, the same intolerance that led him to freeze some of his closest friends and associates out of the Apple IPO over issues of loyalty, the same childish harshness that led him to blow up at one of Pixar's founders over something so petty as commandeering Steve's whiteboard.

All this from one of the towering visionaries of our time, a man who has reshaped three different industries and who, at age fifty, sometimes looks as if he is only just getting started.

Over the years, even the most flagrant flaws may be softened. In an interview when he was forty, Steve Jobs showed that family and experience had smoothed some of his rough edges. Speaking about computers and technology, he said, "This stuff doesn't change the world. It really doesn't." The interviewer replied, "That's going to break people's hearts." Steve said, "I'm sorry, it's true. Having children really changes your view on these things. We're born, we live for a brief instant, and we die. It's been happening for a long time. Technology is not changing it much, if at all."

"Parenthood," he told the authors of a children's book about him and Woz, "changes one's world. It's almost like a switch gets flipped inside you, and you can feel a whole new range of feelings that you never thought you'd have."

Asked on another occasion what he wants to pass on to his children, his answer was equally thoughtful: "Just to try to be as good a father to them as my father was to me." He followed with a remark that was both touching and memorable: "I think about that every day of my life."

For a rock star, adulation means standing-room-only concert halls all over the world and screaming fans. For Steve Jobs, the only technology rock star of the digital age, it means a soaring stock price and the adulation that comes from captivating the investing public.

A few days after Steve's fiftieth birthday, on Monday, February 28, 2005, Apple's stock split for the third time in the company's history. Each of the previous times, it signaled the end of an overheated period of growth and perception. Will the same thing happen this time?

Twenty years earlier, when Steve was thirty, he was an immature young man who had grown up in the cauldron of a public company that led the world in revealing the possibilities brought by technology. He had taken his fascination with electronics parts and stereo systems and crafted a series of devices that launched an industry.

When he was thrown out of Apple, he thought that the magic of Apple was in its hardware. As a result, he tried to build a new company—NeXT—around a new piece of hardware and bought another company, Pixar, that he thought was all about its hardware until he discovered a different reality.

Eventually, he realized that the true genius at Pixar wasn't in the software but in the creativity it enabled. The same thing happened at NeXT. By the time he sold that company to Apple, it wasn't the hardware that mattered, or even the software, but what the software made possible.

With his new focus on software, the next battle that Steve wants to win has come into sharp focus. There is one company on earth that controls software. It is led by the man who stole Apple's crown jewels twenty years ago, and Steve has not forgotten. Now it is Apple, not Microsoft, that has the buzz and the bounce.

Having just extracted himself from one battle of titans, Steve Jobs has now set himself a new battle with, for him, the giant of titans: Bill Gates. When Steve returned to Apple in 1997, there was no doubt who would win. The little Cupertino company was on life support, and it needed Microsoft to survive. Now the tables have turned, the momentum has shifted, and Apple has the upper hand.

Take all of this together, and there is one company that Apple is targeting. It isn't Sony or any of the consumer electronics companies. They are providing boxes, devices, the kinds of products that the young Steve Jobs thought were important. Now, nearly ten years after he rode in to save Apple, Steve has come to understand that the combination of software and content are what make Apple special. "The great thing is that Apple's DNA hasn't changed," he said in a recent interview. "The place where Apple has been standing for the past two decades is exactly where computer technology and the consumer electronics markets are converging. So it's not like we're having to cross the river to go somewhere else; the other side of the river is coming to us."

A wag once said that maturity means knowing what your strengths are, so that you don't need to fight against them anymore. This is exactly what Steve has done with Pixar and Apple.

Steve is no longer an emperor who stands at the water's edge and demands that the river change its course to his command. He is now the captain of a river raft hurtling down the rapids; he's guiding the boat, but he has a team of compadres with oars as well. Whether they are animators at Pixar or a thousand software engineers at Apple, Steve is the leader but now understands that he isn't the only important participant.

No one has changed more than he has. In a world of baby boomers who grew to maturity in the sixties and the seventies, he is now an emblem of hope in a complex world. Maybe we aren't encased in an immutable prison by the age of thirty. Maybe we can change for the better.

In the old days, Steve always considered that a handful of anointed superstars were the magic that made the Macintosh hardware work or gave some other project its glow and glamour. Always the chief superstar among them, in his view, had been Steve himself. He could be gracious when he was being lauded or applauded, but it was never genuine; his arrogance bubbled palpably under the surface. Now his concern for others is genuine.

A friend who ran into Steve during the Christmas holidays of 2004, three months after his cancer operation, said that Steve described himself as "feeling fine, feeling fortunate." He looked robust, the friend said, and recounted his recent pleasure when an analyst gave a positive outlook for Apple, so strong a recommendation that the stock price had jumped up. Steve seemed "gleeful" in describing his reaction. He was smiling and relaxed, and, when complimented on how well he looked, he seemed to genuinely appreciate the comment.

By the following January, Steve was back on track, and so was

Apple. With a receding hairline and graying hair, and no longer trim, Steve was showing his age—just shy of fifty. But he seemed as vigorous as ever when he walked onto the stage for his traditional MacWorld keynote address. When he came to the end of the two-hour presentation, he showed his wisdom.

"I would like you to join me in thanking all the people at Apple who've worked so hard to create all these new products." Then he added, "I want to thank the families and the spouses of all the people at Apple because I know you'd like to have us around a little more."

It was the new Steve: a man who no longer believed that the world started and stopped with what he was interested in. This was a man who still had the qualities of his youth—good and bad—but they had been leavened with time and wisdom and experience. He had rescued his first love—Apple—and made her beautiful again. He had captivated whole families, parents as well as children, with a string of animated stories that celebrate life with a humor that lifted the stories out of the maudlin and made them timeless. He had revitalized the music industry, breathed new life into it, and sent it off to a new digital future.

Up on the heights of Olympus, the view is different. Steve Jobs has proved that he can captivate us all anew, he has shown his children that he is a master of the universe, and he has made money for everyone who has invested in him again. He has taken charge of three industries in an unprecedented hat trick.

Yet there's one more battle he wants to win. It has nothing to do with money, fame, or glory. Like all the best fights, this one is personal. Steve Jobs is going to best Bill Gates. This fight is Shakespearean, elemental, and emotional; watching it unfold should be the most fascinating business story of this young millennium.

We expect our heroes to be flawed. Heroes without flaws would not be successful. Yet in the end, it's not the flaws we need to remember but the achievements.

Acknowledgments

To paraphrase Steve Jobs, "Publishing a book is a team sport." Not only is there an army of unnamed friends, family, and colleagues who have to endure missed birthdays, intense one-sided conversations, and outlandish ideas during the months of reporting and writing, but there are also many people who labor behind the scenes to bring a book to the public.

Gratitude goes as always to our literary agent, Bill Gladstone, who continues to work wonders, and to David Fugate, Ming Russell, and Neil Gudovitz, all of whose efforts have been nothing short of stellar. Wiley editor Hana Lane proved to be a writer's dream: patient, calm, wise, and unflappable; we are in your debt. Helene Godin is an attorney who successfully combines efficiency with kindness and humor. The rest of the team at Wiley—Lisa Burstiner, Naomi Rothwell, Sabrina Eliasoph, and freelance copy editor Patti Waldygo—and their efficient colleagues, all deserve much more praise than would be seemly for us to deliver here. Suffice it to say that we are deeply in your debt.

We have passed ideas, passages, and chapters among friends and colleagues, looking for improvements and inspired reasoning. We've been fortunate to receive this, and more, from many people. They've caught mistakes and clarified our thinking. The errors that remain are ours.

From Jeffrey Young

A writer's family suffers both the trials and tribulations that this life produces. My wife, Janey, has been my mainstay since before I met Steve Jobs, and remains my guiding star to this day. With her I've discovered what forever means, and together we've raised three children who inspire me every day. Without all of them I would be a shadow of the writer I've become.

I would be remiss to forget the two men who set me on this story so many years ago: the late Andrew Fluegelman, and David Bunnell, the creators of *MacWorld* magazine. Also instrumental was the editor of my first book about Steve Jobs, Dan Farber, whose deft touch, gentle humor, and insistent voice made my original effort much better than I could have dreamed. Over the years there've been many who helped refine, define, and expand my thinking about Steve Jobs, but only one who has been a constant sounding board, a relentless iconoclast, and by his example a model for what a great reporter must be: ruthlessly curious, obsessive about the truth, and eternally uncommon in his insights. To Jim Forbes, the sine qua non of Silicon Valley reporters, I owe more than I can express.

Finally, I've been stimulated and embraced by an organization that has provided me with an opportunity for intellectual challenge and personal growth. To Craig Gordon, Jon Gates, and the team at Off the Record Research, thank you for your kindness, humanity, and trust. I couldn't have done this without you.

From Bill Simon

To my darling wife, my inspiration and my light, who suffered less attention and more grouchiness than during the writing of any of my dozen previous books. I'm determined to repay you now that this deadline is over and I don't mind promising in print that you will be showered with lavish attention and the praise you deserve for your patience and your forbearance. As our friends and your many admirers know, life is better with Arynne in it.

For a writer working on a far-ranging biography it's a relief to be able to call on high-quality help with research, organizing, and arranging of material. Jeffrey and I were well served by Sheldon Bermont, Karrie Higgins, Erik Martin, Jerry Starr, and Todd Barmann. Surely each of these folks knows how appreciative I am, as do Angel Sepriano and his daughter Jo Jo, at Umberto's in Beverly Hills, always graciously providing a place for me and my go-everywhere computer. I also want to recognize the kindness and efficiency of my Los Angeles administrative assistant, Brenda Hawkins, and to Marianne Stuber for her super-efficient transcribing of interview material.

During these months I have enjoyed dinner with friends and family who were patient beyond any definition of friendship, suffering my conversation that was heavy with talk of Steve, Apple, Pixar, Eisner, Disney, and the other players in this saga. I ask their forgiveness and vow, now that I am on this last page, that we shall again talk of other things.

Notes

Writing a book together is a special challenge. We were lucky to find each other and discover a mutual fascination with Steve Jobs that spanned more than twenty years. From the time Steve first challenged one of us in the middle of the Macintosh building on Apple's Cupertino, California, campus in the summer of 1983, to the January 2005 MacWorld Expo keynote, we've observed and interacted with him in many situations.

The coauthors of this book have a unique combination of experience that informs this material. Jeffrey S. Young was one of the cofounders of *MacWorld* magazine in 1983, and as such he had a unique ringside seat to the development of the Macintosh computer, both inside Apple before its release, and in subsequent years. He is the author of the book *Steve Jobs: The Journey Is the Reward* (Scott Foresman, 1987), which provides a detailed look at the life of Apple's cofounder through his founding of NeXT Computer in 1985. Throughout the 1990s he was a contributing editor to *Forbes* magazine in Silicon Valley, and covered NeXT, Apple, and many other high-tech companies; as the Northern California editor for *The Hollywood Reporter* in the same period, he reported and wrote extensively about George Lucas and Lucasfilm, Industrial Light and Magic, and Pixar.

Bill Simon wrote scripts for videos, CEO and executive speeches, and live meetings for Apple in the 1980s. He is the author of many books on business and other subjects, and in the mid-1990s coauthored the book *On the Firing Line* (Harper Business, 1998) with Gil Amelio, the CEO Steve Jobs ousted on his return to Apple. As such he brought a deep level of understanding and detail to the crucial period when Steve returned to Apple and the ensuing years.

Steve was offered a chance to contribute to the book. He refused. Because Steve Jobs is violently opposed to friends, associates, or employees speaking for publication, numerous interviews were conducted with the promise of anonymity, and much of the interview material ended up as background. The cutting-room floor is always littered with nuggets—thanks to all of you who spent time with us over the years, especially those whose insights didn't make it directly into this book.

The list of those who've been interviewed by the authors is long, and some have requested anonymity. Our deepest appreciation to all who spoke on condition of anonymity: we salute each of you, and wish we could honor you here individually with the thanks you deserve.

Individuals interviewed are mentioned at the appropriate places in each chapter. Those interviewed also include: Garry Allen, Gil Amelio, Stewart

Brand, Phil Roybal, Larry Tessler, Andy Hertzfeld, Mike Boich, John McCollum, Jay Elliott, Stevan Birnbaum, Burt Cummings, Rich Melman, Chris Espinosa, Jerome Coonen, Phil Schlein, Bana Whitt, Carl Ho, Mike Murray, Lee Felsenstein, Douglas Englebart, Mike Kane, Jim Hennefer, Alex Fielding, Jean-Louis Gassée, Bruce Tognazzini, John Warnock, Alfred Mandel, Brian Fitzgerald, Dick Olson, Al Alcorn, Paul Terrell, Larry Gritz, M. K. Haley, Jef Raskin, Joanna Hoffmann, Donn Denman, Steve Capps, Margie Boots, Ellen Hancock, Paul Heckbert, Joe Hutsko, Bill Atkinson, Regis McKenna, Nolan Bushnell, Bob Henkel, Adam Osborne, Daniel Kottke, Hildy Licht, Jeff Harbers, Ray Wilson of the Ronald Reagan Presidential Library, Susan Berman, Bruce Horn, Larry Kenyon, Patti King, Wendell Sander, Cliff Huston, Peter Quinn, Dave Larson, Barbara Koalkin, Bill Fernandez, Elizabeth Holmes, Ed Riddle, Martin Haeberli, Randy Wigginton, Guy Kawasaki, Fred Hoar, Don Breuner, Ed Ruder, Alex Lamradt, Owen Densmore, Carol Kaehler, Bruce Courture, Linda Lawrence, Alex Schure, Dylan Kohler, Terry Kunysz, Terry Anzur, Joe Shelton, Heidi Roizen, Steward Alsop, Steven Miller, Clifford Miller, Wayne Meretsky, Hilary Rosen, Jeff Eastwood, Bud Colligan, Bob Albrecht, Dan'l Lewin, Todd Rulon-Miller, and Alvy Ray Smith. Pamela Kerwin and a tennis-playing confidential informant deserve special thanks for putting up with so many repeated phone calls. Ditto for Bill Adams, along with deepest respect: his loyalty to Steve is impressive.

While the shelf groans under the weight of many Apple books, there are several that deserve special mention. We especially want to thank author Alan Deutschman, author of *The Second Coming of Steve Jobs* (Broadway Books, 2000) for providing a lead that turned out to be very valuable, and for the contribution of his Steve Jobs biography to the world. The book details the founding of Pixar in exquisite detail and many of the trials and tribulations of the NeXT years; as in science, each person builds on the work of those who came before. Another book that is must reading for anyone wanting to find out about the early days of Apple is Michael Moritz's *The Little Kingdom* (William Morrow, 1984). Steven Levy's *Insanely Great* (Viking, 1994) tells a cheerful version of the making of the Mac, while Guy Kawasaki's *The Macintosh Way* (HarperCollins, 1990) offers a light-hearted view of the inside of the Mac marketing effort by one of the team's early product "evangelists"; they are both counterpointed by Jim Carlton's *Apple: The Inside Story of Intrigue, Egomania and Blunders* (Harper Business, 1998) which paints a much darker picture. To understand the world of the Disney Company and Michael Eisner two books are essential: *DisneyWar* (Simon & Schuster, 2005) by James Stewart; and *Work in Progress* (Random House, 1998) by Michael Eisner and Tony Schwartz.

Several other books deserve to be sought out and read by anyone who wants a deeper understanding of the forces that formed Steve Jobs and created Apple and Pixar, as well as the computer industry. These include: *Fire in the Valley: The Making of the Personal Computer* (McGraw-Hill, 1999, reissue) by Michael Swaine and Paul Freiberger; *Hard Drive: Bill Gates and the Making of the Microsoft Empire* (John Wiley & Sons, 1992) and *Overdrive: Bill Gates and the Race to Control Cyberspace* (John Wiley & Sons, 1997), both by James Wallace; *Gates: How Microsoft's Mogul Reinvented an Industry* (Touchstone, 1994) by

Stephen Manes and Paul Andrews; *Hackers: Heroes of the Computer Revolution* (Doubleday, 1984) by Steven Levy; and finally, *The Soul of a New Machine* (Atlantic-Little Brown, 1981) by Tracy Kidder. All of these are well worth reading and contributed to our work.

Some of the material obtained from published sources is as follows; our thanks to all the reporters, journalists, and authors who provided this silent help. However, the vast quantity of media coverage of Steve and Apple over the years makes it impossible to credit everything, as does the dimming of memory over time and confusion in the face of multiple sources. For anyone we've missed, or missed crediting appropriately, we ask for your forgiveness.

1 Roots

Interview sources for this chapter are Steve Jobs, Clara Jobs (Steve's adoptive mother), Steve Wozniak, Dan Kottke, Randy Wigginton, Bill Fernandez, Al Alcorn, Alex Fielding, Bruce Courture, John McCollum, and Jack Dudman. The quotes about Steve Jobs crying over swim-team losses and being a terror are from David Sheff, "Playboy Interview: Steve Jobs," *Playboy*, February 1985. Paul Jobs's memory of his son forcing the family to move was obtained by Michael Moritz and recounted in his *The Little Kingdom* (William Morrow, 1984). Fred Hoar, a former Apple advertising manager, is the source of the remark about sipping water from a fire hose.

2 A Company Is Born

People whose interviews contributed material to this chapter are Steve Jobs, Steve Wozniak, Dan Kottke, Randy Wigginton, Chris Espinosa, Trip Hawkins, and former executive of Xerox Development Corp. Stevan Birnbaum. Also, Bob Newton, Dick Olson, Rod Holt, Lee Felsenstein, and Richard Melman. Steve's description of selling the Apple I circuit boards to Paul Terrell appears in the Sheff *Playboy* interview cited previously. The explanation given by Steve when he took financial responsibility for Chris-Ann's child is quoted from Moritz's *The Little Kingdom*, previously cited.

3 Let's Be Pirates!

Interview sources for this chapter are Steve Jobs, Steve Wozniak, the late Jef Raskin, Chris Espinoza, Andy Hertzfeld, Dan Kottke, Bruce Tognazzini, Trip Hawkins, Larry Tessler, Bill Atkinson, Stevan Birnbaum, Bill Fernandez, Joanna Hoffmann, Bud Tribble, Donn Denman, Phil Roybal, Mike Murray, Martin Haeberli, Joe Shelton, and Jay Elliott. *Little Kingdom* is also the source of Steve's complaint about Steve Wozniak giving stock to "all the wrong people." The scene of the appearance of the ten-year-old daughter is from *A Regular Guy*, by Mona Simpson (published by Alfred Knopf, 1996).

4 Learning to Fail

This chapter uses interview material from Mike Murray, Jay Elliott, Steve Wozniak, Herbert Pfeiffer, Paul Berg, Bud Tribble, Susan Barnes, and many others. Steve Jobs's remarks to the Swedish journalist are from John Dvorak's article,

"Jobs Breaks Silence on Apple Ouster," in the *San Francisco Examiner*, June 27, 1985. His statements about the following are all from an interview in *Newsweek*, September 30, 1985: his reaction on being fired by John Sculley; giving computers to California schools; and his statements about the issues raised by Apple about "When somebody calls you a thief in public." Information about the events that led to the starting of NeXT includes material from "Jobs Talks About His Rise and Fall," by G. C. Lubenow and M. Rogers, *Newsweek*, September 30, 1985, and from "Behind the Fall of Steve Jobs," by Bro Uttal, *Fortune*, October 14, 1985. The Bill Campbell quote was reported in the *Wall Street Journal*, September 17, 1985. The Mike Markkula statement concerning possible action against NeXT by Apple is from an Apple press release of September 16, 1985.

5   The NeXT Step

A former Disney executive, speaking confidentially, contributed material for this chapter. Information about Christina Redse, in this chapter and later, is from Alan Deutschman's *The Second Coming of Steve Jobs* (Broadway Books, 2000).

The story about Jeffrey Katzenberg's blow-up at Jobs is also from *Second Coming*. This story has been confirmed by the eyewitness who was Deutschman's source. Katzenberg's public relations representative, Terry Press, though she was not present, loyally protects her boss by insisting it couldn't have happened. She maintains, "I have worked with Mr. Katzenberg for seventeen years and I have never heard him speak like this to anyone. It is not possible that Jeffrey said anything like this. . . . I am saying for the record that there is no way he said this."

6   Show Business

People whose interviews contributed material to this chapter are Alex Schure, the man who created the Computer Graphics Lab that was the ultimate genesis of Pixar; Paul Heckbert, a former employee at CGL; a Lucasfilm confidential source; a NeXT confidential source; and former Pixar sales and marketing vice president Bill Adams.

Except for the quotes otherwise attributed, Alan Deutschman assembled the information about Alvy Ray Smith's quest that led him to Long Island, and the insights into the origins and operations of the Computer Graphics Lab; details were originally presented in Deutschman's *Second Coming*, cited previously. The Jobs remarks about the poor quality of individual frames in the early *Star Wars* films are from an oral history interview by Daniel Morrow, executive director, the Computerworld Smithsonian Awards Program, April 20, 1995. The article by Richard Corliss and Jess Cagle, "Star Wars: Attack of the Clones," in *Time*, April 20, 2002, contained Lucas's list of projects he was working on simultaneously. Carrie Fisher's remark was ad-libbed during a live taping of the cable television series "Dinner for Five," February 2005. John Lasseter's background is as reported by Burr Snider in "The *Toy Story* Story," *Wired*, December 1995; by *New York Times* online at movies2.nytimes.com; and on the Pixar Web site. The Catmull quote on hiring was reported in "Pixar: To Infinity and Beyond," *Management Today*, May 1, 2004. Details on hiring Lasseter were contained in Brent Schlender's article, "Steve Jobs' Amazing Movie Adventure," *Fortune*

(Information Technology Special Report), August 18, 1995. The phrase about "the lord in his manor" is from phrasemaker Alan Deutschman, in *Second Coming,* as are details of the stock split on starting Pixar.

Lucas's remark about "We're all Buddhists up here" was made to Jess Cagle and published in *Time,* April 20, 2002. The description of devising Pixar's name comes from the Alvy Ray Smith Web site. Information about the Pixar mission, company organization and work methods, and the Pixar computer is derived from a combination of sources, including new interviews, *Second Coming,* the Smithsonian oral history interview, and the Philip Elmer-DeWitt article, "The Love of Two Desk Lamps," *Time,* September 1, 1986. The *Time* article is also the source of the reaction to the *Luxo Jr.* short at the Siggraph convention. The Catmull remark about the response to this film was reported by Laura A. Ackley in "Pixar's deep talent pool lured by Catmull's vision," *Variety,* July 20, 1998.

7   Master of Ceremonies

Material in this chapter is based in part on interviews with the former Disney executive who also provided information for chapter 5; Dylan Kohler, former Disney software engineer who was a principal contributor to development of the CAPS animation software; and former Pixar executive Pamela Kerwin.

Steve's first encounter with his future wife, Laurene, her trip to Italy, and their wedding are in part from *Second Coming.* Details of her background are from Web sites. Steve told the story about deciding to ask Laurene to have dinner with him on the day of their first meeting to journalist Steve Lohr, recounted in "Creating Jobs: Apple's Founder Goes Home Again" (*New York Times Magazine,* January 18, 1997), and Julie Pitta provided other details about Steve and Laurene's life together and their wedding in the "Informer" section of *Forbes,* October 29, 1990 and April 15, 1991. Steve's blowup at Alvy Ray Smith, recounted in *Second Coming,* is amplified with input from Alvy. Details of the origin of the movie *Tron* can be found on the Web site www.cyberroach.com/tron/tron.htm.

Much of the material on negotiations between Pixar and Disney were provided by three confidential sources, two from Pixar and one from Disney, as well as by Pam Kerwin. Some of the details concerning attorney Brittenham are from the *Los Angeles Business Journal,* February 19, 2001. Material on the production methods and Lasseter's role are based in part on Barbara Robertson's article "Toy Story: A Triumph of Animation," *Computer Graphics World,* August 1995, supplemented by details from other sources including *Second Coming* and Brent Schlender in *Fortune,* August 18, 1995, cited earlier. Details of the Canon investment in NeXT come from Bob Johnstone, "Canon, Lone Wolf," *Wired,* October 1994. Source of the Billy Crystal quote is the Internet Movie Database (imdb.com), August 30, 2001. The Schneider remark about partners comes from a *Business Week* story, "Steve Jobs, Movie Mogul," November 23, 1998.

Material on the story problem on *Toy Story* and how it was solved comes principally from Burr Snider, "The *Toy Story* Story," *Wired,* December 1995; from *Second Coming;* and from a University of Michigan Business School case study, credited as follows: "Catherine Crane, Will Johnson, Kitty Neumark,

Christopher Perrigo prepared this case under the supervision of Professor Allan Afuah." Details of Eisner's heart attack and his negotiations with Ovitz, as well as the break with Katzenberg, for the most part come from the Eisner biography *Work in Progress* (Michael Eisner and Tony Schwartz, Random House, 1998). Steve's complaint to Brent Schlender appeared in his *Fortune* article of 1995, cited previously.

8 Icon

Interview sources for this chapter are Gil Amelio, former CEO of Apple Computer; former Apple chief technology officer Ellen Hancock; Jean-Louis Gassée, former CEO of Be, Inc.; and a senior member of the technical team evaluating Apple's software choices, speaking confidentially. A number of the stories concerning Gil Amelio are from *On the Firing Line*. The Schneider and Eisner quotes are from the Schlender 1995 article, and from Barbara Robertson, "Toy Story: A Triumph of Animation," *Computer Graphics World*, August 1995. Material about the Eisner-Ovitz negotiations and break-up comes from the Eisner biography and from James B. Stewart's article, "Partners," in *The New Yorker*, January 10, 2005; from "Disney's Basket Cases," *Variety*, March 7, 2004; and from information revealed in the stockholders' suit. Steve's comments about Mona Simpson's novel appear in "Creating Jobs: Apple's Founder Goes Home Again," by Steve Lohr, *New York Times Magazine*, January 12, 1997. Information about the prelaunch activities surrounding the upcoming release of *Toy Story* are largely from *Second Coming*.

9 Mogul

Gil Amelio and Ellen Hancock contributed information used in this chapter. Steve's statement about his reasons for returning to Apple and the Internet as an opportunity for the company comes from the *Fortune* interview with him, January 24, 2000. Information on the iMac comes from the Apple Web site and a variety of published sources.

10 Breaking New Ground

Pam Kerwin provided details of the IPO day and of the negotiations and deals between Pixar and Disney, both before *Toy Story* and the subsequent negotiations. A former Pixar executive, speaking confidentially, provided other material used in the chapter. Alan Deutschman is the source of additional material on the effect of the IPO on individuals associated with Pixar. The Motley Fool quote appears on the Internet at www.fool.com/foolu/askfoolu/1998/askfoolu981230.htm. Remaking *Toy Story 2* is based on the account provided by Brent Schlender in "Incredible: The Man Who Built Pixar's Innovation Machine," *Fortune*, November 15, 2004, and the production and success of that film are detailed in Justin Martin's "Inside the Pixar Dream Factory," *Forbes Small Business*, February 1, 2003. The *Business Week* article alluded to is "Steve Jobs, Movie Mogul," by Peter Burrows and Ronald Grover, in the November 23, 1998 issue. The *Time* article that focused on Steve's micromanaging is "Steve's Two Jobs," by Michael Krantz, in the October 18, 1999 issue.

Katzenberg beating Pixar to the screen is based on a confidential interview and on Peter Burroughs's "ANTZ VS. BUGS: The inside story of how Dreamworks beat Pixar to the screen," in *Business Week*, November 23, 1998. Material on the stock package and aircraft presented to Steve by the Apple board is from Jim Davis, "Gulfstream for Steve," CNETNews.com, January 19, 2000; and from airliners.net.

11 iPod, iTunes, Therefore I Am

This chapter uses interview material from former chief executive officer of the Recording Industry Association of America Hilary Rosen; an executive of one of the big-five music companies, speaking confidentially; and Terry Kunysz, former president of Casady and Greene.

The Adam Engst article was "Tower of Song," in the *MacWorld* issue of August 1, 2000. Articles used in developing the iPod are: Spencer E. Ante, "Napster's Shawn Fanning: The Teen Who Woke Up Web Music," *Business Week Online*, April 12, 2000; Jonathan Kantor, "iPod Nation," *Newsweek*, July 26, 2004; Leander Kahney, "Inside Look at Birth of the iPod," *Wired*, July 21, 2004; and Erik Sherman, "Inside the Apple Design Triumph," *Electronics Design-Chain*, Summer 2002. The Jonathan Ive quotes appeared in Kristi Essick's, "The Man behind the iMac," *PC World*, September 18, 1998, in Brent Schlender's "Apple's 21st-Century Walkman," *Fortune*, November 12, 2001; and in Rob Walker's "The Guts of a New Machine," *New York Times Magazine*, November 30, 2003. The Steve Jobs remarks about design and the story about purchasing a washing machine were shared with *Wired*'s Gary Wolf, published in his article "Steve Jobs: The Next Insanely Great Thing" in the February 1996 issue.

The phrase "shined Steve's shoes" is a bowdlerized version of the actual remark.

12 Clash of the Titans

Some information in this chapter comes from an interview with the former Disney executive who also provided information for chapter 5. Other material in the chapter is based on information from the stockholders' suit, from the James Stewart book *DisneyWar* (Simon & Schuster, 2005), and from the following: Devin Leonard, "Songs in the Key of Steve," *Fortune*, May 12, 2003; Kit Bowen, "Pixar's Success May Dampen Future with Disney," *Hollywood.com*, June 3, 2003; Kim Masters, "Fightin' Mike," *Esquire*, September 1, 2003; Ronald Grover, "Pixar Twists the Mouse's Tail," *Business Week Online*, January 30, 2004; Steve Jobs interview, *Rolling Stone*, December 2003; John Markoff "Oh Yeah, He Also Sells Computers," *New York Times*, April 25, 2004; Richard Verrier and Claudia Eller, *Los Angeles Times*, February 8, 2004; Bruce Orwall and Pui-Wing Tam, "Freeze Frame: Pixar Still Lacks a Partner for Post-Disney Era," *Wall Street Journal*, October 25, 2004; Claudia Eller, "Pixar's Flirtations Could Mean Trouble for Disney," *Los Angeles Times*, February 5, 2003; Bruce Orwall and Nick Wingfield, "The End: Pixar Breaks Up with Distribution Partner Disney," *Wall Street Journal*, January 30, 2004; Jay Sherman, "Pixar, Disney to End Partnership Negotiations between Jobs and Eisner," *Television Week*, February 2, 2004; Steve

Jobs interview, *Wired*, February 1996; Duncan Campbell, "The Guardian Profile: Steve Jobs," *Guardian Unlimited*, June 18, 2004; Claude Brodesser, "Feuds," *Variety*, June 7 and 13, 2004; Ron Scherer, "Disney's Real Battle Is to Keep Good Cartoons Coming," *The Christian Science Monitor*, March 4, 2004; Merlin Jones, "Why Pixar's Films Are More 'Disney' Than Disney's," SaveDisney.com; and Steve Jobs interview, *Business Week*, October 12, 2004.

Material for the chapter also comes from Marc Gunther, "Roy Disney's Beef," *Fortune*, January 12, 2004; Claude Brodesser, "Feuds," *Variety*, June 7, 2004; Loren Hunt, "Anatomy of a Mouse," *The Philadelphia Independent*, April 2004; the Pixar Web site, Corporate Information; Austin Bunn, Interview: "Welcome to Planet Pixar," *Wired*, June 2004; Interview, ComingSoon.net, October 25, 2004; Bill Desowitz, Interview: "Brad Bird and Pixar Tackle CG Humans Like True Superheroes," *Animation World*, December 20, 2004; and Jennifer Ordonez, "Mickey's Fight Club," *Newsweek*, November 29, 2004.

The name of the oncologist is fictitious. The physician who provided the information requested anonymity.

13   Showtime

The majority of the material in this chapter is from Steve Jobs's January 2005 keynote address at MacWorld Expo in San Francisco. However, the brief quotes from Steve taken from outside that public appearance are drawn from the story "How Big Can Apple Get" by Brent Schlender in *Fortune*, February 21, 2005.

Epilogue

Material used in the epilogue has been drawn from Steve Lohr, "Creating Jobs," *New York Times Magazine*, January 12, 1997; "Bad Apple," by T. C. Doyle in *VAR Business*, January 10, 2005; and the book *Steven Jobs and Steven Wozniak: Creating the Apple Computer*, by Keith Elliot Greenberg (Blackbirch Press, 1994). The rest is from Steve Jobs himself.

Index

Page numbers in italics refer to illustrations.

Lightning Source UK Ltd.
Milton Keynes UK
UKOW031041091111

181654UK00002B/1/P